A NEW SYNTHESIS OF PUBLIC ADMINISTRATION
SERVING IN THE 21ST CENTURY

A New Synthesis of Public Administration

Serving in the 21st century

Jocelyne Bourgon

First published in Canada 2011 by the School of Policy Studies, McGill-Queen's University Press.

Cover design and photograph by Ahmad Akkaoui, "The Centennial Flame at Parliament Hill, Ottawa, Canada". Layout and typesetting by Michelle Craig & Henri Kuschkowitz.

This book was produced with the assistance of the University of Waterloo, Cisco and Public Governance International (PGI).

This book is printed on recycled paper and is FSC certified.

Library and Archives Canada Cataloguing in Publication

Bourgon, Jocelyne, 1950-
    A new synthesis of public administration : serving in the
21st century / Jocelyne Bourgon.

(Queen's policy studies series)
Includes bibliographical references.
ISBN 978-1-55339-312-2 (pbk.).--ISBN 978-1-55339-313-9 (bound)

    1. Public administration--History--21st century. 2. Public
administration--Philosophy. 3. Public administration--Case
studies. I. Queen's University (Kingston, Ont.). School of Policy
Studies II. Title.

JF1351.B64 2011   351.01   C2011-904854-X

For Francis

Contents

Preface

The New Synthesis Project is dedicated to supporting public sector practitioners, both elected and professional, who are called upon to face the challenges of serving in the 21st century. The project aims to explore the new frontiers of public administration to provide practitioners with an intellectual framework that integrates past practices, lessons learned from recent public sector reforms and the reality of practice in a post-industrial era.

The project began as an individual journey but over time, and in particular, over the course of 2010 to the time of writing, it came to involve numerous people and organizations from various parts of the world. Their contributions enriched the discussion and generated powerful case studies. This helped ensure that the evolving narrative was solidly grounded in the reality of the men and women who, for a time or for most of their career, have accepted to face the challenges of serving the public good in their respective countries. This book could not have been written without their participation. I am grateful and indebted to them.

A number of people and organizations lent their support from the start. They were the early partners and true innovators who supported the initiative and trusted me to make it worthwhile. They included the University of Waterloo, the Centre for International Governance Innovation (CIGI) and, shortly thereafter, Cisco. Their support made it possible to reach out to practitioners and scholars in a number of countries. This made a world of difference. From the university, I benefited from the support of David Johnston, former President; Feridun Hamdullahpur, President; and Ken Coates, Dean of Arts. From Cisco, Simon Willis, Martin Stewart-Weeks and Terry Ansari lent their support to me, the project and the international network that formed around it.

The NS6 is a collaborative international research network of individuals and organizations in Australia, Brazil, Canada, the Netherlands, Singapore and the United Kingdom. The participating organizations included the State Services Authority of Victoria, the Australia and New Zealand School of Government and the Australian Public Service Commission (Australia); the Escola Nacional de Administração Pública, Fundação Getúlio Vargas and the University of São Paulo (Brazil); the

Canada School of Public Service, the Privy Council Office, the Institute of Public Administration of Canada and the Canadian Association of Programs in Public Administration (Canada); the Ministry of the Interior and Kingdom Relations, the Leiden University and Rotterdam University (the Netherlands); the Singapore Civil Service College and the Public Service Division in the Prime Minister's Office (Singapore); and the Institute for Government, the National School of Government and the Sunningdale Institute (United Kingdom).

Each participating country led some aspect of the research work, developed case studies and hosted an international roundtable. In fact, participating countries carried a significant portion of the workload through 2010, and they deserve all the credit for it. I am most grateful to the country co-ordinators for their steadfast commitment to making this project a success: Maria Katsonis and Karen Lau (Australia), Helena Kerr do Amaral (Brazil), Gordon Owen and Marc Sanderson (Canada), Tobias Kwakkelstein (the Netherlands), Yee Ping Yi and Tan Li San (Singapore) and Sue Richards (United Kingdom). They were ably supported by some key people, including Paula Montagner, Luis Henrique D'Andrea, Fernando Simões Paes, Jenifer Graves, Alison Van Rooy, Merel de Groote, Lena Leong and Tim Hughes.

One of the key activities of the New Synthesis Project in 2010 was a series of five international roundtables hosted by participating countries. World-renowned experts and leading practitioners joined the conversation to share their knowledge and experience in some key areas of the project. Their contributions were invaluable. They are too numerous to mention here, so a list is included in Appendix A.

I have benefited tremendously from the advice of three scientific advisors to the project: Peter Aucoin, Eve Mitleton-Kelly and Thomas Homer-Dixon. I thank them for their generosity and their encouragement. I would like to pay homage to Peter Aucoin who contributed to this project until the very end. His premature passing, in July 2011, is leaving a considerable void among the leaders committed to modernizing public administration.

Through this whole adventure, I was supported by a small team of highly dedicated people. Peter Milley was my main collaborator and companion. His unwavering commitment to the project and his careful handling of multiple relationships across the network contributed immensely to making this adventure a rewarding one for all concerned. My able assistant, Jocelyne Comeau, worked tirelessly to make the project a success. We benefited from the support of an exceptional group of students: Ahmad Akkaoui, Amanda Saffioti, Ashley Pereira, Blair Parsons, Farzana Jiwani, Henri Kuschkowitz, Jacqueline Stesco, Jennifer MacDowell, Kofi Kobia, Marian Gure, Patrick Wilson and Yulia Minaeva. They brought ideas, enthusiasm and modern technology to bear on the project. I am grateful to them all. Even the best team may need a helping hand from time to time. When it was most needed, we were able to count on the support of Marie Sassine, James Meddings, Geoff Dinsdale, Andrée LaRose, Sylviane Duval and Brian Johnson. I am especially indebted to Michel Bilodeau for reviewing this manuscript and for his judicious comments.

This book represents the view of its author. Many of the ideas that the reader may find useful, thoughtful or inspiring stem in some way from the contribution of the people mentioned above and others whom I met along the way. I take full responsibility for any shortcomings that the reader may find.

Introduction

Public administration without a guiding theory is risky; administrative theory without connection to action is meaningless. That dilemma is the foundation of a genuine crisis in public administration.

Donald F. Kettl, *The Transformation of Governance: Public Administration for Twenty-First Century America.*

Public administration has been operating without the benefit of a modern theory for quite some time. This situation deprives public servants of a frame of reference to guide their actions. It acts as a barrier to addressing complex issues and finding practical solutions to some of the intractable problems of our times. It places government in a reactive position, unable to anticipate emerging issues or to introduce corrective action in a timely way.

Most practitioners know from experience that the Classic model of public administration does not adequately reflect their reality of practice. In fact, it speaks to a declining fraction of the role of government in society today. A number of scholars, experts and practitioners have reached a similar conclusion.[1]

People willing to take the responsibility of serving the public good and the collective interest need and deserve the support of an enabling framework to guide their decisions and actions. They need an integrated narrative to make sense of 30 years of public sector reforms: they need a set of guiding principles to guide their actions and help them explore the consequences that various public policy choices entail.

Public administration needs a New Synthesis to integrate past theories, principles and practices of enduring value along with the lessons learned over the past 30 years in a manner that resonates more meaningfully with the reality of practice in the context of the world in which we live.

What does it take to resolve peacefully some of the most complex issues and most intractable problems of our time? What do we need to do to prepare government to face the challenges of the 21st century? These are the questions at the heart of the New Synthesis Project.

The New Synthesis Project was born out of a commitment to public servants whose role is more difficult and demanding than ever before. It was created by a group of volunteers from the worlds of practice and academe who were willing to dedicate time and effort to this initiative.

The challenge of the New Synthesis Project is to craft a story powerful enough to transform the way we think of the role of government in society; coherent enough to guide actions and support decisions; flexible enough to embrace a diversity of contexts; and modern enough to prepare government to be fit for the times. Readers will decide if this book lives up to that challenge. For my part, I see the New Synthesis Project as a work in progress. This book creates the opportunity to expand further the conversation on how to prepare government for the challenges of serving in the 21ˢᵗ century beyond those who have contributed thus far to the project, and to deepen the exploration with practitioners and scholars in different parts of the world.

The book is divided into three parts. It does not need to be read from start to finish: each part can be read independently or out of order, depending on the reader's interests.

Part One presents the main storyline of "A New Synthesis of Public Administration." Chapter 1 explains why the Classic model of public administration is insufficient to address the challenges of the 21ˢᵗ century in spite of the public sector reforms introduced over the last 30 years. Chapter 2 argues that there are significant differences about serving in the 21ˢᵗ century compared to any earlier time, including increasing complexity and uncertainty; a transformation of the relationship between the state and citizens as value creators; and the emergence of an expanding public space shaped by the modern communication technologies that are characteristic of the networked societies we live in.

Those already convinced of the need for change may wish to go straight to Chapter 3. This chapter presents the New Synthesis Framework, proposing it as an enabling frame of reference to support practitioners in the 21ˢᵗ century. Chapters 4 and 5 deepen the discussion about the framework and its implications. Chapter 4 explores the new capacities needed to prepare government and society to address complex issues, shape emergent solutions and build resilience. Chapter 5 reflects on how these new capacities transform the administrative systems and practices inherited from the industrial age that served societies well in the past but need to change for the future.

Part Two illustrates various aspects of the New Synthesis Framework through case studies written by authors from the six participating countries. These cases provide powerful and inspiring examples of what is happening in practice to address complex issues, and what some governments are doing to prepare themselves for the challenges of the 21st century. Two cases explore the concept of public results of higher value to society; two others explore how government can leverage the contribution of multiple actors; one explores the concept of resilience; and two more focus on exploration and experimentation. Readers who want to deepen their understanding of what is taking place in practice and be inspired by experimentation and innovation in public administration may want to start here.

Part Three tells the story of the New Synthesis Project and explains how it came about. Readers interested in the methodology used to lead the New Synthesis Project and how it unfolded may want to begin here. The first chapter of this part describes the approach used to engage a diverse and large number of senior practitioners and academics to generate ideas and bridge divides between theory and practice, disciplines and cultures. Subsequent chapters summarize the key findings from the five international roundtables held in 2010.

I believe the New Synthesis methodology provides a promising avenue to advance research work in other areas and other circumstances.

The New Synthesis Project is a work in progress. This is only the beginning. The most challenging and exciting chapters of this adventure are yet to be written. I encourage readers to get involved in shaping the future of public administration by visiting the project website at www.nsworld.org.

Part One

Exploring the New Frontiers
of Public Administration

Chapter 1

Public Administration: Not Entirely of the Past and Not Yet of the Future

If you do not know where you are going, any road will get you there...and if you don't know where you are coming from, you may end up where you began.

Lewis Carroll (paraphrased from) *Alice's Adventures in Wonderland.*

Public administrations have existed since antiquity. From China to Egypt, from Persia to Rome, kings and emperors have relied on public administrations to transform their ideals about society into reality and to oversee the affairs of government. Public administrations have taken different shapes and forms in various parts of the world but they nonetheless have much in common. They contribute to shaping societies. They give shape to concepts and values about the exercise of power in society. They give form to the role of government and definition to the functioning of public institutions and organizations. Public administrations embody a concept about the relationship between people and government from subservient vassal to an expanding concept of citizenship. In short, public administrations embody concepts, principles, conventions and values.

Periodically, profound changes emerge in society, and new sets of values come to the fore that transform the role of government and the practice of public administration. Recent decades have been marked by profound changes and a deep transformation of the world we live in. The last 30 years have witnessed an increasing number of global cascading failures, like the collapse of the real estate bubble in the USA and the resulting financial crises of 2008, the effects of which were felt around the world; events with unforeseen consequences, like the 2010 eruption of the Eyjafjallajökull volcano in Iceland that brought air traffic in most of Europe to a halt; and unpredictable natural disasters, like the 2011 tsunami along the northeast coast of Japan with its devastating consequences for towns and lives, for public health and the Japanese economy. Powerful and unexpected social unrest in the Middle East and North Africa, facilitated in part by modern social networking tools and social media, is rewriting local history and changing the course of global events in unpredictable ways.

These events are powerful reminders that uncertainty, volatility and complexity are characteristics of today's world. They are the result of the growing interdependence and interconnectivity of many of the systems societies depend on, such as food, energy, water supply, banking, communications and transportation systems. They are the result of the changes brought about by the "connected republic"[1] we are part of and of the global stresses caused by a growing world population on a fragile biosphere. Governments are called upon to serve in an unpredictable environment and to address an increasing number of complex public policy issues.

We live in a period of unprecedented potential. As old ways become unstuck, new ways of thinking and new approaches to governance are emerging. Public administrations are in flux. Past practices are insufficient to meet some of the challenges of the 21ˢᵗ century, but a unifying set of principles has not yet emerged to guide practitioners. This provides an opportunity to modernize the intellectual framework of contemporary public administration and to propel it forward as a discipline.

Countries supported by public administrations fit for the 21ˢᵗ century will have a significant comparative advantage. They will be best positioned to anticipate what might be, and influence the course of events in their favour.

PUBLIC ADMINISTRATION

Public administration is both a domain of practice and a field of study. As a field of study, it is barely more than a century old, having taken shape in the late 19ᵗʰ and early 20ᵗʰ century.

As a young academic field, public administration is still plagued with internal debate and dissention on the extent and scope of the field and its relationship to other disciplines, such as political science and public law.

For the purpose of exploring *A New Synthesis of Public Administration*, I propose that, as a field of study, public administration is primarily interested in understanding the relationship between government, society and the people it governs.

Public administration is about transforming political will into public results or, to put it differently, "the translation of politics into reality that citizens see every day."[2] It is interested in how to make feasible what is judged to be politically desirable. This leaves conveniently open the questions: Who has the authority to decide what is desirable? What political process granted this authority? How is the choice of desirable outcome reached?

Public administration is an integrating discipline that draws from many other disciplines, including sociology, political science, administrative law, public finance, economics and more recently, complexity theory, dynamic system theory, organizational development theory, etc.

The study of public administration is not limited to democratic societies. In fact, important lessons may be learned on how societies governed through other means achieve results and ensure social cohesion. However, the foundation of public administration as a field of study can be traced to Western Europe in the late 19th century and to the United States of America during the early 20th century. As a result, the discipline bears many characteristics of the prevailing thinking in societies that were undergoing a dual transformation process of democratization and industrialization.

THE FORMATIVE YEARS

As a discipline, public administration took shape in a period characterized by rapid change associated with the industrial revolution, economic development and the building of modern states in the late 19th/early 20th century in Western Europe and North America. The "Classic" model of public administration, as it is frequently called, was founded on a number of conventions including respect for the rule of law, a strict separation of politics and administration and a meritorious public service operating under the principles of anonymity and political neutrality.

The model was widely accepted and its adoption spread to countries undergoing similar change and to some developing countries (sometimes voluntarily, sometimes enforced by colonial powers) with mixed results. Public administrations shaped around this model share many characteristics. Government is seen as the primary agent responsible for serving the public good. The power structure is vertical and hierarchical. The public service is governed by precisely prescribed rules and is accountable to elected officials. Public servants are expected to exercise minimal discretion in the provision of services.

Some characteristics of this model represented significant breakthroughs. One of its most important foundational contributions was the rule of law.

The Rule of Law

The Classic model of public administration affirmed the dominance of the rule of law. This concept is at the origin of "L'Etat de droit" to designate societies governed by the rule of law. The concept encourages a separation of powers among the legislative, executive and judiciary to provide checks and balances in the exercise of authority and protect society from too much concentration of power. Today, this principle and its associated practices are embodied in most democratic societies.

The rule of law provided the stability and predictability needed for emerging industrial economies to flourish and contributed to social peace. No one, rich or poor, was above the law that granted equal protection to all. Public administrations operating under the rule of law valued impartiality, due process and compliance. These values were well suited to the times, considering the relative youth of many democratic governments during this period. Public administrations operating under these principles contributed immeasurably to the success of countries undergoing industrialization and democratization during the late 19ᵗʰ and early 20ᵗʰ centuries.

While some characteristics of the Classic model are of enduring value, from time to time, it is necessary to ensure that they live up to the initial aspirations. For instance, laws are difficult to change and their cumulative impact may have perverse effects. The challenge is to preserve the merit of a regime of law while avoiding the rigidities that an accumulation of laws, norms and rules may create over time. Nowhere is this effect more visible than in the public sector.

Today, some characteristics of the Classic model act as barriers as governments try to adapt to the changing reality of the 21ˢᵗ century. Different times require different approaches. Past practices need to evolve to take new realities into account. Chief among these practices are a dualistic mental frame and a heavy reliance on scientific management that are ill suited to addressing many of the complex issues characteristic of the 21ˢᵗ century.

Dualism

The Classic model of public administration reflects the dualistic way of looking at the world that was predominant in the 20ᵗʰ century. This view would see a matter as being either public or private. A private matter would be left to the market and individual initiatives. Government would worry about public matters. Once a matter was in the public domain, the role of government would be to contain demand and ration the use of public resources in a fair and equitable manner. As a result, efficiency is the guiding principle of public administration, and performance is improved through controls.

Nothing is as simple in practice. A number of issues overlap public, private and civic interest: they require a pluralistic view of the world and a multifaceted approach to bring about viable solutions.

In fact, this dualistic view lies behind some of the intractable problems that many countries have experienced in recent years, such as increasing health costs due in part to an aging population and the rising cost of medication and new technologies. More public funding does not necessarily mean better public results. Sometimes, finding a different way of framing the issue is the most important step towards finding a viable solution. This may entail a different sharing of responsibility between government, people and society. Countries with the highest level of total spending, the highest level of public spending or the heaviest reliance on market forces do not necessarily achieve the best public health results, including a long life expectancy and a low rate of child mortality. Japan spends significantly less on healthcare per capita and less public funds as a percentage of GDP than the United States,[3] yet it outperforms the United States in most measures of public health results.[4] Healthy life habits at home and in the family and a reasonable standard of living have a significant impact on public health and on public health costs.[5] Multidimensional issues such as healthcare require a multifaceted way of thinking and pluralistic solutions.

Looking at the world through a dualistic mental map is imbedded in the public administration model inherited from the 20th century. It is reflected in the conventional separation between politics and administration and between policy decisions and their implementation. Actualizing these principles in practice has never been as simple as it sounds, and their strict adherence may even lead to significant policy failures.

Public policies are experiments and works in progress. Some start as broad political aspirations that something should be different in society. Reducing poverty or energy dependency, eliminating a deficit or improving public health, for example, are all worthwhile goals. However, leaving the simplest public policies aside, most do not emerge fully formed. They take shape through multiple interactions inside and outside government on possible courses of action and involve decisions at multiple levels.

The choice of delivery instrument sets the contours of the balance of responsibilities between citizens, civic society, the market and the state. Choosing between direct delivery, tax transfers to individuals or transfers to other levels of government has significant consequences on the way societies are governed and leads to very different results.

Policy decisions take shape and become real through an implementation process. New knowledge acquired in practice transforms the initial policy intentions as well as the methods of achieving them. There is no strict separation between public policy decisions and implementation. Both form part of an integrated, experiential learning process in which politics and public administrations share responsibility for the ultimate results.

The Classic model has internalized and institutionalized a dualistic view of the world reflected in multiple separations between means and ends, facts and values, thoughts and actions, policy decisions and implementation.[6] Today, government needs a multidimensional view of the world to address some of the most intricate and complex problems of our times.

Scientific Management

Scientific management was a strong driver of efficiency for organizations and countries undergoing industrialization. Its influence was first felt in the private sector, but was quickly adopted by the public sector. Scientific management contributed to the view that there is "one best way" of achieving results. By breaking down complicated operations into simpler tasks, measuring routines, codifying the most efficient ones and applying rigorous process controls, it was thought possible to improve performance and achieve better results in most, if not all, circumstances.

Scientific management in public administration contributed to the efficient mass production of standardized public services; payments to veterans issued on time and with minimal errors, public works projects undertaken according to plan, standardized curricula in public schools, efficient tax-collection agencies free from corruption or leakage of public funds, etc.

The approach contributed to the efficient functioning of public organizations, and was particularly appropriate for managing tangible public services provided directly by government agencies without intermediaries. Scientific management works best in relatively stable and predictable environments.

Scientific management remains valid today for predictable services that lend themselves to precise routine, repetition and codification. However, these types of service represent a declining fraction of government services. Today, an increasing range of public services are information-and knowledge-based. They require direct interaction between user and provider. The quality and the nature of the service depend on the accumulated knowledge and know-how of the public servant providing it. They defy codification, except in the broadest terms. They require the exercise of a high level of discretion that the Classic model was trying to prevent.

Going Beyond

The Classic model inherited from the 20ᵗʰ century provided a solid foundation for modern public administration, which includes the primacy of the rule of law, a commitment to due process in serving the public good, a concern for efficiency in service delivery and for probity in the use of public funds. It laid the basis for a strong system of accountability that runs through every level of public administration.

Public administrations moulded on this model have proven remarkably stable in different circumstances around the world. But the test of a strong theory is not just its staying power: it is its resilience, which implies an ability to adapt to new and unforeseen circumstances. *Public administration as a discipline lags behind the changes taking place in practice.* It needs to integrate the foundations inherited from the past, the lessons learned over the past 30 years and the imperatives of serving in the 21ˢᵗ century.

THIRTY YEARS OF REFORMS

The current practice of public administration draws from the Classic model of public administration discussed above; the neo-bureaucratic model, built upon rational decision making; the institutional model of the 1950s and 1960s rooted in behavioural sciences; and the public choice model, with its reliance on political economy.[7] In the 1980s, a new generation of reforms took shape, which became known as New Public Management (NPM).

There is no particular need to unpack the underlying principles of each model. Generally, they are an extension of the Classic model. NPM raised to new levels the separation between politics and administration and between public policy-making and its implementation. NPM intensified some aspects of scientific management, leading to a substantial increase of ex ante controls and ex post quantification.

Public sector reforms during the 1980s and 1990s showed some important similarities. Some focused on restoring the fiscal health of government or rebalancing the role of government in society. Some attempted to seize the benefits of globalization while mitigating its negative impacts; but most focused on improving performance, efficiency and productivity. They encouraged integrated service delivery and paid attention to user satisfaction. They adopted various e-government approaches to leverage the power of information and communication technologies.

More recently, some reforms started to explore a different relationship between the state and its citizens. They are experimenting with hybrid models of co-operation that bring together the public, private and civic sectors.[8] They include various approaches to citizen engagement and various forms of co-creation and co-production between public agencies and users.

The reforms of the past 30 years had a number of positive effects, but they *represent an incomplete journey because* they *did not solve some fundamental problems that stem from living in a post-industrial era.*[9] Public organizations are not yet aligned, in theory or in practice, with the global context or with the complex problems they are expected to address.[10] To serve in the 21st century and to meet the challenges of our times, we need a different way of looking at public administration—one that resonates more meaningfully with our experience and the world we live in.

WIDENING GAPS

While most people would agree that one model cannot fit all situations, in reality, this is frequently what happens in the public sector. The public administration model that emerged in Western Europe and the United States of America at the turn of the 20th century has been framed as a set of ideas and prescriptions expected to suit most circumstances.

According to this view, the public sector, private sector and civil society operate in separate spheres, each with its own norms and values. Government operates at a relative distance from society and citizens. In democratic societies, citizens have a periodic connection with their government during elections, which creates the possibility for change and adjustments.

For the most part, our systems of governance are conceived as a relatively closed system where public organizations exercise public authority, and politics are bundled into public institutions. Public institutions contribute to the stability and predictability of life in society. However, they also have the effect of hollowing out politics from society by bringing inside the decisions that give meaning to living in society.

By design, public organizations inherited from the 20ᵗʰ century have a low adaptive capacity. They were built to mass produce public services and achieve predetermined results. They were not expected to adapt to changing circumstances on their own. They were not wired to innovate or discover new ways of fulfilling their missions. In general, public organizations have a low tolerance for risk. Their internal systems cause them to adapt slowly and even to resist change.

Public sector leaders who have led public sector reforms are very familiar with these characteristics. In spite of the unprecedented pace of reforms over the last 30 years and of the heroic efforts of some political leaders and administrators around the world to bring about change, many reforms have come and gone without leaving much impact as the traditional ways reaffirm themselves over time.

With few exceptions, in most countries the fundamentals of public administration today remain more or less the same as at the turn of the 20ᵗʰ century. This is a precarious position for government to find itself in. The gap is widening between theory and practice, between practice and people's expectations and between collective aspirations and the collective capacity to bring about viable solutions to the issues of our times.

Practitioners know about these widening gaps from experience, and a number of scholars have reached similar conclusions by analyzing the situation from different perspectives.[11]

A useful way of appreciating the widening gaps between theory and the reality of practice is to compare, even if cursorily, some of the underlying assumptions of the Classic model with what is happening in practice.

Citizenship

Beginning at the turn of the 20ᵗʰ century, a movement progressed across many democracies that made citizens the bearers of equal rights and obligations under the law. This was a major accomplishment. The law grants the rights and defines the ob-

ligations associated with citizenship. These rights include the right to vote and to select those who represent the interests of citizens and make decisions on their behalf.

The traditional approach to public administration "crowds out" the contribution
of citizens[12] in many ways. It undervalues the role that people, families and communities play in producing public results and creating a society worth living in.

Today, citizenship has taken on a broader definition and meaning. Citizenship
is an integrating concept.[13] People are simultaneously members of their family,
community, country and chosen communities of interest, no matter where those
communities reside.[14] In the connected world of the 21st century, we are all citizens
of the world.

Citizens are political beings. The politics of citizenship is the politics of participation[15] when people act as members of a community to achieve results. Modern
communication and information technologies are transforming the relationship
between citizens and the state. They are allowing people to interact with their public institutions in new ways and to ensure that their voices are heard. As some
countries have recently discovered, the politics of the connected world cannot be
contained within public institutions. The notion that citizens are not merely the
users or beneficiaries of public services but value creators and co-producers of
public results is turning public administration on its head.[16]

The Public Interest

Under the Classic model, political authorities determined the public interest. Their
decisions amounted to carrying out the public will. In this regard, citizens played
no direct role once they elected their representative (in democratic contexts) or
once they conferred legitimacy on or submitted to the rule of political authorities
(in non-democratic contexts).

Today, the public interest can best be described as a collective enterprise that involves government and many other actors. Governments achieve results in a world
characterized by a broad dispersion of power and authority involving the public
sector, the private sector, civil society and citizens.[17]

No government and no country controls all the tools or has access to all the levers
to address the complex problems people really care about. Most government activities and services are not final results: they are intermediate steps in long chains
of activities involving many organizations working across government and across
sectors toward achieving desired public outcomes. Co-ordinating vast operations
that extend beyond the control of government is one of the trademarks of public
administration in the 21st century.

Over the last 30 years, a recurring theme in public sector reforms has been the growth of non-traditional, non-hierarchical and often non-governmental approaches to service delivery.[18] Hence, indirect tools such as grants, loans, insurance, transfers to other levels of government and tax credits account for the bulk of government spending today. These instruments break the link in the traditional accountability model between funding decisions and service delivery since they put public resources in the hands of individuals and organizations thought to be in a better position to achieve the desired public outcomes. New forms of accountability for results are needed to take account of this situation.[19]

We are a long way from government acting as the primary agent in providing direct and tangible public services. Public services today are increasingly indirect, intangible and intermediate steps in achieving complex public results.

The Role of Government

The Classic model saw government as the primary provider of public services. This no longer resonates with the array of roles most governments are called upon to play in the 21ˢᵗ century.

One of government's key roles is to define and search for ways to balance the authority of the state with the reliance on the power of others to advance the collective interest. In other words, its role is to integrate the contribution of government, people and society in a common system of governance able to adapt to changing circumstances, and where government co-evolves with society.[20]

The role of government transforms society and society transforms the role of government. Government forms part of a vast ecosystem where the economic, social, technological and environmental systems are intertwined.

OPEN SYSTEM OF GOVERNANCE

Public organizations exist to serve the public good and the collective interest. This is the normative foundation of the state and the public sector apparatus. However, in today's changing reality, which includes a global economy, networked societies and a fragile biosphere, there is a need to explore anew what it means to serve the public good and the collective interest.[21]

From Closed Systems

A system is a group of elements or units that have a common purpose. Open systems interact with other systems and with their external environment. Closed systems have relatively little interaction with other systems or with the outside environment.[22]

Applying ideas about open and closed systems to public organizations has its limitations, but it can be helpful in breaking away from conventional ways of thinking to explore new ideas.[23]

A closed-system perspective would view public organizations as operating relatively independently of one another and of their environment. In this context, a department or public agency would be expected to operate on its own with minimal interaction with others. As a closed system, a public agency would focus on managing internal matters, such as production, technology, personnel, equipment and finances. All systems have boundaries. In the case of closed systems, the boundaries provide a firm delineation of roles and responsibilities. Something is either in or out.

Closed-system organizations pay little attention to external factors or to their potential impact on the organization because they do not expect these factors to be directly relevant to how the organization functions. Closed-system organizations assume that they do not require complex interactions with their environment.[24]

The public sector was designed and has operated as a relatively closed system, with the political system and the electoral process being its most open parts. This goes some way to explain why public organizations find it difficult to evolve as changes occur in society, why issues reach crisis proportion before corrective measures are introduced and why public sector reforms require heroic efforts. A closed system has great difficulty detecting the early signs of change. It does not have the built-in agility to adapt with ease and parsimony of effort to changing circumstances.[25] This does not bode well for what lies ahead.

To Open Systems

The concept of open systems originated from the natural sciences and has been used in organizational theory since the 1960s.[26] Understanding a concept is one thing: changing things in practice is quite another.

An open concept of governance would see the economic, social, political, technological and environmental systems as intertwined and interdependent. Open-system public organizations would continually exchange with their environment. They would take in information, ideas, energy and resources and then transform and release them with reciprocal effects on the environment.[27] In this context, organizations are part and parcel of their environment.

Open-system public organizations have form and order. This is not a chaotic vision of how government may function. They have sub-systems to manage the multiple interfaces and exchanges across multiple boundaries; exploratory and adaptive systems to collect, process and make sense of information on changing circumstances; management systems to resolve conflict, and allocate resources; boundaries that display flexibility to interact with others; and plasticity to connect and reconnect parts, units and functions as needed.

The main difference between closed and open systems is the complexity and density of the interactions with their environment. The choice between open and closed systems comes down to a judgment about the complexity of the world we live in and a view about the need for governments to acquire new capacities to be fit for the times.

The participants in the New Synthesis Project share the view that the Classic model of public administration inherited from the 20th century is insufficient to prepare governments to face the challenges of the 21st century. The key questions then become What does it take to solve peacefully some of the toughest and most complex problems of our time[28], and What can we do to prepare governments to face the challenges of these times?

Chapter 2

What is Different About Serving in the 21st Century?

The significant problems we face cannot be solved at the same level of thinking we were at when we created them.

Albert Einstein (paraphrased).[1]

What is so different about serving in the 21st century? Every generation, public servants are called upon to face the challenges of their time. While they build on what came before them, they must chart an original course because "we have not been there before."[2] The same is true for the men and women who will accept to shoulder, for a time or for most of their career, the burden of serving citizens in the 21st century.

In some cases, these public servants will be able to stand on the shoulders of those who came before them, but in most cases, they will need to chart a new course since they face new circumstances and unique challenges. They are the first generation of public servants to face simultaneously difficult, complicated and an increasing number of complex public policy issues. They are the first generation to serve in a world where virtual communities contribute to shaping the issues and transforming the context in which public policy challenges must be met. They are called upon to serve in a context characterized by increasing uncertainty, volatility and unpredictability. These are not differences of degree but differences of nature. Such changes and many others transform the role of government, of public organizations and of the people within them.

Public sector reforms before the mid-1990s were essentially related to the challenges of an industrial world in transition. These reforms pre-date the virtual world: today, data, information and content can be transmitted and shared instantly around the globe to be reassembled in unpredictable ways. They pre-date social networking: today, citizens in Brazil can use an Internet blog to collectively elaborate a new framework for Internet governance, and a revolution in Egypt can be triggered on

Facebook, with unpredictable and unexpected consequences. They pre-date the emergence of China, India and Brazil as global economic engines and the transformation of the geo-political worlds that ensued. Public servants serving today and in the coming years will need to find peaceful solutions to an increasing number of complex issues in a world that was inhabited by 1.6 billon people in 1900[3], 6.1 billion in 2000[4] and will soon reach 10 billion.[5]

Their challenge is daunting. They deserve all the help they can get; and this starts by acknowledging that substantial differences exist to serving in the 21st century compared to any earlier time.

DIFFICULT, COMPLICATED, COMPLEX

Governments have always been called upon to make difficult decisions, undertake complicated initiatives and face complex problems characteristic of the period. This is not in dispute. Nonetheless, the current circumstances are different in some ways and more challenging in many others. One challenge is to determine what can be handled in the traditional way and what must be done differently.[6]

Governments have always been called upon to face *difficult problems*. Setting priorities and making choices have always been difficult. For example, eliminating a sizable deficit is "merely" a difficult problem, although it is hard to believe when one is in the middle of such a heart-wrenching exercise. This entails making choices among equally deserving public purposes and making tough decisions about what should be preserved for the future. It requires reconciling future needs with what could garner a sufficient degree of public support in the short term to move forward.

When dealing with difficult problems, governments know what actions are possible, and have relatively good knowledge of their most likely impacts. Some difficult problems are best addressed incrementally, others by swift action. Governments must choose the most promising course of action while recognizing the possibility of unintended consequences. Historical data, computer modelling and expert advice are useful in identifying the preferred course of action. In the end, government will make tough decisions and address difficult problems.

Governments have always been relied on to undertake *complicated initiatives*. These may be complicated because of their scale, scope or the intricate nature of the enterprise.[7] Trade agreements, tax reforms or international treaty negotiations are examples of complicated exercises.

In many cases, the complication stems from the fact that, although there are cause-to-effect relationships, the impact may be difficult to assess because the actions and the results are separated in time.[8] The true impact will only become fully known years into the future. This is the case, for example, for the economic stimulus programs launched by many countries facing recessions stemming from the global financial crisis in 2008. It is also the case for most social policies, which often have deferred impacts over many years. Careful monitoring, data collection and quantification allow governments to assess the impact of the policies and programs they introduce and to make adjustments incrementally. Over time, government actions and their impact will become fully known.

Some initiatives are complicated because of their intricate nature. These initiatives may involve an elaborate web of actions where a single misstep may lead to failure. Sending a man to the moon, for example, is a complicated and intricate operation with high associated risks.[9]

The failure of a complicated initiative may unleash a complex set of events with unknown consequences. Drilling for oil in the Gulf of Mexico is a complicated undertaking that takes place at the edge of scientific knowledge and engineering expertise. A failure can unleash a complex set of events with unknown ecological, sociological, economical and political consequences. A military operation is a complicated initiative. Successful or not, it unleashes a complex set of events with unpredictable consequences.

Addressing complicated problems requires careful planning, staying power and sustained effort, sometimes over many years.[10] Prudence dictates that risk assessment, contingency and mitigation strategies form part of the approach when undertaking a complicated initiative.[11]

Governments today have the added responsibility of addressing *complex issues*. These issues are characterized by a broad dispersion of power and a high degree of interdependence. They are taking shape in the increasingly uncertain context of our global economy and networked societies. They manifest a high degree of unpredictability and display emergent characteristics.[12] They cannot be solved in the traditional way since they cannot easily be broken apart.[13] More knowledge is unlikely to bring about a solution. In most cases, they require a holistic and participative approach since they require the contributions of multiple actors.[14] Multiple micro strategies are more likely to lead to better results[15] than the centrally conceived master plans used for addressing difficult issues or undertaking complicated initiatives.[16]

Shocks, crises and global cascading failures are characteristic of the world we live in. It is highly probable that their frequency will continue to increase.

Complex problems are different from difficult issues and complicated undertakings. They display dynamic complexity when the interactions across systems are so intertwined that the issue can only be resolved by looking at the system as a whole.[17] The problem of deforestation in the Amazon cannot be resolved by focusing on forest management or any other single dimension. The economic, social, environmental and cultural systems are inexorably linked. A viable solution requires a *holistic un-*

derstanding of the whole environment and a multifaceted approach.[18]

Complex problems may display social complexity when the facts and the nature of the problem are contested and when positions are entrenched.[19] Global warming is a case in point, where the existence of the problem is contested and where data are used as ammunition to further entrench positions rather than to find common ground for action. In such cases, the problem definition that matters most (imperfect though it may be) is one that is jointly arrived at by the various parties working together because it may open up the possibility for joint action. Complex issues require a participative approach to problem definition and to concerted action.[20] Viable solutions exceed the capacity of any one actor on its own.

Complex situations also exist when the future is undetermined, when situations are in a state of flux and can go in a number of directions or when the trajectory from the past is broken.[21]

Generative complexity[22] can bring a society to the limit of chaos. It may lead to conflict and social unrest, but it may also lead to a new path and a better future. The events leading to the reconciliation process in South Africa, to the fall of the Berlin wall and the reunification of Germany, and more recent events in the Middle East and North Africa are of that nature. Complex issues are prone to cascading effects.[23] They can have deep underlying causes that go on for years before reaching a tipping point that will irreversibly change the course of events.[24]

Complex issues require emergent solutions,[25] a willingness to co-create[26] and to "learn as we go."[27] Trying to understand complex phenomena by taking them apart and studying their constituent parts is pointless: emergent situations cannot be understood or addressed that way.

For good measure, we can add to this picture the fact that a number of complicated systems that societies rely upon are becoming more complex as the density of connections within and among systems increases. This is the case for food, water and energy supply systems. It is also true for information, communication and financial systems. Complex and densely connected systems are prone to cascading failures. This is how the inadequate trimming of a tree near a power line can cause a cascading failure across a power grid and a blackout affecting millions of people.[28] This is how a small but faulty computer algorithm at a mutual fund company can trigger the largest recorded drop in stock market history in the United States of America.[29]

Different Issues, Different Ways

So, what does it take to solve some of the most complex and intractable problems of our time? Increased complexity and uncertainty do not mean that governments are powerless, far from it. Instead, they need different approaches and different ways of thinking.

Complex issues involve many interacting agents acting simultaneously. Each action has limited effect, but the power of multiple small steps moving in a similar direction can dramatically change the course of events.[30] Each action transforms the context and affects the actions that others take. The behaviour of the overall system is not linear: in most cases, direct cause-to-effect relationships cannot be found. In fact, the interaction among the various elements is the main organizing principle.

The self-immolation of Mohamed Bouazizi, a 26-year-old fruit vendor, in Tunisia on 17 December 2010 became the tipping point that unleashed a sequence of events that resulted in ousting the country's president 28 days later. Within weeks, the protest movement spread from Tunisia to Egypt, Libya, Yemen and Syria. The events surrounding Mohamed Bouazizi may have been the tipping point, but the root causes were multiple and much deeper. Tunisia has long been plagued by high unemployment, food price inflation, poor living conditions and corruption. The region has lagged behind developments in other parts of the world, and citizens lacked some of the rights many people elsewhere enjoyed.

Many different elements interact with one another in complex systems. The interactions produce emergent phenomena that are greater than the sum of their parts and that transform their constituent elements. Complex systems are simultaneously top-down and bottom-up: they can best be approached as nested networks of relationships.[31]

Today, an increasing number of people, groups and organizations make important decisions[32] in an increasing number of places. As a result, there is growing *fragmentation*. Their decisions are influenced by the decisions of others and by the expectation of what others may do: there is increasing *interdependence*. With fragmentation and interdependence come uncertainty, volatility and unpredictability.[33] The ubiquity of modern information and communication technologies means that these changes can spread at the speed of light. Similar patterns may appear and evolve at different speeds and at different scales. The unfolding of the global financial crisis in 2008 is an example. The patterns of troubling mortgage financing practices in some financial institutions were symptomatic of similar patterns in other financial institutions across the international financial system. All of this puts a premium on the capacity of government to anticipate, monitor and intervene ahead of time when the collective interest demands it.[34]

We live in a networked society that consists of a web of networks interacting with each other. In this context, the role of government is more difficult and challenging than ever. Complex issues put a premium on the capacity of government to take account of a multitude of interdependencies among actors, sectors and parts of the world, and to work across boundaries.

Most complex issues cross political jurisdictions, organizational mandates, societal sectors, professions and disciplines. Addressing them requires new forms of co-operation and a willingness to co-create solutions. Complex issues are multi-faceted: they play out differently at different scales. Local issues can quickly become global issues, and issues emerging on a global scale may have devastating impacts at the local level.[35] The implications of global warming for residents in the low-lying coastal areas of Indonesia are vastly different than they are for those in the corporate towers of world capitals.

The search for solutions requires the capacity to think holistically, to discover patterns where none were seen before, and a capacity to design and pursue multiple micro interventions that accelerate the potential for learning as we go.[36] The search for solutions also requires taking preventative action to reduce vulnerabilities and path dependencies.

CITIZENS AS CREATORS OF PUBLIC VALUE

Changes in the global context are transforming the role of government, public institutions and public organizations. But the challenge of serving in the 21st century does not only mean facing new issues: it means doing things differently.

Providing Services to Citizens

The public administration model of the 20th century saw citizens as voters and taxpayers with rights and obligations under the law. People were also users and beneficiaries of public services. Governments were the primary provider of public services *to* citizens who had little or no role to play in the development, design and production of public services.

In the public administration model of the early 20th century, people are credited with little or no ability to solve collective problems. As Nobel Laureate, Elinor Ostrom, points out, "One of the distorted views stemming from the presumption the government should fix community problems is viewing citizens…as helpless and incapable."[37] This approach to public administration has "crowded out" the contribution of society in solving public problems.[38] It has devalued the role played by citizens, families and community groups in the creation of public goods.

This view of public administration has had a number of perverse consequences. It leads to sub-optimal public results at a higher overall cost to society. In other words, no society is rich enough to provide for or to buy those things that people, families, neighbourhoods and communities provide freely.[39]

Public policies built on the assumption that people cannot contribute to addressing issues disempower individuals and create dependencies. Excluding people from the design of public policies and the delivery of public services erodes their self-reliance and depletes the social capital that is essential for society to adapt and prosper in an uncertain environment. Public services designed in this way increase individual vulnerability and undermine social resilience.

When government takes charge of an issue, it "owns the problem." Government becomes responsible for defining the issue, finding the solution and taking appropriate action to bring about the desired outcome. This approach creates an expectation that government has the capacity, the means and the resources to bring about a viable solution. If the results do not meet public expectations, as is frequently the case, government becomes the target of public grievances and faces pressing demands for additional action.

At the root of this situation is the fact that many public policy issues are beyond the reach of government working alone, even when using an increasing amount of public funds. Mounting public costs and declining public satisfaction feed a spiral of declining trust that leads to even more calls for someone—anyone!—to "do something" and "take swift action" even if they are unlikely to bring about a satisfactory solution, since a viable solution would require the active contribution of people working *with* government.

Such situations do not arise because public agencies are doing a poor job or because public servants are somehow wanting compared to their predecessors. They arise because a disconnect exists between what government can actually do and what requires a collective effort that involves government working with citizens, families and communities.

Creating Value with Citizens

People are the main value creators for a number of traditional public goods and an increasing number of public policy issues. To be sure, government is an actor like no other.[40] It can give voice to collective aspirations.[41] It can reconcile conflicting positions and give a sense of direction conducive to collective action. But when it comes to actually producing public outcomes, the capacity of government acting on its own is more limited than is frequently acknowledged.[42] Governments can tax and spend to build public schools; they can provide a publicly funded healthcare system; they can hire and deploy law enforcement officers. Nonetheless, citizens are the main contributors to public health, public literacy and public safety through the decisions they make and the actions they take in their own lives, in the privacy of their homes or in their communities.

Traditionally, public administration has focused on actions within the control of government. This perspective is too narrow to account for the contribution of multiple actors. As a result, it reduces the range of options open to government to achieve better public results at a lower overall cost to society. A government-centric view obscures the long chain of interconnected actions involved in achieving most public results. It leads to an excessive focus on the efficiency of government operations and pays insufficient attention to the potential for effectiveness that a broader perspective would help reveal.

The presumption that government agencies produce most public goods and services is misleading. More schools do not necessarily lead to better educational results. Beyond the role played by government agencies and the use of public funds, other factors are at play. As the work done by the OECD's Program for International Student Assessment (PISA) demonstrates, a country's relative wealth (as measured by GDP per capita) or the level of public spending per student does not entirely explain its educational results.[43] A culture that values education and learning, a supportive family environment and the commitment and efforts of the learners has a significant impact on the ultimate outcome.

Crowding out the contribution of people is "a waste of human and material resources."[44] It raises the overall cost to society of achieving collective results.

Achieving Results with Citizens

Governments have progressively learned about the limitations of past approaches to solving public policy issues and achieving public results. Shifting from providing service to citizens to achieving results with citizens opens up new avenues to integrate the public, private and civic spheres.

An increasing number of public results and public policies must be rethought from the perspective of public results as a shared responsibility of public agencies working with people and communities. A growing body of evidence exists of strong correlations between the active role of people and communities in service design and delivery and user satisfaction[45]; between participation and life satisfaction[46]; and between an active citizenry, self-reliance and community resilience.[47]

The concept of co-production, which is the shared and reciprocal activities of public agencies and people to produce results of public value, helps break away from the traditional concepts of the production of public services through direct government delivery or through contractual arrangements.[48] The central ideas of co-production are that people using public services are not a drain on the system but an asset, and that no country is rich enough to ignore this source of wealth.[49] The relationship between public servants and users shifts from one of subordination and dependency to one of parity, mutuality and reciprocity.

Co-production is a non-contractual arrangement that helps bring government, people and society together. It operates at the individual and societal levels. At the societal level, it brings together the non-market and market economies.[50] It provides an opportunity to restore the balance between what government is best positioned to do, what citizens can do for themselves, and what is best accomplished together.

Modern information and communication technologies are accelerating the pace of change by giving people and government the means to work together in new ways.[51] Web 2.0 technologies and applications are creating new forms of social interaction. Knowledge can be assembled, recombined and repackaged in new and powerful ways to further accelerate the pace of innovation in society. Technology is not simply an enabler or a driver of change: it is part and parcel of the way we live in the 21ˢᵗ century. Governments are undergoing an unprecedented transformation from a "government-to-you" to a "government-with-you"[52] approach that entails a profound shift in relationships and in the exercise of power in society.

SERVING BEYOND THE PREDICTABLE

The role of government in the 21ˢᵗ century is not limited to what government can do on its own or even what it can co-produce with others. Its role extends to serving the public good and the collective interest in all circumstances: when government is directly involved, when it creates an enabling environment for others to act or when society enjoys great freedom to pursue individual interests.

Government is the ultimate guardian of the collective interest, in good times and bad, in predictable and unpredictable circumstances. It is the steward of the collective interests and the insurer of last resort for the worst failures and crises of our times, be they pandemics, natural disasters, economic meltdowns or social unrest.

Governments are called upon to serve beyond the predictable and in the expanding public space forged by the interaction between our networked society and multiple virtual communities. They must act with imperfect knowledge, while knowing that many events are beyond their control. Their role is to leverage the collective capacity to influence the course of events toward a better future and to help society adapt and prosper even in the face of adversity and unforeseen circumstances.

Shocks, Risks and Cascading Failures

In an increasingly uncertain, volatile and unpredictable context, the notions of risk and risk management take on a different meaning. Recent events are stark reminders of the role of the state and the impact of unforeseen events on government. The earthquake on 11 March 2011 in Japan was the most powerful in that country's history. The toll in death and missing people exceeds 25,000. The psychological damage is incalculable. The economic losses are estimated to be over US$300 billion. This far exceeds what private insurers can absorb. A US$50 billion publicly-funded reconstruction plan has been announced, suggesting that households and government will bear most of the financial burden. The Japanese have an admirable resilience and a strong capacity to come together in the face of adversity. Reconstruction will take place and Japan will prosper again.

The role of government in serving the collective interest in the face of catastrophic events with low probability of occurrence extends to prevention, mitigation and decision making on the level of risk society is able to bear. In the end, government and society as a whole will bear the costs. Governments can do much to build the capacity of their societies to absorb unpredictable shocks, and they may be wise to build some degree of redundancy in the most vital systems to help society rebound in the aftermath of unforeseen events.

Crises and shocks are not necessarily the result of natural disasters. They are more frequently the result of human activities. The financial crises and bank failures that began in 2008 were preventable. They may have been the result of a number of factors, including lax oversight functions, weak regulatory frameworks, greed, excessive risk-taking and an excessively laisser-faire approach on the part of many actors, including governments. As a result, massive private risks were converted into public risks as the insolvability of financial institutions was converted into a national deficit and debt, the impact of which society will bear for years to come.

In our globally connected world, the economic, social and political systems are intertwined. A precautionary approach to serving the public interest has implications for the role of government well beyond the programs under its control.

Government functions in an ecosystem of interrelated systems that are constantly adapting to one another and that bring the economic, social, civic and political spheres closer together.

Connected World and Virtual Communities

We live in a connected world where virtual communities play a significant role. Between 2000 and 2008, the number of cell-phone users increased from 1 billion to more than 4 billion, and the number of Internet users from 2.5 billion to more than 10 billion.[53] As of 2011, more than a dozen virtual communities had over 100 million active members.[54]

The growing array of technologies that connect people with information and with each other are not simply enablers or drivers of change in society; they are part of how we live in the 21ˢᵗ century. They make it remarkably easy to access and disseminate ideas and to collaborate close to home or across vast distances. Modern information and communication technologies and the networks of relationships they enable are accelerating the pace of change. This has important implications for government.

The rise of social networking and social media is causing a "disruptive shift" in the traditional balance of knowledge and decision-making power between government and citizens. The best insight about emergent phenomena may not rest with government. It might lie in self-organized social networks and in the multiple relationships citizens have built in their local or globally dispersed communities of interest. The best means of action may not be in government's hands. Citizens and other actors have invaluable information and capacities to offer. Enabled in part by modern technologies, citizens and other actors can devise innovative solutions to public issues.[55] Governments need to leverage the power of others. The knowledge, capabilities and loci for action are broadly dispersed.

To do this, governments need to participate in social media and social networking platforms, most of which are decidedly more open and dynamic than governments are accustomed to.[56] In these virtual communities of interest, the contributions people make are more significant than the positions they hold; relationships involve high levels of reciprocity. Governments cannot simply tap into these communities to "take" ideas—they must "give" as well. The power of social networking is available only to organizations prepared to participate and share.

A more connected world is changing the way public organizations operate. It assumes that it is easy to connect people, knowledge and ideas when and where needed, and that it is possible to connect communities, networks, organizations and institutions at low or no incremental cost. This connectivity enables distributed operating models. It represents a dispersion of power and authority in society. It generates "systemic serendipity,"[57] where distributed knowledge is re-assembled and reconnected in unpredictable ways.

While the Internet and social networks can accelerate the pace of innovation, they create new risks and give rise to new challenges for government. In the Internet age, it is difficult to know "what's what." Before the information and communications "explosion," public servants drew from a limited set of sources for facts, evidence and analysis. They could easily verify the credibility of these sources and the reliability of the information. The exclusivity of this model was its weakness. The connected world offers vast amounts of information from diverse sources. It puts the knowledge of the world at our fingertips and yet makes it increasingly difficult to answer "How do we know what we know?" This puts a premium on government's ability to discriminate credible from non-credible ideas and to extract meaning from diffused and disaggregated information.

In the Internet age, good and bad analysis, trustworthy information and misinformation can all "go viral." Viruses play a positive and negative role. In nature, they connect and recombine DNA in ways that contribute to evolution. They can also have a devastating impact. In the same way, data and information can be problematically recombined, misconstrued and misused. Social networks can be effective instruments for quick mobilization and, just as some viruses spread fast, information can go viral well before government has time to understand an issue or consider a possible response.

Modern information and communications technologies are compressing timelines. Traditional public administration values rational planning that balances short-, mid- and long-term priorities. Those in government today need to manage all these timelines simultaneously, focusing on what is happening in "real time" without losing sight of what matters most for the future.

Like any tool, the Web has potential for good or bad. Unlike other technologies, however, it also has the potential to self-correct the problems it creates with the same ease by which it can spread misinformation. Wikipedia, where contributors and ultimately a hierarchy make sure that the information is as accurate as possible, is a prime example. The question is not whether the Web is good or bad. It is part of the way we live and of who we are as citizens of the world.

Chapter 3
A New Synthesis of
Public Administration

We are not what we know but what we are willing to learn.

Mary Catherine Bateson.

The ideas leading to the New Synthesis Project took shape over several years, but most of the actual work took place between the spring of 2009 and December 2010. The project was launched explicitly to explore the new frontiers of public administration in the hope of providing practitioners with a narrative supported by powerful examples that would better equip them to face the challenges of serving in the 21st century.

> *Public administration needs a new synthesis; one that will coherently integrate past theories, conventions, principles and practices of enduring values with new ones that respond to today's challenges.[1]*

A significant amount of the work was accomplished through an international collaborative network comprised of practitioners and academics from Australia, Brazil, Canada, the Netherlands, Singapore and the United Kingdom. The participants shared the view that there are significant differences to serving in the 21st century. They also shared a common commitment to preparing their respective countries for the challenges ahead. By working together, they were accelerating their own learning and benefiting from the diversity of ideas and experiences that a collective international network can provide. The network was deliberately kept small to ensure rapid progress. Nevertheless, a high level of diversity of practice was ensured by bringing together representatives from countries large and small, densely populated and not, with varying degrees of economic development and different models of governance including presidential and parliamentary systems.

Each participating country contributed actively to the research and provided case studies. The most important discussions took place around a series of international roundtables scheduled over the course of 2010 that brought together world-renowned experts and leading practitioners. The roundtables fostered a free exchange of views and encouraged co-discovery. The case studies played an important role in ensuring that the discussions remained solidly grounded in the reality of the practitioners the network wanted to assist. A full description of the New Synthesis journey, including the project's methodology and brief accounts of the findings stemming from each roundtable, is presented in Part Three of this volume.

The New Synthesis Framework presented in this chapter was developed during the course of 2009. It was presented to the participating countries in a document entitled New Frontiers of Public Administration ("New Frontiers")[2] before the first roundtable in March 2010. It was used as a starting point for the discussion and progressively refined over the course of 2010 as the work progressed. In this chapter, the presentation of the New Synthesis Framework is enriched with case material submitted by the participating countries. These case studies helped deepen the understanding of various concepts and illustrate them in practice. Some case studies are presented in full in Part Two of this volume, others are available online.[3]

The New Synthesis Framework presented in this chapter does not reflect a "negotiated" position among the participants. That is not how the network functioned. Nonetheless, a high level of consensus existed among the participants on most aspects in spite of the diversity of circumstances of their respective countries of origin.

Practitioners the world over are experimenting with similar ideas in response to broadly similar challenges. They describe in similar ways and with the same anxiety their increasing difficulty at reconciling past practices and emerging needs. The New Synthesis Framework remained the frame of reference from the first roundtable to the last. It provided the architecture around which the findings were integrated.

The network adopted a "blended approach," meaning that deliberate efforts were made to bring together in a common exploratory conversation people from a diverse range of academic disciplines beyond the traditional field of political sciences and public law as well as practitioners with a diversity of experience at the national, sub-national and local levels. This approach helped bridge the traditional divide between the world of academia and the world of practice that persists in public administration. Over time, 200 participants contributed to the New Synthesis Project, some of whom participated in more than one roundtable discussion.[4]

In the end, the project may not have generated the powerful narrative some of us were dreaming of: this will be for readers to decide. However, there is no doubt that the work to date represents an important contribution and a step in the right direction to support practitioners and to modernize the field of public administration. It is hoped this work will encourage others to join the conversation on the challenges of *serving in the 21ˢᵗ century* and bring forward their contributions.

AN ENABLING FRAMEWORK

The previous chapters argue that the Classic model of public administration is insufficient for guiding practitioners in this millennium and that the reforms to date represent an incomplete journey. More needs to be done to prepare governments to face the challenges of their times. Furthermore, there are significant differences about serving in the 21ˢᵗ century compared to any earlier time. These differences include increasing complexity, volatility, uncertainty and a profound transformation of the relationship between government and citizens that entails a shift from government as a provider of service to citizens to one of co-creation and co-production of public goods with citizens. Governments are called upon to serve beyond the predictable. The role of government extends to anticipating, preventing and introducing course corrections to reduce the risks associated with unfavourable events when the consequences will be borne by society as a whole and to improve the likelihood of more favourable outcomes. Public servants are serving in an expanding public sphere that combines the virtual public spaces of our connected world with the more traditional public spaces delineated by the public institutions and organizations that help bring stability and predictability to life in society. Participants at the roundtables showed a significant level of consensus about this diagnostic.

To integrate past theories and practices, lessons learned over the past 30 years and today's challenges, there is a need to work from a different perspective, one that brings together government, society and people in a co-evolving system of governance.

> *We need to work from a broader definition of public results; an expanded view of the role of government; and a dynamic understanding of public administration and of the interrelationships between government, people and society* (New Frontiers).

This is the starting point of the New Synthesis Framework.

The New Synthesis Framework is an *enabling framework*. It is not a model proposing yet again to replace those that came before whether the Classic model, the Public Choice model or the New Public Management model. Instead, the framework explores how past systems and practices may co-exist with the new capabilities needed to prepare governments for the future.

A model is a resting place. It affirms a view of reality, describes that reality and proposes an explanation for how things work. It provides answers. Different users can replicate a good model in different circumstances.

In contrast, a framework does not provide answers. It helps frame questions and lines of inquiry. It is a tool that can help practitioners examine their assumptions and explore the full range of options at their disposal. A framework recognizes that there is no single best way of achieving particular results, but it does help reveal the implications that various choices entail. Ultimately, it recognizes that decisions about what to do and how to proceed are highly contingent and can only be made in practice, in the context of each mission and in the unique circumstances of each country.

The New Synthesis Framework aims to help practitioners integrate the solid foundations of the past, the lessons learned over the past 30 years and the challenges of serving in the 21st century. It does not reject past practices; instead it explores how they may fit together and how the new reality of practice transforms them.

The New Synthesis Framework is depicted in Figure 1. It is framed around four vectors. The two vertical vectors help readers clarify the desired public results at the highest level by exploring the interrelationship between public policy results and civic results. The former helps position agency results in the broader context of system-wide and societal results. The latter ascertains how this contributes to building the collective capacity of society to achieve better results over time. These vectors help explore how government, people and communities can work together and share responsibility for producing public results of higher value at a lower overall cost to society.

The two horizontal vectors focus on the use of government authority and the reliance on the collective power of society. They explore the means by which public results may be achieved. In most cases, governments achieve results through a mix of instruments, some direct and most indirect, including tax credits, vouchers or transfers to other levels of government.[5] Since an increasing number of public results exceed the capacity of government working alone, governments rely on vast networks of organizations, some internal and most external, to achieve the desired public results.

The four vectors depicted in Figure 1 are independent from each other. In other words, they are not on a continuum running from +1 to -1 on a common scale.

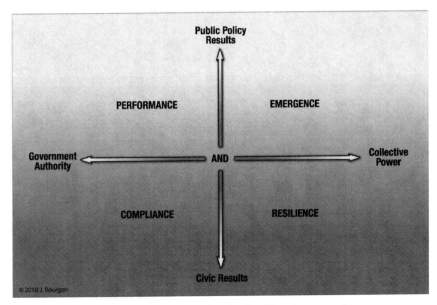

Figure 1: *The New Synthesis Framework—An Enabling Framework*

Taken together, the vectors map out a space of possibilities. They may be combined in different ways depending on the purpose, the circumstances or the existing capacity in government and in society. The possibilities are endless.

The framework is intended to help practitioners explore the space of possibilities, to help them bridge in practice what is judged to be politically desirable with what is feasible and to help them understand what impacts may occur across systems and over time.

There are multiple tensions at the crossroads of these lines of force. Some people prefer to rely heavily on law and order, some advocate relying on market forces and others prefer a different balance between the public, private and civic spheres. Whatever the case may be, the framework encourages decision makers to suspend the expression of their preferences for a time so that they may explore the range of choices open to them more fully.

The greatest potential for innovation lies at the crossroads of the four vectors. This is where issues, tools and capacities may be recombined in new and more productive ways. It is where politics and administration, means and ends must come together, and where conflicting values and preferences must be reconciled. It is where a new sharing of roles and responsibilities between people, government and society may be forged; one that holds the potential for achieving results of higher public value at a lower overall cost to society.

A BROADER DEFINITION OF PUBLIC RESULTS

Achieving public results of value to society is the core business of public institutions and public organizations.[6] *The New Synthesis Framework is proposing that public results are a combination of public policy results and civic results* (New Frontiers). Unlike organizations in the private sector or civil society, public organizations are responsible for achieving public policy results in a manner that contributes to building the collective capacity to achieve better results over time.

Public policy results provide a sense of direction: civic results contribute to collective capacity-building. The former builds credibility; the latter provides legitimacy. Together, they provide a foundation of trust and build resilience (see Figure 2).

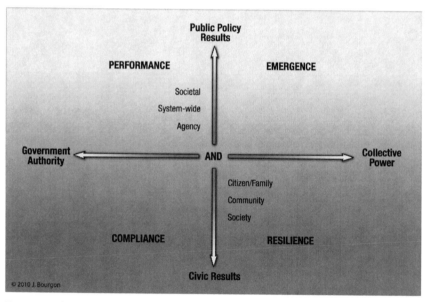

Figure 2: *The New Synthesis Framework and Public Results*

Public Policy Results

In the public sector, *agency results* provide a basis for reconciling inputs, outputs and responsibilities. Agency results are the traditional basis for accountability for the use of taxpayer funds and for the exercise of delegated authority. Agency results provide the basis for improving efficiency.

Every organization, public or private, has boundaries that give its members a sense of belonging. These boundaries help maintain cohesion and accumulate assets in the form of unique expertise or capacities. In the public sector, no organization works alone; no program or service is entirely self-sufficient. Public organizations serve a mission that extends well beyond the walls of their units and beyond the programs and services that they administer at any time. They serve a public purpose.

To fulfill their mission, public agencies must know about, understand and be able to work with other organizations (both inside and outside government) that contribute to the same or a related public purpose. Public agencies form part of system-wide networks of contributing organizations and, as a result, must position their contribution in the broader context of system-wide and societal results.

Public agencies interact with multiple organizations along multiple points of interface. They need the flexibility and the permeability to connect resources and capacities to fulfill their broader mission and support government-wide priorities. An efficient school does not make an effective public education system by itself; nor an efficient hospital an effective health system.

System-wide results provide the basis for interagency collaboration. By defining results at this level, public servants stand a better chance of discovering the interrelationships among multiple systems and the multifaceted interventions needed to address complex issues.

System-wide results open channels for working with others to achieve shared results where organizations working in isolation cannot achieve the desired outcomes or where government agencies must co-ordinate their activities to achieve the priorities set by government. The focus on system-wide results is necessary to connect a diverse array of actors and to broaden the range of options open to government.

Societal results are the most meaningful for citizens and for politicians because they reveal real choices, trade-offs and gaps. They provide information about the overall performance of a country and represent the sum of the contributions made by the private sector, the public sector, civil society and citizens themselves. While it may not be possible to isolate the contribution of a single actor, societal results can be evaluated and made available for all to see. Societal results allow one country's performance to be compared with that of others with a similar level of economic development. This is what the OECD and other international bodies have done for many years and in an increasing number of policy areas.[7]

Societal results provide the basis for achieving progress in areas that require a collective effort. They contribute to public awareness and elevate public debate about the consequences of various choices. Societal results reflect the state of society to citizens and decision makers, and help them shape the collective interests that, in turn, inform government action.

Societal results are multi-dimensional. They cannot be reduced to a single indication, be it GDP growth or GDP per capita. Beyond economic growth, they must take account of factors, such as quality of life, intergenerational fairness and well-being.[8]

Civic Results

The New Synthesis Framework proposes that public organizations have a special responsibility to contribute to civic results. This responsibility is a distinctive characteristic of government and public organizations. Public administration is not separate from people, communities and society. Public administration must integrate the role of government and the contribution of the people and society it has for its mission to serve.

Civic results include an active citizenry, resilient communities and a civic spirit that infuses every aspect of life in society and that is conducive to collective action. Civic results endow society with the energy and the capacity to address complex issues and adapt to unforeseen circumstances. They build the social capital that contributes to the overall performance of society.[9]

Peaceful societies with public institutions that work and are made up of people who collaborate and overcome their differences are better positioned to take risks, innovate and adapt to unforeseen circumstances. This is why similar reforms lead to very different results in different countries. It is also why some countries show a greater capacity for surmounting difficulties and prospering in the face of adversity, while others flounder in similar situations.[10]

Public institutions are expected to live up to some basic principles of good public governance. For instance, they are expected to maintain checks and balances in the exercise of power; allow the legislative assembly to oversee the executive; and ensure that holders of public office are held accountable for the use of public funds and the exercise of authority.

Many countries ensure citizens have access to information and encourage their participation to ensure greater support for government initiatives. These measures contribute to what the OECD calls "open and inclusive government."[11]

In the context of the New Synthesis Framework, however, civic results have a broader meaning and play a more important role. They entail framing public policies, programs and services with the explicit purpose of allowing and encouraging people, their families or their communities to play an active role in producing public results. They approach the production of public results as a shared responsibility that brings government to work with people, families and communities.

Governments deliver thousands of programs and services that are a manifestation of the political will and policy choices made by successive governments over time to express their view of the collective interest. These programs and services have been mediated through a political process and, in some cases, through the electoral process in place in the country. The contribution to civic results of most existing public programs and services can be enhanced by systematically exploring how people, families and communities can play a more active role and how this role may lead to results of higher public value at a lower overall cost to society. As will be seen later, this approach may lead to surprising discoveries.

The active participation of citizens, families and communities may take many forms and different meanings depending on the program and circumstances. The aim is to cultivate the capacity of people, communities and society to contribute to collective public results while meeting their own needs. This approach contributes to building social capital, trust and the willingness to act collectively. Programs designed to encourage active participation have the added advantage of building resilience and encouraging self-reliance. Recent research also demonstrates that active participation contributes to wellness and life satisfaction.[12]

It is relatively easy to improve the contribution of existing programs to civic results by exploring three basic avenues—by providing access, voice and choice.

Better Access

Building on the progress and lessons learned with e-government initiatives, it is possible to improve citizens' access to most government services. This may include integrated service delivery, self-service options or access to services at home and after hours. It may mean better access to experts through modern communication and collaboration platforms, as is the case for telemedicine or telelearning.

Improving access may also include making public data and public information readily available for citizens to use on their own or to create new public goods and services. For example, New York City developed an online Data Mine to increase the public's access to data generated by the city's various departments.[13] More than 170 datasets are available, such as traffic updates, WiFi hotspots, taxi information and restaurant inspection data. Descriptions of the data, the collection method and other contextual material make the datasets easy to use. City agencies control the datasets and update them regularly. Anyone can use the datasets to conduct research or create new applications ("apps"); and the city rewards the developers of the most useful and innovative applications.[14]

Stronger Voices

A growing number of promising avenues exist for people to have a say in public policy and service delivery processes. These range from crowd-sourcing to co-designing and co-creating public services to incorporating feedback mechanisms into the program improvement cycle.

The Brazilian Ministry of Justice led a project to draft and reach consensus on a bill to regulate Internet use that impressed participants at the international roundtable held in that country in May 2010. The Ministry used a blended approach, combining a blog, town hall meetings and other traditional means to reach a broad cross-section of people, including those with various levels of literacy or in remote communities. The discussion moved away from criminalizing what could be done on the Internet to exploring principles to guide its use. As a result of the public's input, the Ministry dramatically changed its initial approach. Previous attempts had failed to garner the necessary political support; this time, the bill gained the support of Congress.[15]

Expanded Choices

Most government programs involve a certain degree of flexibility to respond to diverse needs and circumstances. Public officials who manage the programs and provide the services exercise this discretion. It is often possible to explore how citizens could exercise a portion of this discretion on their own behalf without redesigning existing programs.

In various parts of the world, experiments are under way to give citizens real choices in how they use public services. For example, the Canadian government commissioned the Social Research and Demonstration Corporation (SRDC), a non-profit organization that conducts social experiments throughout the country, to investigate ways of improving outcomes from the Employment Insurance program by giving recipients a choice in how they receive their benefits.[16] The SRDC designs rigorous experiments in which real subjects, real public programs and real consequences are closely monitored to better understand the benefits and costs of providing choice.

One experiment examined the effect of letting recipients decide whether they would benefit more by receiving either larger amounts for a shorter time or smaller amounts for a longer time. While the total dollar amount of either choice would be the same, recipients decided if they needed more money up-front (for example, to help defray the cost of moving to a new city to take up a new job) or if they needed benefits for a longer period of time (for example, to help support them if labour market conditions are particularly bad in their region).

Governments often have more room to manoeuvre than they realize to allow citizens, families or communities to decide how they would like to use public services. Organizing public services in this way can improve results[17] at a lower overall cost to society. It can be done in a manner that respects professional responsibilities and political accountabilities.

Mediating Public Policy Results and Civic Results

Governments have a responsibility to encourage the active contribution of citizens as value creators in their own lives, in their communities and in society. This requires a balancing act to ensure that government focuses on what it does best, that citizens are encouraged to do what is within their power to achieve and that people and government share the responsibility for collective results.

Programs and services designed to encourage the active contributions of citizens as users or beneficiaries hold the promise of improving results.[18] This is because multiple actors share the burden with government. In the process, these measures encourage individual self-reliance and contribute to community resilience.

The New Synthesis Framework is proposing that public administrators must explore how to move the contribution of their organization along the two value-added chains of public policy and civic results (New Frontiers). The challenge is to achieve public policy and civic results of higher value, not one or the other, and not one at the expense of the other. Public administrators must mediate between better public policy results and a drive for efficiency gains in the short term with the need to achieve better civic results to build the capacity to achieve better public results over time. Achieving civic results by providing more access, voice and choice to citizens may take time, but it holds the prospect of building society's capacity to achieve better results over the long haul.

Optimizing public policy results and civic results is a difficult balancing act. It requires fine judgment that can only be exercised by taking into account the unique context, culture and circumstances that prevail in each country.

In recent years, many countries have made great strides towards improving performance, productivity and efficiency. However, these reforms have not paid sufficient attention to civic results, which has distorted our appreciation of the relative contribution of government and of citizens to the overall performance of society.

The challenge of embedding a focus on civic results on an equal footing with public policy results in government activities is not limited to societies with conventional forms of democratic governance. The same challenge applies to countries with or without elections and with or without multiple parties.[19] The world over, citizens are seeking to play a more active role in the areas of greatest importance to them.[20]

In refining the New Synthesis Framework, participants benefited from discussions on powerful case studies. Two cases in particular contributed to a deepening understanding of the interrelationships between public policy results and civic results. One focused on the transformation of the Singapore Prison Service; the other on Brazil's Bolsa Família program. The case studies are presented in full in Part Two of this volume. In this chapter, summaries illustrate how focusing on societal and civic results opens up a broader range of options for government and how this focus may lead to better public results.

The New Synthesis Framework encourages a process of exploration. While the process may be similar in many countries, the policy choices are country-specific.

Learning from Practice:
The Singapore Prison Service Case (Singapore)

In the late 1990s, the Singapore Prison Service (SPS) faced challenges similar to many prison systems around the world. It was plagued by overcrowding, high recidivism and increasing costs. In the span of a decade, however, Singapore has seen dramatic improvements in the rehabilitation and re-integration of ex-offenders. Recidivism has declined from 44.3 percent in 1998 to 26.5 percent in 2007; 1,800 employers have hired ex-offenders; 1,400 volunteers have served in counselling and other activities for inmates; millions of dollars have been raised to support services and programs in communities.

The process of change started with the SPS developing a broader view of its role in society. It transformed itself from an organization "focused on protecting society through the safe custody of criminals" (agency results) to playing an instrumental role in steering offenders towards "being responsible citizens with the help of their families and the community" (societal results).

Positioning an organization in the broad context of societal results helps reveal the interrelationships with other contributors. It provides the basis from which new forms of collaboration can be explored. In the SPS's case, it revealed the need for a more integrated approach that goes beyond security and safety to include prevention, rehabilitation, reintegration into society and after-care (system-wide results).

A vision framed in positive terms and in a manner that values the contribution of others is a powerful invitation to collaboration, mobilization and co-creation (civic results).

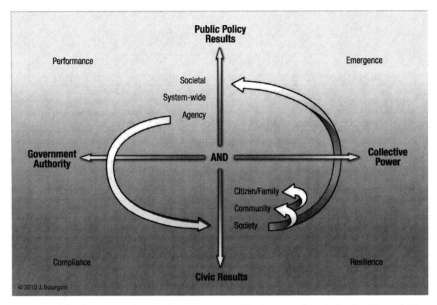

Figure 3: *The Singapore Prison System Case—The Power of an Inclusive Mental Map*

It took years for the SPS to reach internal consensus and still more years to prepare public opinion to give ex-offenders a fresh start in life. Employers found it easier to employ ex-offenders once public opinion became more receptive; family support improved the likelihood of successful rehabilitation; family and community support made it worthwhile for offenders to work hard to make their reintegration successful.

Singapore has ten years of data to document the results. This case illustrates how focusing on the "big picture" and reaching out to encourage the contribution of others make better public results achievable. The SPS has reason to be satisfied with progress to date, and it continues to explore new avenues and experiment with new approaches to achieve even better results. The search for better results never ends. The long-term success of an organization hinges on its preparedness for the future, which in turn depends on its current ability to anticipate and learn.[21]

Learning from Practice: The Bolsa Família Case (Brazil)

Bolsa Família is a national program of conditional cash transfers to families living in poverty. With an annual budget of US$7.4 billon in 2010 and reaching 50 million families, the program is the largest of its kind in the world. It evolved into its current form progressively and over many phases.

Several studies have documented Bolsa Família's impact in terms of reducing poverty, inequality, child under-nutrition and child mortality (societal results). The case material presents some indications of the progress made. For instance, between 2001 and 2008, the income of the poorest families increased by an average of 8 percent per year, while the income of the richest families grew by an average of 1.5 percent. A 2005 study revealed that the prevalence of under-nutrition among children aged 6 months to 1 year was 2.65 times higher in families that were not beneficiaries of the program than in families that were.[22] Today, Bolsa Família stands as a source of inspiration for many developing countries.

Bolsa Família evolved from a process of experimentation and incremental improvements spanning 1995 to 2004. By the early 2000s, a significant number of departmental programs were transferring funds to families, each of which had different registries, administrative procedures, conditions, payment modalities and oversight mechanisms. They reported to different departments with different missions. As one participant indicated when this case was discussed during the roundtable held in Ottawa in May 2010, "People are not divided by ministries."[23] It took political leadership to integrate all the cash transfer programs into a single program (Bolsa Família) and to design the program from the perspective of the families it needed to reach. It took courage to empower families to make their own decisions on how to use the funds transferred to them (civic results).

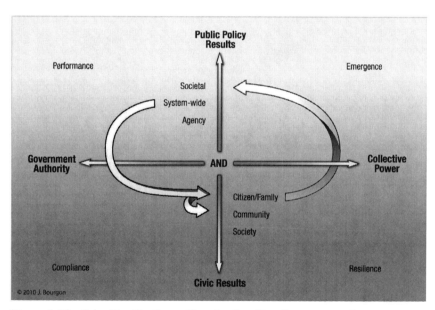

Figure 4: *The Bolsa Família Case—Trusting Families, Empowering Communities*

The program design incorporates a number of initiatives to empower families and build communities (See Figure 4). Funds are provided to families below the poverty line, and preferentially paid to the women in the household directly by means of an automated teller machine (ATM) card. For many, this was an introduction to modern banking and to new technologies.

Families were trusted to use the funds in the manner most appropriate for them in their circumstances. The various conditions and controls previously imposed by departments were replaced by a single limited set of conditions regarding children's health, enrolment in education, the avoidance of being prematurely drawn into the labour market and maternal health, along with a simpler set of controls. Municipalities manage the program at the local level.

The breakthrough in this case was the decision to empower families and communities. Better civic results led to improved public policy results. The results to date indicate that government was justified in trusting and empowering families to make decisions. In fact, a number of more general conclusions can be drawn from this experience, including that trust breeds trustworthiness, and that systems designed based on distrust impose high costs on society and are unlikely to lead to better results.[24]

In its early stages, Bolsa Família was subject to public criticism and intense scrutiny by the media. Inevitably, mistakes were made that led to demands to impose more controls and tighter conditions. The way the government handled the situation provides another important lesson. Instead of giving in to these demands, President Lula said, "We are sensitive enough to correct the mistakes as we find them, and correct our path."[25] Errors will be made. But the risk of error is no justification for not exploring new ways of achieving ambitious results. The most serious error of all would be to fail to learn from the errors we make.

At the time of writing, Bolsa Família enjoys the political support of all parties and strong support from the public.

AN EXPANDED VIEW OF THE ROLE OF GOVERNMENT

Traditionally, government has been seen as the primary agent in serving the public good and the collective interest. According to this view, government sets the agenda for change, proposes new laws and regulations and enforces existing ones, mediates among conflicting interests, collects taxes and uses its spending power to provide public services.

Public agencies that represent both an organizational entity and a policy domain (such as health, education, urban development) were expected to operate without much interaction with others, within the limits of their mandate and with the instruments and resources granted to them.

Today, as we learn that many public results are a collective enterprise requiring the contribution of multiple actors, this view is giving way to a more comprehensive view of the role of government.[26] Organizations of all kinds, in addition to government organizations, hold the resources, capacity and legitimacy essential to addressing an increasing number of public policy issues.

Furthermore, complex issues cut across jurisdictional, organizational, professional and generational lines.[27] Addressing the challenges associated with an aging population, poverty or national security, for example, is beyond the reach of a single public organization working alone. The traditional instruments of government, such as its normative, taxation or redistributive powers, will not suffice.

The New Synthesis Framework proposes that the role of government extends beyond what it can do on its own and incorporates what it can do with others to serve the collective interest. Its role extends to leveraging the power of others across all facets of society[28] and enabling synergies by working across boundaries inside and outside government.[29] *The role of government entails a search for balance between the authority of the state and the collective power of society to advance results of higher value to society* (New Frontiers) (see Figure 5). Too much government authority creates rigidities and brittleness in society; too little dissipates collective efforts and increases the risks for society.

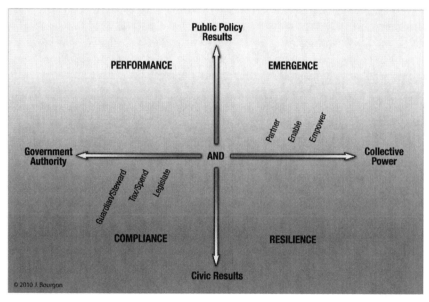

Figure 5: *New Synthesis Framework—Government Authority and Collective Power*

Working across Boundaries

Over the last 30 years, the need to bring multiple organizations together to achieve results has received a lot of attention. As challenges became more complex, governments found that they needed more flexibility and a wider range of options to respond to changing needs and citizens' expectations.[30] Some governments introduced framework laws to give public organizations a higher degree of discretion in responding to a diversity of circumstances. Others explored different distributions of power. They experimented with centralization, decentralization or the creation of additional levels of government. Most governments also experimented with various organizational reforms.

The search for collaborative arrangements took many names and forms. These arrangements were introduced to respond to the common need to work across boundaries as well as some particular needs in each country. In the United Kingdom, "joined-up" government was the leitmotiv in the 1990s. Then came Total Place in the 2000s, which was renamed Community Budgets in 2010. Australia explored whole-of-government models. Canada encouraged working horizontally and community-building across government. France promoted collaborative approaches to address "les grandes questions transversales;" and the Netherlands introduced Program Ministries.

All these efforts entailed, in some way, the recognition that an increasing number of issues do not and will not fit within organizational boundaries.

Complex issues are capable of metamorphosis. They involve a web of interrelationships and require multifaceted approaches that cannot be contained in a single agency. Governments cannot restructure or reorganize themselves out of this dilemma. Reorganization simply creates new boundaries that still need to be crossed. There is no magic bullet and no right way to divide powers and responsibilities.

The ability to work across boundaries and manage multiple interfaces is part of the reality of government in the 21st century. It puts a premium on the capacity of government to bring together in a flexible way the necessary knowledge, know-how, capacity and resources when and where they are needed to make progress and solve complex problems.

The ability to work across boundaries is needed among public agencies, across government and among levels of governments. In fact, it is needed beyond government and across society where public organizations are called upon to operate as platforms of collaboration to leverage the power of others.

Over the past 30 years, most governments have talked about the need for government-wide collaboration. However, because some existing systems and practices inhibit collaboration, a gap still exists between rhetoric and practice. This gap will continue to exist until working across boundaries is recognized as the normal way of doing business in government and until measures are introduced to ensure the harmonious co-existence of networks and vertical hierarchies. There is a long way to go.

Hierarchy and Networks

Networks are powerful assets in generating new solutions. Governments can leverage the power of networks to connect actors, problems and opportunities in new ways to achieve public results.[31] The literature distinguishes between hierarchical, decentralized (hub-and-spoke), networked or distributed models.[32] In the public sector, all three models are at play simultaneously.

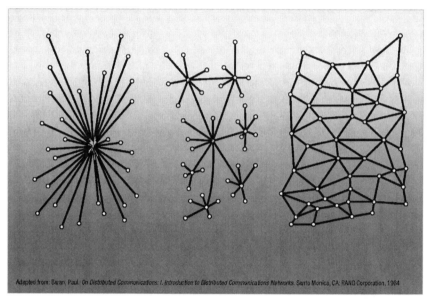

Adapted from: Baran, Paul. *On Distributed Communications. I. Introduction to Distributed Communications Networks.* Santa Monica, CA: RAND Corporation, 1964

Figure 6: *Hierarchy, Hub-and-Spoke Networks and Distributed Networks*

The hierarchical model is the traditional way of running departments and public agencies. It defines the organizational boundaries and sets the jurisdiction of the organization. Authority is delegated vertically. Units are grouped based on responsibility, expertise or function. This model forms the basis for ministerial accountability and reporting on the use of public funds.

Large ministries or highly decentralized departments with relatively autonomous agencies frequently use the *hub-and-spoke model*. Key decisions, such as new policies or budget allocations, are made centrally and in some cases with minimal involvement from the various units or agencies. One such example in Canada would be a provincial department of Health that oversees a large number of hospitals and clinics, which report individually to a CEO and a local board of trustees for their day-to-day operations.

Networks operate with varying degrees of formality and continuity. They do not need formal structure or decision–making power to be effective. The size of their budget or the number of employees does not define their importance, relevance or value. Their strength is in bringing together distributed knowledge and ensuring that various agencies in a related domain of interest take coherent action. Their power resides in the value-added that is brought about by the relationship among participants.

A networked approach is necessary to support government-wide priorities, to bridge policy domains or to compensate for the disaggregation that the fragmented approach among public agencies may cause. Distributed networks display even more flexibility and variability. They connect agencies, people and knowledge as necessary with no need for continuity or permanence beyond the immediate purpose.

In spite of the attention paid to working across agencies, most governments still lack the systems, practices and policies to facilitate the co-existence of hierarchy and networks.

The case study on the Dutch Public Safety Centres that was presented at the roundtable in The Hague in March 2010[33] illustrates these tensions. This case study is presented in full in Part Two of this volume.

Learning from Practice:
Public Safety Centres (the Netherlands)

The case of the Public Safety Centres (PSCs) illustrates potential of new ways of working and some of the challenges associated with working across boundaries.

Public safety issues are too multifaceted to leave to a single agency; reorganization would not solve the problem. The Netherlands introduced PSCs to bring together the contribution of multiple organizations on an as-needed basis. The overall goal was to reduce crime and public nuisance by 25 percent and recidivism by 10 percent by 2011 compared to 2002.

The first PSC was created in Tilburg in 2002. In a short time, it was credited with impressive results, including a reduction in recidivism among young offenders of 50 percent and a general decrease in crime.[34] As a result, the concept was incorporated in the national policy of the Ministry of Justice and expanded to other regions.

The PSCs bring together a blend of expertise in law enforcement, prevention and after-care. They ensure a co-ordinated and multifaceted response to emerging issues involving public, private and community-based organizations. Although their composition may vary from city to city, they typically include the ministries of Justice and of the Interior, the local prosecution office, the local head of police, the mayor, a number of welfare organizations, including mental health and addiction care centres, social housing corporations and probation officers.

Participating organizations share information about individual cases and build a shared file of the case. This is a major shift from the traditional approach in which each agency works in isolation. Representatives from the participating agencies strive to achieve consensus on the best course of action and to co-ordinate their actions. As noted in the case study, while safety problems originate with individual offenders, the problems can be "aggravated by poor co-ordination among public sector organizations."[35]

A PSC is not an organization: it is a network operating as a platform of co-operation. The participating organizations retain their respective mandate, authority and resources. They act on their own and retain full responsibility for their actions even though the knowledge of others contributes to their decision making. Hierarchical structures co-exist with networking arrangements.

In spite of their success, the progress made by the PSCs remains fragile and essentially dependent on individual commitments. The case is indicative of the tensions that exist between traditional hierarchical approaches and networks. It reveals, although obliquely, the need for collaboration between loosely coupled organizations on the one hand and the pull to "formalize," "regularize" or "normalize" informal arrangements on the other hand. Loosely coupled organizations come together when needed to exchange knowledge and work in a concerted way in areas of common concern, but they remain free to pursue their respective mandates on their own.

Networks are agile and nimble. They cut across boundaries and facilitate open exchange at multiple points of interface. They help transform relatively closed organizations into more open systems. Herein lies their strength and value.

The push to "regularize" networks generally reduces the agility that is afforded by working through informal arrangements. A number of measures are needed to ensure that hierarchies and networks co-exist harmoniously.

More than Talk

The harmonious co-existence of hierarchies and networks cannot be left entirely to individual initiative. Individuals must make "heroic" efforts to do so, which exacts a heavy toll on them.

The need to work across boundaries has long been recognized, but the systems and practices are not yet aligned to make it a sustainable feature of public organizations. A number of measures are needed to make a system-wide commitment to working across boundaries more than just talk. Some specific suggestions are discussed in Chapter 5.

LEVERAGING THE COLLECTIVE POWER

An increasing number of public results are beyond the reach of government, even when working across government agencies and with other levels of government. The role of government extends to what can be achieved by working with and through others in society. It extends to leveraging the collective power of society to achieve public results and enabling the contribution of others. Government actions are intermediate steps in long chains of interrelated actions involving the public, private or civic sectors.

Issues ranging from global warming to the global financial crisis, from obesity to illiteracy, from food safety to poverty alleviation, from reducing racial tensions to improving public safety all require the contribution of multiple stakeholders without which government initiatives will falter. In these cases, it is more appropriate to think in terms of *governance* than of *government.*

Recognizing the need to harness the collective power of society, many governments are beginning to complement traditional ways of governing with new ones. As they move towards producing public results with others, an expanded range of options opens up to them.

Partner

Governments can *partner* with others to achieve public results. Partnering is not the same as privatization or contracting out. It is a model of shared responsibility in which each partner contributes what it does best to bring about results of common interests or find shared solutions to common problems. Partnering entails shared responsibilities for shared results. It requires an equitable sharing of the risks and rewards that a joint effort may bring about, along with conflict resolution mechanisms to resolve potential disagreements. Examples of public-private partnerships, which are common in many countries, include providing services such as roads, bridges, waterworks and other infrastructure.

Enable

Governments can *enable* others to produce public results by providing public support to explore new and innovative ways of achieving results. This may involve creating common public platforms and modern public infrastructure or various forms of incentives to encourage innovation and experimentation.

For example, in 1992, two young teachers in an inner-city public school in Houston, Texas, became frustrated with how the system treated minority youth and those living in poverty.[36] They designed the Knowledge Is Power Program (KIPP) for running public charter schools. The program's goal is to help students "climb the mountain to and through college"[37] to combat the tendency of inner-city schools to become "dropout factories"[38] where more than 40 percent of students leave high school before graduating. The KIPP approach is based on creating a community in which individuals are accountable to each other for their success. On entry to a KIPP school, the teachers, parents and students sign a contract that outlines their mutual commitments and accountabilities. As of 2010, KIPP ran 99 charter schools in 20 states. The vast majority of students who attend a KIPP-run middle school (grades 4-9) go on to college.[39]

In the United States of America, charter schools operate with a higher degree of freedom than traditional public schools. They allow for more decision-making latitude in choosing the curriculum, staffing and managing teachers, and responding to community needs. These schools are established with a charter (essentially a performance contract) and are sponsored by a public agency, such as a state government or local school board.

Another example of measures to enable others is to make public data accessible so that it can be blended and recombined in new ways to create new public goods and services. Governments hold large amounts of public data that represent a public asset of great value that taxpayers have already paid for. To encourage new and innovative uses, some jurisdictions have carved public data out from copyright protection. For instance, the Australian Bureau of Statistics and Geoscience Australia are allowing the public to use the data freely using Creative Commons licenses. In the United States of America, many federal government materials are in the public domain and free of copyright.[40]

Co-create

Enabling others to co-create or co-produce public results should not be seen as a new way of cutting public spending or off-loading the costs of public services onto society. Rather, it is the creation of an interdependent relationship between government, society and people to achieve results of higher value at a lower overall cost to society. This may lead to significant savings and better results by combining issues, capacities and resources in new and innovative ways.

Significant experiments and innovations are taking place around different ways of co-creating and co-producing public results in the health sector. The Scottish Centre for Telehealth helps patients with chronic or degenerative diseases actively monitor and assess their own health at home and when required.[41] The results are sent to a community health centre that has complete access to the patients' medical records. Patients can call in for expert advice should they detect any anomaly or unusual result. Expert advice is provided about any necessary actions or if their condition requires going to the hospital. If hospital care is required, the patient's medical record is already in the hands of the medical team by the time he or she arrives. In this example, specialists, community clinics, hospitals and citizens all play key roles, enabled by modern information and communication technologies, to co-create healthcare services.

In a similar vein, in Switzerland, citizens with one of the large healthcare insurers are required to call a medical hotline called Medgate before seeking medical care in person. Medgate connects them with on-call doctors, including specialists, who have electronic access to their medical records and may be able to provide callers with a diagnosis over the phone.[42] In many cases, the doctors provide advice that helps callers treat themselves. Doctors working through Medgate are allowed to write prescriptions if they can make a credible and reliable determination of need. As of 2011, Medgate serves 4.2 million people and fields 4,600 calls per day. The cost of serving patients over the telephone is 50 percent less than serving them in a clinic. France is also exploring the benefits of co-production.[43] Docteurclic and Medecindirect are two services that provide medical consultations over the telephone.

The novelty of these approaches is in the way the factors (patients, medical personnel and facilities, technology, policy, funding) are combined to achieve better public results at a lower overall cost to society.

Empower

Governments can work to *empower* and rely on the power of those best-positioned to act on a given public issue. This does not necessarily mean a formal redistribution of power or resources. It means recognizing that there are multiple sources and forms of power already available in society that can be brought to bear on a public issue or goal. It is about the authority of the state and the collective power of society coming together for a shared purpose. The power of modern information and communications technologies and social media to connect people and information in real time and across great distances is increasing the capacity of people to exercise power and mobilize into action.

The Ushahidi-Haiti initiative[44] played a crucial role in supporting the rescue and rebuilding efforts in the wake of the devastating earthquake in Haiti in January 2010. In the immediate aftermath of the earthquake, a group of graduate students at Tufts University in Boston used an open-source, Internet-based program called Ushahidi to map precisely where rescue efforts were needed and where rescue resources were available. The program used "crowd-sourced" data from an ongoing stream of text messages and radio signals sent by citizens, rescue personnel and on-site aid workers, and from social media networks, such as Twitter. The United States Marines and the US Department of State quickly came on board to support and use the system. Within a day of the quake, the American government declassified satellite imagery and deployed drones over the island to gather more data that could be used in the mapping system. Within two days of the quake, Haiti's cellphone companies issued a short-code emergency number that the Haitian public could use to relay information to assist rescue and aid workers. On the ground, the Marines fed and used the system in their rescue efforts.[45]

During the emergency response phase of the crisis, the Ushahidi-Haiti initiative helped save lives and get crucial aid to thousands of Haitians. At the height of the crisis, more than 300 graduate students worked on the system and more than 1,000 Haitian Creole speakers in the United States of America, Canada and Europe volunteered to translate incoming messages. The initiative also proved useful in the rebuilding phase. Local groups are conducting neighbourhood surveys in Haiti, while in Boston, trained volunteers from the Haitian diaspora are mapping the data.

The Ushahidi platform is not new. It was developed by Kenyan civil rights activists to report incidences of violence in the wake of the 2008 Kenyan elections. It was designed to allow people to report violent exchanges, to alert people in real time as to where violent acts were being committed and to create a permanent record of this information.[46] As a common public platform based on open-source principles, citizens and organizations in Haiti, the United States of America and elsewhere quickly leveraged Ushahidi to work with each other and with government actors to produce public results in Haiti.

Learning from Practice:
The Homelessness Partnering Strategy (Canada)

The role of government in creating or participating on platforms of co-operation in society to tackle complex issues, along with some of the challenges that come with this role, is illustrated in a case study on Canada's Homelessness Partnering Strategy (HPS) that was presented at the international roundtables in Ottawa in May 2010 and in Rio de Janeiro in July 2010.[47] The case is presented in Part Two of this volume.

Homelessness is a complex, multi-dimensional issue that involves diverse underlying factors, such as poverty, affordable housing, employment, transportation, mental illness, family violence and racial discrimination. Homelessness takes many shapes and forms. It is found in developed and developing countries, and can affect every class in society.

The diverse underlying factors of homelessness require a wide variety of responses at the community, sub-national and national levels. No one is fully "in charge." Resolving the issue is beyond the capacity of any one actor.

The HPS was created as a collaborative platform to bring together relevant organizations from the federal and other levels of government, community groups and civil society organizations to look at the challenge of homelessness in an integrated manner at the community level. The Government of Canada's role was to launch the initiative, encourage participation and empower communities to act. The approach involved shared responsibility and co-funding among multiple actors and agencies.

This case study illustrates how government authority and resources can be used to leverage collective power when the results are beyond the reach of a single government or agency. Leveraging is a way of sharing the problem definition and integrating multiple forms of intervention, such as housing, health, social security, labour market and immigration. The role of government is predominantly indirect. Its actions are intermediate steps in a chain of interrelated actions relevant to the collective effort. The case reveals, "The HPS is a leveraging device...intended to address homelessness through building community capacity and bringing a multitude of resources to the table to build locally-defined priority programs and processes." It reports, "The Strategy has been able to leverage C$3 for every C$1 it invests."[48]

Notwithstanding the progress achieved, the HPS case study is also a reminder of how traditional practices designed for direct service delivery by a single public agency and a single government can get in the way of a collaborative endeavour. A heavy burden of reporting requirements, a focus on early results, short-term financing arrangements and frequent staff turnover in government act as barriers to achieving collective results: they undermine the collaborative spirit necessary for a collective enterprise.

Collective endeavours depend on relationships of trust that are built over time. They require special arrangements, including the harmonization of the various departmental financing and reporting requirements to sustain the efforts of the group and achieve better societal results.

The Stewardship Role of Government

Government also has guardian and stewardship roles. As guardian, government is the keeper of a public trust. It is expected to defend and protect public institutions. Public office holders are accountable for the use of public funds and for the proper exercise of the authority delegated to them. They are expected to abide by public sector values and to exhibit prudence, probity and integrity in performing their duties.

Government has a stewardship role to promote and defend the collective interest in all circumstances. In today's context, this presents government with a special responsibility to monitor, anticipate and introduce corrective and preventative measures when the collective interest demands it.[49] The more dispersed the decision making and the more distributed the exercise of power in society, the more important the stewardship role of government becomes. In times of need, citizens will always look to government for action. As various crises illustrate, such as the Severe Acute Respiratory Syndrome (SARS) of 2002-03 or financial crisis of 2008-10, the stewardship role of government cannot be outsourced. Government is the insurer of last resort when the collective interest demands it. Ultimately, the consequences of choices made today will be borne by society as a whole and by future generations. They will have to address the consequences of the financial, environmental or social legacies, assets and deficits they inherit. The stewardship role of government has received insufficient attention in the recent past and was shown to be wanting in some of the crises the world experienced recently.

PUBLIC ADMINISTRATION AS A CO-EVOLVING SYSTEM

Modern governance involves a search for balance between the public, private and civil spheres. It entails a search for a delicate balance where the state authority is used to leverage the collective capacity of society to achieve results of higher public value.

In acting in this fashion, government is not taking a laisser-faire stance, nor is it reducing its position relative to other actors in society. Instead, it is exercising a more sophisticated blend of roles on behalf of the collective. In this light, *the role of government is taking shape in an expanding space of possibilities where public organizations, public servants, citizens and other actors in society form part of a co-evolving system of governance.* Government transforms society and is transformed by society.

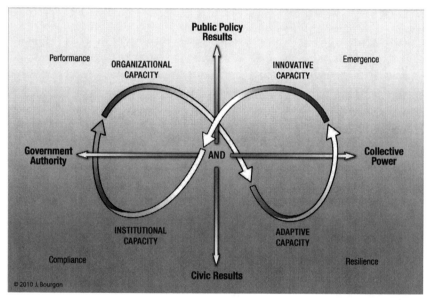

Figure 7: *New Synthesis Framework—Public Administration in an Expanding Space of Possibilities*

The New Synthesis Framework provides a schematized illustration of a co-evolving system of governance (See Figure 7). Taken together, the four lines of force—public results and civic results, government authority and collective power—shape a space of possibilities where issues, capacity and resources may be combined in new and different ways to achieve public results.

As an enabling framework, the New Synthesis Framework encourages practitioners to focus on achieving results of higher public value by positioning the contribution of their programs and organizations in the broader context of system-wide and societal results, and by contributing to civic results through giving citizens and communities an active role as value creators.

The framework encompasses the conventional uses of state authority along with newer forms of collective effort. It opens up the possibility for government to exercise an expanding range of roles in working with others.

The framework does not tell practitioners what to do: instead, it helps them explore the vast array of pathways open to them. It lifts the constraint that comes from the belief that there is one best way of doing things and frees the energy that comes from exploration and innovation in an open and dynamic system of public governance.

Chapter 4

Preparing Governments for the
Challenges of the 21st Century

It is not the strongest species that survive, nor the most intelligent, but the most responsive to change.

Charles Darwin (paraphrased).

Governments are called upon to address an increasing number of complex issues in an environment characterized by heightened levels of uncertainty. This situation is the result of a growing interdependence among the multiple systems that society depends on and of the changes brought about by the "connected republic"[1] of which we are all part. The Classic model of public administration is insufficient to support practitioners in this context. Furthermore, the public sector reforms to date represent an incomplete journey.

The New Synthesis Project is exploring what is different about serving in the 21st century, what new capabilities are needed to prepare government, and how these capabilities may work with current public administration systems and practices. In the end, for government to be fit for serving in the 21st century, everything must coalesce. Chapter 3 discussed the significance of the four vectors (public policy results, civic results, state authority and collective power) and explored their dynamic interrelations. This chapter goes deeper. The vectors map out four sub-systems through which government, society and people interact as part of a common system of modern governance. They reflect the need for compliance, performance, emergence and resilience, which are discussed in more detail in this chapter and the next, and which explore some of the capabilities needed to prepare government to face the challenges of our times.

The compliance sub-system includes constitutions, conventions, rules and norms that govern how we live in society. It includes the public institutions that have evolved over long periods. These institutions make and oversee the implementation of political decisions on behalf of society and give form to societal values.

Public institutions contribute to stability and reduce uncertainties. They ensure that society is governed by the rule of law. Public institutions provide legitimacy to the exercise of formal powers in society and give shape to collective aspirations. They evolve slowly, and so they should.[2]

A peaceful society with public institutions that work, with an efficient private sector and with an active civil society has a solid foundation on which to face the challenges of its times and to pursue an ambitious course for itself.

The performance sub-system transforms public purpose into concrete action. It includes the public organizations that give shape to public policy decisions by combining government authority, policy instruments, organizational capacity and public resources to achieve the desired public results. This sub-system also includes the public platforms of co-operation that allow public organizations to work across boundaries in government, among governments and with other organizations in society to achieve system-wide or societal results. Public organizations provide a solid basis for accountability for the use of taxpayers' money and the exercise of delegated authority. They need to reconcile hierarchical accountability with shared responsibility when working with others to achieve system-wide, government-wide and societal public results. Public organizations work best when they balance a concern for efficiency with a drive for the effectiveness of the whole.

The emergence sub-system helps build government's capacity to anticipate and detect emerging issues and phenomena. It helps introduce proactive interventions to mitigate the risks associated with undesirable events or to improve the likelihood of more favourable outcomes for society. This sub-system encourages the development of practical and emergent solutions to some of the complex issues of our times. It is necessary for government to serve the collective interests in unpredictable circumstances and to improve the likelihood of "smart" interventions even when governments are called upon to make decisions with imperfect knowledge and in uncertain circumstances. The emergence sub-system encourages the development of an innovative society with a high capacity for social innovation and experimentation.

The resilience sub-system provides the ultimate reality check to the adaptive capacity of government and society. Notwithstanding the efforts of government and society to anticipate issues, discover emergent solutions to the most challenging problems of our times and introduce proactive measures to deflect risks, unforeseen events will arise and unpredictable shocks will occur. The role of government in the 21ˢᵗ century extends to building the resilience of society to adapt, absorb shocks, embrace change and prosper even in the face of adversity. Resilience ensures that government and society have the capacity to bounce back and seize opportunities in the midst of crises. Resilience takes shape progressively as people, communities and governments work together and learn that they can count on each other in all circumstances and in times of need.

This chapter and the next illustrate some of the capacities needed to support each sub-system. They also consider how new capabilities transform the systems and practices inherited from the past. A key challenge is to ensure that, taken together, old and new capabilities amount to a more open system of governance, one where government has the capacity to explore emerging issues, shape emergent solutions, conserve energy and use collective resources with parsimony, exploit avenues for working with others to achieve results of higher public value at a lower overall cost to society and adapt to changing circumstances (see Figure 8).

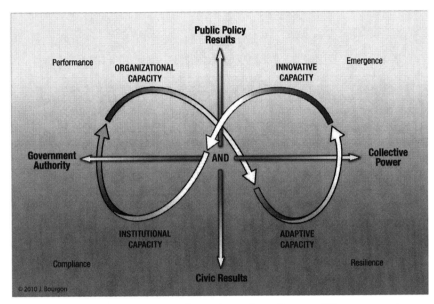

Figure 8: *New Synthesis Framework—A Co-evolving System of Governance*

Participants in the international roundtable discussions made a number of important observations on how to prepare governments to face some of the challenges of the 21st century. This section draws from the lessons learned from those discussions.[3] The key question is whether the proposed changes and adjustments will be sufficient to support a co-evolving system of governance where government transforms society and is open to being transformed by society.

SERVING BEYOND THE PREDICTABLE: EMERGENCE

Governing in the 21st century entails dealing with complex issues in an uncertain environment. The main difficulty for government is that public organizations were not devised or designed to deal with complexity and high levels of uncertainty. Their strength is in providing stability and predictability. What is an asset in some circumstances becomes a liability in others. Relying on traditional approaches, government runs the risk of being left in a reactive position, unable to anticipate or detect emerging patterns in a fast-changing landscape and therefore unable to intervene in a timely way.

The topics of emergence, resilience and how to prepare government for the challenges of serving beyond the predictable were discussed at the roundtables in The Hague in March 2010 and in Singapore in September of the same year. The conversations revealed the importance of improving the anticipative, innovative and adaptive capacities of government and society. Much can be learned by exploring what some countries are doing in practice to improve their anticipative capacity and the innovative capacity of society.

Borrowed from complex systems theory, the term *emergence* refers to the process by which new patterns arise out of a multiplicity of interactions between different systems.[4] Applied to public administration, the theory would recognize that the economic, social, political, technological and environmental systems are dynamically intertwined and continually impact each other.

Successfully addressing complex issues requires concerted efforts to improve the capacity of government to anticipate emerging trends and encourage timely, proactive interventions. Countries with the capability to anticipate and the ability to use these insights to make better decisions and intervene ahead of time will have an important comparative advantage. They will be best able to adapt and prosper in unknown circumstances and to influence the course of events in their favour.

ANTICIPATIVE CAPACITY

We may not know the future but we can envisage and understand a range of possible futures. Furthermore, the actions taken today will have direct and indirect consequences in the future; they shape the landscape for tomorrow. Focusing on the future helps government deflect risks and chart a better future for society. It helps improve today's decisions by providing better insights about their potential downstream consequences.

Futures work is not new; much can be learned from the work to date in the private and public sectors. Futures work and anticipatory work form part of the capabilities needed to prepare governments to be fit for their times. It is one of the most important roles that policy units in departments, ministries or the centre of government can perform. Anticipatory work can help government and society think more systematically about the future and build a broad-based consensus about what constitutes a preferable future and how to get there.

Futures work serves a number of purposes. It helps assess and manage risks, identify and mitigate vulnerabilities and detect opportunities.[5] It also helps challenge assumptions that may lead to unproductive results at great costs to society. For instance, evidence is emerging that the rate of violent crime is declining in many countries, such as the United Kingdom and Canada.[6] However, public perception is that the opposite trend is occurring. In response to public concerns, government may invest in public safety measures and infrastructure that are not warranted by the evidence.[7]

Futures work encourages preventive action. Crises are inherently costly and, in many cases, wasteful of resources. It is easier, more effective and less costly to introduce corrective measures when the early signs of emerging problems appear rather than reversing a downward trend once the problems have taken root. For example, the government in the United Kingdom has a multifaceted strategy in place for tackling rising rates of obesity now in order to ward off negative impacts on public health and public expenditures in the future. This strategy was informed, in part, by work done by the United Kingdom's Foresight Program.[8]

Forward thinking allows public organizations to understand what can be done today to prepare for an uncertain future. It allows them to rehearse potential strategies and to garner a deeper understanding of the choices, options and consequences of possible futures in the process. The conversations and rehearsal processes about alternative futures play a key role in building the creative capacity and agility of organizations to respond to unforeseen events.

While a multitude of variations exist on how to conduct foresight work, it is essentially comprised of three broad steps. The analysis phase focuses on finding patterns in a variety of data and addresses the questions: What are the facts? What do we know? What can be detected? The interpretation phase attempts to extract meaning: What is really happening and what does it mean? Finally, the prospection phase focuses on what might happen. It develops a deeper appreciation for alternative futures.[9]

Many tools are available to support this work. Traditionally, they have included horizon scanning, trend analysis, scenario planning, modelling, simulations and gaming in varying degrees of sophistication. Horizon scanning facilitates systematic evidence gathering across government and from multiple sources beyond government. Scenario planning helps construct a fully developed image of possible, plausible and probable futures. It encourages a deep, proactive conversation and facilitates a mutual understanding of a preferable future among participants.[10]

Some countries have a lot of experience with futures work; others are still in their infancy in this regard. Whatever the case may be, participants in the New Synthesis roundtables shared the view that *a strong anticipative capacity is necessary to prepare government to serve in the 21st century.*

Learning from Experience

Among the participating countries, Singapore, the United Kingdom, and the Netherlands have the most experience with futures work. Their approaches are different and fulfill different needs, but important lessons can be drawn from their experiences. The network also benefited from the experience of the Government of Finland, whose approach was presented and discussed at the roundtable in Singapore.[11] The Finnish approach integrates the contribution of Parliament, government and all departments, and encourages broad-based public discussion and consensus building.

The United Kingdom's Foresight Program was introduced in 1994, and a Foresight Horizon Scanning Centre launched in 2005. The Foresight Program focuses on issues that entail some aspects of science and technology and have a cross-sectoral reach. The selected projects look five decades into the future. The centre serves as a locus of expertise in futures work for all departments and agencies, and provides support and training for departments.

In contrast to the permanent horizon scanning in the United Kingdom and in Singapore, the Netherlands conducted a single project in 2007. The project extended over two years and involved government and the general public. It led to a report and a broad "state of the nation" presentation.[12]

Singapore has a long tradition of looking far into the future and of long-term strategic planning and decision making. Scenario planning, at the global and national levels, has played a key role in decision making since the early 1980s. The Risk Assessment and Horizon Scanning Program (RAHS)[13] introduced in 2009 is probably the most sophisticated of its kind in the world.[14] These efforts have been complemented by the addition of the Centre for Strategic Futures in 2009.[15] The centre combines the strength of scanning and scenario planning with a strong focus on experimentation and discovery.[16] These initiatives are supported by a sustained effort called PS21 that aims to create a culture of innovation in the public service.[17]

Finland ranks high in terms of international comparisons of standard of living, quality of life, competitiveness and innovation. Like others mentioned before, Finland conducts futures work and foresight exercises. But unlike other countries, Finland has a Parliamentary Committee for the Future. The committee conducts research and facilitates discussion about the future between the governing body and Parliament. Its work contributes to raising public awareness about potential risks and the action needed to make progress over time. The committee helps forge a broad-based consensus across political parties that guides the actions of future governments.[18]

A number of lessons and observations may be drawn from these examples and from the roundtable discussions. Futures work and foresight exercises help challenge underlying assumptions, reveal blind spots and detect patterns and emerging risks. They help garner a better appreciation of the impact of today's decisions on the future and reconcile short-term action with mid- to long-term needs. Futures work is a necessary complement to the traditional policy research work conducted by most departments, which tends to value causality and linear thinking. This is insufficient to detect emergent phenomena. Anticipatory work brings a more dynamic and systemic perspective to the mix that is better suited to detecting weak signals and potential wild cards.

While data and technology may help anticipate emerging trends, the most important knowledge is not in the data but in the conversations about the data and the insights forged by the different perspectives and lines of questioning that various actors bring to the discussion. These insights may draw from traditional knowledge, expert opinion and institutional memory. Futures work is strengthened by a diversity of perspectives coming from the interaction of participants with a variety of skills and academic backgrounds. It is enriched by a diversity of approaches where linear thinking, non-linear systems-thinking and emergent understanding co-exist.

The best knowledge and the most useful intelligence on emergent phenomena are dispersed across society and at the scale of our globally networked world. They take shape and circulate in self-organized social networks and in the multiple relationships citizens have in their local communities or globally dispersed communities of interest.[19] Improving the anticipative capacity of government entails reaching out beyond expert knowledge and circles of government "insiders." The broader the conversation and the greater the diversity of perspectives brought to bear in the conversation, the better the chance of detecting emerging trends and emergent phenomena.

One of the key benefits of futures exercises is the process of engagement that brings together decision makers from across government and, in some instances, outside it. This helps forge a consensus about a preferable future. Futures programs need political support and political engagement. The findings must be discussed at the highest levels and integrated into government decision-making systems. Foresight projects and futures programs can be used to improve public awareness and develop a better public understanding of the consequences that various risks entail. Used this way, futures work contributes to building the public support needed to address complex issues, in particular when short-term costs or sacrifices are necessary to reap mid- to long-term benefits.

Implications for Government

In addressing complex issues, government faces a number of challenges. The first is to avoid the danger of oversimplification; the second is the equally dangerous tendency to exaggerate the complexity of the issue.

Not everything is complex or wicked. As discussed in Chapter 2, it is already challenging enough for government to make difficult decisions or undertake complicated projects. That being said, oversimplifying genuinely complex issues may lead to policy failures because it fails to anticipate the downstream consequences of policy decisions in other systems or parts of the system. An example would be a policy aimed at encouraging the production of ethanol that did not take account of the downstream impact on agricultural production, the use of farm lands, the impact on water supply, the global consequences for food prices and the availability of food for humanitarian aid.[20] Oversimplification may unleash a cascading series of events that leads to even more complex or intractable issues.

One challenge for government is to better understand the nature of the issue at hand and the dynamic interrelationships among systems. Another challenge is to strike a balance between short-term demands for action, the downstream impact of those actions and long-term needs.

In many countries, policy units can be found in departments and at the centre of government. Their role is to conduct policy research and provide policy advice that takes account of past experiences and the capacity to deliver. Policy units must adapt to the changing circumstances faced by government in the post-industrial era by helping decision makers recognize the linkages among multiple systems and by focusing on the future impacts of today's decisions and actions.

Policy units should contribute to the anticipative capacity of government. Their role is to help improve decision making in the short, medium and long terms.[21] As one of the participants in the roundtable in The Hague indicated, the overall purpose "is not to improve predictions but to improve decisions that lead to better results."[22] A number of participants in the discussions noted the importance of working with Parliament or Congress to develop a better appreciation of future challenges and opportunities.[23] A deeper understanding of future challenges among elected officials will help overcome political divides on some complex issues. It may also help reduce the risks of unforeseen mid- to long-term effects of decisions made today.[24]

Participants noted that, in some cases, the demand for policy research and futures work is anti-cyclical. In other words, demand is highest after a crisis when it is too late to take preventative actions, and lowest when no major shocks have disturbed society for a while. Policy research and futures work should be conducted on an ongoing basis, whether there is a strong demand or not. This is necessary to ensure that the public service is able to provide full and sound advice to support decision making and to ensure the relevant knowledge is available when it is most needed. Futures work needs to be embedded in the political decision-making process.[25] Over time, it contributes to creating a culture for looking ahead and learning.

It is sometimes too late to change a prevailing situation, but governing is about preparing a better future. For that, it is never too late.

INVENTIVE CAPACITY

There is vast literature on innovation generally and on innovation in the public sector. Some observe that there is not enough innovation in the public sector, and they propose various ways of removing obstacles and various measures for creating a more supportive environment.[26] Some have noted that several of the most powerful innovations of the past 50 years, including the Internet and the World Wide Web originated in the public sector.[27] Many have noted that there is no shortage of innovators and entrepreneurs in the public sector and that public servants innovate in spite of the barriers prevailing in many bureaucratic settings.[28]

The New Synthesis Project brings a different angle to the discussion on innovation. It returns to the question: What does it take for government to be able to address peacefully some of the most complex and intractable problems of our times? From a New Synthesis perspective, the primary area of interest is ensuring that the collective capacity to invent and implement practical solutions keeps pace with the increasing complexity of the problems faced by society.

As there is abundant literature on innovation, there are also many definitions. In the private sector, the distinction between innovation and invention is easy: innovation converts new ideas into wealth and return on investment. In the public sector, the distinction is more difficult. A useful definition for public innovation is: "new ideas that work at creating public value."[29]

However, innovation is not always the answer to some of our most complex or intractable problems or at least it is not the whole story. Innovation does not always require "new" ideas. Sometimes it requires practical solutions adapted to the context and that use the resources available in the circumstances. These practical solutions may not entail the level of novelty normally associated with the concept of innovation.

In some cases, the best way of addressing a complex issue may be to use old ideas, and even very old ideas, in a way that combines a parsimonious use of resources, inventiveness and ingenuity for creating alternative approaches. It may involve a recombination of existing factors. The newness, if newness there be, may not rest in the ideas themselves but in the way various factors, including ideas, local resources and capacities, are assembled, combined or recombined.

In the 1980s and early 1990s, municipalities in Brazil were having great difficulty ensuring the delivery of safe drinking water and sewerage services to citizens. It was too costly for local governments to build and maintain the necessary infrastructure, especially to modern engineering standards. Moreover, regulations meant that citizens were limited in improving their own sanitary conditions, even though they had the skills and time to solve some aspects of the problem. Intractable problems require thinking differently. In this case, it meant using much smaller "feeder lines" from the main trunks of the system and giving local residents an active role in planning, building and maintaining the feeder lines that service their homes. Residents decided on the layout of the system, which affected the cost of the system and the charges that they paid. They installed and maintained the feeder lines. This solution was adapted to local needs and means. It involved old ways of doing things at small, local scales and marrying these with new requirements. This recombination of old and new ideas "dramatically increased the availability of lower cost, essential urban services to the poorest neighbourhoods in Brazilian cities."[30]

Addressing complex or intractable issues requires that governments and citizens discover and successfully implement practical solutions that achieve a higher public value across systems and over time. It is not sufficient to achieve better results in the short term if it means that society will be confronted with problems of even greater complexity or intractability in the future. The management of the Atlantic fisheries, water management in the Middle East and public farmland management in some parts of Russia and China all produced "public results." They contributed to community and regional economic development, and increased food supply. They even reduced poverty in some regions, at least for a time. Some of these initiatives were innovative in the conventional sense, some even entailed innovation breakthroughs. But they also pushed tougher decisions and more complex issues to the background, as some of the measures resulted in the collapse of the fish stocks[31], increased desertification[32] and famines.[33] The measures taken at the time did not take sufficient account of downstream consequences nor did they build more resilience to unforeseen developments in the future.[34]

To prepare for the challenges of the 21st century, governments need a heightened appreciation of the impact across systems and of the downstream consequences of today's actions and decisions.[35] We need *inventive government*. In the context of the New Synthesis Project, I propose that *inventiveness is the capacity to generate and implement practical solutions that bring about ever more valuable public results to society.* The outcome would be a society better able to adapt and address the problems of the times.

As discussed in the previous section, this requires a strong anticipative capacity to help government detect emerging issues, reveal the interdependencies across systems and over time, and ensure an ongoing focus on the future. This is a starting point. But preparing government to face the challenges of the 21st century also requires a sustained effort at exploring and experimenting to find out what works in practice.[36] It requires a willingness to encourage social innovation[37] and to co-create solutions with citizens and other actors.[38]

In the context of the New Synthesis Project, some preliminary work was done to explore these concepts, but much remains to be done. The following section presents some of the early ideas that emerged over the course of the discussions in 2010.

Exploration

Public policy decisions and public service reforms are context-specific. To be successful, they must take into account the unique set of circumstances that characterizes each country in light of its culture, values, needs, resources and capacities.

Great ideas can be found the world over. They have been tested through implementation. They represent a vast reservoir of practical solutions that have been used by governments to address issues of public concern in various contexts. While some have proven very successful and have achieved their desired outcome, in other cases, the costs exceeded the overall benefits to society. As a result, these ideas were modified or abandoned. Some ideas and practices failed outright or died a natural death. But in all cases, governments can learn from the experiences of others in different parts of the world.

Exploration is about bringing in a constant flow of ideas. It is a process of discovery.[39] It starts at home by documenting and capturing the lessons learned through successive initiatives and experiments: otherwise stated, government needs to know what it knows and make this knowledge readily available. This provides an important basis from which to explore new and better ways of achieving results of higher public value. While it may sound gratuitous, it is no small task for government to "know what it knows" considering the number and diversity of organizations involved. However, some countries do better than others at this. The United Kingdom has a long tradition of capturing, discussing and sharing lessons learned from experience. In so doing, it builds collective intelligence and enriches the knowledge of others.

The best ideas and the most promising avenues are not limited to what was invented at home. The most powerful learning, the most important discoveries and breakthroughs on how to address complex issues may come from countries facing very different circumstances and with vastly different levels of development. I am particularly struck by the dynamism of the experimentation process and by the richness of the learning in developing and emerging economies.

Exploration is about detecting and unearthing powerful, practical ideas with some potential for replication in other circumstances. This is difficult to achieve but well worth the effort. Part of the difficulty is that, in many cases, no documentation exists or it may only become available years later. Public sector leaders need to stay abreast of promising avenues in real time. In this regard, nothing replaces face-to-face discussions among people leading similar reforms or facing similar challenges. This is why international collaborative research efforts, such as the New Synthesis Project, are important. These projects facilitate and accelerate exchanges among and across countries.

A small team of dedicated public servants with the explicit mission of scanning, identifying, documenting and disseminating the lessons learned by various approaches in areas of interest to government may seem like a costly proposition but, in fact, it is a wise investment. No one can afford to not learn from experience, whether their own or that of others: and no one can afford to introduce policies that have been proven to be deficient or that have had serious unintended effects. Among the participating countries, Singapore has the most systematic approach of scanning, exploring and reinventing promising ideas in the context of its particular landscape. Exploration helps government build on the knowledge and experience of others by identifying ideas that have worked in practice. The most important part of an exploratory process is discovering why an initiative has been successful or unsuccessful, what the drivers, the enabling conditions and the constraints were that led to the observable results. Exploration reveals which initiatives are worth testing at home. It improves the likelihood of smart interventions and helps ensure that scarce public resources are used to greatest effect.

Emergent Solutions

Practical solutions to complex problems are contextual. In the case of the Singapore Prison System, the successful reintegration of ex-offenders was the result of a bottom-up initiative and a transformation process initiated from within.[40]

Top-down political leadership was at the origin of the process of change initiated in the context of Bolsa Família to reduce poverty and disparities in Brazil.[41] The program design was preceded by an extended period of experimentation at the local and the community levels. Practical emergent solutions to complex problems may be bottom-up, top-down, inside-out or outside-in.

The Registered Disability Savings Plan (RDSP) is a Canadian example of a solution that started as a private initiative before becoming a government program. The RDSP provides a means of improving the financial security of disabled people. It is a tax-deferred savings vehicle that allows disabled people access to government grants and bonds, depending on their level of income, in addition to other income assistance programs already available to them.[42] This solution came from a social movement aimed at improving the long-term economic security of disabled people. One family initiated the idea. It rapidly grew into the Planned Lifetime Advocacy Networks (PLAN), which put "flesh on the bones" of the idea that garnered support from national and provincial governments, financial institutions and other organizations.[43]

Emergent and practical solutions take form in an organic way. The key phases of development vary depending on the issues and the circumstances, but most of them display some common elements, including an awareness of the significance of the issue; sustained commitment and leadership to bring about solutions; a different way of thinking that breaks from the past; and a willingness to learn and adapt along the way. Emergent solutions are not fully formed ideas, and they are not enacted by definitive, top-down decisions. They exceed the capacity of any one actor acting alone. *Emergent solutions require inventiveness, ingenuity, and a form of "bricolage" in putting ideas, local resources and communities to productive use.*[44] No one is totally in control. Generally, the end result requires the active support and contribution of government, multiple actors and the active participation of citizens.

The importance of emergent solutions is best understood by considering examples. Successful examples provide reasons to be optimistic about the collective capacity to address the intractable problems of our time.

Learning from Practice: HIV/AIDS (Brazil)

In the 1980s, Brazil was experiencing an AIDS epidemic comparable to that in South Africa,[45] with reported cases increasing at an alarming rate.[46] Conventional cost-benefit analyses conducted by the World Bank suggested that developing countries such as Brazil did not have the financial resources or the capacity to reverse the trend in the short term.[47]

Conventional thinking leads to conventional solutions and, in many cases, to solutions that far exceed the financial or institutional capacity of the country facing the problems. Furthermore, conventional approaches tend to focus on weaknesses, deficits and deficiencies rather than the assets imbedded in the communities.

Expert studies revealed that Brazil faced a number of difficulties in addressing the HIV pandemic. There were problems of affordability (the fiscal capacity was insufficient to pay for expensive drugs). There were problems of capacity (not enough hospitals, not enough beds, not enough qualified personnel, including doctors and nurses). There were also access problems. In a country as vast as Brazil with a large number of remote communities and inadequate medical infrastructures, it was judged to be nearly impossible to reach those affected to limit the spread of the disease. Furthermore, these difficulties were compounded by the illiteracy, poverty and hunger that prevailed in many remote communities.

Expert opinion and advice to the government of Brazil was to focus on prevention to protect future generations and those as yet not infected.[48] The pandemic would run its course, and eventually the problem would resolve itself over an extended period, although at the cost of much suffering and loss of life. Brazil chose a different path. By 2002, the HIV infection rate in Brazil was 0.6 percent and stable. In contrast, it was 25 percent and climbing in South Africa.[49] What accounts for such a difference?

Brazil started to address the issue as early as the 1990s. Broad awareness led to mobilization—individual citizens, government officials, community and church groups and healthcare workers joined forces to tackle the problem. Broad-based conversations framed the issues differently than the experts that had been consulted. No one, no matter how poor or illiterate, would be left behind. Treatment would be provided to all who needed it. Prevention strategies would enlist the support of those already affected to bring about behavioural changes even in the most remote communities.

Dialogue and debate was the first phase, leading to different lines of inquiry and with them different ways of framing the issue and different solutions. Practical solutions are imbedded in the context and must be able to put available resources to productive use. The problem of affordability became how to drive down the costs. In the end, it meant staring down the pharmaceutical companies through the World Trade Organization to produce generic versions of antiretroviral drugs and give them free to those infected with HIV and suffering from AIDS.[50] The problem of medical capacity was turned on its head by enrolling 600 NGOs, the churches and food distribution centres to support existing hospitals and clinics. The problem of reaching those affected was addressed by enrolling trustworthy individuals and groups in the communities. A country may be poor in financial resources but rich in the power of its networks.

The approach was systematic and participatory. The government played a leadership role. It drew on the collective ideas and innovativeness of Brazilian society. Most importantly, the solutions were embedded in Brazil's context and culture. While AIDS still causes great suffering for millions of people in Brazil, this story gives hope to countries facing similar problems.

The Brazilian response to the HIV/AIDS epidemic provides a good illustration of the exploration of the "space of possibility" framed by the four vectors of the New Synthesis Framework presented in Chapter 3. The response relied on the active participation and contributions of individuals, communities and civil society organizations (civic results) to achieve the desired public health results (public policy results). The desired public results were beyond the reach of government working alone. They required a sharing of responsibility across sectors and among multiple actors to leverage the collective capacity to shape an emergent solution and to achieve the desired outcome. Emergent solutions are a collective enterprise that entails a sharing of responsibility between government, people and society.

Learning from Practice: The Truth and Reconciliation Process (South Africa)

South Africa has provided the world with one of the most inspiring examples of emergent solutions during the reconciliation process that took place in that country after the collapse of the apartheid regime in 1990. The birth of the Truth and Reconciliation Commission (TRC) that followed was "something of a miracle."[51] It was a way to pursue justice through a restorative healing process on a uniquely human level.

The TRC emerged as a central component of an imperfect but workable solution to a seemingly impossible problem. By 1990, South African President, F.W. de Klerk of the ruling National Party, announced negotiations with Nelson Mandela, leader of the opposition African National Congress, to end apartheid and establish a democratic system of governance. The National Party had ruled the country since the 1940s with an apartheid policy of legal racial separation that severely curtailed the rights of the majority of "non-white" inhabitants while ensuring minority rule by white people. The people and nation of South Africa were at a crossroads. The apartheid regime was clearly ending, but this had not necessarily changed the hearts and minds of the people who supported it. Moreover, those who had been victims of the regime and the conflict it engendered were not necessarily ready to forgive and forget.

A delicate course needed to be steered in the constitutional negotiations to prevent further violence or societal breakdown. The journey toward a democratic society was fraught with dangers and risks.

A traditional legal process aimed at investigating and prosecuting those involved in perpetrating crimes under apartheid would not work. It would drain an economy already in disrepair and likely further divide the country. South Africa needed a process that could help people and the country heal and still achieve justice. Any solution had to strike a delicate balance between those who cried "prosecute and punish" and those who demanded "forgive and forget".[52] Some people began to think through a restorative justice approach. The solution of "healing through truth" became an important step along the path to a better future.

Under the leadership of Desmond Tutu, three committees were formed to establish a process that would bring closure and heal a broken society. They were the Gross Human Rights Violations Committee (to hear, recognize and pay reverence to the stories of victims); the Amnesty Committee (for those who committed crimes to confess voluntarily with the possibility of receiving amnesty); and the Committee on Reparation and Rehabilitation (for those seeking some form of reparation for harm done and to help with their healing).

The TRC held hearings throughout the country, with thousands of victims and witnesses giving testimony.[53] People were encouraged to tell their stories in their own way, and to be heard and respected for their willingness to share. The approach ensured even-handedness, as there were victims on all sides of the conflicts. The hearings provided a means for people to grieve together and to begin a process of reconciliation. The TRC allowed people to have a truthful conversation about how they had lived in the past and how they wanted to live together in the future. No traditional legal process could have achieved these outcomes.[54]

By using the New Synthesis Framework presented in Chapter 3, this initiative could be summarized along the following lines. The desired outcomes included both social justice (a public policy result) and national reconciliation (a civic result). These results were beyond the scope of the traditional instruments of the state. Legal measures (government authority) could only form part of the solution. People defined the issues and gave shape to the emergent solution (collective power). In the process, South African society gained a strengthened capacity for a better collective future.

The examples of combating HIV/AIDS in Brazil and post-apartheid reconciliation in South Africa illustrate that emergent solutions form part of the social fabric and take form by using and harnessing the resources and the capacities present at that time and at that place. Emergent solutions are unique. They cannot be replicated. However, they provide important lessons and contain elements of solutions that have replicating potential in other circumstances.

INNOVATIVE SOCIETY

Focusing on public results and public value opens up an expanded space of possibilities. There are many contributors in this space. As discussed previously, it is a mistake to consider government as the primary agent in producing most public results. In fact, this view undervalues the contribution of multiple contributors in society and fails to take into account the increasing number of public results that are beyond the reach of government acting alone.

An innovative society recognizes that there are many contributors to results of public value. Besides government, there are many independent sources of public value in society. This view reinforces the importance of a framework of public administration that embraces the contribution of government, market and society. It underpins a concept of governance where *public results are a collective enterprise and a collective responsibility.*

The public administration of the 21ˢᵗ century needs to be plural and pluralistic to address some of the complex issues of our time. Plural because of the contribution of a large number of agents and contributors; pluralistic in the diversity of perspectives and approaches used to produce results of higher public value at a lower overall cost to society.

This view of modern governance recognizes the co-existence and interaction of government, market and collaboration-based approaches to creating public results and public value. It opens up the possibility of a broader discussion on the appropriate means of pursuing government priorities and achieving results of value to society.[55] It encourages a shift from a narrow discussion on the efficiency of government programs to a broader conversation about the collaborative efforts needed to lift the contributions of society as a whole.[56]

An Enabling Environment

Through various forms of collaboration, people explore and experiment with innovative ideas to address practical problems of concern to them. They produce results of value to society with or without the participation of government.

An innovative society has the capacity to develop new ways to achieve results of value to society. Governments have a special role to play in building societies' capacity for innovation and in helping ensure that the benefits accrue to society as a whole. This role is multifaceted. It starts by valuing the contribution of others and providing them with an enabling environment.

Public Utilities

Now as in the past, governments play a special role in providing the modern public infrastructure necessary for society to function. This infrastructure extends beyond the roads, harbours and airports necessary to ensure the circulation of people and goods; beyond basic utilities, such as running water, electricity grids, energy distribution systems or telecommunications. Today, access to modern information and communication technologies is a public utility. It is necessary to encourage innovation and to give people the means of addressing the problems of importance to them. Internet access, high-speed broadband and smart grids give people access to leading-edge knowledge, new means of exploration and new forms of collaboration.

This also presents new challenges for government. Not everything on the Web is to everyone's liking and not every use of the technology is beneficial to society. However, these technologies are changing the world we live in as well as how we forge relationships among people and with government. Checks and balances are needed and corrective measures will be necessary, but information and communication technologies are transforming the world as surely as the steam engine and the combustion engine did during previous eras.

Governments cannot help society prepare for the challenges of the 21ˢᵗ century by holding on to the practices and ideas of the 20ᵗʰ century. Poverty takes many forms. In today's world, poverty encompasses all the dimensions previously acknowledged plus the debilitating consequences of being cut off from the knowledge the world has to offer and the potential of collaboration that modern information and communication technologies provide to improve one's conditions.[57] Narrowing the digital divide and using the power of modern information and communication technologies to achieve results of value to society is part of the fight against poverty.[58]

Public Data

Public data are generated by public agencies using public funds. Public data constitute a public asset of great value to society. As a matter of course and as a matter of principle, public data should be made publicly available and freely accessible with as few exceptions as possible. Public data sets can be made available on public websites relatively easily in digital and standardized formats to facilitate their use by the largest number of users possible.

Governments collect and create public data to support public decisions and to gain an understanding of issues relevant to society. They should maintain an inventory of all data sets to ensure the quality of the data and provide accurate information on the sources and the methodologies used to generate the data. Their responsibility should extend to making public data available in a portable, usable and timely way.

Governments hold no particular responsibility for how the data will be used once released. Users are free to combine, recombine and integrate data with other data sets. They can create new applications and new services to address particular needs.

Beyond collecting, creating and releasing public data, governments may choose to play a more proactive role. For instance, they may create public platforms to animate discussions or participate on existing platforms to encourage the sharing of ideas on issues of interest to government. Governments can transform their role from keeper of public data to connector and sharer of data to encourage the creation of innovative solutions where users build value by using each others' contributions. For example, everyblock.com allows people to see what is going on in their neighbourhood or other neighbourhoods in a number of cities in the United States of America. It integrates and maps open data from a range of sources, such as governments, police and news organizations, and offers a range of collaborative tools so that users can solve problems and make their neighbourhoods "a better place."[59]

Participants in the roundtables were well aware of the challenges, risks and opportunities associated with open government. This was the subject of discussion, in particular, in London in November 2010.[60] It comes down to a judgment about how far and how fast governments are prepared to go to reap the benefits of collaborative innovation. One participant provided judicious advice by outlining a three-step process: lay the foundation, foster culture change, and catalyze and nurture innovation.[61]

Some governments have put policies in place to encourage the release of public data. This is an important first step, but only a step. The benefits of openness come from opening up to others. In the United States of America, the Obama administration has launched its "Open Government Initiative" based on a presidential directive, an Internet portal (www.whitehouse.gov/open), a common platform for innovation (www.Apps.gov), open data (www.Data.gov) and an incentive platform (www.Challenge.gov). In the United Kingdom, a new Public Sector Transparency Board (www.data.gov.uk) was established in 2010 to ensure that all key public data sets are released to the public and that standards for releasing data are implemented across the public service. In Australia, the Commonwealth Government's Government 2.0 Taskforce observed in 2009 that data collected by and for the public service are "a national resource which should be managed for public purposes…and should be freely available for anyone to use and transform unless there are compelling privacy, confidentiality or security considerations."[62] In March 2011, the government launched its open data platform (www.data.gov.au), which includes data sets, examples of applications and a number of incentives for people to use the data, such as competitions.

Social Innovation Policy

Businesses innovate for profit, society innovates for social return. Of the two, the latter may be the more important in the long run; yet, while many countries have an innovation policy for the private sector, most lack a coherent and comprehensive social innovation policy.

Many social innovation initiatives are small or of limited impact. Many are underfunded. A social innovation policy helps build capacity in society to explore, test and experiment with innovative approaches to addressing social needs. Not every problem can or should be addressed by government; a strong capacity for social innovation builds the potential for self-help and collaborative initiatives.

The Social Innovation Europe initiative funded by the European Commission has started to sketch the contours of what a policy aimed at encouraging social innovation may look like.[63] For instance, it may include support for social innovators to help them forge a mutually supportive community to accelerate learning from each other; financial support for testing and prototyping concepts and promising ideas; and a systematic approach to documenting, evaluating and encouraging the dissemination of innovative ideas.[64] Social innovation requires experimentation and the ability to scale up or spread promising ideas at the level of cities, regions and states, or even at the global level.[65]

Governments can promote social innovations by encouraging social experimentation as a way of improving policy decisions.[66] This allows decision makers to identify the likely impact and the unintended consequences of future social policies or programs. Social experiments are not about "trying things out and hoping for the best." They involve a rigorous approach to testing in practice and on a small scale the possible designs of future public programs.[67] They are an opportunity to explore in practice how program design may encourage the active participation and contribution of users, families and communities, and how they contribute to wellness and life satisfaction.

Experimentation accelerates learning within government and also in the communities where the experiments are conducted. In Canada, the Social Research and Demonstration Corporation is a not-for-profit research organization created specifically to develop, field test and rigorously evaluate future social programs using experimental methods, such as randomized field trials.[68] The corporation provides support to national, sub-national and municipal governments as well as to other public and non-profit organizations. Reports and findings are made publicly available to accelerate learning and further encourage innovation and experimentation. Experimentation takes time and may be expensive. Prototyping may provide a quick and cost-effective alternative for exploring what works. It can help "fail fast, safely and smartly."[69] This is a precondition for innovation.

Learning from Practice:
The NorthLight School Experiment (Singapore)

During the roundtable that took place in Singapore in September 2010, delegates were taken on a "learning journey" to NorthLight School, a wellspring of lessons on social innovation. Established in 2007 by Singapore's Ministry of Education, NorthLight is an experimental school for students who were having repeated difficulty passing the national Primary School Leaving Examination and who were at risk of leaving the school system at an early age.[70]

Soon after the Ministry announced this experiment, offers of help came in from other government agencies, businesses, community groups and the general public, all of whom recognized the merits of the experiment. Within the first three years of opening its doors, the growth and motivation of NorthLight students surpassed all expectations. Its innovative strategies include the use of advanced technologies in the classrooms (such as smart-boards, laptops and Internet) and different approaches adapted to learning styles. Students undertake projects that have a direct connection to their life-worlds. They have a say in parts of the curriculum and participate in running some aspects of the school, ranging from gardening, working in the cafeteria or running a gift shop. The NorthLight School approach has been replicated in other schools, and not only those with similar student populations, in Singapore and abroad.

A number of factors contributed to the success of this initiative. Political leadership created an enabling space for experimentation within the broader educational system. Selecting a principal keen to make this experiment a success proved crucial, and equally important was the decision to give her significantly more autonomy and discretion than usual. Another important factor of success was that teachers had to compete for the honour of working at the NorthLight School rather than being posted as was the normal practice. This created a highly motivated professional community in tune with the mandate of the school.

Teachers have significant discretion to try out new approaches. They share their findings at monthly sessions or on the school's information management portal. The sharing of information extends to all lesson plans and student progress reports. Families are encouraged to be involved. There are parent support groups, including one for fathers, and regular initiatives to ensure families feel welcome and are contributing to the school community.

In the case study, the desired public policy result was achieving better educational outcomes for students with special needs. The desired civic result was for students to become self-reliant. The government provided the impetus and created the conditions for experimentation. The engagement and the active contribution of students, families, community groups and employers ensured the success of the initiative. NorthLight has become a laboratory for spreading a successful experiment by teaching others how to replicate the approaches in other classrooms and schools.

Social Innovation Incubators and Hubs

Social innovation incubators and hubs already exist in a number of countries. Notable examples are Denmark's MindLab, Spain's Social Innovation Park (DenokInn—the Basque Centre for Innovation, Entrepreneurship and New Business Development), and the United States of America's Unreasonable Institute. Incubators encourage experimentation, often through rapid prototyping. They provide a way to "fail fast, safe and smart" on the way to generating social innovations. Just like innovation processes in business, social innovation needs to be taught, nurtured and fostered in a formalized way to build capacity; incubators and hubs provide a locus for this.

MindLab is an innovation centre that works largely with public servants from its parent ministries in the Danish government: the Ministry of Economic and Business Affairs, the Ministry of Taxation and the Ministry of Employment. It helps these ministries see their policies and services from the "outside-in;" that is, from the perspective of citizens. MindLab helps generate possible solutions to reduce the amount of "red tape" that citizens encounter when interacting with the government, therefore improving service delivery and citizens' experience with government.[71]

Created in June 2010, the *Social Innovation Park*, managed by DenokInn, focuses on forming relationships among social innovation bodies to create an international ecosystem for social innovation. Conceived as a "social Silicon Valley," the park provides physical space and innovation support services for a diverse mix of non-profit organizations, social entrepreneurs and small businesses.[72] The park uses an enabling platform of four labs: InnovaLab: for creativity and concept design; FabLab: for prototypes and rapid fabrication; FormaLab: for training, and AppLab: for social entrepreneurship.

Each year, the Unreasonable Institute runs a competition to choose 25 social ventures worthy of development. Social innovators from all over the world are chosen to participate in a six-week intensive program to transform their ideas into realities. The ideas must be sustainable and globally scalable. Chosen projects range from ventures to end honour killings in India to pre-paid taxi and bus services designed to reduce drunk driving and provide safe transportation. The institute encourages mentoring and facilitates capital investments in promising social ventures.[73]

Social innovation does not simply emerge on its own. As in the business sector, it requires support systems, enabling environments and supportive public policies.[74]

BUILDING RESILIENCE

Focusing on resilience may be one of the most promising avenues for modernizing public administration. The New Synthesis Framework proposes that the role of government extends to serving the public good and collective interests in all circumstances, whether predictable, probable, plausible or unpredictable. In the end, society as a whole bears the impact of complex and unpredictable events. *The role of government extends to encouraging self-reliance and building the resilience of society to adapt and prosper, even in the face of adversity.* Resilient societies are better able to shoulder the burden of inevitable crises, avert preventable shocks and learn from adversity.

Governments are the stewards of their country's collective interests.[75] They are called upon to play an active role in reducing unfavourable risks, the costs of which would be borne by society as a whole, and to initiate proactive action to improve the likelihood of more favourable outcomes for society.

This puts a premium on government's capacity to anticipate what might be, prevent what can be prevented and help build the resilience of society to adapt and prosper in all circumstances, whatever the future might hold.

Sometimes, change takes place gradually; at other times, more abruptly. There are some indications that abrupt changes may increase in frequency, duration and magnitude for a variety of reasons in the foreseeable future.[76]

Resilience refers to the capacity of various systems to absorb perturbations while continuing to regenerate without slowly degrading or flipping into less desirable states. It is the capacity of a system to absorb disturbances while retaining its essential functionality.[77]

The New Synthesis Project approached the concept of resilience from the perspective of the capabilities that enable individuals, communities and societies to adapt to change and prosper in all circumstances, particularly in periods of rapid and abrupt changes. Resilience includes the capacity to recover from disastrous events, whether they are caused by internal or external shocks, disturbances or crises.[78] It refers to the capacity of people, communities and society to gain an awareness of risks and vulnerabilities, respond to and recover from shocks, and create and seize opportunities when unforeseen events take place. It is not about fortifying society to maintain the status quo in the face of a changing world. Continual change and adaptation are at the heart of resilience.

All the measures discussed so far in this chapter contribute to building resilience in some way. They help improve the anticipative capacity of government. They leverage the capacity of government, society and citizens to work together to shape emergent solutions to address complex issues or intractable problems. They encourage social innovation and experimentation and the active contribution of multiple actors.

In the end, however, no matter how smart government and citizens are at anticipating events and introducing proactive actions to prevent and mitigate risks, unforeseen events will occur and unpredictable crises will happen. Ultimately, society as a whole bears the impact of change in a complex and unpredictable world.

Resilience is the "soft-power" that explains why some societies weather crises and emerge stronger than before, while others do not.[79] Resilience cannot be conjured up in times of need or bought when it is most needed. It is built day-by-day and over long periods. It is found in self-reliant individuals who have the ability to take charge of their lives and shape their future. It is in the supportive relationships forged among people, families and communities that allow them to come together in times of need and know they can count on each other. It is in the bonds and relationship of trust found in communities able to take proactive action to prevent or reduce their vulnerabilities and find solutions to the problems they face.[80]

The literature on social capital formation offers some insight on how government policies and programs can help build resilience and grow the stock of social capital that enables people to act collectively.[81] Of particular importance is the concept of "bridging" forms of social capital that links diverse people, groups and communities, and circulates new information, perspectives, ideas and opportunities.[82]

For resilient people, communities and societies, change (even disruptive change) can create opportunities for development, renewal and innovation. However, for the most vulnerable, even small changes may be devastating.[83] Events around the world, ranging from natural disasters to financial crises, highlight vividly the consequences of the differing capacities of societies to recover from relatively similar shocks. Governments in a number of countries are paying increasing attention to the concept of resilience and are exploring how to improve community resilience. This is the case, for instance, in New Zealand where the government started focusing on creating more resilient communities in the early 2000s. The explicit purpose was to ensure that the awareness and management of risk would become broadly embedded in government, business and communities, thereby increasing the overall resilience of society.[84] The New Zealand approach emphasized the importance of linking resilience strategies and day-to day actions.

The concept of resilience was explored on several occasions during the New Synthesis Project, in particular during the roundtables in The Hague in March 2010, Ottawa in May and again in Singapore in September of the same year.[85] Participants deepened their understanding of the concept and refined their thinking about the role of government by drawing from behavioural sciences, complexity theory, economic theory and recent research on well-being.

A number of case studies contributed to exploring various aspects of the concept of resilience. One of these was developed by the State Services Authority of the Government of Victoria in Australia. It provided important insight about the recovery and reconstruction phases that began immediately after the devastating bushfires that raged across that state in 2009.[86]

Learning from Practice: The Victorian Bushfire Reconstruction and Recovery Authority (Australia)

In February 2009, bushfires ravaged parts of the state of Victoria in Australia, causing unprecedented devastation. One hundred and seventy three people died, over 3,400 properties along with almost 430,000 hectares of forests, crops and pasture were damaged or destroyed. Damage was done to 950 local parks, 467 cultural sites and 200 historic sites.

Within three days of the disaster, while fires were still burning, the state government established the Victorian Bushfire Reconstruction and Recovery Authority (VBRRA) to co-ordinate the restoration and recovery of affected regions and communities. The case study illustrates aspects of crisis management, reconstruction and recovery phases. It reveals how action taken during the crisis may facilitate reconstruction; and it also reveals the need for a different approach during the reconstruction phase compared to the crisis phase.

The Emergency Response

Crisis management requires quick responses, swift decisions and concerted action. The success of the operation depends to a large degree on existing capacity and preparedness. In the bushfire case, the immediate establishment of a government authority tasked with recovery and reconstruction provided the necessary focus for the operation. The scale and urgency of the operation required agility and responsiveness. The VBRRA's organizational structure, decision-making and management processes facilitated this. Six teams reported to the Chief Executive and Chair. Daily meetings gave people the authority to take action. Decisions were made expeditiously. If needed, adjustments were made promptly. The case provides a good illustration of many exemplary practices for emergency response.

The Reconstruction and Recovery Phase

The VBRRA's recovery and reconstruction framework put "people first." The needs of local communities were at the centre of the strategy. People in the communities designed the recovery plans and owned the decisions. Implementation took place at their pace. Each affected community was encouraged to establish a local recovery committee to prepare plans and put forward projects to support the recovery process. While the VBRRA provided guidance, each committee set its own priorities and tapped local people and organizations to forge consensus. The role of government case workers was to assist the communities.

Centralized decision making and unilateral action by government would have been faster. Governments have the capacity and the means to tear down damaged houses, remove the ruins and rebuild new houses on the sites of the old ones. This is not in dispute. But the result that matters most in circumstances following a disaster such as the one in Victoria is not the removal of rubble, but the recovery of devastated communities.

Community consensus building and decision making may be slower in some ways, but they are the fastest way of helping communities recover from traumatic events and emerge strengthened and better equipped for the future. A slower pace led to better and faster overall results.

This case is an illustration of how a public policy result (recovery and reconstruction) and civic results (community building and resilience) are interrelated and mutually reinforcing. Government leadership was the main driver for crisis management. During the reconstruction phase, the wise course of action was for government to follow the lead of the communities.

The VBRRA's approach focused on community-led recovery, capacity building and decision making at the local level. The case indicates that despite adversity, communities were strengthened through their recovery efforts. The approach engaged the natural resilience of individuals and their communities. By being part of the recovery process and recovering at their own pace, communities tailored the recovery strategy to meet their needs and reduced the risk of creating ongoing dependencies on government.

The case illustrates the factors that contribute to community resilience. These include using a diversity of approaches, building supportive relationships, contributing to social capital and trust, and sharing risks and responsibilities.

The case leaves open a number of questions that will be answered over time. As a result of the traumatic events of 2009 and of the reconstruction efforts, are the communities better able to prevent a similar occurrence? Have they, and has government, learned from this experience? Is the learning transferable to other communities to prevent similar crises? Bushfires and floods are regular occurrences. Resilience is the capacity to absorb shocks and rebound; but it is also the capacity to foresee and prevent similar occurrences.

PUBLIC POLICIES AND RESILIENCE

The Australian bushfire case study provides a number of important insights on how public policies and programs can contribute to building community and societal resilience. The first is that resilience already exists. It is not created by government. It is in the people, in their relationships with each other and in the community. The first principle for government is to avoid taking action that might erode natural resilience either by creating harmful dependencies or by increasing vulnerabilities. The corollary is that while government cannot create resilience, it can nurture it.

This principle has a number of implications for government. It signals the need to build on strengths and to seek the active and direct contribution of the people and communities most directly concerned. Government must be able to work simultaneously at different scales and at different speeds. In the bushfire case, this was illustrated by the quick pace of the emergency response and the slower pace of the reconstruction phase. A slower pace in the recovery phase was necessary to achieve deeper and more sustainable results: in the end, it may even be faster. Quick fixes may be "quick" but they may not "fix" much: in fact, they may even erode the natural resilience of society by disempowering people and communities.

Strategies aimed at building resilience should focus on people and on capacity building. Crises present opportunities for learning and disseminating new knowledge that may prove useful in other locations facing similar circumstances or that provides a base from which to address new challenges. The learning is central to building the adaptive capacity of society.

Public Policies

One of the key findings of the discussions on resilience is that "resilience is all around us."[87] Based on research on human development[88] that was discussed in The Hague, resilience is naturally supported by the adaptive systems that humans have developed to protect themselves.[89] Resilience is part of the evolutionary process that has made humans what we are today. Resilience depends on "ordinary magic," including strong attachments to and positive relationships with other people, organizations and institutions.[90] This signals the need to shift the focus of public policies from deficit-based models to positive frameworks that take advantage of the existing strengths, assets and adaptive capacity in people and social systems.[91]

This view received a powerful echo a few months later during the roundtable in Ottawa, where participants learned more about recent research on well-being. An invited expert in this area articulated three key propositions: "positive trumps negative, social trumps material, and generosity pays".[92]

Based on ideas from research on human development and well-being, the roundtable discussions and some personal observations, some factors would help shape public policies that encourage resilience.

Do no harm. Many public policies and programs traditionally have been designed from the perspective that users and beneficiaries have a limited capacity for self-help. These have the effect of "crowding out" the contribution of society and discouraging the active contribution of citizens and communities. An important first step towards building resilience is to challenge this assumption and review existing policies and programs from the perspective of deliberately creating an active role for citizens and communities whenever relevant. Besides contributing to resilience, this has the added benefit of revealing a broader range of options to achieve results of higher value at a lower overall cost to society.

Build on strength. Public policies and programs should approach complex and intricate problems by focusing on building a society where people have an elevated view of what they can accomplish together. A positive view of the future and of what people, government and society can accomplish together builds resilience and encourages innovation. This approach is in opposition to a focus on deficit reduction and on negativity where the dominant paradigm is to "fix," "fight" or "declare war" on complex problems. The most important problems of our time are beyond quick fixes. Negativity erodes confidence and quick fixes may lead to even more complex issues in the future.

Go fast, go slow. One of the greatest challenges for government is to reconcile the short timelines of modern politics with the longer timelines needed to build the collective capacity and societal resilience with which to respond and adapt to change. Time is a continuum. Each generation builds on the contribution of the one before. Action taken (or not taken) today creates the society future generations will inherit tomorrow. Slow is good when it leads to more resilient results across systems and over time, and when it builds the collective capacity for better results over time. Fast is good when it anticipates and deflects risks and reduces the overall costs that society would bear now or in the future.

Design for collaboration. Prevention, reducing exposure to risk and facilitating protective mechanisms contribute to building resilience. Social capital and supportive relationships are powerful protective mechanisms and primary factors of resilience. They can be fostered by using collaborative networks and citizen engagement in the design of public policies and programs and by building public policies and programs where helping others is built into the design of the service delivery system.[93]

Use a narrative of hope. Some collective aspirations are more conducive than others to building resilience. Narratives of hope that marry aspirations for material progress, social progress and intergenerational fairness are powerful instruments of change that contribute to building collective resilience. Fear, hatred and negativity are default mechanisms that indicate a failed capacity to adapt and change. They further erode self-confidence and resilience. Positive narratives of hope can help resolve tensions in society and generate the optimism and energy needed to transcend issues and reach collective goals.

Self-reliance and Resilience

A resilient society is characterized by self-reliant individuals and resilient communities. A number of factors contribute to self-reliance, including caring and supportive relationships within and outside the family that offer reassurance and help bolster a person's resilience. Care-givers, families and schools are key contributors to individual resilience.

Resilient individuals have a number of characteristics.[94] They display a solid grounding in reality, neither unwarranted optimism nor negativism. They believe that life is worth living and can be improved. They know how to improvise and use the tools at their disposal.

Resilience is the capacity to be robust under stress and to adapt in response to changing circumstances. Resilience cannot be achieved by individuals alone nor can it be available in the community and in society without being built at the individual level.[95] This has a number of implications for government.

Resilient communities rely on a critical mass of people with the motivation, skills and confidence to act to meet their needs and those of their family and their community. These people have solid, durable relationships in their community and beyond. These assets may be put to the service of their community when needed. These people can mobilize to respond to challenges and shape solutions in areas of common interest.[96]

Resilience is acquired and expanded by doing.[97] It is based on a stock of trust, mutual understanding, knowledge and know-how that allows people to act, learn, adapt and evolve collectively.[98] It develops through individual bonds and collective efforts over time, in the family, in the community and in society. These bonds weave a strong net of relationships that protects and lifts everyone up when times are good and reduces the risks when the going gets tough.

But what happens when resilience is weak? What are the implications for communities, and what can government do to strengthen resilience? Some elements of information can be gleaned from a case study on the Tarwewijk neighbourhood in Rotterdam.

Learning from Practice: Rotterdam Tarwewijk, a Resilient Neighbourhood? (the Netherlands)

At the roundtable in The Hague in March 2010, Dutch experts presented a case study on community building approaches to foster resilience in the neighbourhood of Tarwewijk, Rotterdam.[99] This case focused primarily on how community resilience can be cultivated and the barriers to doing so; but some interesting insight on individual resilience and its relationship to community resilience formed part of the sub-text.

According to the Dutch government, dozens of problem neighbourhoods face a combination of difficult issues, including high unemployment, poverty, school drop-out rates and crime, and insufficient integration of "new" Netherlanders. Sustained attention and investment by various levels of government made significant progress in some communities, but in others, such as Tarwewijk, major gains are elusive and the issues seem intractable.

Tarwewijk was built in the 1930s to house port workers. Today, the vast majority of residents live in rental accommodation that is of poor quality and in disrepair. Over 40 percent of the population is under 25 years of age, and 78 percent of inhabitants belong to an ethnic minority. The neighbourhood has become a place where newcomers to the city live. It is also a place where "slum lords" and drug dealers have carved out a niche. Poverty, drug-related crime, illegal housing, social injustice and unemployment are features of daily life in Tarwewijk. It is a transient community with a high turnover rate of residents.

In 2007, Tarwewijk was one of 40 neighbourhoods targeted for more intervention. It received extra funding and support for housing, work, education, integration and safety. Through the *Action Plan for Empowered Neighbourhoods* (APEN), the aim was for the government, municipal authorities, housing corporations, local organizations and residents to work together to define local goals and collaborate in reaching them. The case study identified a number of small successes; however, the challenges were numerous and overall the results underwhelming.

A powerful insight that emerged from the case is whether it is possible to pursue a strategy aimed at building community resilience when there is an insufficient level of individual resilience in the community. The case seems to suggest that it may be advisable to address some of the most pressing individual needs first or at least at the same time as community-building efforts. Many residents of Tarwewijk face stressful challenges, including poverty and unemployment, on top of the shock of adjusting to a new country and learning a new language. Most of their energy is focused on meeting survival needs. It is not entirely surprising if they cannot engage in creating a "liveable neighbourhood" at the same time. Moreover, the transience of the area makes it difficult for people to build relationships with each other.

Some of the basic foundations of individual resilience are under threat in Tarwewijk. This suggests that a complementary strategy to APEN may be needed to build individuals' self-reliance as a necessary condition for community building. This might include reducing exposure to risks, such as unscrupulous landlords or criminals, and building strengths through retraining, labour-market access programs or language training. Doing this in ways that connect residents with people experiencing similar challenges and with supportive community organizations could provide relationships that protect them and get closer to the goal of community building.

The Tarwewijk case study illustrates how addressing the multifaceted challenge of helping a neighbourhood in distress (a public policy result) involves working at multiple scales (individuals, groups and community) and requires a diversity of interrelated interventions.

Resilient Communities

Community resilience is built and accumulated over time. It manifests itself in the capacity of communities to define issues, find solutions to the challenges they face and act with or without government support.

Community resilience requires a delicate balance in the role of government. An all-encompassing role by government may erode societal capacity, increase dependency on government and encourage individual vulnerability to change.

The way governments go about their business is as important as the policy results they strive to achieve. Encouraging people to play an active role in their community, along with social innovation, co-creation and co-production are examples of measures that contribute to building community resilience and enhancing the collective capacity to achieve better results. Resilience is in people and in their relationships with other people, organizations and institutions. The building of capacity is in the doing.

ADAPTIVE CAPACITY

Some shocks can be foreseen, even if only as possibilities. They have a high probability of occurring, even if their exact time and place are unknown. Hurricanes in the Caribbean and earthquakes along known fault lines are examples.

Some shocks cannot be foreseen, prevented or mitigated. These events are beyond the realm of normal expectations at the time they occur. The 2001 terrorist attack on the World Trade Center in New York is an example. In other cases, even though shocks might be foreseen, the timing, location or impact may be a surprise. This was the case, for instance, for the outbreak of the Severe Acute Respiratory Syndrome (SARS) epidemic in Hong Kong, Singapore and Toronto, and of the impact of the Icelandic volcano's eruption on air travel in Europe.

The role of government is not to attempt to predict or control all potential shocks. This is impossible and counterproductive. Trying to protect society from disturbances may create "brittle" communities, institutions and societies as it undermines the collective capacity to learn and adapt.[100] Delaying change can increase the risk of larger-scale crises in the future.[101] Change is inevitable and can be healthy,[102] although the benefits and costs may be unevenly distributed.[103]

The ultimate test of resilience and adaptive capacity is when unforeseen and unexpected shocks occur. This is where the strengths and weaknesses of the ecosystem of resilience that has been built over time are revealed. These strengths and weaknesses include the capacity for self-organization and collaboration under intense and stressful conditions; the capacity to draw from acquired knowledge from diverse sources and to use knowledge in uncharted circumstances; the capacity to chart new trajectories; and finally the capacity to generate learning that will further improve the adaptive capacity of society to unforeseen circumstances in the future.

Resilient societies with strong adaptive capacity do not waste perturbations; they use them to accelerate learning. They test the capacity of various systems to absorb pressures and undergo changes. Crises help reveal more desirable pathways for society's development in the face of the increasing frequency of particular types of perturbations.[104]

Resilience and the adaptive capacity of society are essential to forge a system of governance adapted to the challenges of the 21ˢᵗ century and able to co-evolve with society. As the following case study illustrates, adaptive capacity takes leadership, trust, strong networks and reliance on social capital accumulated over time.

Learning from Practice: SARS Revisited, Insight from Singapore (Singapore)

At the roundtable in Singapore in September 2010, a case study was presented on that country's response to the Severe Acute Respiratory Syndrome (SARS) pandemic that broke out in early 2003.

SARS was the first pandemic of the 21ˢᵗ century and Singapore's first ever. The virus hit the country on 1 March 2003, when three women developed atypical pneumonia. A week later, healthcare workers started falling ill. By 13 March, the government issued its first SARS update. By the following week, infection had spread to four healthcare institutions and a wholesale vegetable market. In addition to its threat to human health, SARS had the potential to severely impact Singapore's economy as a city-state that relies on its openness with the rest of the world for survival.

While SARS posed a novel challenge, the discipline of preparedness for threats and surprises had always been a central concern to Singapore's government. Existing capabilities in emergency response, scanning, risk assessment, and scenario and contingency planning across government were immediately put to use. Singapore modelled its response on procedures from the Centers for Disease Control and Prevention (CDCP) in Atlanta. The government used every conceivable communication tool to explain the outbreak and to rally action across the public service and society.

In Singapore's response to the crisis, "learning-by-doing" and innovating "on the run" stand out. The response consisted of progressively improving on the CDCP procedures. Central to this process was the generation of new ideas, the best of which were rapidly prototyped and tested on a small scale, quickly adjusted and, if found workable, put to use on a larger scale.

Some successful innovations included a case management system that integrated contact tracing, epidemiology, disease control and frontline operations; a variety of quarantine monitoring technologies (such as radio frequency tags); confidence boosting initiatives, including fever screening technologies for the public (for example, thermal body scanners); SARS-free transportation and shopping corridors; a multi-agency image management task force that monitored and corrected misinformation about Singapore's SARS situation; and a "blitzkrieg" that used every possible communications channel, including a dedicated television station.

Singapore's sustained focus on building capacity for learning and innovation in government and society helped it weather the SARS crisis and prepare for future shocks and surprises.

Implications for Government

Serving in the 21ˢᵗ century entails serving beyond the predictable. This chapter explores some of the capacities needed to deal with the heightened levels of complexity, intractability and uncertainty that are characteristic of our times. It explores how some countries are undertaking initiatives to prepare for the challenges that lie ahead. They are placing their emphasis on bolstering the anticipative capacity of government and society to improve foresight, prevention, risk assessment and mitigation. They are building the capacity to shape emergent solutions through exploration, experimentation and by encouraging social innovation to tackle complex issues and intractable problems. They are experimenting with various ways of encouraging self-reliance, community resilience and improving the adaptive capacity in society.

These new capacities must co-exist with practices inherited from the industrial age. The challenge is to see how a focus on emergence and resilience in public administration can work in practice in the public institutions and organizations that have been designed to encourage stability and ensure predictability. This is the subject of the next chapter.

Chapter 5

Government Fit
for the Future

There is a crack in everything,
That's how the light comes in.

Leonard Cohen, *Anthem.*

Public administrations embody concepts, principles and values about the role
of government in society and about the relationships between government,
people and society. Many of our public institutions and public organizations
were born in the late 19th and early 20th centuries. They retain some fundamental
characteristics from that era.

The world has changed since "scholars posited two optimal organizational forms,
two types of goods, and one model of the individual."[1] This means a view of the
world where the market is the optimal way of producing and exchanging private
goods, the role of the state is to ration public demand, goods are either public or
private and individuals are fully rational and informed about all options available
to them as well as about the consequences that may result from their choices.

Today, economics, the social sciences and many other disciplines give us a view of
the world that defies a "one-size-fits-all" approach to problem solving. We live in a
world where multiple actors are simultaneously taking actions and making decisions
that transform the course of events and affect the performance of countries and the
well-being of citizens in faraway places. Public administration is taking shape in an
ecosystem of interrelated complex systems that co-exist and influence each other.

Preparing government for the challenges of the 21st century requires viewing the
role of government through a different lens than the one inherited from the industrial age. The New Synthesis Framework proposes a different mental map to think
through the complex issues and intractable problems of our times by bringing
together the contributions of government, people and society. In Chapter 4, we

discussed some of the capabilities government needs to do things in different ways and to improve the capacity to forge emergent solutions.

When different ideas and different ways of doing things come together, the old ways become unstuck. The potential for transformation is greatest at that moment. A new reality may take shape, bringing with it the potential for transformation, should the environment be hospitable to change and organizations display sufficient adaptive capacity. Otherwise, new ideas may linger for a time, but will most likely disappear as the traditional way of doing things reaffirms itself.

In this chapter, we ask, What can be done to improve the adaptive capacity of the public sector? What changes to public administration systems and practices would make the public sector more hospitable to new ideas and new ways of doing things? What changes would help government co-evolve in harmony with the changes taking place in society? These may be the most important questions of all: they go to the core of the capacity of the public sector to fulfill its mission in the future.

Different countries will choose different paths. Some will prefer a public sector that relies heavily on traditional compliance systems; others will seek to build the capacity of government to serve beyond the predictable. Whatever the choice, it will affect the capacity of government to face the challenges of the 21st century, the performance of society as a whole and the capacity of society to prosper in an environment characterized by complexity, uncertainty and volatility.

A SOLID FOUNDATION

There is no such thing as good governance without good government, no matter how one chooses to define these terms. Nor is there such a thing as good government without sound public institutions and well-performing public organizations. Institutional and organizational capacity provides the starting point for preparing governments to be fit for the future.

Public Institutions Matter: Compliance

Institutions contribute to social order by governing the behaviour of people in their communities. Public institutions have a central concern for the law, rule making and the enforcement of the law. They define the rules of the game in government and society. They provide legitimacy for the exercise of power and embody the values, norms and constitutional conventions that have evolved over time.

Public institutions incorporate history, traditions and conventions. In many countries, they are expected to live up to a number of democratic values, including accountability for the exercise of power and the use of public funds, along with the expectation that public office holders will exhibit integrity, probity and impartiality and behave in a manner deserving of the public trust.[2] Public institutions support a state apparatus able to make and enforce laws, to tax and to redistribute public funds without "leakage" and without corruption. Many countries maintain a significant degree of separation between the legislature, executive and judiciary to provide checks and balances in how the state exercises its considerable power.[3] These factors and many others contribute to the *institutional capacity* of the state.

Governments and societies have focused on building institutional capacity for many decades and indeed centuries. Public servants and public office holders have a special responsibility to defend, protect and ensure that future generations benefit from public institutions fit for the times.

A society with solid institutions is better able to absorb shocks and drive an ambitious agenda for itself. This was evident, for instance, during the reunification of East and West Germany. In spite of all the difficulties, the process was considerably facilitated by West Germany's strong public institutions, well-performing private sector and strong civic institutions as well as East Germany's residual market-based economy and active civic groups.[4] The absence of well-performing public, private and civic institutions or weak institutions are a cause for worry. When autocratic regimes break down, it is often the case that few institutions are left behind since the regimes inhibited the development of public, private and civic institutions in the country.

Public institutions set the normative framework for the functioning of the public sector. They provide the starting point and a solid foundation for preparing government for the challenges of the post-industrial era. Public institutions were designed to reduce uncertainty and provide stability. They value predictability, due process and compliance.

In the context of the New Synthesis Project, the key question is: How do we ensure that public institutions designed for stability, predictability and compliance can also improve the capacity to anticipate, innovate and introduce proactive interventions in a timely way when the collective interest demands it? What adjustments would help improve the adaptive capacity of the public sector to changing circumstances and changing needs?

Public Organizations Matter: Performance

Public organizations transform public purpose into concrete actions. They are the instruments through which governments bring together policy purpose, resources and the capacity to achieve results. They implement the public policies and programs that were mediated through prior political processes and give shape to the priorities of the governing body. They help reconcile inputs, outputs and results. They provide a basis for accountability in the exercise of delegated authorities and the use of taxpayers' money. They are created and governed by rules.

Improving *organizational capacity* has been the centrepiece of reforms in many countries since the 1980s. Reforms have focused on making government more productive and efficient.[5] Today, most public agencies pay greater attention to user satisfaction than before. The use of modern information and communications technologies has contributed to reducing the number of intermediaries and empowering users in the service delivery process.[6]

As public policy issues became more complex, governments experimented with various organizational models in an attempt to bring under one roof the relevant agencies, programs and services to address a set of complex issues or respond to a government-wide priority. While organizational restructuring is useful in some circumstances, it cannot meet the need to work across multiple boundaries. Reorganization simply creates new boundaries that will need to be crossed to address the next set of issues, or even the same ones since complex issues tend to metamorphose over time.

Public sector reforms to date amount to an incomplete journey: the most challenging transformations are still ahead. Public organizations need to find solutions to a number of unresolved challenges.

Firstly, there is no alternative to working across multiple boundaries and managing an increasing number of interfaces.[7] To fulfill their mission, public organizations must increasingly work across disciplines, functions and structures.[8]

Secondly, public organizations must become platforms of collaboration, experimentation and innovation. To do this, they must reconcile their vertical accountability for delegated authority with the need to operate through vast networks of organizations to achieve shared and collective results. This transforms the role of departments from operating as vertical silos to being hubs of vast networks. It transforms the role of the centre of government to one of ensuring coherence in the interagency space of modern governance.

Thirdly, public organizations must keep pace with changes in society. When organizations are locked into a fixed way of working, they fall victim to a rigidity trap where they waste energy preserving the status quo. When they operate as closed systems, they fall victim to a poverty trap where no new ideas are brought in to renew them and ensure their ongoing relevance. Avoiding these traps requires a level of adaptability, openness and inclusiveness that has proven difficult for most public organizations to achieve.

The challenge is to discover what changes would help public organizations operate as platforms of exploration to bring in new ideas, as platforms of experimentation to discover new ways of doing things and as platforms of collaboration to co-create public policies and services.

The way forward will vary among countries, which makes learning from what is happening in real time and in practice all the more important. That said, preparing public institutions and organizations for the challenges of the 21st century entails various ways of opening up existing administrative systems and moving from a relatively closed system of government to a more open system of governance.

The New Synthesis Framework recognizes the continued contribution of the traditional public administration (*compliance*) and the need for a sustained focus on performance that was introduced by New Public Management (*performance*). The rule of law and due process are fundamental in a public sector setting, so is a commitment to better quality, productivity and performance. These functions are best suited to predictable tasks performed in a relatively stable environment. A strong capacity for *emergence* and building *resilience* in government and society must complement these functions in order to face the challenges resulting from increasing levels of complexity, uncertainty and volatility in the world we live in.

The most powerful element in the New Synthesis Framework is arguably the word "AND" that stands at its centre (see Figure 9). It illustrates that *modern governance requires the coming together of systems of compliance, performance, emergence and resilience*; that the old and the new must co-exist. In the future, public administration will be open in some respects and closed in others. A modern system of governance must be able to bring in new ideas, conserve energy, use resources with parsimony and exploit internal and external capacities to achieve results of higher value and of lower overall cost to society across systems and over time.

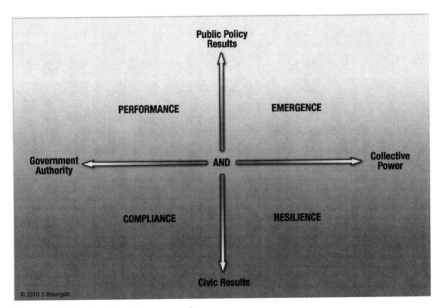

Figure 9: *New Synthesis Framework*

The four sub-systems illustrate the multidimensionality of modern governance. The following sections explore some changes to traditional concepts, systems and practices that would help open up the public sector to change. They draw freely from the discussion during the roundtables and the difficulties practitioners encountered. I hasten to say that they reflect the views I have formed through practice over the years rather than the position of any particular country, participating organization or individual participant.

ACCOUNTABILITY REVISITED

Accountability is central to public administration. It helps ensure that public funds are used for their intended purpose and that officials exercise their authority in a manner that is respectful of the law and public sector values.[9]

The traditional system of accountability worked as if most actions were under the control of a single minister and of a single agency without much interference from others. This does not reflect today's reality.[10]

In reality, no public agency is an island; all public organizations must work with others to fulfill their missions. As discussed in Chapter 3, an increasing number of public policy issues are beyond the reach of a single agency. They require the active contribution of other agencies, citizens, families, communities and society. Furthermore, complex issues respect no boundaries: they require the co-ordinated efforts of multiple actors.

The focus on the accountability of individual agencies for results presents a distorted picture of how public results are achieved in practice.[11] There are indications that such a focus acts as a barrier to interdepartmental co-operation and may lead to suboptimal results.[12] *The concept of accountability must take account of the shared responsibility of multiple agencies for shared results and government-wide priorities.*

Shared Accountability for Shared Results

In most cases, the concept of shared accountability for collaborative efforts can be implemented within existing laws and conventions. Various authors[13] and supreme audit organizations from various countries, including Australia[14] and Canada,[15] share this view. Shared accountability can be achieved by using memoranda of understanding to outline roles, responsibilities and accountabilities among various public agencies or with external partners. Collaborative efforts and collective results can be reflected in the annual reports normally produced by individual departments and ministries.[16]

Looking forward, enabling legislation that creates new public services or programs could be used to recognize the need for and the expectation of interagency co-operation across government.

A lot of time and energy could be saved if government policies explicitly recognized the need for shared accountability, encouraged it in practice and facilitated its implementation. Considering the prevalence of situations where organizations are called upon to work with others, the question is how best to ensure that shared accountability arrangements become the "new normal" rather than exceptions requiring case-by-case negotiation. The changing landscape of modern governance is such that it is difficult to imagine how a department could fulfill its mission without some shared arrangements for working with and through others.

Shared accountability for shared results involving the contribution of multiple agencies in government and actors outside government requires a number of supportive conditions. It starts by recognizing that the desired results exceed the capacity of any one agency working on its own and that partners have shared responsibility for results and to each other. Such arrangements generally require mid- to long-term commitments, an agreed-upon level of resources for the duration of the joint effort and common reporting modalities that replace individual agency requirements.[17]

In the context of a collective effort, direct causal links between the contribution of each agency and the overall results are unlikely.[18] The focus should remain on the overall results, which should be monitored and reported on collectively to evaluate progress and accelerate collective learning.

The difficulties that agency-based reporting requirements engender in the context of a collective effort were manifested in some of the case studies discussed at the international roundtables, including the cases of Canada's Homelessness Partnering Strategy, Brazil's Bolsa Família and the Dutch Public Safety Centres. These case studies are presented in Part Two of this volume.

Public Accountability to Citizens

The most important form of accountability is to the public.[19] There is a need to ensure that citizens have a reasonably informed view of their country's overall performance over time and compared to that of other countries with a relatively comparable level of development. It is generally recognized that reliable information is needed for the market economy to function properly: the same holds true for public governance. Relevant and reliable information is needed to encourage public awareness and to elevate public debate.

Societal results represent a country's "scorecard." They are the sum of the contributions of the public sector, private sector, civil society and citizens themselves. In essence, societal results are about the overall performance of a country. While it might not be possible to isolate the contribution of a single actor, overall results can be measured and made available for all to see. Societal reporting encourages a long-term view and an understanding of the collective responsibility for public results.

The reporting system must be relevant to elected officials, credible to the public and professionally competent. It should be based on statistically valid methodologies and administered consistently over a multi-year horizon.[20] Economic indicators are insufficient measures of societal progress.

The discussions during the course of the New Synthesis Project revealed the need for a basket of indicators, including economic results, quality of life, intergenerational fairness and well-being.[21] Measures of well-being involve asking citizens about their life satisfaction, their social well-being and their satisfaction with public services. These measures provide a different and complementary perspective to efficiency measures.[22] These findings are in line with the work of a commission created by President Sarkozy of France and headed by Nobel Laureates, Joseph Stiglitz and Amartya Sen. In 2009, the commission, comprised of 21 international experts, submitted its report calling for measures of economic growth to be complemented with measures of societal well-being.[23] Within Europe, Eurostat is leading in implementing the commission's report. This work involves 15 countries. The OECD has also taken action to implement the recommendations in collaboration with the member countries (France in particular) by releasing its "Better Life Index" in May 2011.[24]

Some countries, such as Finland, have made significant progress in developing a national "scorecard." The Finnish initiative is instructive in terms of what was done and how. Societal reporting is also useful at the sub-national level. A Canadian example is the British Columbia Progress Board, which produces benchmark reports on how the province is faring relative to other provinces on economic growth, standard of living, environmental quality, health outcomes and social conditions.[25]

Learning from Practice: The Findicator System (Finland)

The "Findicator" system (Findikaattori) was launched in 2009 by then Prime Minister, Matti Vanhanen. The system aspires to be at the vanguard of distributing information on the overall performance of Finland to citizens in a user-friendly way. The system includes domestic and international information on a number of topics, including welfare, economy, environment and social conditions. It includes more than 100 indicators chosen through a collaborative effort between the Prime Minister's Office (PMO), Statistics Finland, data producers and users, including the media.[26] The system is very popular and has been expanding at the request of users. In 2010, Prime Minister Mari Kiviniemi announced a new phase of development for the system aimed at incorporating various well-being indicators and providing a broader perspective. A working group chaired by the State Under-Secretary, Economic Affairs (PMO), was tasked with the initiative that involved various departments, universities and civic organizations.

More than Process

As more and more public results exceed the reach of a single agency acting alone, agency-based reporting has become progressively less relevant. This has led to a greater focus on "process accountability," which means that how things are done has become the main focus of accountability rather than what has been accomplished. This trend can be observed in a number of countries by the questions raised in the legislature, the focus of discussions in public accounts committees, in audit reports or in the media coverage of various public policy issues. Taken to the extreme, this focus means that the requirements for public accountability could be met successfully by an agency that complies with everything but achieves little of value.

Elected officials can do much to ensure that system- and government-wide results remain the focus of analysis and of political attention. They could focus committee work on the long chain of intermediate results that lead to significant societal results. Drawing from the case studies presented in Part Two of this volume, this would mean focusing on reducing homelessness rather than on individual initiatives administered under the Homelessness Partnering Strategy in Canada, monitoring poverty reduction rather than concentrating on the modalities of the Bolsa Família program in Brazil or looking beyond prison management in Singapore to monitor improvements in public safety and the successful reintegration of ex-offenders.

Committees of the legislative body can hold hearings involving multiple agencies and even several levels of governments to focus on mid- to long-term system-wide and societal results.

These are but a few examples of measures that could help the oversight function of the legislature over the executive focus on results. The oversight function is about more than process. It is about ensuring that public institutions remain focused on finding solutions to the most complex issues and the intractable problems of our time.[27]

COMPLIANCE REVISITED

One of the liveliest discussions in the context of the New Synthesis Project was whether it is advisable to disentangle control systems aimed at ensuring compliance from other systems aimed at learning, improving decision making and achieving better public results. By extension, this would mean disentangling audit as an assurance function to ensure compliance from evaluation and policy functions aimed at experimenting and discovering new ways of achieving better public results.

This deserves some explanation. I would start by noting how striking it was that concerns about the impact of an expanding array of controls on the performance of public organizations was raised in some fashion at every roundtable discussion over the course of 2010.[28] It was a subject of concern for senior public officials working in vastly different domains of activity and in countries facing very different challenges. These concerns on the part of practitioners deserve serious consideration.

The concerns can be summarized as follows. Controls and reporting requirements of all kinds have been increasing steadily since the 1980s.[29] This trend is not likely to abate since new controls are added each time new problems are identified, whether or not control mechanisms are relevant to the issues at hand.[30] This trend is creating a compliance culture that is adverse to innovation. Some would say that the increasing use of controls creates a climate of fear; others would describe it as a "blame and shame" approach that is not conducive to learning and continual improvement.[31] The growing cost of controls is of concern since it is financed by using funds intended to provide services to the public. In essence, the cost of controls constitutes a hidden tax paid by taxpayers without debate, accountability or reporting obligations. There is anecdotal evidence that, in some instances, the cost of controls and reporting requirements may be as high as 25-30 percent of the total budget of some public programs.[32] There is a risk that the size of the levy imposed to meet internal requirements has become disproportionate to the benefits for taxpayers.[33] This trend, if confirmed by a more scientific approach, gives rise to ethical, transparency and accountability concerns beyond the scope of the New Synthesis Project. There is a need for empirical research to establish the facts. It is timely to take stock and assess the path that has been followed over the last 30 years.

In the context of the New Synthesis Project, the main concern is to explore how to open up public administration systems and practices to ensure compliance while building the capacity for innovation and experimentation that government needs to serve in a post-industrial era.

The Cost of Controls

All organizations, whether public or private, operate under some controls and constraints. It is generally recognized that public organizations operate under a heavier burden of controls and constraints than do private organizations and, as a result, public sector efficiency is somewhat diminished.[34] Control systems in the public sector are needed to ensure compliance with laws and rules and to ensure due process. These systems are aimed at reducing the risk of mismanagement, including the risk of corruption and the abuse of power by office holders.[35]

Process controls set the limits within which public office holders can exercise discretion and set the parameters of acceptable behaviour in a public sector setting. To be efficient and contribute to compliance, controls must be objective, rule-based, enforceable and verifiable. At the most fundamental level, they should apply to all public organizations irrespective of their mandate and therefore be non-negotiable.

Since the 1980s, there has been a proliferation of controls and an expansion of the use of controls beyond their normal utility. *Input controls* set constraints on the nature of the resources an agency is allowed to use to fulfill its mission. These may limit, for example, the number of employees, pay bands and classification levels. They may introduce barriers between those funds used to pay salaries and those used to finance operations or buy equipment.

Ex Ante controls require public agencies to seek and obtain permission to use the funds already voted and allocated to them by the legislative body. For instance, a public hospital with an approved allocation for a program for disabled children may need to seek further approval from its ministry or a central agency before it can rent space, recruit staff or buy equipment to implement the program. Ex Ante controls may also be used to limit the duration of the approval granted or oblige the public agency to seek approvals at regular intervals.

In recent years, *output controls* have been added to the mix. A ubiquitous example is when various performance indicators used to monitor results are converted into "performance targets." When this happens, performance indicators cease to be a source of information to improve results and instead become control mechanisms. A significant body of research, in particular from the United Kingdom, has established that the use of targets transforms the strategic behaviour of the individuals and organizations subject to them, often with the consequence that the specific targets may be met but not in a way that translates into better agency or system-wide results.[36] In some countries, output controls are associated with various incentives or disincentives, including performance pay and budget allocation. These measures may further reinforce a compliance culture. Furthermore, it was noted that, in many countries, the reporting requirements and the number of oversight agencies have increased over the period.[37]

Controls add up and accumulate over time.[38] If their expansion is left unchecked, they will negatively affect the capacity of public organizations to fulfill their missions.[39] Governments periodically review the impact of regulatory requirements on the private sector; it is arguable that a similar, deliberate effort is also needed in the public sector to limit the cost of controls.

Controls should be used primarily to reduce the risk of mismanagement and to ensure that public funds are used for the purpose and in the manner intended by legislators. There are better, more efficient and less costly ways of improving public policy decisions and public results.[40]

A compliance system must work in synergy with other public sector management functions, but it also has a separate and distinct role. Focusing each administrative system on what it does best improves the overall performance and the adaptive capacity of governments.

The ultimate test of an efficient compliance system is to reduce the cost of controls necessary to achieve compliance and reduce the risk of mismanagement. It is necessary to reduce controls in low risk areas and to target areas with higher risk.[41] This approach should be supported by training, monitoring, early detection, prevention and corrective action including legal recourse, where necessary.

Documenting, monitoring and reporting publicly on the cost of controls and reporting requirements in government would help keep the cost of controls within reasonable limits. It would also be advisable for controls and reporting requirements to be subject to "sunset" clauses and periodic reviews.

Audit for Compliance

Auditors general and supreme audit organizations play an essential role in supporting the oversight function of the legislature over the executive. An audit function also provides independent advice and assurance to managers by examining, evaluating and monitoring the adequacy and effectiveness of internal control mechanisms.[42]

Before the 1980s, the work of external auditors focused primarily on "audits for compliance" and forensic audits. The work of audit organizations progressively expanded to include such things as "value-for-money" audits.[43] In some cases, audit and evaluation functions were combined and, in some countries, audit functions extended to providing management and policy advice to decision makers.

A similar development took place in the private sector, where large accounting firms expanded their business lines to include management consulting and other services. By the early 2000s, serious problems emerged from this practice. The new business lines had generated conflicts of interest that undermined the integrity of the auditing process. The collapse of Enron Corporation and other accounting scandals during the period stemmed in part from this development.[44] As a result, measures were introduced to disentangle audit work from management and strategy consulting work, and legislation was passed to increase the independence of auditors.[45]

In the public sector, expanding the audit function to include value-for-money and program evaluation as well as for various aspects of management and policy advice functions should also give rise to concerns, although the issue has not received much attention. The effect in the public sector may include a reduced focus on audits for compliance and forensic audits, causing some problems to go undetected; an increasing confusion of roles between audit and management functions; and a tendency to query policy choices made by the governing body, which entails a risk of politicizing the audit function.

The combined effect of the expanding use of controls and the expanded role of audit functions has had a number of unintended consequences. In particular, this environment is less hospitable to new ideas and new ways of doing things at a time when experimentation, exploration and innovation in the public sector are needed more than ever.[46]

No system can be all things to all people.[47] In the context of the New Synthesis Project, an argument is made that controls and audit functions should focus on ensuring compliance; it is an assurance function aimed at reducing the risk of mismanagement. Program evaluation, experimentation, exploration and policy work, for their part, should focus on results: they form part of a performance function aimed at improving the likelihood of achieving better public results.[48]

Both functions are needed, and both play a crucial role. However, a clearer delineation of roles and of the interrelations between compliance and performance would better prepare government for the challenges of the 21st century.[49] It would also help ensure that public institutions are hospitable to new ideas and adaptable to new ways of doing things in a manner that is guided by principles of accountability and respect for the rule of law.

PUBLIC ORGANIZATIONS AS CO-OPERATION PLATFORMS

Achieving public results is a collective enterprise that requires the coming together of multiple actors, sectors and agencies. In government, this means that hierarchy and networks must co-exist and operate in a seamless way.[50] This transforms the role of departments as well as the role of the centre of government. It requires that public agencies operate as platforms of co-operation inside government and beyond to leverage the contribution of others and bring in new ideas.

Working across multiple boundaries is a characteristic of public administration in the 21st century; yet most countries still lack the systems, practices or policies to facilitate the co-existence of hierarchies and networks.

Those working in a network are often conflicted between accountability to their home organization and their responsibility to a network of organizations supporting government-wide priorities.[51] Traditional practices and systems militate against a collective approach even when the benefits of working through networks far exceed the cost to the participating organizations.[52]

There are many reasons for organizations to work vertically and horizontally simultaneously. Working across boundaries and through horizontal networks is necessary to achieve results that exceed the capacity of a single agency. Equally important, it is also necessary in order to gain a holistic view of issues, appreciate the linkages across systems and garner a multidisciplinary understanding of complex issues.[53]

Gone are the times when the dominant view was that public agencies could operate more or less independently and with minimal interference from others. Much can be done to facilitate the co-existence of hierarchies and networks and help public administration internalize the need to work across multiple boundaries.[54]

Interagency Collaboration

As a first step, senior leaders must recognize explicitly the need for both hierarchies and distributed networks. This could be done in a policy statement from the highest authority. It may be reflected in mandate letters to ministers and deputy heads.

An expectation of interagency collaboration could be recognized in the financial appropriations of public agencies. In effect, funds could be set aside in departmental budgets to cover the costs associated with interagency collaboration. While the amount might be small, such a measure would have a powerful symbolic value: it would recognize that specific individuals and organizations bear the cost of collaboration while the whole of government reaps the benefits.

A more ambitious measure would be to reflect the need for interagency co-operation in the job descriptions and performance agreements of some public servants and all public sector managers. This would recognize the expectation that managers, administrators and decision makers are responsible for working across boundaries whenever the need dictates to fulfill their public purpose.

Rewards and incentives should support interagency co-operation. These range from formal recognition programs to training and development plans and promotions. Some countries have implemented performance pay and performance bonus schemes. An argument could be made that these should be used to reward achievements that reach beyond departmental responsibilities and transcend the jobs for which people are paid.

Interagency collaboration and working across boundaries are needed at all levels, including the highest one. A powerful incentive to a whole-of-government approach comes from the way ministers work together when tackling complex issues that cut across multiple agencies. Collaborative approaches that facilitate information-sharing among departments and encourage debate on the merit of various policy options can strengthen interagency collaboration and send powerful signals to public servants about what is expected of them. Some policy decisions are best made by restricting the discussion to a small group of actors; however, most decisions benefit from a broader airing of the issues.

A Centre of Government Fit for the Future

The centre of government may consist of one, two, three or even more central agencies. Some of these may have the authority to set the normative framework within which other public agencies operate, while others play a leadership role because they enjoy the confidence of the head of government and the governing authority. The most important role of central agencies is to help ensure that the interface between political actors and the public administration functions effectively and harmoniously. This role ensures that the professional public service is mobilized in support of the government's priorities and is ready to respond to unforeseen circumstances and challenges.

An important role of central agencies is to help government focus on the future. This includes focusing on decisions that may reduce preventable risks for society or improve the likelihood of more favourable outcomes over time. Central agencies have a special role to play in improving the anticipative capacity of government. Examples of what some countries, such as Finland, Singapore and the United Kingdom, are doing in this regard are presented in Chapter 4. These initiatives require a strong and active role by the centre of government.

The role of the centre is to help ensure coherence in the interagency and intergovernmental space of modern governance.[55] This means using the convening power that the proximity to the highest authority in government confers to help ensure a co-ordinated approach to government priorities. It also entails creating an environment conducive to government-wide collaboration. The centre has a special responsibility to ensure the availability of a sufficient cadre of leaders in the public administration who have the knowledge, diversity of experience and abilities needed to meet future challenges.

PUBLIC ORGANIZATIONS AS INNOVATION PLATFORMS

Because of their daily interaction with citizens and users of public services, public organizations are well positioned to detect emergent issues and risks. They are also best positioned to experiment with new ways of doing things and test new ideas in practice. It is at that level that government can bring in new, practical ideas most efficiently, and where innovation and experimentation can most effectively take place.

Public organizations, in essence, *need to operate as public platforms for innovation, exploration and experimentation.* Their contribution is of critical importance in creating a more open system of governance and in building the capacity of government to adapt to the changing landscape of the post-industrial era.[56] Some ways of accomplishing this, such as releasing public data and providing incentives for their innovative use or creating an enabling environment for social innovation, are discussed in Chapters 3 and 4.

It is well established that public organizations and public servants innovate.[57] The problem is that, in many cases, it is happening in spite of the constraints that bureaucratic settings tend to impose. Many innovations are random "one-offs" and depend on individual initiative that sometimes borders on the "heroic." The challenge is to make innovation, experimentation and exploration part of the normal fabric of public organizations. For that to happen, it must be supported in a systematic way.

While the public sector can readily accommodate incremental improvements and productivity gains, it is not wired for innovation or for breakthrough innovations. This is not entirely surprising since the public institutions inherited from the 19ᵗʰ and 20ᵗʰ centuries were designed to encourage conformity and reduce the exercise of discretion.

So what can be done to introduce the gene of innovation into the "DNA" of public organizations? There are promising signs that this is happening in countries such as Denmark, Sweden, Australia and Singapore to name a few. Promising initiatives are also taking shape at sub-national levels, where the work done by the Government of Victoria in Australia and the Government of British Columbia in Canada comes to mind.

Few significant private organizations would prosper without a commitment to researching and developing new products, services, business models or operating methods. Yet, while the public sector accounts for a significant proportion of GDP in most countries (in member countries of the OECD, government spending accounts for approximately 40 percent of GDP),[58] most countries do not have a formal innovation policy for the public sector. It is unlikely that the public sector will make the transition from a relatively closed system to a more open and innovative system without systemic adjustments and systematic efforts to remove some of the barriers to innovation.

Innovation Policy

Some countries have introduced national innovation strategies that include a focus on the public sector. The United States of America introduced such strategies in 2009, for example, and the Finnish and Norwegian governments did the same in 2008.[59] These governments recognized the importance of innovation in public policy and administration. The Innovation Action Plan launched by the state Government of Victoria, Australia, in February 2010 is particularly interesting because it specifically addresses the challenges of innovation in a public sector setting.[60] Every chief executive in government signed and endorsed the plan, sending a powerful message about their commitment to innovation. The plan focuses on four key areas: the need for strong networks; building the innovative capacity of the public sector; aligning rewards and incentives; and opening up and sharing data, information and knowledge across government.

Government-wide innovation policies, strategies or action plans are important. They provide public organizations with the context necessary to develop targeted innovation plans and initiatives. That means organizations may deliberately use innovation and experimentation funded through departmental budget to address unresolved issues. Some of these issues may be of interest to individual organizations, while others may cut across several of them, in which case, they can pool resources and conduct experiments jointly.

Dedicated resources, such as venture capital or innovation funds inside government, have been used to encourage public sector innovation. For example, in the mid-2000s, the Government of Canada established and the Canadian Centre for Management Development administered a Learning and Innovation Seed Fund.[61] Some of these initiatives had limited success, in part because the workload necessary to access the funds was high and the amounts involved were relatively small. Some countries also created social innovation funds, as did the United States of America in the spring of 2009.[62]

It would be relatively easy to draw from successful experiences to design a public sector innovation policy and related initiatives adapted to the needs of particular countries. The key is to keep the approach light, agile and fast.

Innovation Labs

One promising approach that has recently emerged is the creation of dedicated innovation labs to test ideas and conduct experiments.[63] Some of these are mentioned in Chapter 4 in relation to social innovation, but they may also be useful as part of an innovation strategy within the public sector, where they can help breed a culture of innovation across government.

Innovation labs within government enjoy some level of core funding, in some cases as a result of pooling resources among the founding departments. MindLab is one example.[64]

Innovation labs benefit from a critical mass of projects. This facilitates the accumulation of expertise and the development of a core capacity to encourage innovation and experimentation across government. Innovation lives in "places."[65] Experience shows that it is particularly difficult to preserve these "places" in line departments exposed to day-to-day crises. Innovation labs provide an alternative to resolving this problem since they operate at some distance from such pressures. They are built to support a number of departments or agencies,[66] which encourages cross-fertilization and generates efficiency gains. Innovation labs provide a "safe space" that reduces the traditional concerns associated with the risk of failure.

Openness

Openness should not be confused with transparency. Over the past 20 years, many countries have enacted legislation to establish people's right of access to government-held information. This has been and continues to be a cornerstone of transparency in governance.

Openness rather than transparency is the subject of primary interest in the context of the New Synthesis Project.[67] Openness has a number of dimensions. It includes open exchanges, open systems and open minds.

Open exchanges are about the processes public organizations use to exchange information and ideas with their environments. Ideas brought in are transformed before being released in new forms. In this way, public organizations are part-and-parcel of their environment. This is the case, for instance, when government collects information and makes the resulting data freely and publicly available in digital format to facilitate its recombination with other information and the creation of new products or services. It is also the case when government encourages the "in-sourcing" of ideas from people outside public organizations.

Singapore and Australia have used "crowd-sourcing" to encourage innovation and bring in new ideas in various policy areas, ranging from business policies to social innovation.[68] Brazil has experimented with open-source policy development. One example, discussed at the roundtable in Brazil in July 2010, was the development of a legal framework for the use of the Internet.[69] Contributions to this policy were received through an online platform built by the Brazilian Ministry of Culture. Citizens commented on the draft legal texts paragraph by paragraph directly on the website. In addition, the Brazilian government harvested blog posts, tweets, articles published in mainstream media and institutional and individual contributions sent by email.[70]

The most ambitious application is taking place in Iceland where tech-savvy Icelanders are actively contributing to the work of a constitutional council to overhaul the constitution for the 21ˢᵗ century. The draft constitution is due to be completed by the end of the summer of 2011.[71]

Open systems in the form of modern information and communication technologies offer powerful tools for generating open exchanges. The main challenges are not related to the technologies themselves but to the degree of freedom that public servants enjoy to engage and participate in open exchanges. This presents particular difficulties for government as exchanges on totally open public platforms, such as blogs, Facebook or Twitter, may give rise to political controversies as well as some security and privacy issues.

The appropriate level of openness must be addressed in practice taking into account the mission, the culture and the circumstances. The Commonwealth Government in Australia, for instance, struck a "Government 2.0 Taskforce" in 2009 to make recommendations on how it could move forward in the age of digital governance.[72] In 2010, the government accepted 12 of the 13 recommendations, which included requiring public agencies to engage online and finding ways for public servants to do so as well.[73]

Open minds are needed to explore new ideas and to be receptive to new ways of doing things. A number of measures may contribute to this facet of openness, including training that familiarizes public servants with the tools, instruments and methodologies available for various types of innovation and experimentation. This may include design work, ethnographic analysis and co-creation processes. Human resource management that encourages interagency mobility and a diversity of experiences also plays an important role. Professional associations may contribute to the dissemination of new ideas. Active participation in conferences and international events exposes practitioners to a diversity of practices and approaches used in other countries to address similar issues.

A Systemic Approach

An innovation policy targeting the challenges specific to the public sector combined with other measures, such as the availability of venture funds, the creation of innovation labs and a commitment to openness would create an *innovation ecosystem*[74] in the public sector.

Some will note that these measures require funding and may question the advisability of proceeding at a time when governments in many countries are facing fiscal difficulties. The question is, How can governments afford not to? The challenge for governments in times of fiscal difficulties is to invent new ways of addressing public issues at a lower overall cost to society. The complex issues and seemingly intractable problems, such as aging populations, increasing healthcare costs, energy supply and environmental pressures, cannot be resolved by doing more of the same, even if governments had more financial resources at their disposal. Rather, addressing fiscal imbalances requires new ideas, new ways of doing things and a different sharing of responsibilities between government, people and society. This is what some authors have called "radical innovation."[75] It may prove to be less radical and less costly than traditional cutting exercises that erode the collective capacity to achieve public results even if at a lower overall cost to society.

PUBLIC POLICIES AS EXPERIMENTATION PLATFORMS

A public policy is more than a decision; it is an experiment in progress. The policy decision itself, while important, is only one step in a system of interrelated actions that ultimately lead to the success or failure of the initiative.

When a national policy is launched without prior testing, governments are in fact conducting an experiment with the whole population. It may work, but it is also high risk. This approach may be appropriate for policies that confer an advantage on those with prior knowledge of the proposed measures. Such may be the case, for example, with tax measures. In most cases, however, it is preferable to test ideas on a small scale and to discover in practice and ahead of time what works and what does not, what unintended consequences might ensue and what other approaches might better achieve the desired outcome.[76]

Experimentation

A successful public policy is one that achieves the desired outcomes at the lowest overall cost to society and with the fewest unintended consequences. In general, it makes sense to improve the likelihood of success of public policies through experimentation or at least through some testing. Public policies aimed at addressing complex issues require more testing, more experimentation and more interaction than before to discover their downstream effects across systems and over time. They also benefit from co-creation, co-design and co-production processes to reach an effective balance of responsibility between government, people and society.

Public policies do not emerge fully formed. While the initial intent or the desired outcome may be reasonably clear, public policies take shape and evolve through multiple actions and interactions. By doing, through trial-and-error and experimentation, public organizations discover how to achieve better results. It is an iterative process that takes shape through course corrections and incremental adjustments;[77] the learning is in the doing. Experimentation includes the development and evaluation of demonstration projects conducted in real-life contexts.[78] It helps gather evidence about what works, in what circumstances and why.

Co-creation

Co-creating policy responses with people and in particular with potential users helps understand their needs, preferences and concerns. More importantly, it helps discover how to build on their strengths. Co-creation does not refer to public policy consultation where government seeks people's views on particular issues. It is not about polling, opinion surveys or focus-group testing. It involves a methodical process of working directly with people in designing, developing, testing and experimenting with potential solutions.

Governments in a number of countries are actively using co-creation in various circumstances.[79] As a result, a body of documentation and empirical evidence about what works in practice will accumulate rapidly over the coming years.

Some co-creation initiatives use *ethnographic research*. This research focuses on how people live the experience of interacting with government as a taxpayer, as a person with a disability, as a family in distress or as a patient with complex medical issues navigating through public services. *Service journeys* are another method used in co-creation processes. They provide a detailed map of the step-by-step interactions between a user of public services and the service providers, whether existing or proposed.

The combination of ethnographic research and service journeys may be very revealing. The Danish National Board of Industrial Injuries, for example, discovered the tragic irony that, from an injured worker's perspective, the process of accessing and using services was so intricate and time consuming that "you have to be healthy to be able to" do it.[80] During a roundtable in London in November 2010, a similar dynamic, unearthed by the social enterprise Participle using similar means, was reported on concerning families in a chronic state of crisis in the United Kingdom.[81]

The maze that people describe in using these methods is comparable to the maze public servants must navigate within the public administration to provide services. A detailed map of both realities is a powerful starting point to redesign and reinvent a more satisfactory reality.

Design Work for Public Policy

Design work, also known as *Design Thinking*, entails using specific methodologies that put service users at the centre of the creative process.[82] Used in public policy settings, design work brings together public purpose, collective capacity and societal means to test concepts in practice. Design work helps bring together policy design, policy implementation and the desired policy outcome to make the approach as valuable as possible through all its downstream effects.

Design work helps reduce the risk of policy failures that result from poor decisions, poor design or a poor appreciation of the downstream consequences of policy choices. A number of countries are giving heightened attention to design work methodologies to co-create policy and service designs with users.

Learning from Practice: National Health Conferences and Participatory Processes (Brazil)

A case study on the creation of Brazil's public universal healthcare system, presented at the roundtable in Rio de Janeiro in July 2010,[83] was the most ambitious example of co-creation discussed as part of the New Synthesis Project.[84] It illustrated how Brazil's deliberate use of large-scale social participation in governance, which began with the end of military rule in the mid-1980s, provided an enabling context that resulted in the Unified Health System (SUS).

The case placed particular emphasis on the policy work done at the 8th National Health Conference in 1986 that involved government officials, healthcare professionals and technocrats as usual, but also academics, graduate students, trade unionists, healthcare users and other actors from civil society. All told, 4,000 delegates participated, with more than 1,000 of them coming from civil society and trade unions.

Before the 8th National Health Conference, the delivery system for healthcare was both centralized and institutionally fragmented. It was financed through insurance premiums paid by those with incomes. Access to healthcare was financially exclusive and regionally uneven.

Many conference delegates from civil society and the unions were actors in the

Sanitary Movement. This movement was set on creating a universal and free healthcare system that would cover the entire population and be based, in part, on the institutionalized participation of communities. In the fertile political context following the end of military rule, the government invited members of the Sanitary Movement to help organize and participate in the national health conferences.

The 8ᵗʰ National Health Conference was a watershed moment. It provided a space in which participants co-created a dramatically new health policy and governance processes. The conference report proposed the implementation of a universal healthcare system and "became the cornerstone for the Charter of Health in Brazil's 1988 Federal Constitution."[85] This meant all Brazilians were constitutionally entitled to full health assistance through a model of shared responsibility between all levels of government, with municipalities being the main government actors. The conference report also led to the creation of a new legal framework that provided for community participation in, and "social control" of, the health system through local conferences and councils.

The case illustrates how the model that emerged in the mid-1980s of co-creating policy and co-producing results remains at the heart of the Brazilian health system. The mobilization of local non-governmental organizations and other community resources in response to the HIV/AIDS epidemic, discussed in Chapter 4, is cited as one example. Another is the 13ᵗʰ National Health Conference that took place in 2007 and mobilized 1.3 million participants from across sectors and regions of Brazilian society.

Learning from Practice:
Paediatric Complex Care—Taming of the Queue (Canada)

This case contains elements of co-design, co-creation and experimentation associated with a rigorous scientific evaluation process. The initiative is the result of leadership at the agency level. The pilot project was initiated in 2009, designed and funded by the participating agencies and is ongoing as of 2011.[86] It gives rise to the classic problems of the dissemination of successful initiatives, the incentives needed to encourage innovation beyond the start-up phase and the financing of successful experimentation when the costs are borne by individual agencies yet the benefits are system-wide and accrue to society as a whole.

The Children's Hospital of Eastern Ontario (CHEO) is a tertiary care academic hospital serving a population of 1.5 million in Ontario, Quebec and Nunavut, Canada. Several years ago, a Family Forum was created to advise CHEO on areas requiring priority attention from the perspective of parents with sick children. In early 2009, the forum recommended that children with very complex health problems receive priority attention. These are children with chronic illnesses requiring interaction with various medical specialists to ensure the co-ordination of care, reduce duplication and the risk of medical errors resulting from the complexity of the case. The children are three times more likely to require intensive care and hospitalizations than other children. Some hospitalizations may be preventable. Parents experience high level of stress, burnout is frequent and their lives are profoundly disturbed.

A pilot project was designed based on a family-centred approach. It was developed jointly by CHEO, the Ottawa Children's Treatment Centre (OCTC), an out-patient rehabilitation organization, the Community Care Access Centre (CCAC), physicians and two parents from the Family Forum. It aims to improve the co-ordination and navigability of the overall system, reduce the need for hospitalization and its duration, and improve family health.

The project team conducted a literature review to learn from similar experiences elsewhere in Canada and the United States of America. They developed project design criteria for the selection of children and developed a detailed map of the eligible population of children with very complex health problems in the region. One hundred children were identified. The pilot project includes a number of innovations, including a "Most Responsible Physician," a "Nurse Care Co-ordinator" and a "Family Co-ordinator" to ensure co-ordination and help navigate the system across the three organizations. A multi-agency patient record was created and medical roadmaps were developed to map out the relationships with service providers from the family and user perspectives. This is equivalent to the ethnographic research and the service journey mentioned before. The CHEO Research Institute developed the evaluation framework and will conduct a formal evaluation in June 2011.

The two-year pilot project started in April 2010. It involves 25 randomly selected children and a control group of another 25 children receiving care in the traditional manner. It is too early to assess the results; however, after one year, early indications show high family satisfaction. The evaluation will reveal if the satisfaction translates into lower stress levels and improved quality of life. The evaluation is expected to reveal a reduction in external visits and a decrease in hospitalizations.

If the evaluation confirms these results, decisions will be needed at a higher level to continue, expand or abandon the project. The case reveals a classic dilemma in public sector innovation, where the benefits and the savings are societal and system-wide but the costs are incurred at the local and agency levels.

PUBLIC SERVICES AS CO-PRODUCTION PLATFORMS

A broader view of public results, one that extends beyond agency results, opens up new perspectives on the production of public goods starting with the question: Who is the producer? Until the 1970s, the dominant view focused on government production and the mass production of government services. Government was seen as the primary producer of public goods and services. Little attention was given to the role played by the users of public services in the production of public results. Efforts to improve results essentially meant improving the productivity of the programs and services directly delivered by public agencies.

In the 1980s, in part in response to growing fiscal pressures in many countries, the focus shifted to the marketization of public services. This included various forms of privatization, deregulation and contracting out. Over time, however, problems associated with contracting out were uncovered.[87] For instance, contracting out does not necessarily reduce costs, and it works better when governments can specify their needs ahead of time. For many public policy areas, particularly those associated with complex issues and intractable problems, these factors are not in place.

Co-production

Co-production processes open up an alternative approach to government-centric services or contracting out. They are receiving more attention in a number of countries where they have been used in areas ranging from the delivery of postal services and assistance for unemployed people to tax administration.[88] This heightened interest is due to the fact that many governments face stringent fiscal conditions combined with a growing awareness that ignoring the contribution made by people and service users discounts a significant source of capacity and resources in society. *Public agencies that are not exploring the potential of co-production arrangements are, in fact, reducing the range of options open to government.*

As a concept in the context of the New Synthesis Project, co-production represents the shared and reciprocal activities of people and public agencies to produce results of public value. The concept has broad application and is anchored in a few basic principles, such as people are assets. There is always a way to put assets to productive use and there are enough resources to go around if we put them to good use.[89]

Learning from Practice: From "Care Trap" to "As Long as Possible in Your Own life" (Denmark)

This case study is from the Department for Elderly Care, Health and Labourforce in the Municipality of Fredericia.[90] It includes elements of co-creation and experimentation, but its most important aspect is how co-production is used to encourage the self-reliance of elderly people to "live their own life as long as possible." The experiment began in 2008 in Fredericia, a town of 50,000 people, and spread to other towns and cities. Similar to many other developed countries with low birth rates, Denmark has an aging population, which puts significant pressure on services and resources aimed at providing care to seniors. There were serious concerns about the sustainability of the existing system and the quality of care that could be provided in the future.

The traditional approach was embedded in a culture that sees seniors as vulnerable and in need of assistance. Typically, the service flow for eldercare starts with some in-home assistance and progresses to placement in a nursing home and, finally, to intensive care at the end of life. This system provides care but, at the same time, it considers its users as passive and provides very little encouragement for them to remain active. The services aimed to compensate for the "deficit" in the capacity of seniors to look after themselves. However, research and experience began to show that this approach became a "care trap," where its beneficiaries progressively lost their ability to cope with everyday life. Research also showed that seniors who manage their everyday lives as long as possible have happier lives. These findings are consistent with the roundtable findings on resilience.[91] This was the starting point of a new approach to eldercare in Denmark that is based on strengths, self-reliance and resilience.

The new approach was based on a concept of co-production aimed at encouraging self-reliance through a shift from passive consumption to active participation. It was based on the evidence that seniors want to be responsible for their lives and want to retain their physical and intellectual capabilities as long as possible. The approach required that service providers help seniors regain their self-sufficiency. In some ways, this means success is when the public service is no longer needed.

The program starts with a face-to-face session between each senior and the relevant professionals. The conversation centres on the question, What would you like to be able to do again? Responses led to some modest demands on caregivers but, interestingly, some of these demands did not fit into the range of services previously provided. Typically, seniors needed fewer services than they were getting under the conventional approach. They also used their physical and intellectual capacities much longer. The program used a concept of "everyday rehabilitation" that saw actions in everyday life as a way of rebuilding strength and developing cognitive ability. The key is that seniors were responsible for defining the services they needed and were empowered to be active in realizing the outcomes.

The results have been quite remarkable. Based on an evaluation of close to 450 participants in Fredericia, 45 percent are now self-reliant "in all matters of everyday life," 40 percent need less care than previously and 85 percent have a better quality of life. For the municipality, it has meant a lower cost and a greater capacity to face the challenge of an aging population. Results in other municipalities, such as Odense, are also very positive.[92]

In summary, Chapter 3 presented an enabling framework for public administration in the 21st century and Chapter 4 explored the new capacities for serving beyond the predictable. This chapter has explored how these new capacities transform public administration systems and practices. The questions now are, How does it all fit together? And are these changes sufficient to prepare government for the challenges of the 21st century?

Chapter 6
The New Synthesis Journey
Continues

Life is an unfoldment, and the further we travel the more truth we can comprehend.

Attributed to Hypatia of Alexandria.

The New Synthesis Project was launched to support practitioners who face the challenges of serving in the 21ˢᵗ century.[1] They are called upon to serve the public good and the collective interest in the face of increasing complexity, uncertainty and volatility. Their task is more difficult and demanding than ever.

The project has evolved over a number of phases. The most intensive period of work took place over the course of 2010, when a collaborative international research network involving practitioners and scholars from six countries held five international roundtables. That phase of the project is now over.

With the publication of this book, the New Synthesis Project will once again enter a new phase. This time, the focus will be on expanding the conversation by engaging practitioners and scholars in other parts of the world. It will also be on deepening the exploration of various aspects of the challenges associated with implementing ideas and practices associated with the New Synthesis Framework in the countries that have participated to date.

ALONG THE WAY

The New Synthesis Project has been a rich human experience and a stimulating process of discovery. It brought together a number of organizations from six countries into an international collaborative network.[2] Close to 200 participants from academia and from the world of practice contributed their ideas and experiences, shared their insights and expressed their aspirations about preparing their respective countries to address the challenges of the 21st century.[3]

Exploratory discussions took us to The Hague, Ottawa, Rio de Janeiro, Singapore, and London, as well as Melbourne, Perth, Auckland and Wellington. Each encounter enriched the participants' appreciation of the breadth of the transformation taking shape in government and in public organizations. The richness of the process of experimentation that is under way in countries with different cultures, histories and geographies, as well as different governance models and varying degrees of development provided new insight on how governments are responding to the challenges of the 21st century and the problems that stem from the post-industrial era.

The New Synthesis Project was designed to explore the new frontiers of public administration by bringing together experts from different fields, different disciplines and diverse areas of practice. This approach helped bridge the divide between theory and practice. It also expanded the conversation to a broad spectrum of disciplines beyond those conventionally associated with public administration, including social and behavioural psychology, wellness, resilience, ecology and complexity theory.

Despite their different circumstances and the diversity of programs and services they administer, the practitioners involved provided strikingly comparable descriptions of the challenges they face. They described with the same passion their aspirations to build a better future and prepare their countries for the challenges of the 21st century. They used similar words to voice their difficulties in reconciling in a meaningful way past practices with the changing circumstances of a world characterized by increasing complexity, uncertainty and volatility. Practitioners the world over have a lot in common and much to talk about.

The project revealed there is no shortage of good ideas, powerful experiments and breakthrough innovations in public governance and administration. There is no lack of courage, passion or commitment. What may be lacking is a frame of reference to guide the actions of practitioners and decision makers.

There is a thirst for a narrative supported by powerful examples to help integrate harmoniously the past practices of enduring value, the lessons learned over the past 30 years of public sector reforms and the challenges of our times in a manner that resonates more meaningfully with the reality of the world we live in. This is what the New Synthesis Project is about.

The project has taken us this far. Along the way, a more integrated picture than was available at the start of the project [4] began to emerge. The New Synthesis Framework is inspired by what already exists in practice. In that sense, it is not entirely new. Furthermore, a vast amount of academic literature is available on the core functions to which this book refers, including accountability, compliance, performance and networks. Detailed analysis of relatively new concepts and practices, such as futures work, co-production and co-creation, is also readily available. The New Synthesis Project was not conducted to deepen the understanding of particular public sector reform initiatives or techniques. Instead, it is principally concerned with how key ideas, functions, systems and practices may come together and interact in a manner that enhances the capacity of government and society to achieve results of higher public value in predictable, unpredictable or unforeseen circumstances, across systems and over time.

A NARRATIVE

At the time of writing, the central narrative that has evolved over the course of the New Synthesis Project could be summarized as follows:

> *The role of public institutions and public organizations is to enhance the collective capacity to achieve results of higher public value and at a lower overall cost to society, in all circumstances, across systems and across generations.*

This statement is subjective, debatable and perfectible. It will no doubt evolve as the journey continues. Others who participated in the roundtable discussions in 2010 may distill it differently. For me, this statement encapsulates the essence of the findings of the New Synthesis journey thus far.

Focusing on *results of higher value for society* helps overcome the introspective approach in public administration that has given so much weight to the internal structures, systems and practices that govern the functioning of public agencies. The role of public organizations extends beyond the public programs they administer and the services they provide. It extends to contributing to system-wide and societal results with others. Furthermore, public organizations must achieve results in a manner that builds the collective capacity for better results over time. In democratic societies, the public will ultimately determine what is of value to society. This judgment may be made directly or indirectly, in real time or over time.[5] People speak directly to what they value when they act on their own, with others or with government to produce public results. They speak indirectly about their preferences when they mandate elected officials to make decisions on their behalf. Periodic elections give the public the possibility to pass judgment on choices made on their behalf and to introduce course corrections as they see fit.

Focusing on *collective capacity* recognizes that there is much more to creating and producing public results than what public organizations actually provide. Public results of benefit to society are created by multiple actors. Some public results and services are created and provided by government. Some are created by individual citizens and groups of citizens. Some are co-created and involve the coming together of government, citizens and various other actors in society. It is in government's interest to optimize the value of public results irrespective of how they are produced and with whom. Focusing on results of value to society and on the collective capacity in society to produce them opens up a broader range of options for government. It helps reveal how new forms of collaboration are possible. It draws attention to the danger of undermining the collective capacity for results through public policies that create dependencies. It also attracts attention to the perils of undermining resilience when public services exclude the capacity for self-help, erode self-reliance or increase vulnerabilities.

Achieving public results of higher value for society is a "net" concept. It is a reminder to stay focused on the "big picture" of the benefits of system-wide and societal results and on the *overall cost to society*. Public results are not produced out of nowhere and for nothing: something is contributed from somewhere. Moreover, the costs are not equivalent to a public organization's expenditures. The costs to society take many forms. Some are paid through taxes. Some stem from the time and the energy invested by individuals, families, communities and other actors in society. Public results are a collective enterprise and entail sharing the costs and responsibilities. Finally, some costs take the form of constraints on the way people live to benefit society as a whole. For instance, applying a postal code to a letter or sorting garbage to facilitate recycling is a constraint that limits individual freedoms in order to create a greater good.

The role of government is to serve the collective interest in all circumstances. This means in relatively stable environments as well as in unforeseen circumstances, including times of crisis. Addressing complex public policy issues and finding solutions to intractable public problems requires that government, people and society discover and successfully implement solutions that achieve evermore valuable public results to society across systems and generations. It recognizes that economic, social, technological and environmental systems are intertwined. No real progress is made and no higher value is achieved when the solutions to a complex problem are beneficial in one system but detrimental in another, when solutions to short-term economic problems generated by a specific set of actors result in high costs being borne by society as a whole or when measures taken in the short term mean that society will confront even more intractable and complex problems in the future.

AN ADAPTIVE SYSTEM OF GOVERNMENT

The New Synthesis Framework is meant to help practitioners see their work and context from a broad perspective; one that integrates government, people and society, one that can help them appreciate that government is acting simultaneously at multiple scales and at different speeds. Governments perform predictable tasks in a reliable way. This encourages predictability and reduces uncertainty in society. At the same time, governments are called upon to serve beyond the predictable. They are responsible for building the collective capacity of society to absorb shocks and prosper even in the face of adversity. This calls for new systems, capacities and skills to complement existing ones. It requires a heightened capacity to detect emergent issues, to make sense of intricate interrelationships across systems and, in some cases, with differing impacts over many years. It requires a strong and deliberate focus on the future; a focus aimed at forging a shared appreciation of a more favourable future. This does not happen by accident. It requires sustained efforts to explore, experiment and discover emergent solutions to complex issues or to give rise to practical solutions to the intractable problems of our time. It requires a willingness to challenge the status quo and the courage to change.

Emergent solutions require the inventive use of assets people have at their disposal and a willingness to rely on the strength of others. Emergent solutions require the active contribution of government, multiple actors and citizens. As a result, no one is entirely in control. Resilience is about building strength in others by recognizing and cultivating those strengths. Seeing public administration in that way opens up an expanded space of possibilities. It transforms the way we think as well as the way we do things. In such a context, public policies are experiments in progress that open up the possibility for co-creation and accelerate collective learning. Public services are instruments of co-production that build self-reliance and community resilience.

The New Synthesis Framework presents public administration as a dynamic system with the capacity to adapt to changing circumstances and where governments have the capacity to co-evolve with society. Everything is connected to everything; government transforms society and is transformed by it. (See Figure 10.)

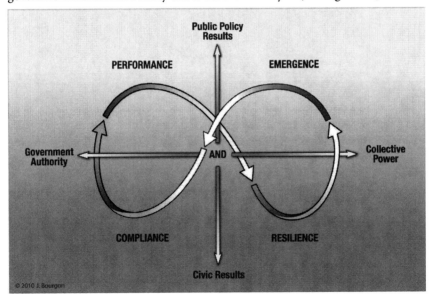

Figure 10: *An Adaptive System of Government*

An enabling framework does not provide answers. It facilitates the exploration in practice of the broad range of possibilities open to government. It helps reveal the consequences that various choices entail and the potential for new types of relationships. *There is no single solution and no approach fit for all seasons. There are choices and possibilities; both are important, as therein lie the potential for a better future.* These choices must be made in practice, in the unique circumstances of each country. They must align collective aspirations, resources, means and capacity. This is what governing is all about: it is beauty, grandeur and dilemmas.

A DYNAMIC SYSTEM

While what has been presented above may only sound like a small change compared to what is already happening in some countries, in reality, it represents a profound shift from a relatively closed concept of government where public organizations operate more or less on their own and act as the primary provider of public services to a more open, dynamic concept of governance.

An *emergence function* helps improve the capacity of government to anticipate emergent issues and opportunities, to reap benefits from social innovation and to stay focused on the future.

A *compliance function* provides government with an organized way of setting priorities and making choices. It is needed for public institutions and organizations to internalize new ideas and adapt to new ways of doing things. One of the greatest difficulties in sustaining a dynamic system lies in cultivating the capacity to rethink, reconsider and reinvent what worked well before.[6] Path dependencies and vested interests in the old ways of doing things lead to resistance to change. This is why a culture of experimentation and innovation is so crucial to preparing government for the challenges of the 21ˢᵗ century.

A *performance function* helps government think across systems and work across boundaries, sectors and disciplines. It brings together the contribution of the private, public and civic spheres to achieve results of higher public value across sectors and over time. It uses public organizations as public platforms of collaboration, exploration, experimentation and innovation to co-create solutions.

A *resilience function* builds the collective capacity for better results through co-production and the active participation of citizens, communities and society. It recognizes that collective learning builds the civic spirit necessary for society to weather unforeseen circumstances and prosper even in the face of adversity.

A CO-EVOLVING SYSTEM

An adaptive and dynamic system of governance would see economic, social, political, technological and environmental systems as intertwined and interdependent; where public organizations constantly exchange with their environment and where government and public organizations are part-and-parcel of their environment. In such a case, the public, private and civic spheres would display the capacity to co-evolve in a manner that supports the overall performance of society.[7]

It requires deliberate efforts to develop a shared understanding of a more desirable future. In this process of co-evolution, partners identify issues of mutual concern that eventually lead to emergent solutions. There is no pre-determined master plan; rather, a progressive convergence of views and a congruence in the actions of multiple actors emerge that would not otherwise be possible. Emergent solutions encourage the integration of divergent interests in the design of public solutions. The co-design and co-creation of public policies and services strengthen the potential for co-evolution.

AND, THE JOURNEY CONTINUES...

Where will the New Synthesis Project go now? What does the next chapter contain? What new forms will the project take? No one knows yet, but for now, I am simply happy that it was possible to bring the project this far.

Publishing this book is already beyond what the partners and I had envisaged to do at the start of this project. This last phase gave me the opportunity to tell the story of the New Synthesis journey, to honour its many contributors as well as those who believe in the importance of preparing government for the challenges of the 21st century. Since sharing ideas is central to learning, writing this book gave me an opportunity to clarify my thinking and refine some of my ideas.

Above all, this project remains a work in progress. This book is an attempt to share the results to date in an effort to open up and expand the conversation to practitioners and scholars in many parts of the world and in a diversity of circumstances.

This book will be initially launched and discussed in the six countries that participated in the journey during 2009-10; this is as it should be. Some readers will choose to deepen the conversation by engaging managers at various levels. Some will explore how the findings transform the preparation of future public sector leaders. Still others will explore how to reflect the key findings in the curricula of schools or faculties of public administration.

Whatever the form the next steps take, the key is to pursue the conversation about what it takes to resolve peacefully some of the most complex issues and intricate problems of our time. What do we need to do to prepare government for the challenges of serving in the 21st century?

And so, the journey continues...

Part Two
Case Studies: Bridging Theory and Practice

Chapter 7
The Changing Reality
of Practice

The best way to learn about where public administration is going is to study what public sector leaders are doing in practice. Great things can be learned from every country and from innovative public servants at all levels.

The scholarly literature will eventually catch up with some of the most visible or publicized initiatives. Unfortunately, that may take years, and time is not a luxury practitioners can afford. Moreover, some of the most inspiring initiatives may be overlooked.

Case studies reveal what worked, what did not and why it worked at that time, in that place and in that way. These are the lessons practitioners are looking for.

Case studies played a key role in the New Synthesis Project. Each participating country committed to preparing at least two case studies. In the end, 17 cases were prepared over the course of 2010. Each was presented and discussed at one or more of the international roundtables.

These cases provided participants with a wealth of insights. They help explain the changing nature of public administration in various parts of the world. They reveal how profoundly the role of the public sector is changing. They show how public organizations do not operate in the orderly and well defined environment that the conventional doctrine of public administration would have us believe. By necessity, public organizations manage multiple interfaces with an increasing number of organizations inside and outside government. They are platforms of co-operation reaching out well beyond their organizational borders to fulfill their public missions. Their operating environment is dynamic and turbulent.

The cases illustrate how policy decisions are not the exclusive prerogative of the people on "the inside" or "at the top." They illustrate how policy decisions and their implementation are more intimately related than conventional wisdom would have it. Policy decisions flow from in-out, up-down processes. They evolve through multiple interactions and take form through implementation. The cases show how public administrators are agents of change who are actively promoting innovations and reforms to achieve better public results.

Almost every practitioner we met through the course of the project commented on how increasingly difficult it is to reconcile some of the practices inherited from the past with their current reality of practice. The cases highlight how, despite these gaps, public officials in different parts of the world are working to reconcile traditional systems and practices with the need to work in new and different ways.

Beyond the merit of individual cases, the discussions helped participants identify similar trends and difficulties in responding to changing needs and circumstances. From Rio to The Hague, Auckland to Ottawa, London to Singapore, public administrators provided surprisingly comparable descriptions of the challenges they were facing and of the experiments they were conducting. They used similar words to describe how they are struggling to transform past practices to adapt to the world we live in and respond to the expectations of the people they serve.

We met exceptional people. Listening to them and learning from them was an inspiring experience.

Seven of the case studies prepared for the New Synthesis Project are presented in this book. The others are available on the NS World website.[1]

In the following chapters, the case studies are grouped into four themes of particular importance to the New Synthesis Framework. Two cases explore the New Synthesis concept of public results that embrace both public policy and civic results. The second grouping examines how governments are called upon to combine forces with multiple actors to address complex issues. The cases reveal the tensions between traditional approaches and the need to work across multiple boundaries. One case study is presented to help readers gain a better appreciation of the concept of resilience. Finally, two cases demonstrate the importance of exploration and experimentation to ensure that governments acquire the capacity to adapt to the challenges of serving in 21st century and to co-evolve with society.

In this chapter, we provide a brief discussion for each thematic group to help readers explore the connections between these practical examples and the New Synthesis Framework. Obviously, there is much more to each case than these preambles capture. Readers will find they contain many other important insights and lessons.

ACHIEVING PUBLIC RESULTS

The New Synthesis Framework argues that public results are a combination of public policy results and civic results. The former helps move society forward: the latter builds the collective capacity for better public results over time. The two are necessary to address complex issues and adapt in unpredictable circumstances.

In this context, the roles of public organizations and public servants extend beyond the walls of their agencies. To fulfill their public purpose, they must position the contributions of their programs and organizations in the context of broader societal results. Doing this opens the door to an expanded range of possibilities. It provides a mental map to think in new ways about how to achieve results of higher value at a lower overall cost to society. By thinking about the role of their organization as a contributor to broad societal results, public servants stand a better chance of discovering the interrelationships among multiple systems and the multifaceted interventions needed to address complex issues.

Past practices that focus primarily on agency results and what government can do on its own have crowded out the contribution of society and devalued the work of citizens.

Public services and programs designed for the active participation of citizens and societies improve the likelihood of achieving better results. In the process, government encourages individual self-reliance and contributes to building communities able to take charge of their own affairs.

The case studies on the Singapore Prison Service and Brazil's Bolsa Família help explore these concepts.

The Singapore Prison Service case illustrates the power of a broader mental map when mission and desired outcomes are cast in broad societal terms. It is also a powerful illustration of bottom-up innovation in the public sector, where a public organization transforms its role and, in the process, transforms the view of society on ex-offenders.

Bolsa Família is one of the largest direct-funding transfer programs to citizens of its kind in the world. It was designed to empower families to make their own decisions about the use of public monies transferred to them. The case reveals a powerful story about how taking the risk of empowering and trusting people paid off. It shows how the emphasis on civic results and the active role of family were key to achieving measurable progress on a number of fronts. It is also a story of about how innovations initiated at the local level ended up shaping national policy.

Singapore Prison Service

This is the story of an organization that transformed itself by pursuing a mission reaching beyond the walls of the prisons it oversaw. Its vision encompassed its customary role of ensuring security and discipline in the prisons along with a new leadership role in rehabilitation. Casting its role at the level of societal results in addition to organizational results meant steering ex-offenders "towards becoming responsible citizens with the help of their families and the community."

This broad vision helped both management and officers explore a long chain of interconnected public results—in this case going beyond security and safety, to rehabilitation, after-care and reintegration of offenders into society.

Focusing on societal results opened up new possibilities. It encouraged a different sharing of responsibilities between inmates, prison officers, inmates' families, employers and the general public. It transformed the role of prison officers. By sharing the responsibility for public results more broadly, it became possible for officers to focus on higher value-added tasks, such as coaching and mentoring. As a result, staff motivation improved.

By sharing the responsibilities more broadly, it was possible to achieve better results at a lower overall cost to society. This is an important lesson for countries facing severe fiscal constraints. The challenge is not so much to look for cuts but to look for a different way of thinking, one that entails sharing responsibilities and costs to achieve results of higher value at a lower overall cost to society.

Ten years of positive results speak for themselves. In the late 1990s, the Singapore Prison Service featured overcrowded facilities, high staff turnover and staff shortages, increasing costs and undesirable rates of recidivism. The service is now one of the most effective in the world, and recidivism rates have dropped by 50 percent between 1998 and 2009.

It is a powerful story of professional leadership where public administrators see their role as agents of change and where political leadership is receptive to exploring new ways of achieving public results.

Bolsa Família: Brazil

Over a fifteen-year period, Brazil undertook an ambitious reform agenda that simultaneously addressed issues of social inclusion, the reduction of inequality, the strengthening of democracy and the promotion of economic stability and sustainable growth. In light of its progress over a relatively short period, Brazil became a source of inspiration for developing countries in the region and elsewhere.

Bolsa Família is one such success story. It is one of the largest transfer payment programs in the world, benefiting some 50 million people. Its fundamental purposes are to reduce hunger and poverty and to pull people out of the poverty trap. The program is designed to empower families, and in particular women, to play an active role in achieving these results and to make good decisions by themselves.

Bolsa Família is an example of how focusing on civic results through a co-production process involving public agencies and families contributed to achieving multiple policy results, including the alleviation of poverty, access to education, the reduction of child mortality, community building and the strengthening of the pact between different levels of government in the Brazilian federation.

Bureaucratic controls and program conditions were reduced to empower families and engage communities. This meant trusting individuals to make the best decisions for their families in their situations. The impressive results of the program show that the risks involved were well worth taking. An important lesson flowing from this case is that administrative systems based on trust encourage trustworthy behaviour. By and large, people responded in a responsible manner.

The case also shows the considerable political leadership it took to design Bolsa Família from the perspective of those who need help and to introduce the administrative changes required for the program to work. Political leadership was also needed to accept the risk of reasonable administrative errors and to stand up to the pressure of introducing more controls each time a mistake was uncovered. This is a case where political leaders stood up for the need to learn by doing and to introduce improvements as lessons were learned. It is refreshing to see that the "blame and shame" approach in vogue in some countries has not taken hold everywhere.

PUBLIC RESULTS AS A COLLECTIVE ENTERPRISE

The New Synthesis proposes that an increasing number of public policy results are beyond the reach of a single public agency, or even of a government, working alone.

Governing in the 21ˢᵗ century incorporates what public agencies can do on their own and what they can best achieve by working with others across government, with various levels of government and with multiple actors. Governing is a search for balance between using government authority in a traditional way and relying on the collective power of society when the latter is needed to achieve results. It is a delicate balancing act where the role of government is to optimize the use of state authority to leverage collective capacity in society.

Two case studies are presented to explore how governments are working across boundaries to leverage the power of others: the Homelessness Partnering Strategy (Canada) and the Public Safety Centres (the Netherlands).

The Homelessness Partnering Strategy is an example of collaboration across government, among levels of government and with community groups. The goal is to build collective capacity that will ensure a co-ordinated response to homelessness at the local level.

The case of Public Safety Centres illustrates the need for public organizations to work across organizational and professional boundaries to share knowledge to develop a comprehensive view on complex issues of common interest. Networking across multiple interfaces is part of the daily reality of the organizations and individuals involved in improving public safety in the Netherlands through these centres.

The traditional approach to public administration did not pay much attention to boundary crossing and the need to manage multiple interfaces. In fact, most public agencies were expected to deliver on their own, without much interaction with others. This is not the reality that practitioners experience today. The complex public issues they must respond to do not respect boundaries. They need the contribution of multiple actors. Solutions depend on a coherent response from "the whole" rather than an efficient response from one or more of "the parts."

Both cases illustrate very well the tensions that currently exist between the traditional approaches and the new reality of practice, between vertical organizational authority and the need to operate through distributed networks. Organizational boundaries define the outer limits of organizational authority, but most missions require a sustained input of knowledge from other sources and the mobilization of other relevant entities. Networks act as platforms for collaboration. They help government renew and adapt to changing circumstances.

Tensions between formal organizations and informal arrangements will continue to exist until interagency collaboration is recognized as the normal way of doing business in government, and until interagency co-operation finds institutional expression in such things as agency budgets, job descriptions, performance assessments and career advancement decisions.

Homelessness Partnering Strategy: Canada

Homelessness is a complex, multi-dimensional issue. It involves diverse underlying factors including poverty, affordable housing, employment, transportation, mental illness, family violence and racial discrimination. Homelessness can take many shapes and forms. It is a problem found in developed and developing countries. It can affect every class in society.

As the underlying factors of homelessness are diverse, a wide variety of responses are required at the community, sub-national and national levels. No one is fully "in control," and resolving the issue is beyond the capacity of any one actor.

The Homelessness Partnering Strategy was created as a collaborative platform to bring together relevant organizations from the federal government, other levels of government, community groups and civil society to look at the challenge of homelessness in an integrated manner at the community level. The role of the

Government of Canada was to launch the initiative, encourage participation and empower communities to act. The approach could be described as collaborative governance involving shared responsibility and co-funding among multiple actors and agencies.

This case study illustrates how government authority and resources can be used to leverage collective power when the results are beyond the reach of a single government or agency.

This case study is an important reminder of how traditional practices designed for direct service delivery by individual public agencies can get in the way of an endeavour that involves many other actors. A heavy burden of reporting requirements, a focus on early results, short-term financing arrangements and frequent staff turnover in government act as barriers to achieving results and undermine the collaborative spirit necessary for a collective enterprise.

The case shows how collective endeavours depend on relationships of trust and require special arrangements, including the harmonization of the various departmental requirements, to sustain the efforts of the group.

Public Safety Centres: the Netherlands

Public Safety Centres are networks of organizations formed to stimulate co-operative approaches for dealing with crime and public safety through information and knowledge-sharing. They are comprised of public and civil society organizations working together on an as-needed basis and employing a blend of strategies including law enforcement, prevention and after-care. They are platforms for co-operation, not formal organizations.

This case provides a practical illustration of how modern public organizations and professionals can work across boundaries and interact through the multiple interfaces of the various agencies involved in addressing complex issues. It reveals how hierarchical structures can co-exist with networking arrangements and how networks contribute to the sharing of knowledge and information that helps prevent problems resulting from poor co-ordination among agencies.

The case reveals the tensions and the push-and-pull between hierarchical approach and networks. It illustrates the "oscillations" between the need for collaboration among loosely coupled organizations on the one hand and the pull to "formalize," "regularize" or "normalize" informal arrangements on the other hand. Loosely coupled organizations come together as needed to exchange knowledge and work in a concerted way on a problem of common concern. Otherwise, they pursue their respective activities on their own. Formalizing such arrangements generally tends to defeat the purpose since it reduces the agility and the usefulness of working through informal networks.

RESILIENCE

The New Synthesis Framework proposes that the role of government in the 21st century extends to building the resilience of societies to adapt, absorb shocks, embrace change and prosper in predictable and unpredictable circumstances.

Some shocks can be foreseen. In these cases, building resilience entails preventing and mitigating vulnerabilities. However, some of the most significant shocks and crises cannot be anticipated. In these cases, the role of government is to act in ways that promote resilience in society on an ongoing basis.

Resilient societies have a number of characteristics. This includes a positive perspective about the future, an active citizenry consisting of a critical mass of people with the capacity to act when the needs of their society demands it and solid networks of community groups able to mobilize resources to address common challenges.

Government, citizens or organizations working alone cannot achieve resilience. It accumulates over time through the experience of working together. It makes a powerful difference in the ways societies mobilize in the face of crises and rebound in the aftermath of disasters and inevitable shocks.

The Victorian Bushfire Reconstruction and Recovery Authority: Australia

The case study provided by Australia on the Victorian Bushfire Reconstruction and Recovery Authority was the most important one presented to the network for exploring the concept of resilience. The case focuses on the recuperation process undertaken after a series of devastating bushfires raged across the state of Victoria in early February 2009.

There are two stories in this case. One provides insight into how crisis management can be done well. It shows how a quick response on the ground, interagency co-ordination, rapid decisions (including unfettered access to the highest levels in government), clear leadership, flexibility and agility are crucial elements of an effective emergency response. It is fascinating to see that governments often do very well in periods of crisis many of the things they find difficult in "normal" times, including horizontal co-ordination, working across boundaries, deliberately learning and course correcting.

From a New Synthesis perspective, the most interesting storyline in the bushfire case is the reconstruction and recovery efforts that began even as the crisis was unfolding. The case elegantly illustrates many of the theoretical findings on resilience that were discussed at the international roundtable in The Hague.[2]

The case revealed important lessons. The rapid establishment of a recovery agency and its immediate actions injected much-needed support, resources and, most importantly, a sense of hope. The reconstruction and recovery efforts put the needs of people and communities first. All affected communities were supported in coming forward with their own reconstruction plans. They were allowed to make decisions at their pace. This was in stark contrast with the fast pace of the emergency response efforts. In fact, a slower pace on the recovery front allowed people to devise solutions to their own problems and helped ensure a more rapid and harmonious implementation than would otherwise have been possible.

Community engagement played a key role in the reconstruction process and contributed to building resilience. The case shows how "people recover better when they engage in their own recovery." By working together, citizens in affected areas developed stronger relationships and a stronger sense of community. Putting communities in charge of reconstruction decisions restored a sense of collective empowerment and helped accelerate the grieving and individual recovery process.

The factors contributing to community resilience are clearly displayed in the case: these include using a diversity of approaches, building relations, contributing to social capital and trust, and sharing risks and responsibilities.

EXPLORATION, EXPERIMENTATION AND LEARNING-BY-DOING

The New Synthesis Framework proposes that, to prepare government for the challenges of the 21st century, we need to work from a perspective that encompasses a broader understanding of public results, an expanded view of the role of government in society and a deeper appreciation of the dynamic interrelationships between government, citizens and society. In essence, the framework puts forward an adaptive concept of public administration; one where government transforms society and where society transforms the role of government. The framework integrates the contribution of government, people and society.

This is a significant departure from the traditional concepts of public administration. By design, governments have a low adaptive capacity and a built-in resistance to change. They were built for reliability, predictability and to reduce uncertainties. They were not designed for innovation, agility or creativity. More often than not, public servants innovate in spite of built-in rigidities and barriers. In some countries, the public service is experiencing an overwhelming amount of oversight that further erodes its adaptive capacity. This is creating a culture that is both defensive and risk averse at a time when innovation, agility and creativity are more needed than ever. The New Synthesis is exploring how to turn the situation around and what can be done to improve the adaptive capacity of government.

Two case studies illustrate the importance of exploring new ideas and experimenting with what works in practice. The Singapore Workfare case study focuses on the challenge of growing income disparities. The Citizen-centred Public Services in the United Kingdom is exploring various ways of dealing with families in distress. Both approach public policy making as an exploratory and experimental process where the policy intent and the means to achieve it are perfectible and are transformed as the learning takes shape in practice.

Building the adaptive capacity of government is a learned process that requires a shift in thinking, discipline and strong leadership. It is about discovering how to combine in new ways issues, tools, capacity and means to address complex challenges and help government to be fit for the times.

It involves exploration. This entails the scanning of ideas, learning from the experience of others, framing issues in broad societal terms to expand the scope for innovation. It requires a commitment to experimentation. This includes the testing of ideas to refine the concepts incrementally and to accelerate the collective learning about what works and what does not. It requires a willingness to learn and to introduce course corrections as needed.

Workfare Income Support Scheme: Singapore

This case study was the most comprehensive illustration presented to participants of how an adaptive approach to governance may work in practice and how it can encourage innovation. It touches upon many of the elements of the New Synthesis Framework.

The scheme framed the issue of growing income disparity and what to do about it in broad societal terms. The goal was to develop "a new social compact that... would not shelter Singaporeans from global competition, but would instead redistribute some of the benefits of economic growth to lower-income groups." As a result, the approach embraced both public policy results (addressing growing income disparity and the impact on low-income earners) and civic results (improving social cohesion).

The Singapore government has a long tradition of intelligence gathering, horizon scanning, experimentation and learning-by-doing. Not surprisingly, the process of exploring how to achieve the desired outcome of creating a new social compact began by scanning what other countries were doing to address similar challenges. By learning from what had been done in practice elsewhere, the government was able to bring greater definition to the desired outcomes as well as the adverse effects it wanted to avoid. Subsequently, a workfare program was designed to integrate the desired public results based on Singapore's unique context, circumstances and needs.

The deliberate testing of ideas contributed to refining the program design incrementally. This accelerated the collective learning about what worked and what did not. It also increased public acceptance and support for the new program. Formative results and unintended consequences are monitored carefully. While the program is still in its early stages, results indicate that significant progress has been achieved. In addition, systems are in place to adjust or course correct as circumstances warrant. These aspects of the case illustrate many of the key features of an adaptive system of governance able to encourage innovation.

It is also worth noting that the workfare program was designed to enrol the contribution of families, communities, businesses and beneficiaries. In the process, it reinforced the values of self-reliance and social resilience. Program design took the multiple facets of the issue into account and paid attention to inter-related results, including support for families in need, skills training, job opportunities, support for children of low-income families and financial support for low-wage workers. Multifaceted policy interventions such as these reduce vulnerability and improve the likelihood of success when dealing with complex issues.

Citizen-centered Public Service: United Kingdom

Total Place (recently "rebranded" Community Budgets) is a national initiative designed to improve the efficiency and effectiveness of government programs. The working hypothesis is that this can be achieved by moving from a centralized, prescriptive and target-driven approach to a location-based approach for delivering public services. At the macro level, Total Place is an experiment about reconnecting public institutions, communities and citizens in new ways. At the micro level, Total Place pilot projects reveal an interest in local experimentation. The case unveils a search process that is under way to find local mechanisms to engage citizens in addressing the issues that are most important to them in their families and communities.

In the London borough of Croydon, one pilot project experimented with a support program for families, while a project in Swindon provided insight into an experiment in which families in distress were actively involved in designing public services to support themselves and others in similar circumstances. The core of the program is a new type of relationship between public services and families to develop capabilities, networks and resilience.

The experiments described at the national and local levels in the case are in the early stages of development. They signal the possibility of a different relationship between public service providers and citizens, where services are co-designed and potentially co-produced with citizens.

Beyond its particulars, this case is a reminder that institutional reforms are never over. This is true for developing countries facing the challenge of building public institutions to govern their society. It is also true for emerging economies that must reconcile economic growth, social justice and the exercise of power in society. And it is just as true for a mature economy and an old democracy like the United Kingdom exploring different ways to delineate roles and responsibilities, exercise power and authority and align public purpose, means, actions and accountability in new ways.

CONCLUSION

All the cases provide powerful insights about the trends that are transforming public administration as a domain of practice. Taken together, the cases illustrate various aspects of the New Synthesis Framework and help deepen our understanding of what a co-evolving governance system may look like in practice.

Chapter 8

The Story of the Singapore Prison Service: From Custodians of Prisoners to Captains of Life

Lena Leong, Senior Researcher
Centre for Governance and Leadership
Singapore Civil Service College[1]

The Singapore Prison Service (SPS) transformed itself from an agency focused on protecting society through the safe custody of criminals to a leader in rehabilitation. Between 1998 and 2009, the recidivism rate dropped significantly from 44.4 percent to 26.5 percent.[2] The SPS is also one of the most cost-effective prison institutions in the world, with an average cost of incarceration of S$75 per day and an inmate-to-staff ratio of 7.6:1. Yet, security and discipline have not been compromised: there have been no escapes or major riots, and the assault rate has been kept low. Staff morale has also been high, with about 81 percent of officers indicating their satisfaction with work in the organization.[3]

This case chronicles the change journey of the SPS: how a traditional command-control agency faced with challenges of an increasing prison population, high staff turnover and poor public perception, engaged its staff, stakeholders and eventually the community to create outcomes that changed the lives of inmates and their families. It illustrates a change that started within the organization and cascaded outwards to the rest of the community.

The case also explores the following elements of the New Synthesis Framework:[4]

- The roles of government as a law enforcer and custodian, as well as a facilitator and an enabler of change;
- The possibilities that open when the focus on results is shifted beyond the agency to the societal level; and
- The possible impact when government includes other stakeholders rather than acting alone.

CHANGING FROM WITHIN

Context for Change

In 1998, the SPS was confronted by two pressing issues—an overcrowded prison that was straining existing infrastructure and resources, and a shortage of staff due to difficulties in recruitment and retention.[5] Prison staff members were overworked and morale was low. Poor public perception of the organization and its work did not help.

Even though rehabilitation had always been articulated as a component of SPS work, rehabilitation efforts were fragmented, *ad hoc* and considered to be the responsibility of specialists, like counsellors. The role of prison officers remained mainly custodial. Rehabilitation programs for offenders (limited to work, education and religious counselling) were not systematically monitored and assessed for effectiveness.

Taken together, these obstacles were hindering the SPS's ability to deliver on its mission.

New Leadership

In late 1998, the SPS had a change in top leadership (see Figure 1 for a timescale of change at the SPS). Chua Chin Kiat, who had held several key positions at the Singapore Police Force, took over as Director of Prisons. He felt that a mere increase in staff headcount would not address the SPS's problems, nor would an increase be sustainable in the long term. Chua also realized that he alone could not bring about change; he had first to convince his senior management team of the need. On behalf of the team, Chua visited a number of prisons overseas, most of which had progressive rehabilitative programs in place. The visits gave the senior team fresh perspectives on how prisons in Singapore could be managed.

Figure 1: *Milestones in the SPS Transformation Journey*

Year	Events
1998	▪ Chua Chin Kiat appointed as Director, SPS. ▪ Re-organization of prisons and setting up of Research and Planning Branch.
1999	▪ Development of new vision and revision of mission statement. ▪ Housing Unit Management System conceptualized.
2000	▪ Strategic Framework introduced (FY 2000–02). ▪ Prisons Rehabilitation Framework launched. ▪ Kaki Bukit Centre Prison School established. ▪ Prison Management System launched. ▪ Community Action for the Rehabilitation of Ex-offenders (CARE) Network established. ▪ Home detention scheme introduced. ▪ Ethics structure launched. ▪ Women deployed in male institutions. ▪ Level of Service Inventory-Revised tool introduced.
2001	▪ Singapore Quality Class awarded. ▪ A new set of departmental values promulgated. ▪ Balance scorecard tool adopted. ▪ Tele-visits introduced. ▪ Public awareness campaign "Rehab, Renew, Re-start" launched.
2002	▪ Family Friendly Firm Award won.
2003	▪ Strategic Framework introduced (FY 2003–05). ▪ Community Involvement Framework launched. ▪ ISO 9001:2000 achieved for the Intake Rehabilitation Classification. ▪ Public Service Award won.
2004	▪ Cluster A construction completed. ▪ Awarded Singapore Innovation Class Award. ▪ Operations philosophy revised. ▪ First Yellow Ribbon Project launched.
2005	▪ Awarded Singapore Service Class Award. ▪ Director of Prisons received Public Administration Medal (gold). ▪ Awarded Distinguished Public Service Award. ▪ Government amended the Criminal Registration Act to strike out ex-offenders' criminal records for minor offences provided ex-offenders remained crime-free for a specified period of time.

Figure 1: continued next page

Figure 1: *continued*

2006	▪ Prisons' Leadership Competency Model launched. ▪ Awarded Singapore Quality Award. ▪ Awarded Top Public Service Award for Organisational Excellence.
2007	▪ Named Hewitt top ten best employers. ▪ Ng Joo Hee appointed as the new Director, SPS.
2008	▪ Successful combined re-certification of three Business Excellence Niche Standards: People Developer, Innovation Class and Service Class. ▪ Yellow Ribbon Project concept exported to Fidji.
2009	▪ Inaugural Prisons-NUS Research Seminar launched. ▪ New Prisons Business Framework unveiled. ▪ Named Hewitt top ten Best Employers. ▪ Cluster B construction completed.

Re-thinking the Prison's Reason for Existence

New Vision

Chua realized that the SPS's focus had been on maintaining security and safety within the prisons: it did not have an articulated, overarching vision of its role in society. In 1999, more than 800 staff members and strategic partners from the Ministry of Home Affairs (SPS's parent ministry) and voluntary welfare organizations were invited to share their vision for the SPS. A variety of platforms (retreats, facilitated dialogues and online intranet forums) were employed. The exercise challenged the way SPS staff saw their role and their impact.

The visioning exercise was not all smooth sailing: there were pockets of resistance and scepticism at the ground level. While some prison officers wanted to do more to help inmates under their charge become contributing members of society, not everyone was receptive. It took about a year to confirm the new vision: "We aspire to be captains in the lives of offenders committed to our custody. We will be instrumental in steering them towards being responsible citizens with the help of their families and the community. We will thus build a secure and exemplary prison system." That vision was instrumental in giving shape and direction to many SPS strategies that would follow. The fundamental change was the shift beyond security and safety to the rehabilitation and reintegration of offenders into society.

Cascading from the vision, SPS also developed a set of core values to articulate what it wanted to preserve and how it would operate as it pursued its goals. These values are: honour our vision by placing it above self-interest and inspiring others to our cause; excel in our work because we care enough to want to be the best; be agile by being innovative and open to new possibilities, overcoming adversity through continuous learning; respect our fellow colleagues and the community we come into contact with; and foster teamwork by coaching, guiding and inspiring one another in our workplace. In the process of articulating its vision, SPS also re-crafted its mission.[6]

Changing the Way the Prison Thinks

New Mindset

While a compelling vision may be a powerful driving force, old ways of thinking often hinder its translation into practice. From the outset, Chua was mindful that without significantly increasing staff numbers, he had to find new ways of freeing up staff time for the real work of reforming the prison system. His habit of challenging assumptions and getting staff to critically re-examine old ways of doing made many uneasy, but it also forced them to re-think, explore new possibilities, develop new solutions and achieve breakthroughs. Consequently, many redundant processes were discarded. The SPS was one of the pioneers in the Singapore public service to outsource non-core functions, such as medical services, kitchen management and escorting lower-risk prisoners to attend court and medical appointments.

New Roles

In the past, prison officers were rotated periodically to avoid compromising security, but as a result, most officers did not know the inmates well. Chua's challenge to tell him everything they knew about the inmates under their charge stumped many, but it also caused staff members to realize they could not help offenders change if they did not understand them.

In 1999, the Housing Unit Management System helped close that gap (see Box 1). The system emphasized engaging inmates in a meaningful and purposeful manner. A dedicated team of prison officers was assigned to manage all matters relating to inmates in a particular housing unit. Officers were no longer just custodians of prisoners; they had to take on roles as disciplinarians, mentors and para-counsellors. They were empowered to make decisions as long as their decisions helped inmates change for the better.

Box 1: Implementing the Housing Unit Management System

The SPS leadership team anticipated that not all SPS officers might be ready for change. Inevitably, some would still hold to the lock-and-bolt mindset. Many were likely to find balancing the multiple and seemingly conflicting roles of disciplinarian and rehabilitation officer overwhelming. New skills were also needed before transitioning to the new roles. Hence, instead of a full-scale roll-out, volunteers were invited to test the system. Six of the 14 SPS institutions responded. In the end, the Housing Unit team leaders' commitment and hands-on approach to improving the system were pivotal to the success of the year-long pilot.

To address ground concerns of security lapses and manipulation by inmates, the SPS subsequently also instituted an ethics structure, a team-based approach and a coaching framework.

Officers soon discovered the value of the Housing Unit Management System. Besides rehabilitating inmates, it helped officers gather intelligence, therefore augmenting the level of security, discipline and control in the prisons. They experienced the power of teamwork: working and learning together indeed enhanced the quality of decisions and outcomes.

Re-designing Supporting Infrastructure

New Structure

In 1998, a restructuring exercise was conducted. Chua believed that an organization's long-term success hinges on its preparedness for the future, which in turn depends on its current ability to anticipate and learn. A Research and Planning Branch was set up to conduct research, network with external research institutes and co-ordinate the planning and implementation of key organization-wide initiatives. One of the outcomes was the adoption of the LSI-R (Level of Service Inventory—Revised) tool in 2000. The SPS sent a team to Canada to learn from that country's experience with the tool. The tool enabled the SPS to allocate resources by assessing, categorizing and matching inmates to different rehabilitation programs based on their risk of re-offending and their rehabilitation needs. New learning resulting from the Branch's activities challenged SPS staff's established ways of thinking and doing. Establishing the Branch was instrumental in helping staff embrace change and create a culture of learning and innovation within the SPS.

A Program Branch was also subsequently set up to give greater focus to rehabilitation. Inmates were encouraged to help with simple duties, including peer-support counselling and tutoring. Some participated as members of work improvement teams, an initiative under the PS21 (Public Service for the 21st Century) movement that empowers officers on the ground to seek improvements. These initiatives relieved the officers' workload, improved the inmate-staff relationship and also became an essential part of the rehabilitation process.

New Behaviour

Internal systems and structures were put in place to encourage behaviour to support the operational strategies. For example, twice-a-week, informal "agendaless" breakfast meetings among senior management, heads of staff units and superintendents were started to encourage dialogue, exchange ideas, and strengthen the quality of relationships and trust within the leadership team. The leaders took turns to meet with recruits at induction programs, walk the floors and connect with ground staff to seek out diverse and fresh perspectives.

At the staff level, cozy coffee corners were created to encourage informal interaction and exchange of ideas. A learning centre with a resource library, broadband Internet access and training/meeting rooms was set up to provide an environment conducive for sharing and brainstorming. Online platforms were developed to facilitate sharing among officers across departments. Notes of senior management meetings were posted on the intranet so that all officers could follow the thinking behind decisions. To encourage ideas from the ground, a system was developed to capture and track all suggestions generated. With these new supporting systems and structures in place, prison officers picked up new behaviour, new ways of learning and new capabilities over time.

These internal changes opened the way for more effective rehabilitative programs, such as the establishment of Kaki Bukit Centre Home Detention Scheme Prison School. Other initiatives included the Home Detention Scheme, deployment of female officers in male institutions, tele-visits (see Box 2) and virtual court sessions for remand inmates—all of which fundamentally changed the way the SPS operated. These initiatives freed SPS resources for other areas of need and gave SPS staff the confidence to explore new solutions beyond the prison walls.

Box 2: New Learning, New Solutions

The SPS observed that chances of rehabilitation were higher if inmates had the support of their families, yet divorces were common in the prisons. Family Resource Centres were set up to help inmates' families cope with incarceration. Subsequently, the SPS also introduced family visits during Father's Days and Mother's Days, other family celebrations within the prisons and tele-visits to enhance family bonding.

HARNESSING THE COLLECTIVE EFFORTS OF SOCIETY

The Next Phase of Change

The SPS realized that even if rehabilitation efforts within the prisons were successful, chances of recidivism would still be high if after-care support for ex-offenders were weak. The transition from the controlled incarcerated environment into a society not quite ready to receive them could generate a culture shock. The inability to cope with the stigma and stress could turn ex-offenders back to crime. The realization that internal resources would not be enough to meet inmates' after-care needs forced the SPS to venture beyond the confines of the prisons to engage the wider community—a new move for the SPS.[7] Its vision consisted of a system of well established rehabilitation and reintegration programs with a strong emphasis on family and societal support.

In 2000, the SPS mapped out its primary functions (secure custody of offenders; rehabilitation, prevention and after-care) and its most important stakeholders (staff, families of offenders, the community and the Board of Visiting Justices).[8] Through a series of dialogues at the ground level, 96 strategies organized along four focal areas were developed: enhanced operational capabilities, staff development structure, integrated in-system care for inmates, and co-ordinated after-care for ex-offenders. Of these strategies, 15 projects were prioritized over three years. The levers for change in each area were identified as technology, knowledge management and community resources (see Figure 2).

Figure 2: *Prison Service Reform, Focal Areas*

Focal Areas		Enablers
2000-02	**2003-05**	
1. Enhanced operational capabilities	1. Enhancing inmate management capability	Technology, Knowledge management, Community resources, and Mass media (added in 2003)
2. Staff development structure	2. Developing staff to make a difference	
3. Integrated In-system care for inmates	3. Maximizing inmates' reintegration potential	
4. Co-ordinated after-care for ex-offenders	4. Preventing offending and re-offending	

In 2003, these focal areas were further refined. This time, input was sought not only from prison officers but also from inmates and community partners. It became clear from the strategic conversations that in-system care and after-care should not be implemented separately. These two elements were merged into Maximizing Inmates' Reintegration Potential, acknowledging that reintegration really begins on the first day of incarceration. A key thrust under this focal area was to "improve public perception of ex-offenders," where mass media were identified as key enablers in shaping the population's mindset. A new focal area, Preventing Offending and Re-offending, with the goal of significantly reducing the incarceration rate, also surfaced. To achieve that goal, the SPS realized that it needed to work more closely with family members and community partners like the Singapore Corporation of Rehabilitative Enterprises (SCORE),[9] the Singapore After-Care Association, and the Singapore Anti-Narcotics Association.

Branding: Captains of Lives

New Partners (the Media)

A public perception survey in 2000 revealed that the public had little knowledge of the SPS's work. Poor public image led to difficulties in recruitment and threatened growth. The SPS Public Affairs Branch was charged with revamping the organization's image. A series of advertisements aimed at changing public perception was launched in 2001. The media campaign, Captains of Lives, Rehab, Renew, Restart, followed in 2002, in which the SPS opened its doors to the public and reporters were given prison tours. Success stories of reformed prisoners reinforced the key messages behind SPS rehabilitation efforts that were then carried over into print media, local radio and television stations, as well as billboards. SPS television advertisements became the talking point in public places and radically changed the public's understanding of prison officers' work. In 2002, the SPS won the Creative Circle Awards (bronze) in the Television and Cinema category and the "TV Campaign of the Year" awarded by the Institute of Advertising Singapore. The success of the campaigns led the SPS to adopt an even more ambitious media strategy in 2003, which aimed at educating and garnering the support of the community for rehabilitation work and generating acceptance of ex-offenders into the community.

With its public image boosted, the SPS staff's sense of pride in their work grew. The positive experience helped reinforce the desired changes in mindset and strengthen commitment to the vision. The SPS' staff shortage problem also gradually eased as more qualified officers and volunteers were recruited to serve with the organization. Additional resources could therefore be released to look at other areas of need, such as efforts to reintegrate ex-offenders into the community.

Networking within Government and Beyond

To strengthen after-care support for ex-offenders, the SPS adopted four sub-strategies: development of structured and co-ordinated after-care programs; development of a networked governance structure to oversee the co-ordination of after-care services; investment in family education to help family members cope with problems arising from incarceration and prepare them to receive ex-offenders upon release; and the building of community acceptance and non-rejection.

New Partners (the CARE Network)

The Community Action for the Rehabilitation of Ex-offenders (CARE) Network was one of the 15 projects identified for implementation in 2000-02. In 2000, the SPS brought together eight major community and government organizations responsible for rehabilitating ex-offenders to form the CARE Network to promote seamless in-system care and after-care support for ex-offenders. Co-chaired by the SPS and SCORE, its other six members comprised representatives from the Ministry of Home Affairs; the Ministry of Community Development, Youth and Sports; the Industrial and Services Co-operative Society Ltd; the National Council of Social Service; the Singapore After-Care Association; and the Singapore Anti-Narcotics Association. A government-initiated informal network, the CARE Network held annual retreats and met quarterly to set direction and co-ordinate the strategies and efforts of all eight agencies as well as others in the after-care sector. Their focus: to maximize resources and results through alignment and collaboration.

One of the CARE Network's first initiatives was the Case Management Framework Program established in 2000. Under the framework, case managers from the Singapore After-Care Association and the Singapore Anti-Narcotics Association met inmates one to two months before their release to go over their after-care needs with them and then follow up to ensure that they received the support up to six months after release. This work was co-funded by the SPS, SCORE, the National Council of Social Service and the respective after-care agencies. Another project, Singapore's first community movie, "Twilight Kitchen" in 2003, featured an ex-offender seeking a second chance in life. A private movie company that supported the cause funded the publicity efforts for the movie.

One of the CARE Network's most successful initiatives was the annual "Yellow Ribbon Project" (YRP), a series of public education efforts started in 2004 aimed at creating awareness of giving second chances to ex-offenders, generating acceptance of ex-offenders and their families into the community and inspiring community action to support rehabilitation and reintegration of ex-offenders (see Box 3).[10] Inspiration for the name originated from the 1970s pop song, "Tie a Yellow Ribbon Round the Old Oak Tree," that told the story of an offender's request to his wife to forgive and accept him. A yellow ribbon was picked as the symbol for its simplicity and because it embodied the message of acceptance and forgiveness and resonated with the community.

Box 3: The Message Behind the Yellow Ribbon

- Every offender encounters two prisons: physical prison and psychological/ social prison.
- Who holds the key to the physical prison? Offenders' families, friends, neighbours, employers, colleagues the community?
- Help unlock the second prison!

The YRP organizational structure consisted of a steering committee led by SPS and SCORE senior officers, a secretariat anchored by a SCORE team, and chairpersons of the various sub-committees. Attempts have been made over the years to encourage volunteers, community partners and other members of the CARE Network to take up more leadership roles.

The YRP's activities were fully government-funded in the initial years, with growing corporate support more recently. Once the CARE Network had endorsed the theme and overall concept plan for the YRP, events were managed autonomously by the chairpersons of the various sub-committees. Only issues that affected other sub-committees or the entire campaign would be raised at the steering committee. Support functions that required co-ordination across sub-committees (such as finance, publicity, sponsorships, invitation of guests of honour) would be centrally managed by the steering committee. The secretariat periodically monitored progress to ensure consistency of themes and objectives.

A Yellow Ribbon Fund was separately set up with its own management committee to provide financial support specifically for rehabilitative and after-care services, other programs aimed at raising public awareness of the needs of ex-offenders and inspiring community involvement, and support services for family members of inmates (see Figure 3). To ensure good governance, two sub-committees were formed to advise the Yellow Ribbon Fund Committee on the disbursement and fund-raising activities.

Figure 3: *The Many Helping Hands Approach to Rehabilitation and Reintegration of Inmates and Ex-offenders*

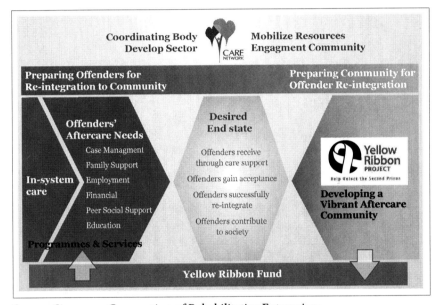

Source: Singapore Corporation of Rehabilitative Enterprises

For the Community, by the Community

Every year, September is set aside for intensive YRP activities. The initial focus was on organizations more open to the message of giving second chances to ex-offenders, such as religious groups and schools. Gradually, the work extended to the rest of the community. Activities in the first two years (2004-05) aimed at creating awareness. The next two years (2006-07) focused on deepening the community's understanding of the rehabilitation journey and profiling the contribution of reformed ex-offenders. Serving inmates and ex-offenders were also mobilized to contribute to society through community service. In 2008-09, the themes shifted from raising awareness to generating acceptance and inspiring action.

New Partners (the Community)

At the inaugural launch of the YRP in 2004, the SPS invited targeted groups such as volunteer groups, employers, policy makers and students to tour various prison institutions to deepen their understanding of life in prisons and their role in the rehabilitation journey (see Box 4). Talks held in schools and open house events heightened awareness of the needs of ex-offenders and their families and sparked new ideas of action that groups could take to support the reintegration process.

Box 4: Community Involvement Framework

In 2003, the SPS developed a Community Involvement Framework. A stakeholder analysis was conducted and community resources were segmented and mapped to needs. Emphasis was placed on volunteer management, including recruitment, screening, placement, orientation, training, recognition and exit. Groups with high leverage were identified. The framework required shifting the mindset from seeing volunteers as "outsiders" to seeing them as "partners" and critical resources to be tapped.

The Community Involvement Section was set up to bring more focus to the work. Regular dialogues with volunteers were instituted to better understand challenges on the ground, seek feedback to improve processes and identify new avenues for community contribution. Critical issues were escalated for discussion at the annual SPS and SCORE joint work plan seminars attended by all staff and community partners. These interactions between the SPS, SCORE and their partners greatly enhanced understanding between the groups and enabled them jointly to find new solutions to old problems and spot new issues.

The Singapore National Employers Federation and National Trades Unions Congress Income supported the skills competition and talent showcase launched in 2004. About 200 employers were invited to visit prison training facilities and witness the inmates' IT, multimedia and cooking skills, and encouraged to hire them. Subsequently, job fairs, employers' networking sessions and forums to discuss the reintegration of ex-offenders into the workplace were also organized. Corporate organizations were appointed as rehabilitation ambassadors and encouraged to contribute to YRP publicity efforts. Awards were given annually to recognize exemplary employers and corporate donors.

The "Wear-A-Yellow-Ribbon" campaign was a key event in the YRP's annual calendar to engage the community at large. Inmates' hand-made yellow ribbons were distributed on the streets by ex-offenders and inmates from halfway houses (for an optional donation), encouraging members of the public to support ex-offenders and their families. In subsequent years, fairs and road shows were held at major city and heartland malls throughout the country to reach out to different segments of the population. To attract all ages and interests, a range of activities was organized, including performances by artists and ex-offenders, testimonies by ex-offenders and interactive games (see Box 5). Various volunteer groups hosted booths aimed at educating the community on the rehabilitation process and selling products and crafts made by inmates. Art exhibitions showcasing the talent of inmates were also held at public places.

Box 5: Poetry Competition

The National Library Board (NLB) wanted to bring reading programs into the prisons. The YRP team seized the opportunity to organize a poetry competition for inmates in 2007. The NLB appointed the judges and sponsored the event. The collection of poems from the competition was later compiled and published, and is now available in all national libraries in Singapore.

Songwriting competitions, open to inmates, ex-offenders and after-care agencies, were organized with local songwriters and musicians invited as judges. Winning entries were showcased at annual YRP charity concerts, another key event where local and overseas artists perform alongside inmates and ex-offenders to raise funds for the Yellow Ribbon Fund. The President and the First Lady graced the inaugural concert. Mass walks led by ministers, community leaders and celebrities were also organized. In 2009, Deputy Prime Minister, Teo Chee Hean, led the first public run that cut through the prisons compound.

The inaugural YRP conference was held in 2005 to align and inspire community action through the sharing of case studies, best practices and research. Participants included foreign delegates, ex-offenders and community partners, such as employers, volunteer groups and grassroots organizations. With their plenary sessions and concurrent workshops led by local and foreign practitioners and academics, the YRP conferences became important events for groups involved in rehabilitation and reintegration work to come together to share experiences, tap into collective wisdom and develop more integrated approaches. In 2006, ex-offenders from the Industrial and Services Co-Operative Society Ltd youth wing played a key role in organizing the conference.

The YRP team was surprised how the project grew over the years. What started as branding and public education efforts had gained momentum and, with support of the media, corporate organizations and individuals from all levels of society, seemed to have taken on a life of its own. Most recent was the community service project with the Singapore Lions Club. The club, which also works with the elderly, approached the YRP team to host a joint lunch for the elderly in 2009. On that day, inmates cooked the meal while ex-offenders served it. Funding came from the Singapore Lions Club and the National Arts Council, which sponsored the entertainment program. The event was covered by the media and helped further reinforce the YRP's message to the rest of the community.

New Partners (Inmates/Ex-offenders)

Besides changing the community's perception of ex-offenders, it was equally important to educate inmates and ex-offenders about the need to seize the second chances given to them (see boxes 6 and 7). In 2003, the inmates (as part of their work routine with SCORE) contributed to the nation's efforts to fight SARS by washing hospitals' laundry. In 2009, inmates volunteered to fill the fun packs for the National Day parade. The same year, Hanniel Chong, a reformed drug addict, teamed with a prison officer and SCORE officer to take part in an Ironman race to raise S$10,000 for the Yellow Ribbon Fund.

Box 6: Tattoo Removal

The owner of GiGATT International Marketing Private Ltd acquired the distribution rights for a type of laser machine that could also be used to remove tattoos. The organization called the YRP hotline to see if the YRP could use these machines. Tattoo removal then became a means for inmates to pledge their commitment to change. As of 2010, 174 inmates had benefited from the pilot.

Box 7: Nicodemus

Nicodemus was a finalist in the YRP's songwriting competition in 2004. On release from prison, he formed a band to take part in a national music competition, "Super-band" (similar to "American Idol"), and won. Nicodemus has since continued to volunteer at YRP events.

Although the events and stories may change, the YRP's message of acceptance and renewal remains the same each year. The YRP receives tremendous recognition and support from the media, and an increasing number of individuals, communities and corporate organizations come forward to volunteer, donate and employ ex-offenders. A nationwide public perception survey in 2007 revealed that 94 percent of respondents expressed awareness of the YRP and 70 percent were willing to accept ex-offenders as either a friend or colleague. Between 2004 and 2008, about 300,000 Singaporeans had participated in YRP events, 690 new employers were added to SCORE's database, 720 new volunteers were recruited, more than 400 inmates and ex-offenders were mobilized and S$3.9 million was raised for the Yellow Ribbon Fund's work. In support of the YRP, the government amended the *Registration of Criminals Act* in late 2005 to strike out ex-offenders' criminal records for minor offences provided they remained crime-free for a specified period.

ORGANIZATIONAL, PUBLIC AND SOCIETAL OUTCOMES

Over the years, the SPS transformed itself from a custodian of prisoners to a leading rehabilitation agency without losing its key focus on security.[11] Today, more than 1,800 employers have come forward to offer employment to ex-offenders and about 1,400 volunteers serve alongside prison staff in counselling and various personal development activities for inmates. The recidivism rate has also steadily declined from 44.4 percent for the cohort released in 1998 to 26.5 percent for the cohort released in 2007. The SPS is one of the most cost-effective prison institutions in the world—without compromising security or discipline.

In 2006, SPS won the top Public Service Award for Organisational Excellence and the Singapore Quality Award.[12] In 2007 and 2009, it was voted one of the top ten best employers in Singapore by the global human resource consultancy, Hewitt Resources, and now has little difficulty recruiting the talent it needs.

Key Lessons

The New Synthesis Framework

The case illustrates a government agency stepping beyond its traditional role of guardian to that of facilitator and enabler of change, first by clarifying a shared vision and purpose, then by creating channels and empowering and equipping its staff, other members of society and even its beneficiaries to contribute. The case illustrates the possibilities that open up when a government agency begins to frame desired outcomes beyond the organizational level to the societal level and also to help other members of society do likewise. Government was able to leverage its unique position and expertise to harness the collective efforts of society towards a common purpose. Finally, the case illustrates the impact that can result when a government agency moves beyond acting alone to involving other stakeholders and members of society, tapping into their aspirations to co-create the change agenda, building collective wisdom and designing interventions so that the whole becomes more than the sum of its parts.

As SPS work attracted new believers, first internally and then externally, more resources were made available to deepen its mission. Positive results attracted more believers and resources—a reinforcing loop. The quality of relationships within the organization and with partners enabled collective thinking and improved planning and actions, which led to higher quality outcomes that improved relationships and deepened trust—further improving outcomes; another reinforcing loop. The process began with "Think big, start small": a shared desire to see the lives of those whom they serve change. The circle of influence started with individuals, then the organization and cascaded to the rest of the community.

Compelling Mission and Vision

Although the change was triggered by the need to address a problem, it was driven by a compelling vision and sense of mission. These were pivotal in shaping strategies and aligning organizational plans, priorities, systems, processes, resources and people. Ownership of the vision and mission at all levels of the organization also energized its officers to contribute more creatively to its desired outcomes, making transitions more natural and intuitive and enabling the vision to grow beyond the SPS to the inmates, their families, after-care agencies and finally the community at large. Change was facilitated by building shared goals and perspectives.

Strong Leadership

Chua Chin Kiat galvanized the organization and his staff through an inclusive approach. He did so by listening and learning from the ground level, creating safe environments for open and deep conversations. He developed a strong leadership team and built trust by empowering others, sharing ownership, and taking risks. Together, management helped the officers see new meaning in their work and a new future with stakeholders and inmates. Their influence rippled beyond the prisons' four walls to the after-care agencies. Their essence of leadership was one of stewardship of the organizational goals they served and the people they led.[13]

The Power of Mental Models[14]

New ways of perceiving their work, role and relationships with inmates and stakeholders helped prison officers see new possibilities and solutions, form new structures, networks and relationships, build new capabilities and create outcomes that they had never before imagined. Applying the same principle, prison officers realized that when inmates acquire new ways of perceiving the world and thinking and are equipped with new skills, they too can learn to make different choices and contribute to society. Likewise, the community began to respond differently when it understood more of prisons and rehabilitation work, which changed its perception of inmates and ex-offenders. Results were sustained because of changes in thinking and therefore choices, actions and outcomes.

Chapter 9

Bolsa Família Program: Funding Families for Development

Frederico Guanais[1], Head
International Cooperations Office
Escola Nacional de Administração Pública (ENAP)

B razil faces enormous challenges: it is the fifth largest country in the world and home to deep income inequality.[2] It is also extraordinarily complex to govern: co-ordination is needed among 26 states, 5,564 municipal governments and one federal district—each of vastly differing capacity but subject to the same rules governing the implementation of public policy. Municipalities, for instance, have populations that range from 800 people to 11 million people and a total yearly GDP that ranges from US$1,000 to US$77 million.[3]

Yet despite these challenges of size, poverty, and complexity, recent Brazilian governments have pursued simultaneous agendas of social inclusion, reduction of inequality, strengthening of democracy, macroeconomic stability and acceleration of sustainable growth.

This case study presents one of these initiatives: *Bolsa Família*, a program of conditional cash transfer to poor families. It is an enormous undertaking that has made important strides in addressing poverty and complexity in Brazil's reality.

SOCIAL POLICY IN BRAZIL: A BRIEF HISTORICAL CONTEXT

The colonial past left an immense social debt in Brazil. During the formative years of the nation, millions of people were forced from their homelands in Africa to work as slaves in Brazil. Indigenous populations were decimated to a mere fraction of their original numbers. Furthermore, as the country declared independence in 1822, abolished slavery in 1888 and became a republic in 1889, no inclusion mechanisms were put in place for either indigenous peoples or descendants of slaves, perpetuating a cycle of poverty that still has lasting negative effects.

As a republic, Brazil has a history of political patronage and clientelism that characterized its social policies during the majority of the 20th century. In the 1930s and

1940s, the first social rights were introduced in the form of pensions, maximum daily work hours and paid vacation time. However, these rights were restricted to the few urban labour groups, such as the railroad, port and telegraph workers, that could mobilize and affect economic activities in a decisive manner. It was not until the 1970s that pension rights were extended to workers in the rural sector, partly to alleviate potential social unrest in the countryside.

From the 1960s until the turn of the millennium, the main approach to poverty alleviation was based on a belief that growth is good for the poor. A *coup d'état* gave rise to a military dictatorship in 1964 and, for the following ten years, the economy expanded rapidly, with annual growth rates reaching peaks of 14 percent. But as the country grew, income concentration worsened. Supposedly an "economic miracle," very few actually benefited from the changes. Government officials insisted that a cake must rise before it can be shared.

The second half of the 1980s was marked by the end of the authoritarian period. Drafting a new Constitution was an important cornerstone of the process of democratization. The 1988 Constitution at last introduced legal guarantees to a broad set of social rights, including rights to healthcare, education, social protection, pensions and housing, among others. However, despite the legal mandate, policy implementation has shown mixed progress.

In the 1990s—the first decade under the new constitution—public policy emphasized structural adjustment reforms focused on macro-economic stabilization, fiscal austerity measures and privatization of services. From 1993 to 1995, previously rampant inflation finally came under control, which made a significant dent in poverty rates.[4] However, for the eight years that followed, average real incomes stagnated and poverty and inequality rates remained high. While important social programs were introduced during this period, they still had limited reach.

By 2001, over 58 million Brazilians lived in poverty, earning approximately less than US$2 a day per capita.[5] Of those, 25 million lived in extreme poverty, subsisting on less than US$1 a day per capita.[6] These figures provide the overall initial scenario in which the Bolsa Família program was designed and implemented.

FORMATIVE YEARS: FROM LOCAL LEVEL INITIATIVES TO A NATIONAL POLICY

The success stories associated with Bolsa Família in the national and international public policy communities frequently overlook the importance of the learning and experimenting process that took place with earlier basic income policies in Brazil.

The first Brazilian initiatives of conditional direct cash transfers to poor families took place at the local level. In 1995, the local governments of the cities of Campinas and Brasília pioneered initiatives that made cash payments directly to the families as an incentive to make sure that their children attended school regularly. In both cities, the programs were called *Bolsa Escola* (School Fund). From these early experiences, variations started to appear in various city, state and federal administrations. By 1998, at least 24 sub-national income transfer initiatives were in progress with varying scopes and ranges.

At the federal level, conditional cash transfer programs took place in a highly frag-mented fashion during the Cardoso administration (1995-2002) and in the first year of the Lula administration (2003). In 1996, the federal government started the *Programa de Erradicação do Trabalho Infantil* (Child Labour Erradication Program), which made payments to poor families whose children were at risk of engaging in labour activities, with the purpose of keeping them in school instead of at work. In 2001, the federal Ministry of Education launched a program called also Bolsa Escola, giving cash to poor families whose children attended school regularly. Also in 2001, the Federal Ministry of Health launched a program named *Bolsa Alimentação* (Food Fund), which provided cash to poor families who were at risk of undernourishment. In 2002, the federal government launched yet one more cash transfer program for poor families under the name *Auxílio Gás* (Cooking Gas Aid) that supplemented the incomes of those registered for other social programs with a small stipend to compensate for rising prices in cooking gas.

At the end of the Cardoso administration (December 2002), at least four different government agencies were transferring cash to poor families to alleviate poverty. Each agency was using its own registry, payment mechanism, administrative pro-cedure and, perhaps more interestingly, the same policy to justify the pursuit of different organizational missions—education, health, child labour and energy.

Around this time, President Lula was elected on a platform that focused heavily on the reduction of poverty and inequality: it was the first time that the Workers' Party had managed to win presidential elections. In his inaugural speech, Lula an-nounced the *Fome Zero* (Zero Hunger) policy, stating that the human right to ad-equate food and the fight against poverty were the key priorities of his presidency.

To implement the Zero Hunger policy, President Lula created a government agency that was named the Extraordinary Ministry for Food Security and Fight against Hun-ger, known in Portuguese by the suggestive acronym *MESA*, which means "table." José Graziano, a long-time activist in the fight against hunger and a close ally of the presi-dent, was appointed as the first minister to head the agency responsible for implement-ing the policy. Its first relevant initiative in early 2003 was the creation of yet one more form of cash transfer to poor families, called *Cartão Alimentação* (Food Card).

The Food Card was not conditional on behaviour (for example, going to school), but families had to spend the funds on food. The control mechanisms were local committees of organized citizens, called *Comitês Gestores* (managerial committees) that were to oversee family expenditures. Behind this design was the idea that managerial committees and the ensuing discussions would empower citizens, strengthening critical thought and self-awareness.

Administrative and political problems arose very soon, however. At the time, Brazil had no system comparable to the United States of America's Food Stamps program, which electronically restricts the disbursement of funds to pre-authorized items. One proposal was that poor families prove their spending by publicly displaying their grocery store receipts. A huge controversy followed. An interview given by Minister Graziano to the newspaper *Folha de São Paulo* vividly illustrates the public debate:

> Folha de São Paulo: One of the criticisms of the requirement to present receipts is that it would not only create a market of counterfeit sales receipts, but it would also generate excessive red tape.
>
> Graziano: I repeat that we have no fiscal objective. At the discretion of the local committees, the proof of [food] purchases could be made with a formal sales receipt, handwritten notes from the owner of the grocery store or even the testimony of the salesperson.
>
> Folha de São Paulo: Did the government have access to the survey that indicates that families in basic income programs already spend 70 percent of their money on food purchases?
>
> Graziano: There are several studies showing that families spend 70 percent or even 80 percent of their funds on food. These data suggest that the discussion has been focused on details only. In our view, it doesn't matter how the expenditure was made. The important issue is how people organize through participation in the Food Card program committees. The difference between the Food Card and the School Fund is not the link with the type of expenditure. The difference resides in the fact that one program promotes schooling while the other one creates the embryo of local organization: the citizen oversight committees. And, with the Food Card, which associates income with food purchases, beneficiaries will have more money to build their own citizenship.[7]

In late 2003, the federal government already had at least five cash transfer programs, including the policies initiated by the previous administration and the new Food Card program. Once more, such programs had differences in requirements, amount of funds transferred, administrative structures, governance structures and oversight mechanisms. But all of them had one key overlapping characteristic: they were poverty alleviation programs focused largely on the same target population: people living below the poverty line.

The programs were managed by five different ministries, each trying to use similar tools (cash transfers) to achieve different public policy results in the fields of social work, health, education, food security, energy and child labour. As the controversy over different programs, agencies and requirements grew into a public debate (and with no real evidence linking them to poverty reduction), President Lula launched a task force to unify all the cash transfer programs and their databases into one single program. From the citizens' perspective, the organizational distinctions did not make sense: people are not divided into ministries.

According to one of President's Lula top aides at the time and currently the federal Minister of Planning, Miriam Belchior, the role of presidential leadership was crucial in the decision to unify the programs and in its success:

> The second point is the issue of leadership. An issue that does not value a matrix framework will not succeed in making the administration achieve goals of such magnitude. Then, what role did the President play? The President of the Republic arrived at the [Interministerial] Social Policy Commission and said: the income transfer programs must be unified. "Wait, but…" No, there is no "wait, but." The programs must be unified, but they must be unified in a way that takes into account the views of all of the ministries that are involved with the issue. There must be an open dialogue. And a process in which everyone may express their views and contribute to the overall construction.[8]

The result of that presidential determination was the creation of Bolsa Família in October 2003, merging the previously existing Bolsa Escola, Bolsa Alimentação, Cartão Alimentação and Auxílio Gás.[9] In the new program, families had no restrictions on how to use funds, but payments were preferably to be made to the women in the household, and conditions were linked to the use of health and education services. In response to problems of compliance, the design of the program was made *more* flexible, rather than stricter. Instead of assigning the infant Bolsa Família to one of the ministries responsible for the parent programs, the President decided to create an executive secretariat located within his own office to manage it.

However, the underlying differences of opinion in the overall approach to poverty alleviation and to the implementation of Fome Zero—the strategy that later became an international trademark of President Lula's administration—did not end with the integration of programs. An important debate over the role of civil society in the oversight of the program persisted even after the merger.

Some presidential advisors insisted that the management of the cash transfers (including the selection of beneficiaries, audit and control) be conducted mainly by citizens organized in the managerial committees. They argued that such a design would help alleviate poverty through cash transfers and also increase social mobilization and citizen empowerment. Yet, a second group of presidential advisors defended the idea that the management of Bolsa Família should strengthen the federal pact rather than civil society. These advisors proposed that states and municipalities should be responsible for managing the program and verifying legal compliance.

This dispute was made clear in a letter sent in December 2003 from Carlos Alberto Libânio Christo (known as Friar Betto, one of the top presidential advisors) to José Dirceu, who was then Chief of Staff of the President's office:

> Bolsa Família: in my view, the duplicity over Bolsa Família and Zero Hunger has not been properly resolved. It seems as if they are different programs, and that the one which was announced later [Bolsa Família] replaces the other one [Zero Hunger]. I hope that the [impending] ministerial reform settles this issue.
>
> It is important to maintain the managerial committees in each municipality composed of a majority of the civil society. It is important to stress that these committees should not lose their powers related to the selection of registered beneficiaries. My proposal is that the current criterion should be kept (…): two thirds of the committee members should be representatives from organized civil society and one third should come from government.
> (…)
>
> I believe in the role that states and municipalities have in the development of the program, but it is essential to maintain balance, especially in all of the municipalities in Brazil, and the managerial committee favours such balance.[10]

In fact, the managerial reform anticipated by Friar Betto took place soon afterwards. In January 2004, a new ministry was created, integrating functions of social assistance, food and food security, and income transfers, absorbing Bolsa Família's responsibilities. This new agency was named Ministry of Social Development and Fight against Hunger. Patrus Ananias, federal congressman and former mayor of Belo Horizonte, was invited by President Lula to be the minister.

Also in January 2004, the provisional measure that created Bolsa Família was converted into Federal Law number 10836. The law established that the existing cash transfer programs would be unified. The cash benefit would be paid directly to the families on an ATM card issued by Caixa Econômica Federal, a public bank owned by the federal government. The beneficiary would preferably be female and, to receive the benefits, the families should be below the poverty line and comply with a set of conditions. The law also stated that municipal governments would be responsible for designing the mechanisms for social control and participation in the program. Therefore, it meant the end of the proposed managerial committees with a majority of representatives from civil society. Instead, the mayors were the main authority responsible for managing the program at the local level.

FROM EARLY STAGES TO PERMANENT NATIONAL POLICY

When Bolsa Família was created in the last quarter of 2003, its parent programs served 3.6 million families through cash transfers. During 2004, Bolsa Família was submitted to intensive scrutiny from the press. It was far from being seen as a unanimous success.

In October 2004, during Bolsa Família's first anniversary, televised media prepared a series of investigative reports showing so-called inclusion and exclusion errors: some relatively wealthy families who should not be receiving the transfers had benefited, while some extremely poor families were still excluded. The contrasting images of rich and poor made for strong public opinion against Bolsa Família, and the report was mentioned by President Lula in a public speech:

> I thought that the news report that came out on TV recently was important to us. Some people thought that the report was a criticism. I think that we have to learn to accept things as they are. It is true that all of us politicians would like that, every day, the headlines in the news were favourable, but we are not like that even in our private lives. So why should we ask others to do so? What we have is just the consciousness and the certainty that we are doing our best and that we are sensitive enough to correct the mistakes as we find them, understand that they are mistakes, and correct our path.

> Every now and then people say, "But the registry of beneficiaries of Bolsa Família does this, [and] does not do that." Well, if even a large chain of supermarkets such as Pão de Açúcar accepts the possibility of one percent of losses to shoplifting, imagine what can happen to a program that works with five million ATM cards. There could be some fraud. There could be.[11]

In his speech, the President also referred to potential problems in the registry of beneficiaries. From the beginning, the program relied on a registry called *Cadastro Único* (Single Registry), a massive database that contains data on all families in the country that are at risk of poverty (defined as being below an income threshold). This registry is maintained by the federal Ministry of Social Development and Fight against Hunger, but municipal governments are responsible for collecting data on poor families and entering data into the registry. This practice was one of the sensitive points that led to the creation of Bolsa Família: some in government wished to assign to civil society organizations the responsibility of selecting the beneficiaries and entering them into the registry, while the other officials wanted municipal governments to perform the task. The latter idea prevailed.

After being entered into the registry, families are selected to receive the benefit by the federal government. The funds are then directly paid to the families with the use of an ATM card issued by a federal bank, and the money may then be with-drawn from banks, post offices, lottery shops and other forms of banking services. Families may use the benefits freely and are not required to report their expenses. In approximately 95 percent of cases, the ATM cards are registered under a female in the household. The average value of the monthly benefit is US$65, but it may reach US$137, depending on the characteristics of the family.

To receive the benefits, families must comply with conditions that are designed to build human capital. The education conditions require minimum school atten-dance rates of 85 percent for children aged six to 15 years and 75 percent for teen-agers aged 16 or 17 years. The health conditions require that children aged zero to six years be immunized and receive growth monitoring, and also that pregnant women attend sessions of pre- and post-natal care. Finally, social assistance condi-tions require that children at risk of being used as child labour participate in after-school activities. All these services are universally available and free of charge.

Despite the complex program design in the early implementation stages, the press focused much of its attention on two issues: the errors of inclusion and exclusion, and the role of school quality and attendance. Kathy Lindert, a Social Protection Specialist working at the World Bank, undertook an extensive analysis of media coverage of the program.

> From the point of view of the PBF's [Programa Bolsa Família] objectives and expected roles, however, it can be said that the press coverage some-times is out of focus, as in the case of reporting on inclusion vs. exclusion errors or on its role in promoting school attendance (via conditions) vs. school quality (out of the realm of the PBF). Similarly, from a technical point of view, there are important differences between administrative errors and intentional fraud (both of which are present to some degree in all programs), but these concepts are sometimes blurred in reporting on the program. The analysis should be useful to help the press itself identify new hooks for its reporting and to better understand the program's broad nature and role, as well as key implementation aspects.[12]

Having survived a difficult first year of intense media scrutiny, the biggest test came with the presidential election of 2006—the first national election since the creation of Bolsa Família. At the time of the election (October 2006), the program had already reached its target coverage of 11.1 million families estimated living under the poverty line.

Candidates running in the election publicly mentioned their support for the program. For President Lula, it meant one big success story in the reduction of poverty and inequality—one that translated into electoral support in his campaign for re-election. For his main opponent, Geraldo Alckmin, the votes of 11.1 million families could not be ignored, and he could not dispute the "paternity" of the program since it had originated from initiatives of previous administrations at federal and sub-national levels. Rather than attacking the program, opposition parties declared that they would expand and improve it. Electoral results made clear that a large fraction of civil society saw the program as an asset they wanted to keep.

As of March 2011, Bolsa Família has reached 12.85 million families in every Brazilian municipality and the federal district, with an annual budget of approximately US$5.7 billion. The program costs nearly 0.4 percent of Brazilian Gross Domestic Product each year. Another round of presidential elections was held in October and November 2010 and, once more, all major candidates publicly declared their support for the program. Current president, Dilma Rousseff, publicly renewed her commitment to the program, approving an average increase of 19.8 percent in the amount of the benefit in March 2011.

DOCUMENTED IMPACT

Bolsa Família is considered one of the largest programs of its kind in the world,[13] benefiting approximately 50 million people in the entire country. Its stated rationales are fighting deprivation and hunger as a means of short-term alleviation of the most urgent effects of poverty; breaking the intergenerational cycle of poverty through health, education and social assistance conditions; promoting access to public services, also by the means of conditions; and finally, integrating and rationalizing the social safety net.

It seems to be working. Several studies have documented the impact of Bolsa Família on poverty and inequality reduction,[14] improvement of the local economy, reduction of child undernutrition and other food security outcomes.[15]

Perhaps the most important public policy impacts have been the reduction of poverty and inequality. Between 2001 and 2008, the average annual growth rate of per-capita family income was a little under three percent for the entire population.[16] However, when the data are disaggregated, one important distinction is revealed: the income of the poorest ten percent grew at an average of nearly eight percent per year, while the income of the richest ten percent grew at a much lower average of nearly 1.5 percent per year. The continuation of this trend has produced an important reduction in income inequality, which has reached the lowest levels since baseline data began in 1976.[17]

Despite the great importance of the reduction of inequality, partially attributable to Bolsa Família and other social policies, evaluations also point to positive outcomes in other domains, such as food and food security. A cross-sectional study done when the program was expanded in 2005 documents that the prevalence of undernutrition among children from six months to one year of age in families that were *not* beneficiaries of the program was 2.65 times higher than in beneficiary families.[18]

Representative surveys of beneficiaries show that their top expenditures of Bolsa Família funds are on food (indicated by 87 percent of the families), school supplies (mentioned by 46 percent of the families), and clothing (37 percent of the families). These results are significant, given the early debates about ensuring that the families spent the money on food purchases. The results also reinforce evidence that women are more careful spenders than men. In 95 percent of the cases, the benefit is paid directly to a female in the household. Another important consequence captured in the surveys was that 40 percent of women reported an increase in decision-making power in their household after receiving the funds.

The global economic crises of 2008-09 provided a further test for the claim that social policies may act counter-cyclically to mitigate the effects of external shocks through incentives to internal markets and household consumption.[19] The country was considered one of the least affected by the global crisis.

FINAL NOTES: BROADENING THE EXPANDED PUBLIC SPACE

Perhaps as important as the traditional impact evaluations is the possibility that Bolsa Família may promote an integration of public and civic results. Above and beyond the program's stated rationale and intended results, it became clear that the success of Bolsa Família depended on a broader set of changes, both in the public and civic spheres. The strong leadership behind the implementation of the program created momentum for other items on the social policy agenda, and so contributed to the expansion of the public space in several domains.

First, a considerable percentage of the poorest Brazilians had no form of official identification and therefore were denied access to public services. In an interview given in 2005, then Minister of Social Development and Fight against Hunger, Patrus Ananias, laid out the difficulties and achievements experienced:

> It is a matter of citizenship to make sure that people obtain their official registration. We are making partnerships with social organizations to help people get their identification papers. Several families that strictly comply with the program rules still do not receive the money because they do not exist from a civic perspective. Those are people that have never had a birth certificate, a marriage certificate, or anything comparable. I do not see a political or electoral interest in this. We have partnerships with every single local government in the country.[20]

Second, the new spending power of poorer families had an important influence on the economic dynamics of the country. Large food corporations have made new investments in factories in the poorer Northeastern region of the country to serve these new markets. Even the food products themselves have changed, with packages being made in smaller portions and simpler wrapping materials to make them more affordable to people with low incomes.[21]

Third, the main mechanism of payment used by the Bolsa Família program—the ATM cards—paved the way for several other public initiatives. The bank is starting to convert some of the ATM cards into simplified banking accounts. In this program, families gain access to a new set of financial products, such as small loans, savings accounts and other services that help include them in the formal banking system.[22]

Fourth, the discussion about accountability and control over the payment of benefits created strong incentives for greater transparency. Anyone with Internet access may check whether any given person is a recipient of Bolsa Família (and other government programs as well) at www.portaldatransparencia.gov.br.

Finally, the main electronic database used to manage the program, the Single Registry of Beneficiaries, has enormous potential for the design, implementation and evaluation of other social policies. Once the database was built, new initiatives were planned using geospatial analysis techniques to identify needs and monitor delivery of public services to the population. So far, these possibilities have not been explored to their full potential, but their future impact may be very important.

Within the New Synthesis expanded public space, Bolsa Família may suggest interesting possibilities. It is the story of a policy that was initiated by local governments, made its way up to a national policy, then was incorporated as an asset of civil society. From the perspective of social and civic results, the program has promoted an integration of policies and had an impact that surpassed its original purposes, showing that funding families at the micro level may be a way to achieve developmental outcomes on a much wider scale.

Chapter 10

Vision, Collaboration, Persistence and Hard Work: the Canadian Federal Government's Homelessness Partnering Strategy[1]

Andrew Graham
School of Policy Studies
Queen's University[2]

Homelessness is not just a problem of failed public policies and programs: it is also a bone-crushing, right-to-the-core experience of loss of all of those things that we value and believe to be so near and dear to us.[3]

This is the case of the federal government of Canada's role in addressing homelessness. The story offers an overview of how one level of government leveraged limited resources to help align and bind together the considerable and varied efforts of three levels of government, the not-for-profit sector and individuals to tackle a growing and complex public problem.

By any definition, homelessness is a wicked problem. The effort to solve one aspect may reveal or create other problems: poverty, housing, health, mental health and security of communities. The very term homelessness, itself a relatively new public policy designation, actually masks the complexity of the problem.

Solutions to homelessness are similarly contentious. With multiple causal inputs, there are also multiple interventions that can make a difference. Yet intervention choices are owned by various players, differ across communities and often demand collective action that needs intense co-ordination and common purpose. The instruments of public policy are neither public nor private but both: both governmental and voluntary sector, both collective and individual.

This case explores how states can address complex issues by applying power *through* others (via funding) and *with* others (through processes of collective governance). Indeed, in this case, the federal government's efforts involved very little direct action but a great deal of capacity building for local action. For the traditional notion of government power and authority—one that stresses direct government intervention or a single programmatic solution applied across the country—this is a challenging new approach.

The story is not all roses, however. Where the distributed governance model described here did make a difference in decision making and innovation, it failed to build a similarly shared model of accounting for money invested. Old accountability measures, designed for a different command-and-control model, became the Achilles' heel of an otherwise exciting collaborative model.

HOMELESSNESS IN CANADA

Defining Homelessness

Surprisingly, the very concept of homelessness is a recent one. As David Hulchanski of the University of Toronto put it:

> By the early 1980s we needed a new term for a widespread mass phenomenon, a new social problem found in many wealthy, developed nations. The response was to add yet another suffix to further qualify the word homeless, to give us that odd job word, homelessness. Adding the suffix –ness makes the simple and clear word homeless into an abstract concept. As such, it allows users, readers, and listeners to imagine whatever they want. It tosses all sorts of problems into one handy term. We thus have the ongoing problem of defining what homelessness is and isn't. There is no single correct definition, given the different mix of problems that goes into the hodgepodge of issues, and depending on who is using the term.[4]

That "hodgepodge" shows up in the debate on the definition of what it means to be homeless and in the steps deemed necessary to address it. Researchers rightly refer to homelessness as "an odd job word, pressed into service to impose order on a hodgepodge of social dislocation, extreme poverty, seasonal or itinerant work, and unconventional ways of life."[5] In 2008, the Library of Parliament published a paper titled *Defining and Enumerating Homelessness in Canada*. In it, homelessness was described along a continuum of vulnerability to losing shelter, regardless of cause:

> Homelessness is a broad term that can encompass a range of housing conditions. These can be understood on a continuum of types of shelter:
>
> - At one end, absolute homelessness is a narrow concept that includes only those living on the street or in emergency shelters.
> - Hidden or concealed homelessness is in the middle of the continuum. These include people without a place of their own who live in a car, with family or friends, or in a long-term institution.
> - At the other end of the continuum, relative homelessness is a broad category that includes those who are housed but who reside in substandard shelter and/or who may be at risk of losing their homes.

Another way of understanding these categories is as levels of a pyramid, where absolute homelessness is only the "tip of the iceberg."[6] Some organizations propose that for every homeless person visible on the street, there are four whose homelessness is hidden.[7]

There are, however, no accurate national statistics in Canada to help us know the full scope of the problem. The lack of reliable data may limit the country's ability to address homelessness and has been a focus for international criticism. During a visit to Canada in October 2007, then UN Special Rapporteur on adequate housing, Miloon Kothari, reported that he "was disappointed that the government could not provide reliable statistics on the number of homeless."[8]

Factors Shaping Homelessness

There is some agreement on the range of factors that shape homelessness in Canada. The most obvious are the lack of adequate affordable housing and poverty: yet other forces are also at work. The gradual deinstitutionalization of mental health facilities in the later part of the 20th century, for instance, and the concomitant failure to grow community-based mental health capacity certainly had an impact. Criminal activity is another factor. As individuals move through the correctional systems and return to the street, they often face homelessness as one barrier among others that prevents their reintegration into society.

Still another contributing element is ethnicity. In Canada, homelessness strikes First Nation people disproportionately. Homelessness for them has two faces: inadequate or non-existent housing on First Nation reserves and urban homelessness. Fully 25 percent of Toronto's homeless population is of Aboriginal descent, compared to the two percent of Aboriginal people who form the ethnic makeup of Toronto.[9] These numbers are even more dramatic in the western part of the country where First Nations urban populations are larger: in a single one-day count of the homeless in Edmonton, 38 percent were identified as of First Nation origin.[10]

Responses to Homelessness

Just as the underlying factors are diverse, so too have been the types of response at individual, community, municipal, provincial and federal levels, and the expectations of each level for "success." As one interviewed official noted, What is the problem being solved? Is it placement in housing? And, if so, for how long? And at what level of economic, personal and social self-sustainability? From the municipal perspective, homelessness may mean getting people off the streets. From the social order perspective, it may mean the effective reduction of drug use and trafficking. From the provincial perspective, it may be the reduced reliance on social welfare. From the federal perspective, it may mean less reliance on social assistance or greater justice for minority groups.

In any case, the capacity of the federal government to act on its own is limited, as many of the instruments of policy and delivery are the responsibility of provincial and municipal governments. For instance, social welfare policy, while funded in part through federal transfers, is the shared responsibility of the provinces and municipalities. Public safety, while driven by the federal responsibility for criminal justice, is in fact a direct delivery responsibility of the provinces and municipalities. The reality is that the vast majority of first responder-type activities associated with homelessness (emergency shelters, social housing, and food, medical and drug addiction services) are provided locally, often through voluntary and not-for-profit agencies. The federal reach is constricted by jurisdiction and capacity to intervene directly.

Shifting Policy Landscape and Impacts

Responsibility for homelessness policy has shifted among the various levels of government over the years. In fact, the shift of the federal government away from a direct role in social housing in the 1980s and early 1990s may well be key to understanding how a new role for the federal government was able to address an emerging crisis in the late 1990s.

Historically, the federal government provided direct support for adequate housing and supports for low-income Canadians. However, beginning in the 1980s, global and domestic changes in the economy led to a push for smaller government, lower taxes and spending cuts. The government responded through gradual spending reductions on social programs, including affordable and social housing in the 1980s, the termination of spending on new social housing in 1993 and the almost complete transfer of responsibility for social housing to the provinces in 1996.[11]

These changes in social and housing policies had a profound impact on low-income Canadians. Once considered a minor problem afflicting a small number of transient single men, homelessness began affecting a much broader spectrum of individuals and families in the early 1980s. By the late 1990s, it had become a matter of public and media concern.[12] Seen as a problem beyond their capacity and resources to resolve, the mayors of Canada's big cities began pushing for direct funding from the federal government rather than through the provinces as intermediaries.[13] From the federal perspective, this was an opportunity to establish relationships with big cities at a time when big-city issues were on the rise. By the summer of 1999, the federal government felt pressured to act. In developing a response, a new role emerged for the federal government that moved away from direct funding to *collaborative* governance and co-funding with partners at multiple levels.

THE HOMELESSNESS PARTNERING STRATEGY

In December 1999, the federal government announced the precursor to the Homelessness Partnering Strategy (HPS): the National Homelessness Initiative (NHI), a three-year, C$753 million demonstration initiative designed to respond to the perceived emergency situation in major cities. Although most funding went to enhance existing federal programs, it also included the new C$305 million "Supporting Communities Partnership Initiative" (SCPI) which provided flexible funding to 61 communities to plan and implement local strategies to prevent and reduce homelessness.[14] In 2003, the NHI was extended for an additional three years before being replaced in 2007 by the HPS. The HPS (as was the NHI) is funded and administered by Human Resources and Skills Development Canada (HRSDC).

The HPS builds on the existing community-based model established through the NHI to develop deeper partnerships and more permanent and longer-term solutions to help individuals out of homelessness. The strategy targets the development of transitional and supporting housing, and supporting programs, such as health and treatment programs and skills training. The HPS has seven funding streams: Designated Communities, Outreach Communities, Aboriginal Communities, Federal Horizontal Pilot Projects, Homelessness Knowledge Development, the Homeless Individuals and Families Information System (HIFIS) and the Surplus Federal Real Property for Homelessness Initiative (SFRPHI).

The HPS promotes the development of community plans that are required for designated communities (the 61, mostly urban communities, with significant problems with homelessness), but optional for outreach (small cities and rural areas) and Aboriginal communities. In general, the HPS is delivered using two financial administration models: a Community Entity model, whereby a Community Advisory Board (composed of homelessness stakeholders in the community) recommends projects to the community entity (normally an incorporated organization), which makes the decisions regarding project proposals (HRSDC does *not* make decisions: it is responsible only for managing the contribution agreement). The second method, a Shared Delivery model, involves the same Community Advisory Board in recommending proposals to HRSDC, and both Service Canada and the community then work in a joint selection and decision-making process.

These models have given focus to the HPS work as a community integrator rather than a direct service provider. As Margaret Eberle, a housing policy consultant, said in testimony before a House of Commons subcommittee, "One of the things that SCPI or the Homelessness Partnering Strategy has done is to bring players to the table that were not involved before. If you look at some of the homelessness tables around the country, foundations and private sector people are involved. Local governments are definitely on board."[15]

Beyond the community-based initiatives taking place at the regional level, the

HPS also includes the Federal Horizontal Pilot Projects (HPP) component. The HPP explores harmonization with programs in other federal departments and agencies, as well as with other programs delivered by HRSDC to ensure that federal ministries are working together to be part of the solution. HRSDC therefore funds a number of pilot projects to stimulate other parts of the federal government to act on homelessness or develop their own capacities through experimentation (see Box 1).

Box 1: Examples of Horizontal Pilot Projects

- Pre-discharge Support for Federal Offenders: Provided identification documents to offenders before release to reduce the risk of homelessness. Location: Kingston, Ontario. Partners: Correctional Service of Canada and Office of the Federal Interlocutor for Métis and Non-Status Indians (OFI).
- Employment Support for Homeless Youth: Provided skills development to marginalized street youth to help them establish employment and long-term housing. Location: St. John's, Newfoundland. Partner: HRSDC Employment Programs.
- Nutritional Health: Provided a life skills program focused on nutrition to improve capacity of Aboriginal women living in a family shelter to become self-sufficient. Location: Brantford, Ontario. Partner: Status of Women Canada.
- Tending the Fire Leadership Program: Provided transitional housing, counselling and life skills training to encourage better outcomes for homeless Aboriginal men. Location: Regina, Saskatchewan. Partners: Public Safety Canada, Canadian Heritage and OFI.
- Integrated Employability and Transitional Housing: Provided transitional housing with life skills training for people involved with the criminal justice system. Location: Ottawa. Partners: Justice Canada and Health Canada.

Through HPS program elements, a growing sense of trust among players has developed. Members see the day-to-day interactions through the initiative in a positive light *because* it is collaborative. The strength of that collaborative model has carried the program, but tensions have existed. Throughout the program, the federal government insisted on fairly onerous reporting that did not always match community organizations' understanding of the desired outcomes. Moreover, the reporting information collected was little used and does not seem to have played a significant role in federal decision making for the 2009 renewal process. Simplified reporting requirements put in place for the 2011 review period were expected to help somewhat in reducing the burden.

Other tensions had to do with the continual cycle of funding justification. The renewal processes were often at the last minute, requiring a scramble to renew contractual funding arrangements quickly to ensure continuity. With the renewal processes linked to policy reviews, evaluations and budget cycles, various players entered the picture, asking for information, clarification and answers. "Ten years is not temporary any more. It wears you down. Do I have to go to defend this again?" was one observation of a long-term program official.

A further cause of friction was staff turnover. While it is clear that trust and a deep knowledge of the local scene are crucial to the success of collaborative partnerships, the federal government was plagued by staff turnover, most notably in its regional offices. Staff unfamiliar with the local culture and not adequately embedded in the local system turned into visiting bureaucrats. (By way of contrast, the national office provided some consistency: a number of senior officials within the Homelessness Partnering Secretariat in Ottawa have been involved with the program for many years).

Today, however, the future of the program looks strong. Although the HPS is not part of the base funding of its home ministry, it has been given rolling approvals: first, a two-year, then a five-year commitment with requirements for Cabinet approval for the last three-year segment. Remarkably, the HPS and its predecessor, the NHI, have been extended over the life of two governments of different political parties and have enjoyed considerable grassroots support (indeed, the federal government does not even provide the majority of funds). The lessons of the Homelessness Partnering Strategy, both in addressing homelessness and thinking about the future of governance, are worthy of close examination.

PRACTICAL LEARNINGS

A recent Canadian Senate Report on poverty singled out the NHI and HPS as a success story:

> The Government of Canada's National Homelessness Initiative and Homelessness Partnering Strategy have been widely praised and held up as a model for how the federal government can work with all stakeholders to tackle a problem in its local peculiarities. Most witnesses who addressed either homelessness in particular or approaches to local issues more generally flagged these programs as examples to be sustained and replicated in other areas.[16]

What made the HPS work? Why is it considered a success worthy of replication? Here are some of those factors of strength and weakness, both in terms of practical steps in the design of the program and the larger New Synthesis issues they raise.

Trust-building

The various initiatives that made the strategy work (such as the Community Advisory Boards) needed time and sustained support to be effective. Keeping the relationship going takes more than sound formal governance agreements: it demands that relationships of trust and common purpose be forged with people over time.

One risk to that trust in such multi-layered and cross-agency enterprises is the impact of change. Government directions and personnel turn over, and new relationships must be forged. For changes in personnel:

> Governments must pay more attention to their internal succession planning and knowledge transfer with respect to comprehensive community initiatives. The success of this work is rooted in personal relationships that are built by working collaboratively. Consequently, when public servants are transferred, the remaining partners feel a sense of loss. It is easier for new relationships to form with the incoming public servants if they are personally introduced to the partners by their predecessor and have been well briefed on the initiative. While the same principles hold true for other partners, staff turnover is much lower.[17]

A similar rule holds true for changes in government. The Secretariat has been able to weather changes in government by using its wealth of relational credits created over the past decade. As one senior official said, "The leveraging we get from these relationships goes way beyond just good will. Often it means that someone will connect the dots along the value chain of the program to find more resources, bring in a new funder and, most important of all, smooth over any threats to the total program by one change, reduction in funding or shift in emphasis."

Adaptability

Part of the success is also due to the government's adaptability to local demands. The HPS, while presenting clear requirements for eligibility, was highly flexible in the ultimate application of funding. Creating an environment that permits local adaptation meant a leap in thinking from a traditional bureaucratic model, articulated by one program official as the reality that there is "more known outside of Ottawa than inside." As noted by Liz Weaver, the Director of the Hamilton Roundtable for Poverty Reduction:

> Where we have seen a bit of a difference is around the national Homelessness Partnering Strategy, where there has been flexibility for local communities to help design what the community requires. There is some challenge around the shortness of that funding option, but it has allowed government, citizens, service providers and the development community in Hamilton to come together and identify strategies for that whole continuum of social housing that is effective and relevant to our community. That is the type of solution we are looking for.[18]

Leveraging

The value of the HPS lies in its strength as a leveraging device. The HPS is intended to address homelessness through building community capacity and bringing a multitude of resources to the table to build locally defined priority programs and processes. By finding ways to engage provincial and municipal actors, the strategy has leveraged approximately C$2.61 for every C$1 it invests. To ratchet up that investment, it avoided the common problem of distorting local priorities and overriding local and provincial decision making through its funding influence. For instance, no funding for any HPS project in Newfoundland is approved without provincial agreement. This practice ensures greater alignment of resources, increasing the likelihood of impact and building trust among partners who see their contributions valued.

Measurement

The HPS suffered from tension between transactional reporting and a focus on outcomes. Federal players funded others to act on a larger (ill defined) goal, but then attempted to measure short-term results that focused strictly on the use of federal money. As one program official noted, "All our tools now measure what we spend. We do not measure the impact on homelessness itself or on how communities work together."

Moreover, the very idea of "a result" for the federal government's homelessness policy has changed over the years. At first, "partnership" was an intermediary result intended to bring resources together. Money was seen as a strategic leveraging tool. However, as the focus moved to "results-based initiatives:" the emphasis became what the money actually does. As one program official said, "We began to look at what our money does and taking credit for that. That means less focus on the cumulative focus, taking into account what others did and what we were all doing together." The focus on results, however, became increasingly short-term and narrow, generating a potential conflict between accountability and results.

Permanence

Since 2007, the HPS has been subject to a number of reviews and extensions, requiring considerable administrative effort on a nearly full-time basis. Such impermanence, however, also destabilizes relationships with partners as the future of the program always remains in question. There is some encouragement in having had two different governments renew the HPS and its predecessor, the NHI: the impermanence of the strategy does not seem to reflect any ambiguity of political will. Perhaps such impermanence creates a temporary role for the federal government as communities mount their successful efforts. The model of building a temporary agency to address temporary challenges is seductive and can be good public policy. The question in this case is whether the model will work for wicked problems that do not easily go away.

NEW SYNTHESIS LEARNINGS

Wicked problems like homelessness are alike in many ways. They are large, complex and seemingly insolvable problems that require a different way of thinking about what governments can and should do. Here are some broader reflections from the Canadian case that speak to a New Synthesis understanding of any wicked challenge.

Dealing with Complexity

Homelessness is deeply rooted in complexity. Responses demand individual and localized approaches, unlike many federal programs that produce a single standard or entitlement for all Canadians. This is uncomfortable territory for federal actors who designed a far different program in the HPS—one that built in organizational adaptability to local circumstances to manage that complexity. That was its key strength.

Identifying Results

Where federal officials did *not* manage complexity well, however, was in taking on a short-term view of results (and insisting on short-term financial reporting on the federal slice of those results). But what would be the larger view? When, indeed, does homelessness end? With the elimination of homelessness? With the elimination of poverty? Societal goals are by their very nature contentious, seldom well defined and subject to continual re-scoping. Navigation on this plane requires a different set of governance skills than we saw at play in Canada.

Building Civic Engagement and Civic Results

The HPS is built on the model of civic engagement. In fact, it enabled many of the 61 designated communities engaged in the strategy to build stronger working arrangements, leverage resources in a more effective way, distribute risk and focus action. According to a 2009 report on homelessness by the Standing Senate Committee on Social Affairs, Science and Technology, the impact was palpable. "The 20 agencies visited by the committee and the dozens of agencies that submitted briefs, participated in roundtables and appeared as witnesses, all inspired the committee with their innovations, passion and effective programs."[19] Engagement engendered results at the civic level far above what government could have achieved independently.

Fluidity in Governance Models

The shift to *collaborative* governance and co-funding with partners at multiple levels was a genuine innovation. A veteran official who worked with both programs noted that "Homelessness is one of those areas that demands an asymmetrical response, one that is probably counter-intuitive to the bureaucratic mindset of program and compliance." Addressing homelessness from the federal perspective meant accepting a level of local variance uncommon to federal programming. Little was going to happen on homelessness unless communities were able to coalesce around the issue and marshal resources to address the specific problems each community faced.

The number of players and issues that affect homelessness make greater flexibility in governance inevitable. In the context of the New Synthesis, responsibility is actually distributed according to circumstance. The potential for confusion about accountability is real, however, and part of an ongoing debate among partners. The file is so complex and has so many dimensions that "It doesn't settle down," as one of those interviewed noted. There is the constant potential for debate in which nobody owns it or everybody owns it. As one public official added, "We are constantly rehashing those ideas. These questions are unresolved and unclear."

However, such fluidity is not necessarily negative. Bureaucracies like certainty and predictability: homelessness does not offer such comfort. The problem does, however, require that those driving the policy spend more time on process and take a longer-term perspective. Policy leaders saw that many communities were fragmented, NGOs were competing for resources and there was no co-operation. Therefore, in building capacity and sustainable governance, community plans proved to be the most important tool for addressing homelessness at the community level and giving the federal government some kind of hook upon which to hang its role and resources. As one program official explained, "It created a focus on priorities. We made communities do policy exercises."

Program leaders also noted that as communities developed their initial plans and created Community Advisory Boards, they grew in sophistication and capacity. In some cases, boards were able to leverage municipal and provincial funding through a relatively small amount of federal funding. In another example, faced with conflicting provincial and federal concerns, one board developed a decision-making protocol that ensured all parties *signed off* on new program development. This increasing governance capacity at the local level is yet another positive result.

Adaptive Governance

The HPS was built on a concept of shared and adaptive governance. The small case in Prince Albert, Saskatchewan, points to two elements that stood out in the fact-gathering stage (see Box 2): the deliberate pursuit of a community-based governance strategy, combined with the integration of existing community arrangements.

Box 2: Prince Albert, Saskatchewan

The City of Prince Albert is a good example of a community coming together to address homelessness and how the HPS made that co-operation possible. The city evolved its former Housing Committee into a Community Advisory Board to pursue the funding available from the federal government. It then used the CAB community planning and analysis model to identify real needs and brought together groups to discuss how to measure the outcomes (as well as comply with contribution funding regulations). The city's 2007 report states:

> "Not only does [HPS support] mean that meagre resources will be used more efficiently, but it also means that collective wisdom can be brought to bear on this overall plan as it emerges. When a community works together in a strategic fashion, they will not only use their resources better, they will also be able to leverage other funds because of their collective action and capacity."[20]

Adopting such a strategy meant both encouraging the creation of community boards and providing enough flexibility to support variation to meet local circumstances. The approach also meant creating information and knowledge-sharing tools that enable effective governance and reporting.

Multi-party and Multi-dimensional Risk

The issue of homelessness is rife with risk: strategic risks (the investments do not work or produce unintended consequences), political risks (something terrible happens to an individual directly linked to a government-funded activity, political conflict among the various levels of government calls for greater political action by opposition parties or activist NGOs), compliance risks (in a complex chain of delivery, the potential of something going wrong rises quickly) and performance risks (one party does not play its role or deliver on its promises). Despite the potential for disaster, the risk did not deter many of the actors from moving ahead. The risk is, however, in constant flux among the various parties, most notably among the Community Advisory Boards, the bureaucrats and the politicians. While the risk environment is complex, there seem to have been few systemic failures. Why is this so?

It appears that risk management took place at various stages of the process, despite an apparent lack of a systematic and singular approach. This case might best be described as multi-dimensional risk-gridding. Traditional concepts of risk management involve the application of risk analysis and the definition of mitigation strategies in a linear fashion for a single organization. However, in this case, the initiative crosses all levels of government, the civic sector and the non-for-profit sector. Elements inherent in multi-dimensional risk-gridding include spreading risk throughout the system, avoiding single risk targets and decentralizing response. There is evidence of sustained efforts to ensure that risk in this case *was* distributed in a multi-dimensional way.

Systems of Performance Management and Accountability

The very concepts of performance management and accountability are built on the ability of organizations to learn and share information. Learning and sharing has been a challenge for the HPS for a variety of reasons: an over-emphasis on micro-level reporting requirements prevented people from focusing on the important issues; a constant churn of those involved meant that knowledge is not easily retained; and achieving results on an issue such as homelessness is a long-term process; however, performance was often judged and managed in the short term. As one program official noted, "We are not good at learning from all this information we gather. People move on, memories are lost. You have to know how to handle the ingredients of success, but have to put it together within the context."

The metrics of accountability have changed over time. These are some of the contributing factors:

- **Shifting Goals.** The exact goals of homelessness programs can shift over time, making the successful measurement of performance more difficult. This shift is certainly valid as needs change. However, it takes place among players in the whole process so that short-term goals, often quite intractable in themselves, begin to be the only concern. In this way, the longer-term goals are ignored.
- **Multi-level Measurement.** Engaging three levels of government, an array of NGOs and local groups will always be a formula for confusion when it comes to defining what gets measured and how. In a time of increasingly prescribed accountability arrangements, each government will have its own view on what needs to be measured, by whom and when. In the longer term, it means placing a greater focus on coming to a mutual understanding of the measurements needed to satisfy these requirements, not obviate them.
- **Action Learning.** This is a case in which performance and accountability have to keep pace with increasing knowledge about the phenomenon itself. An example of both successful action learning and confusion about what needed to be measured is the "housing first" strategy, an approach that recognized shelter as a precondition to self-sufficiency and full participation in society. The adoption of "housing first" illustrates successful action learning in that this policy arose from the experience of those involved in the issue. Confusion regarding performance measures occurred because the immediate goal of "shelter," often temporary and transitory, was difficult to measure. Further, this goal clouded the longer-term concern that housing, as important as it might be, was only one component of a homelessness strategy.

Systems of Compliance and Control

The HPS represents an environment in which issues of centralization and decentralization compete. Issues of compliance with rules and control over inputs, processes and outcomes were sometimes set in *competition* with steps deemed necessary by some to reach the ultimate desired outcome. As one program official stated, "There is a blind spot on performance management and control. They drive you to the pursuit of the measurable. This distorts you towards standardization of approach in a public policy area that begs for specialization." While policies evolved based on partnerships and collective leadership allowing for a range of generally predicable alternatives, this variation was hard for governments to manage.

From a New Synthesis perspective, the very definition of compliance could be taken apart. Is it compliance with the rules of the various players or of the chief funder? Is it compliance with the intended program outcomes? Within a wider Canadian context of tightened financial accountability, the tension is real; many actors within the HPS clearly identified a narrow version of accountability as a major impediment to sustaining the focus on reducing homelessness. As one interviewee pointed out, "We have had to act with some considerable stealth to avoid flooding the various communities with compliance requirements."

The HPS, like most federal government programs, has seen an increase in annual reporting requirements and short-term audits even though neither the overall objective nor individual interventions are limited to a single year. Such reporting requirements distort organizational behaviour and encourage short-term actions that can be measured within an audit cycle. These timelines are incompatible with what might be called the appropriate policy/implementation cycle of a complex set of responses and strategies. "We would just like to get one thing done before we start reporting on our compliance," said one interviewee.

Several of those interviewed helped summarize the main issues affecting compliance and control in the HPS environment with distributed responsibilities, powers and governance.

- Difficulties in harmonizing multiple accountabilities, rules and systems of compliance created by the multiple actors.
- Lack of consensus on intermediate goals, final outcomes (aside from "elimination of homelessness") and shared metrics of success.
- A profound mismatch between the long-term view and the immediate short-term, audit-driven reporting effort.
- A focus on short-term surrogates for long-term results meant a poor allocation of resources on actual outcomes.

SUMMARY

The case study of the HPS illustrates how, in the face of homelessness, the federal government used state authority and resources to leverage collective power. It shows how people and resources from multiple government departments, several levels of government and community organizations came together at local levels under the auspices of the HPS to tackle homelessness. It reveals how this entails government and actors from other sectors drawing on an expanded repertoire of roles and relationships. It emphasizes how the federal government attempted to align resources across various departments and to play effective roles as a funding partner, convener and enabler of unique approaches and actors at the community level.

The case also reveals difficulties in establishing workable systems of shared commitment and responsibility for results, largely as a by-product of issues such as short-term funding arrangements, the heavy burden of reporting requirements and controls, and a performance measurement system that looks mainly at the micro level rather than at higher level outcomes.

Despite these difficulties, the future of the program looks strong. Not only will it carry on addressing the issues of homelessness, but from a research and learning perspective, it will continue providing valuable lessons for ongoing and future practice—both in addressing homelessness and thinking about the future of governance.

Chapter 11
Public Safety Centres in the Netherlands[1]

Jouke de Vries, Harry Kruiter and Martin Gagner
Centre for Governance Studies
Leiden University

Unheard of a decade ago, Public Safety Centres (PSCs) are a recent and relatively unknown phenomenon within the Dutch public sector. While the first was formed in 2002, there are now 47 PSCs across the Netherlands, with most having emerged over the past two years. This study aspires to shed some light on the processes relating to the PSCs and how they have come to be viewed as an effective tool in dealing with complex challenges relating to public safety.

Dutch public sector work has long been characterized by a propensity to specialize. While this process has enabled public organizations to attain advanced levels of knowledge and skill, it has also become difficult to co-ordinate efforts in an effective way. This lack of co-ordination is perhaps particularly true in the area of "social safety," which involves multiple and disparate challenges. In trying to reduce crime and public nuisance, problems frequently prove to be too complicated and multifaceted for single approaches to be effective. Providing public safety is a complex task as related challenges are constantly changing and problems are in constant motion. Against this background, the PSCs represent an approach to overcoming compartmentalization, to co-ordinating individual efforts effectively and to stimulating co-operation in the pursuit of public safety.

PSCs are networks of organizations formed to stimulate co-operative approaches in dealing with crime and public nuisance and, hence, share office space. Each network is comprised of public and private organizations working in some area of public safety, organized to deal with cases referred to them by the contributing partners. Once a case has been reviewed and action agreed upon, representatives from partner organizations communicate the agreements back to their own organizations for implementation. Because of their inclusive approach, PSCs are seen to be of great value in supporting the government's mission to increase safety in Dutch urban areas. Operating under the principles of short communication lines, integrated approaches, co-operation, effectiveness, efficiency and balancing punitive measures with prevention, PSCs are (on paper) well suited to dealing with the complex issue of social safety.

In the following pages, we elaborate on how the PSCs—by connecting national policy and local realities—are expected to strengthen the anticipative capacity of the Dutch public sector in dealing with safety. After exploring the development of PSCs, we turn to the processes of identifying, interpreting and dealing with problems. In the last section, we point to a number of existing tensions and considerations that ought to be taken into account when attempting to connect local-level practice with policy.

POLICY CONTEXT

Over the past decade, as part of a broader emphasis on public safety and security, social safety has gained prominence in Dutch public debate and climbed high on the political and policy agenda. In 2007, the government presented a general policy program outlining 74 targets spread over six themes,[2] which the Balkenende IV Cabinet[3] aspired to achieve by the end of its mandate in 2011.[4] Within the public safety and security theme, 15 targets were mentioned, one of which states that the government will establish PSCs in larger cities.[5] The general policy program also included ten more specific programs, one being "Safety Begins with Prevention," which deals in part with the creation of PSCs.[6] The new policy broadened the concept of public safety and security and aimed to complement punitive measures with prevention.

The overall goals of the Dutch safety program are to reduce crime and public nuisance by 25 percent and recidivism by 10 percent by 2011, compared to 2002 levels. These goals, inherited from an earlier program and policy framework,[7] along with measures to monitor performance, are the result of the wide-ranging decentralization of Dutch public sector activities. The process of devolving responsibility for public safety and security to local authorities was intensified in 1997, with the introduction of the Justice in the Vicinity (*Justitie in de buurt*) policy framework. Initially focused on problem-ridden neighbourhoods in four Dutch cities, the purpose of the framework was to better connect Ministry of Justice activities with local authorities (including the police), thereby shortening communication lines. The framework was further developed and broadened, leading to the introduction of Justice in the Vicinity—New Style in 2004.

It is worthwhile to elaborate briefly on the current ethos of broadening approaches to complex problems, as this is relevant to how the PSCs function. The "Safety Begins with Prevention" program involves six ministries,[8] and represents one part of the government's efforts to stimulate integrated approaches based on multiple perspectives. A key feature of this program (explained later in more detail) is also a characteristic of the PSCs: a carefully mixed blend of law enforcement, preventive measures and post-incarceration after-care. To create this blend, ingredients are sourced from both the public and the private sectors, including agencies connected to various ministries, housing corporations, civic organizations and organizations providing care and education.

"Discovery" of a Tool

The first PSC was created in the City of Tilburg in 2002 through the initiative of the local Public Prosecution Service. Although safety organizations had co-operated before, there was room for improvement. At the time, the local head of police, the senior public prosecution officer and the mayor of Tilburg were concerned about the lack of safety in the city. They reasoned that by sitting together in one building, the various actors involved in safety-related activities could better connect their processes, the collaboration would have a positive effect on the level of safety in the city and communication lines would be shorter. With the support of these three senior public servants (representing the Ministry of the Interior and Kingdom Relations, the Ministry of Justice and the municipal government), nine organizations were invited to participate in the new collaborative venture. During the first three or four years of its existence, the PSC focused primarily on processes related to criminal law.

In 2002, the Municipality of Tilburg commissioned a local criminology professor to conduct a comprehensive study on the state of public safety in the city: it painted a very grim picture.[9] The report states that residents of the municipality experienced unacceptably high levels of crime and public nuisance, and generally felt unsafe. The study portrays the PSC as a fundamental building block and concludes that its position had to be strengthened if the city were to increase social safety. In addition, the study recommends that the municipality take on a co-ordinating and more proactive role in providing social safety. According to the manager at the local PSC, the municipal government fully adopted the recommendations and was to implement them within four years.

An evaluation performed at the end of this period concludes that the work at the PSC was a great success, as the overall picture of public safety had improved. Among the oft-quoted improvements were a reduction in recidivism among young people of approximately 50 percent, a lower number of first-time offenders and a general decrease in crime in the public sphere.[10] If such good co-operation could be achieved within the sphere of the penal system, it was reasoned, Why not extend this approach to organizations in the mental health care sector?

What took place in the Tilburg PSC was not an isolated case—it matched a general trend in the Netherlands of pursuing an integrated approach to addressing the complex issue of public safety. Nevertheless, the Tilburg PSC gained national attention and was visited by politicians, municipal governments and senior public servants. This profile was due in part to a local scholar who enthusiastically propagated the importance of the PSC in improving public safety. As a result, the Minister of Justice, with his strong connections to Tilburg, ensured that the PSC concept was incorporated into the national general policy program.

In Tilburg, the government had found a tool that supported the policy framework, appeared suitable for dealing with the complex challenge of increasing public safety and, through a number of key actors, was adopted as part of a national program. In its initial form, the PSC was not a ready-made tool that could be adopted at the national level. Rather, it had developed through continual contact with high-ranking public servants active beyond the local context.

Developing National Coverage

The Tilburg PSC has been held forth as a prime example of how a co-operative and integrated approach to safety can contribute to the achievement of the government's goals. This locally conceived experiment, built on popular concepts found in national policy frameworks, fit the zeitgeist of Dutch public sector activities. With the support of some key actors, the national government included the expansion of PSCs in its general policy program, and they are now found in all larger cities in the Netherlands. With only a handful of PSCs operating in 2007, 47 are now spread across the country, and the Balkenende IV Cabinet reached its target of creating a nationwide network.

There has been great enthusiasm for the PSCs overall; however, the varying degrees of support, commitment and resources found in each locality may influence the level of success. The manager in Tilburg, who took part in creating the first PSC, strongly emphasizes that, "*people* are the most important factors in creating a success or a failure." He offers a word of caution regarding the development of new PSCs:

> What I tell people is "I'll tell you my story—how we did it here—and you take whatever suits you best. But you have to take your own little steps. You can't start with 20 organizations at once. In every city, in every village, people already co-operate. Sometimes it's just a couple of people, sometimes three, sometimes five. Start with that as your basis. [...] Really, you've got to start on a small scale. Keep it simple, and slowly build from below. Don't make it too complicated at once; let it develop. And another thing that you have to count on is that it takes time. You've got to deal with different organizations, all with their own culture."

Given that historical background and the drivers that led to the expansion of the model, it is time to explore how the PSCs work on a day-to-day basis.

OUTLINE OF THE PUBLIC SAFETY CENTRES IN PRACTICE

The most basic feature of a PSC is the co-operation of representatives from several organizations concerned with some aspect of public safety, all working together at one location. Although managers tend to be keen on sketching an organizational chart for the PSCs, one of the intentions of co-operation is the adaptive nature of the network, where partners are engaged on an as-needed basis. It is often suggested that a PSC is not an organization, but rather a platform for co-operation, manifested in the physical location shared by individual participants. One of its fundamental principles is a network-like and non-hierarchical structure where representatives of participating organizations remain employed by their parent organizations, but are present at the PSC on an assignment basis.

The PSCs' main task is to contribute to reducing crime and public nuisance. According to the directives, PSCs are to contribute to increasing safety by facilitating co-operation. This is not a flaw. These broadly defined outcomes allow space for collectively identifying problems and defining areas of attention. Typically, the constituents and activities of a PSC differ from city to city; however, three partners remain constant. They are the Ministry of Justice, the Ministry of the Interior and Kingdom Relations and the municipal government (represented by the local public prosecution officer, the local head of police and the mayor). A number of welfare organizations are also represented, including mental health and addiction care, housing corporations and probation.

In keeping with the integrated approach, the work at the PSCs is organized around different "cluster tables." Generally, a PSC has four to eight cluster tables, including juvenile delinquents, (adult) multiple offenders, domestic violence, multi-problem families and post-incarceration care. In addition, PSCs may form other themes or area-based clusters depending on local needs.

Individual cases are addressed at cluster table meetings by representatives (attending on an as-needed basis) of partner organizations. The most frequent participants are representatives of the municipal government, the police (often a neighbourhood police officer who knows the individuals being discussed) and a public prosecution officer (when the case involves criminal activity). Other participants, depending on the case, may include representatives from child protection services, mental health care organizations or youth workers. In addition, other professionals may be invited to share information considered relevant for forming a more complete picture of the individual(s) discussed. During these meetings, tasks and responsibilities are determined, and representatives communicate the agreements back to their organization (See Box 1). By offering a spatial nucleus for co-operation, significant changes in process are visible in how problems are interpreted and handled, and how networks centred on PSCs perform.

Box 1: Example of a Case Discussion within a Cluster for a Specific Neighbourhood

Once a week, one of the four selected neighbourhoods is discussed during a meeting. The following people gather around the table: a municipal employee from an agency dealing with public order and safety (who chairs the meeting), two youth workers, a neighbourhood police officer, and representatives from the child protection services, a youth probation office and a youth care agency. Five cases will be discussed in the hour-long meeting.

For each case, at least three or four participants know the individual and some aspect of his or her particular situation personally. They hold different knowledge and views on the case derived from their relationship to the individual. Taken together, a multifaceted image of the individual is sketched out, including family relations, school performance, track record of delinquency, leisure activities and social network. To illustrate an approach facilitated by the cluster meeting, we can look at how participants handle the case of one youth seen as being "on the wrong track" (hanging out with older petty criminals) but otherwise "not a bad apple."

One of the youth workers tells the other participants a bit about the family situation, pointing out that the parents are also concerned about their child but do not know what to do. Both parents are worried that the government, if involved, will try to take their son away. The father bears a grudge against the police, so it is preferable that they do not approach the family. Other than that, the youth worker argues, the parents are an easily approachable couple. The municipal employee suggests that he offer the family some support from the municipality and suggest solutions. The youth worker emphasizes the need for a considered approach, which the parents are more likely to welcome and trust. The youth worker and the municipal employee agree to talk to the parents together, but will first speak to the youth's uncle (a well respected resident of another neighbourhood who has previously worked with the municipality) and ask him to introduce them to the parents.

It is decided that the youth will be offered a place in a municipality-sponsored after-school program and that the parents will be invited to a talk with a family coach. Furthermore, the case will be brought to the juvenile delinquency cluster to ensure that no overlaps take place and that relevant information about the case has not been missed.

Having reached agreement on the first case, the meeting proceeds with the remaining cases, all handled through a similar multi-perspective approach. At the end of the meeting, the decisions are summarized and participants return to their organizations to undertake the agreed-upon actions, all aware of each other's activities. The cases will be reviewed and discussed in one month's time (should nothing drastic happen in the meantime), when the next meeting about this particular neighbourhood takes place.

Interpretation of Problems

According to the PSC perspective, problems relating to safety originate with individuals and are aggravated by poor co-ordination among public sector organizations. To address these issues, an individual, "person specific" approach is taken, and organizational deficiencies are handled through better co-operation.

The person based approach provides participants with a greater awareness of the frequently multifaceted nature of a case. The stories about individuals, offered from the multiple views of participants, serve to nuance interpretation, thus avoiding a limited view of the person discussed. This nuance may have a profound influence on how a case is approached, even from a judicial standpoint. A representative of the Public Prosecution Service consulted for this study was keen to point out that the Service's goal is "not [to] advocate as long a sentence as possible, but [to advocate] the most appropriate measure for the case at hand." Moreover, he claimed that multiple views frequently facilitated the identification of an appropriate measure. For other organizational representatives, in particular the care oriented ones, multiple viewpoints often led to better insights.

From Multiple Viewpoints Towards "New" Problems

Working together regularly entails discovering problems. Through the intense organizational relationships playing out at PSCs, overlaps, contradictions and gaps may be identified faster and more easily. Although deficiencies in public sector organizations may not be immediately remedied, awareness is a first step. Deficiencies are collectively identified by representatives sharing information and experiences. Through this practice, they also attempt to anticipate new problem areas.

Multiple organizations working together at the PSCs seem to offer greater opportunities for identifying emerging problem areas. Occasionally, they mobilized resources to handle problems more rapidly than had the network not existed. At more established PSCs, this dynamic has resulted in new theme-based clusters being added to their activity area. One example is a "pimp boys" cluster that uses the multi-organizational approach to deal with young men who force their girlfriends into prostitution. Also at the more recently established PSCs, new clusters begin to take shape as organizations share their experiences of street-level work. One example of this process is the identification of a growing number of Central- and Eastern-European citizens who are seen to have a negative impact on social safety because they cannot find work in the Netherlands and therefore end up on the streets. Another example is immigrants who have been denied asylum or a residence permit but who do not exit the country. These individuals do not have a legal right to public services, but may of course still need them. These are but some examples of the many cluster problems that may emerge when safety and care oriented organizations work closely together. Although clear approaches to such problems may still be lacking, their joint identification may enable faster and better co-ordinated action than was possible before.

Practices in Dealing with Problems

The steps towards genuine co-operation involve sharing information, experiences and perspectives. In the newer PSCs, establishing co-operation involves building files around the cases. Although this may seem trivial, the active sharing of information about individual cases represents a major shift in practice. Awareness of other organizations' activities regarding a case enables action to be more effectively co-ordinated. This initial information-sharing is as much about becoming familiar with the case as getting to know the other partners around the table. With differing core businesses, perspectives and organizational cultures, building relationships and trust requires time and effort. It is only once trust and a thorough knowledge of each others' competences and limitations are established that the network at the PSCs can begin to generate innovative approaches.

Dealing with the problems caused by individuals, or an individual's problem, starts with collecting information and building a shared file of the case. This information is then discussed among the representatives at one of the cluster meetings. Representatives also consider appropriate measures and decide on a course of action.

Where this situation is unclear or agreement cannot be reached, the case is discussed at greater length at another meeting to which additional participants may be invited to share relevant information. Once appropriate measures are identified and action is agreed upon, the decisions are communicated to the representatives' organizations for implementation.

Development of Different Routines

There are significant differences in the interpretation and resolution of problems by the clusters and also in the style of approaches taken. It is not possible to generalize along cluster lines, as each group of professionals develops its own culture, determined partly by the character of the participants and the cases at hand.[11] To illustrate these differences, however, we can explore the two most common clusters: juvenile delinquents and (adult) multiple offenders. Although these examples have limitations, they show the considerable effect of problem interpretation on the range of selected actions.

Participants around a cluster dealing with juvenile delinquency most often include a neighbourhood police officer, a youth worker who knows the person discussed, representatives of the municipal authorities and the Youth and Family Centre and, if relevant, representatives from mental health care, child protection agencies and parole offices specializing in young offenders. Other parties, such as school teachers, football coaches or family members may also be invited. As can be expected, the participants frequently have differing relationships with the person and often hold highly divergent views. With these multiple viewpoints, the image of the individual becomes increasingly intricate, and a better understanding of the uniqueness of the case evolves.

Within clusters dealing with adult multiple offenders, there is less optimism for a positive outcome, and the approach tends to lean towards getting troublesome individuals off the street by punitive means. Many cases in this cluster involve drug or alcohol abuse, and individuals often have a history of mental health problems. Frequently, they have exhausted a range of legal measures without much improvement. As the severity of their offences rarely justifies longer-term imprisonment, many of these individuals continue to commit petty crimes and cause a public nuisance. One of the more common measures suggested for these cases involves the Institution for Persistent Repeat Offenders (*Inrichting voor Stelselmatige Daders* or ISD).[12] Through an ISD, an individual committing even a petty crime is kept off the streets for two years while receiving treatment in a closed institution. While in many cases participants around the cluster table view this as an appropriate measure, it is the duty of the representative of the Public Prosecution Service to inform them about the limitations of this approach. Indeed, where many resources have already been exhausted and where there appears to be little belief in the opportunity for positive change, the preferred measures tend to be punitive rather than preventive (see Box 2).

Box 2: Hunting 'em Down

PSCs are thought to play a central role in dealing with multiple offenders causing a nuisance and committing petty crime. "That's where the PSC comes in...," says a representative from a mental health care organization, "...to deal with those cases that fall in between—people who are not really criminals but cause a lot of nuisance. For example, people who are constantly drunk and walk around the train station, talking to people, urinating in public and then yelling at the police when approached. Those people are thus the target...those causing offences that don't justify long [prison] sentences. [...] You know, the legal system is not set up to deal with that kind of stuff." A common practice in dealing with this is to ask particular neighbourhood police officers to pay extra attention to these individuals; in essence, to "hunt" them down.

The primary intention of this practice is to reduce the number of offences these individuals commit. In practice, however, it often means that the individuals simply get caught for committing offences more frequently than before. As a consequence, they build up an extensive list of offences with the police, which is subsequently passed on to the PSC. When reviewed at the PSC, these individuals are seen as major obstacles to social safety and, lacking alternative instruments, a stay at an Institution for Persistent Repeat Offenders is often recommended.

Bounded Innovation

In addition to applying the tools at hand from a multi-actor perspective, dealing with problems at PSCs often involves thinking beyond standard procedures and existing measures. While the absence of a clear structure and the vague definitions of tasks allow space for developing new approaches, the extent of innovation is unsurprisingly limited by existing rules and regulations governing work in the public sector. But even working within administrative and legal frameworks, new interpretations do take shape. One successful way of dealing with a problem that has been attributed to co-operation at the PSCs is the approach to post-incarceration care and prevention.[13] Where individuals used to be released from prison with little more than a train ticket in hand, participants at PSCs are now co-ordinating action to provide a decent living for ex-convicts, including making housing arrangements, assisting in finding employment and, if necessary, providing counselling. These improved services are thought to reduce recidivism and thus contribute to public safety through prevention.

Another example of a non-traditional measure conceived at a PSC is the "discouraging talk." These involve high-risk youths with little evidence of criminal activity who are invited to the police station for a one-on-one discussion. Once in conversation, the police reveal that they have been told that the youth is involved in illegal activities and is being monitored. Furthermore, the youth is "considered warned," told to stay away from such business and cautioned that the "discouraging talk" will be taken into consideration should the rumours turn out to be true. In having these talks, it is assumed that the behaviour of the high-risk youth will change for the better, and safety will be improved through prevention. Whether these talks have any effect is uncertain, but their existence shows a desire to develop and try out new approaches to deal with uncertainty.

The ability and willingness to experiment at PSCs is largely due to the space given for such ventures, combined with the multiple perspectives and resources available through participating representatives. It is also due in part to the status of a PSC as something of a last resort. As one participant mused, "If we are not able to deal with it, who is?"

Performing Networks

The networks associated with the PSCs are neither stable nor static; they need continual and considered action by participants to function effectively. One ongoing task of participants is to ensure that the work adds value to the partner organizations, given their ongoing investment of resources. Likewise, representatives are expected to ensure their organization's work has visibility and contributes to the objective of social safety through effective co-operation with other organizations. The first step involves getting to know the competences, cultures and limitations of other organizations. In taking this step, sharing a physical location seems to contribute to a positive experience of co-operation.

Creating a Common Language

In anticipation of critique from adversaries, PSC proponents frequently claim that they are "not just talking, but *doing*." In fact, much of the time at PSCs is spent talking. But talking *is* doing, to the extent that information and experience is shared and networks are created, strengthened and maintained. A high percentage of time at the PSCs is dedicated to meetings and, as well, there is quite a lot of unscheduled, informal interaction between representatives of partner organizations. Almost all representatives consulted for this study mentioned the possibility of "just walking in next door to speak with someone" from a partner organization as one of the immediate and most obvious benefits of participating in the PSC. Although everyday interaction seems to fill an important function at PSCs, the peak of information-sharing takes place at the cluster tables, where concrete cases are discussed and analyzed, and where organizations come together for a shared purpose.

While sharing information is an essential component of building trust between participants, this is not enough to create a functional network. Beyond information-sharing, the common effort to identify problems and articulate some form of shared objective seems to play a vital role in grounding co-operation. Part of this process involves developing a common language among participants (see Box 3). With backgrounds in various disciplines and different organizational cultures, it

Box 3: An Open Exchange of Information?

At times, tensions that arise at the PSCs may be the cause of diminishing trust between representatives. An enduring challenge is to determine what information on individual cases is relevant and whether it should be shared. This challenge was evident at an event that centred on a PSC a few years back.

A youth committed a serious offence that gained a great deal of media attention. When the matter escalated, the youth regretted his action and told a youth worker that he wanted to tell the truth. This youth worker, a PSC participant, told the other participants around a cluster table (including a police officer) that he knew who the perpetrator was and that the youth wanted to tell the truth. An agreement was made to let the youth speak with one of the municipality's aldermen before reporting to the police station. At the last moment, the youth changed his mind. At this point, however, the police officer from the cluster table had already informed his supervisors of the plan. When the plan changed, the police officer was ordered to identify the youth worker involved. The youth worker was taken in to the police station and during interrogation he revealed information that the youth had given him in confidence. As can be expected, this event severely strained the trust between the participants and also damaged the youth's trust in the youth worker.

Most PSCs have set up privacy covenants to prevent situations like this. In practice, however, the extent of information-sharing appears to present an ongoing dilemma. Whereas it may be possible to clearly regulate information relating to criminal activity, the matter becomes increasingly difficult when dealing with information concerning the mental health of individuals. Participants are left to act upon their own judgment.

may prove difficult for participants to reach the understanding necessary for co-operative relationships. But with time, willingness and focused effort, participants may strengthen their bonds by developing collective knowledge expressed in a similar understanding of concepts, ambitions and visions.

Building Personal Relationships

Linked to the creation of a common language among representatives at PSCs are the individuals' roles as translators between organizations. While representatives need to develop the skill to communicate the intricacies of their own organization to other participants in the PSCs on the one hand, they also need to communicate effectively the activities, agreements and decisions in the other direction. Representatives' performance in this role is critical for the functioning of the network, as they constitute the connecting lines. In practice, this communication role entails a careful balance between complying with their organization's culture and structure, and meeting the demands for flexibility and dedication to the PSC.

With each organization having only a few representatives, people get to know one another more easily, which improves the performance of the networks. The fact that most participants meet frequently (often daily and at least weekly) helps create and maintain relationships, and deepens the understanding of each other's actions or lack of action. When organizations have direct links through personal connections at the PSCs, it is easier to hold other organizations accountable for agreements made.

All for One...

Another essential component in the performance of networks at PSCs is the principle that all organizations participate on equal terms and through non-hierarchical relationships. This may prove difficult in practice, as some organizations have more resources, some representatives have stronger mandates or there may be histories of strained organizational relationships. One way the PSCs have promoted equality is to let participants from different organizations function as chairpersons during cluster meetings, thereby attempting to avoid the establishment of hierarchical relationships among participants. As the function of the network depends on voluntary co-operation, the full commitment of all participants is in everyone's best interest. By discouraging forms of organizational hierarchy, co-operation seems more likely to occur.

CONCLUDING REFLECTIONS

The first PSC emerged as a collaborative network at the local level and, with political and academic support, developed into a concept that was implemented in various contexts. The story raises the questions of whether a network can be designed and implemented and, if so, what considerations should be made.

As a phenomenon, the PSC can be viewed as a new form of governance network emerging from interactions around concrete problems at the local level. Conversely, it can be viewed as a policy instrument intended to remedy organizational deficiencies in the public sector. Although both views can be argued validly, tension arises when attempting to formalize an emerging development at the policy level. In this process, the practices of particular individuals in particular settings have been integrated with policy objectives and transferred and transformed into solutions for different problems. Despite attempts to formalize these networks, they remain unstable because they depend on loose relationships among individuals. These relationships, however, may serve to strengthen anticipative and adaptive capacity within the PSCs.

Because PSC networks are unstable and non-static, they require careful negotiation. In the absence of organizational structures, co-operation ultimately depends on individual participants' capacity to create and maintain mutually beneficial relationships by generating trust in and knowledge of other partners. Acting as organizational links, participants fulfill a translating function in the networks and bridge different organizational cultures, core businesses and competencies. In this sense, the networks are continually maintained by the individual actors, who must balance the integrity of their organization with the needs within the network.

An apparent strength of the PSCs is the opportunity to collectively pursue creative approaches to problems identified through co-operation—a strength that may be enhanced by the absence of routine and stability. Stabilizing the networks could limit the uniqueness of approaches at PSCs and consequently undermine their value. At the same time, PSCs depend on voluntary partnerships with formal organizations connected through individual representatives. The lack of stability puts increased pressure on these participants. Balancing the need for flexibility within the networks and the integrity of participating organizations is an ongoing issue.

Another issue is the challenge of providing discernable and clear results. Until now, PSCs have largely been spared performance targets, however, it is just a matter of time before demands to legitimize expenses arise. It is indeed very difficult to indicate the performance of PSCs, given their stated objectives of facilitating collaboration around specific problems and contributing to broadly defined policy goals, such as providing public safety. PSCs have no mandate of their own and rely on the work undertaken by partner organizations for their achievements. The essence of a PSC is co-operation, but how can co-operation be measured? All or any of the organizations involved could claim that their actions are responsible for reducing crime and public nuisance. It is unfeasible to isolate the actual effect of a single PSC, let alone all PSCs. This attribution problem, however, does not mean that attempts to show effect have not been made. Until now, a small number of evaluations of individual PSCs have portrayed the entire phenomenon as both effective and successful.[14]

Participants will also want performance indicators to justify their ongoing participation. Whatever the measurement of performance, it has to give partner organizations a sense of the value of their participation. Furthermore, an indication of effective performance could give individual representatives recognition that their efforts do make a difference, and thereby give impetus for continued endeavours within PSCs.

Chapter 12

Victorian Bushfire Reconstruction and Recovery Authority: A Case Study on Agility and Resilience

State Services Authority[1]
Government of Victoria

The Victorian Bushfire Reconstruction and Recovery Authority (VBRRA) was established in February 2009 as a time-limited government agency in the state of Victoria charged with co-ordinating the initial two-year phase of recovery and reconstruction following the most devastating bushfires in Australia's history. The scale and urgency of the recovery task created an imperative for public sector agility and responsiveness that involved VBRRA taking on high priority operational roles in a complex operating environment that crossed jurisdictional, portfolio and sectoral boundaries. The VBRRA's recovery and reconstruction framework puts local communities at its centre. Community-led recovery presents challenges, including time costs and resource costs for building capacity. However, its rewards lie in better decision making and stronger community recovery. Community-led recovery also has the potential to strengthen the resilience of communities and their capacity to foresee and adapt to future challenges.

This case study was prepared in March 2010 and examines the VBRRA at the halfway point of its two-year operating timeframe. This means that the full story of the organization is not yet known. Nevertheless, the VBRRA's rapid start-up and eventful first year provide a useful starting point for a conversation about public administration in complex operating environments, public sector agility, governance and operating challenges, and building community resilience.

ABOUT VICTORIA AND GOVERNMENT IN AUSTRALIA

Australia has three levels of government: Commonwealth (national), state and local. The Australian Constitution establishes a federal system of government and defines the boundaries of law-making powers between the Commonwealth and the states.[2]

Victoria is a state within the Commonwealth of Australia. Victoria has its own state Constitution and can make laws on any subject related to the state. The state government is responsible for a wide range of services including policing, emergency services, public schools, roads and traffic, public hospitals, public housing and business regulation. The Premier is the head of the Government of Victoria.

Within Victoria, there are 79 local government councils. These councils are established and operate under state laws. Councils provide a diverse range of services, including property, economic, human, recreational and cultural services. They also enforce state and local laws relating to matters such as land use planning, environment protection, public health and traffic management.[3]

THE 2009 BUSHFIRES IN VICTORIA

With a week of extreme heat and a day of unprecedented fire danger approaching, the Premier of Victoria had warned that 7 February 2009 would be the "worst day in the history of the state."[4] But the unanticipated scale of the devastation that followed shocked the entire nation. Black Saturday's fires claimed the lives of 173 people. Many others were injured. Communities were traumatized. Homes, businesses and townships were destroyed.

Police Chief Commissioner Christine Nixon's planned retirement was only weeks away when her police helicopter landed in Marysville. Looking around, she observed absolute devastation. Days before, the resort town had been a popular tourist destination. But now, most of the houses in the town and its commercial hub had been destroyed.

Standing on the steps of the Marysville emergency command post, Premier John Brumby asked Christine Nixon what she planned to do in her retirement. Although the Premier already knew the answer, he and the Prime Minister had a new proposal. "I'd like to ask you," said the Premier, "would you run the reconstruction and recovery authority?"

Christine Nixon accepted the job. It was clear that an enormous reconstruction and recovery task lay ahead. The full extent of the tragedy was only just becoming apparent. Grieving and traumatized communities—people who had lost family, friends, homes and livelihoods—would face the daunting prospect of rebuilding. See Box 1 for the full impact of the 2009 bushfires.

Box 1: Impact of the 2009 Bushfires[13]

By the time the 2009 Victorian bushfires were contained:
- 173 people had died and many more had been injured;
- almost 430,000 hectares of forests, crops and pasture were destroyed or affected;
- more than 2,000 properties were destroyed; another 1,400 were damaged;
- over 55 businesses destroyed and many hundreds significantly impacted;
- three primary schools and three children's services destroyed, with 47 primary schools partially damaged or requiring cleaning;
- more than 5,000 households accessed case management assistance;
- 366 households required direct housing assistance and up to 500 households assisted into the private rental market;
- over 420 km of arterial roads had been damaged;
- over 10,000 kilometres of fencing had been damaged (private, road and Crown land boundaries, and internal), the equivalent of two return trips from London to Moscow;
- over 11,000 farm animals had been killed or injured;
- an estimated 1,000,000 wildlife were lost;
- over 3,550 agricultural facilities, including dairies, hay, wool and machinery sheds had been damaged;
- around 211,000 tons of hay had been lost;
- 70 national parks and reserves, 950 local parks, 467 cultural sites, more than 200 historic places were damaged; and
- the electricity supply to 60,000 households was cut.

VICTORIAN BUSHFIRE RECONSTRUCTION AUTHORITY: EARLY ESTABLISHMENT

Fires were still burning when the Victorian government established the VBRRA three days after Black Saturday. The VBRRA is responsible for co-ordinating the restoration and recovery of regions, towns and communities affected by the 2009 Victorian bushfires. Given the massive scale of the disaster, this involves overseeing the largest rebuilding program in the state's history. The bushfires affected 109 communities in 25 of Victoria's 79 local government municipalities. See Box 2 for the VBRRA's terms of reference. An overview of the VBRRA's institutional and governance arrangements is in the "governance challenges" section of this case study.

Box 2: Victorian Bushfire Reconstruction and Recovery Authority Terms of Reference[14]

1. Advise governments, co-ordinate efforts and develop an overarching plan for the restoration and recovery of regions, towns and communities affected by the 2009 bushfires.
2. Work closely with the communities in the process of rebuilding and recovery, and ensure that individuals and communities are consulted closely—with such consultations to be transparent and sensitive to local needs.
3. Analyze and advise governments on the impact of the bushfires on the communities, economy, infrastructure and environment in affected areas.
4. Co-ordinate activities and the work of relevant organizations to help regions, towns and individuals re-establish their communities once it is safe to do so, and in a way that is respectful of individual and community needs.
5. Ensure that services to affected people are easily available and co-ordinated across all levels of government and community organizations.
6. Work with communities to develop co-ordinated plans to deal with the effects of the disaster on local economies, communities, infrastructure and the environment. These plans should cover the immediate recovery requirements and longer-term development.
7. Have overall responsibility for ensuring that communities are rebuilt and projects are delivered quickly and efficiently.
8. Work closely with all funding sources, including the Red Cross Victorian Bushfire Appeal Fund, to ensure effective and co-ordinated expenditure of funds.
9. Report to the Premier of Victoria and consult with the Commonwealth Government as required on reconstruction and recovery efforts.
10. Report regularly on progress to both governments and to communities.

Initially, with just a handful of people, the VBRRA commenced its co-ordination and leadership role with limited resources, but also with enormous resolve and goodwill. Offers of help were immediately forthcoming. Individuals and organizations stepped forward to equip the new organization, setting up office space, computers and information systems. Public service departments and private sector businesses provided experienced and capable staff with expertise in policy, planning, logistics, media, information technology, communications, small business, local government, service systems and the natural environment.

In the early days and weeks after Black Saturday, the VBRRA worked alongside dedicated emergency response, recovery and relief agencies. Access to water, food, clothing, medical treatment and shelter were immediate priorities, as was the restoration of essential services. Scores of agencies had already mobilized. The state's police, fire and emergency services agencies were supplemented with personnel from the Australian Defence Force as well as from federal, interstate and overseas agencies. Government, volunteer and community sector organizations administered medical treatment, paid emergency relief grants, arranged temporary accommodation, managed public health and safety risks, and established a registration and inquiry system to record and account for those affected by the fires.

The scale and urgency of the recovery task created an imperative for public sector agility and responsiveness. There was little room within the VBRRA's internal structures for hierarchy. The organization's structure was flat, with six teams reporting to the chief executive and chairperson. Information was shared freely and decisions were made swiftly. Christine Nixon used the daily meetings to update staff on what had happened the day before—where she had been, whom she had spoken to and what resources she had committed. VBRRA staff managed the interface back to federal and state government agencies to follow up on these commitments, which ranged from insurance issues to counselling needs.

Daily staff meetings set the agenda for the upcoming 24 hours. Staff focused on immediate priorities: What is the issue? What is its status? What decision needs to be taken today to make the day productive? Each team would raise issues, and a discussion and decision would follow. All issues were registered in an issues log. The issues log gave staff three timeframe options for dealing with each issue: 24, 48 or 72 hours.

Each daily meeting's objective was to give people enough authority to take action. Staff did not need to go away and write a brief to get something approved. Decisions were made. If they were wrong, they were fixed. VBRRA Interim Chief Executive Jeff Rosewarne emphasized, "The one thing we didn't want was delay or a sense that no one was in a position to make a decision."

The VBRRA's early days and weeks were characterized by rapid organizational activity. The VBRRA convened decision-making and advisory groups, met with local governments, built a website for public information, engaged communities in a series of open meetings and established a media presence. The VBRRA needed to bring together the people who would undertake lead roles in recovery and reconstruction—from the Premier to individual members of the 109 affected communities.

The VBRRA supported a range of decision-making and advisory groups. These included the Bushfire Reconstruction and Recovery Committee of Cabinet comprising state and federal ministers; an interdepartmental committee of departmental secretaries; an interagency taskforce of senior officials; an expert reference group, including non-government agencies; an industry champions group; and local community recovery committees.

RECOVERY AND RECONSTRUCTION FRAMEWORK

With the adoption of a recovery and reconstruction framework, the VBRRA developed a more long-term and strategic approach to its activities. The framework puts local communities at its centre around which it encompasses four elements: people, reconstruction, economy and environment. The framework recognizes the interdependencies of local community recovery with each of these four elements. Figure 1 shows the framework and the guiding principles that underpin the VBRRA's activities.

Figure 1: *Recovery and Reconstruction Framework*

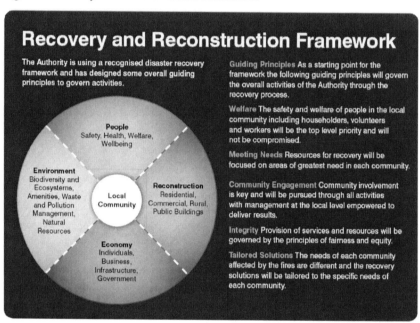

Source: VBRRA, 12 Month Report, 2009, p. 3

The framework provides a structured and interactive approach to recovery and reconstruction, keeping the needs and aspirations of local communities at its centre. Both the framework and the VBRRA's terms of reference (see Box 2) involve working with communities, three tiers of government, departments and other organizations to develop co-ordinated plans for recovery and reconstruction. This includes supporting community recovery committees in developing plans for their local area and co-ordinating a Statewide Plan for Bushfire Reconstruction and Recovery.

COMMUNITY-LED RECOVERY

The VBRRA made an early commitment that communities and individuals would have the opportunity to participate in their own recovery and rebuilding process. Each local community would be supported in identifying issues of local concern and in developing plans to address those issues. This approach was designed to maximize opportunities for communities to determine their futures.

Over a two-month period, the VBRRA held or attended 29 community meetings. These meetings were open events. They provided a forum for individuals and communities to raise issues and concerns and for government, through the VBRRA, to listen.

Community members used the meetings to pose questions to VBRRA. These questions ranged from the general (What is VBRRA?) to the specific (How can you help resolve this problem with my bank?). Other questions sought information on the reliability of rumours that had begun to circulate (Is it true that the drinking water is unsafe and that the government is going to cancel the football season?). Publicly airing and settling rumours provided an opportunity for the VBRRA to reassure the community.

VBRRA representatives needed to establish credibility with communities. If they did not know the answer to a question, they would admit it and offer to find out. Where individuals or communities raised issues not within the control of government, the VBRRA took an advocacy role. For example, bushfire-affected households raised concerns with the VBRRA about issues with private sector companies such as insurers, banks and utility providers. While the VBRRA had no formal authority over private businesses, it could at least ensure that every insurer, bank and utility provider heard the problem and understood the community's position. VBRRA staff would make phone calls on behalf of bushfire-affected residents. Companies would at least take their call, listen and consider the concern.

Community Recovery Committees

As part of emergency management arrangements in Victoria, each bushfire-affected community was encouraged to establish a community recovery committee. In some areas, this model was quickly enacted. Indeed, some of the 25 local government councils affected by the fires were already establishing and supporting citizen-based groups. Other councils preferred to operate through municipal-level emergency recovery structures that did not necessarily have broad-based participation models or membership from each location within the municipality.

The VBRRA did not have formal powers to enforce its preferred model. Rather, it relied on relationships, education, conversation and influence to advance its preference. This proved largely successful. The VBRRA remains clear that it is engaging with communities through citizen-based and local community recovery committees.

The VBRRA continues to work with 33 community recovery committees. Each committee provides community leadership for recovery and reconstruction in its local area. The committees work alongside other agencies, including regional recovery committees, the VBRRA, local councils, government departments, and other local groups.

Community recovery committees have prepared 30 community recovery plans. These plans identify ideas, needs and proposed projects that will help each local community recover. Over 1,000 proposed projects cover all aspects of recovery: personal health and well-being, built and natural environment, business and economy, and community strength and well-being. Projects range in their scale, complexity, timeframe and urgency. They include rebuilding community facilities, improving local infrastructure, holding social events and well-being programs, restoring sport and recreation facilities, installing fire safety systems and restoring parks and habitat.

Community recovery committees and plans represent a departure from well established models of government-community consultation. The VBRRA provided guidance and templates for developing and refining the plans. However, each community recovery committee set its own priorities and retained complete and uncensored authorship over its plans. Each recovery committee tapped into its own local organizations and networks to generate support for its plan.

The VBRRA incorporated projects identified by communities into a state plan. The plan brings a co-ordinated approach to recovery and reconstruction that crosses jurisdictional, portfolio and geographic boundaries. The state plan is funded by the Government of Victoria, the Commonwealth Government, the Victorian Bushfire Appeal Fund[5] and other donors. The VBRRA is working with communities to further develop the projects featured in the state plan, helping solve problems and ensure that communities are well placed to deliver the projects on time and in accordance with community expectations. This means that communities are supported to deliver on their own priorities. VBRRA Community Engagement Teams also work with community recovery committees to identify alternative options for developing, funding and delivering projects that have not been incorporated into the state plan.

Challenges and Rewards of Community-led Recovery

The VBRRA's commitment to community-led recovery was not without challenges. Community participation models can incur time and resource costs. Decision making through community consensus can be slower than through individual agencies. Rather than immediately replacing schools, kindergartens, fire stations and other infrastructures precisely as they were, community-led recovery leads to broader debate about how infrastructure should be redeveloped. In some cases, this can lead to replacement facilities that are different from the original infrastructure.

Achieving consensus within diverse communities was challenging, particularly for many individuals who were recovering from traumatic experiences of survival and grieving over the loss of family, friends and property. Furthermore, some communities were working together for the first time and had little or no experience of government processes. They may not have previously been involved in running meetings, engaging stakeholders, resolving issues, scoping projects, managing consultancies and developing formal plans. This meant they needed to develop these capabilities through the bushfire recovery planning process.

The rewards of community-led recovery can outweigh its challenges. People recover better when they can engage in their own recovery process.[6] Giving decision-making capacity back to individuals and communities is fundamental to restoring a sense of empowerment and control. This is why the VBRRA sought to create participation opportunities for all individuals and communities who were able and wanting to engage.

Participative models of recovery can lead to better results. Communities made decisions that might not have happened if government had immediately commenced rebuilding public infrastructure. For example, communities have said, "Wouldn't it be great to have the primary school and kindergarten right next door to each other rather than down the road?" These kinds of suggestions can lead to time-consuming debate. Yet these debates are fruitful more often than not. They can result in solutions that might not have emerged in a process imposed from outside the community.

Marysville and Triangle Urban Design Framework

The development of an Urban Design Framework for the town of Marysville illustrates the challenges and rewards of a participative recovery model. Rebuilding Marysville has been the subject of extensive consultation and heated debate. Nine months after the fires, the new Marysville and Triangle Urban Design Framework was released. The framework sets out a long-term vision for rebuilding and linking the town with neighbouring communities in Buxton, Taggerty, Narbethong and Granton. See Box 3 for an overview of the framework, previously published in the Statewide Plan for Bushfire Reconstruction and Recovery.

Box 3: Rebuilding Marysville[15]

The once-thriving resort town of Marysville was devastated in the bushfires: 34 people lost their lives, and the main street and town centre were almost completely destroyed.

Four further fatalities occurred in nearby Narbethong, and some 538 properties were destroyed by the Murrindindi fire.

The task of rebuilding Marysville and surrounding communities is a formidable one, but it is taking shape as the clean-up is completed, people return to the town and the community focuses on its future.

In September, following extensive community consultation, Premier John Brumby, Federal Parliamentary Secretary Bill Shorten, Murrindindi Mayor Lyn Gunter and VBRRA Chairperson Christine Nixon released the new Marysville and Triangle Urban Design Framework, which sets out a long-term vision for rebuilding the town.

The framework provides design guidelines for developing Marysville as a safer, more sustainable town with a distinct character that complements the surrounding environment. The framework includes plans for an iconic new town centre; a new community hub that incorporates a primary school, a children's centre, health services and recreation facilities; the rebuilding of the police station, petrol station and general store; better links with other Triangle communities; and the reinstatement and expansion of the oak tree landscape.

The Statewide Plan for Bushfire Reconstruction and Recovery funds the next phase of this process, including detailed master plans for five key areas in the town (the "heart of Marysville," the main street and business hub, the remainder of Marysville, Gallipoli Park and the community hub site); civil engineering and technical assessments for sites and projects; and detailed project briefs for reconstruction projects that will be managed by the VBRRA, the local council, government agencies and community groups.

While this planning and consultation process continues, work is proceeding on a number of rebuilding projects that conform to the framework, including the redevelopment of the Marysville Motor Museum site, a new Rebuilding Advisory Centre and the restoration of community and visitor facilities.

The development of the Urban Design Framework allowed the community to discuss how Marysville should be rebuilt. Extensive community consultation enabled people to participate and have their say about the future design of their town. For example, the framework sets aside a lot on the corner of the main street to become the "Marysville Heart." Before the fires, this land was occupied by the police station. Had government prioritized efficient replacement of infrastructure over community participation, the police station would likely once more be located on one of the best lots in the centre of town. Instead, the police agreed to give up that lot for the "Marysville Heart" and rebuild the police station elsewhere.

The community determined that the "Marysville Heart" will be a precinct where people can gather. It will be a focal point for the local community and for visitors. The details for the precinct are yet to be decided. The community needs time to decide how to realize its aspirations and achieve an appropriate mix of business, cultural and social activities on the site. The participative recovery model continues to offer to communities support and time to recover in their own way and at their own pace.

Building Community

In some areas, one of the less tangible benefits of community-led recovery has been the creation of a civic spirit. Tony Ferguson, Chair of the Hazelwood-Jeeralang Community Recovery Committee, noted that, "Before the fires, we were just a locality…For the most part, we knew our immediate neighbours but that was pretty much it…The future is brighter now as the community is much tighter. You now find that more people have the time for a chat on the side of the road. That's got to be good."[7]

The value of community spirit is difficult to quantify. However, its effects are nevertheless real. It means that working as part of the community is individually rewarding as well as collectively productive. It means that communities are better equipped to lead their recovery, drawing on their own resources as well as support from government and from other organizations.

OPERATIONAL CHALLENGES

Although the VBRRA is primarily a co-ordinating body, it also undertook operational responsibilities, including three of five "extraordinary" commitments extending beyond government's usual areas of activity. These were establishing systems for managing material aid and donations; overseeing the clean-up of sites destroyed by the bushfires; and constructing temporary villages in three townships.

The Department of Human Services (DHS) is leading the government's two other extraordinary commitments. These are a case management service for every affected household and the establishment of ten community service hubs to serve as one-stop-shops for services including financial support, housing and counselling. Over 5,000 households have accessed the case management service. The DHS has played a significant leadership role in bushfire recovery efforts and is one of the VBRRA's key partners in managing co-ordinated recovery efforts.

The VBRRA's operational responsibilities centre on those activities that do not have a logical "fit" within existing agencies' core business, so its broad terms of reference provide the flexibility to take on operational roles as required. This includes the three extraordinary roles mentioned above and outlined in the sections on "Clean-up," "Material Aid and Donations" and "Temporary Villages" below. It also includes other initiatives, such as providing free portable showers and toilets to people living in temporary accommodation on their land while they rebuild. This allows a degree of agility to respond to community needs as they arise and to shape recovery efforts in accordance with these needs. It enables the VBRRA's role to evolve as needs emerge and change over time.

Clean-up

Senior staff at the VBRRA consider the clean-up operation as one of the agency's most notable successes. Three weeks after the fire, the government contracted private company Grocon to clear debris from thousands of properties. A considerable break from usually protracted procurement procedures and negotiations, the VBRRA progressed from preparing a request for tender document to a signing a contract within six days.

Grocon cleared all properties that owners wanted cleared. Wherever possible, the clean-up operation engaged local contractors, with 69 percent of work undertaken by non-metropolitan contractors located within or close to affected areas. The operation cleared 3,053 properties in four and a half months (almost two months ahead of schedule), removing 400,000 tons of material. This involved clearing up to 300 properties per week at the peak. It included a central role for the Environmental Protection Authority, which ensured the safe disposal of hazardous waste, including asbestos.

The clean-up program received considerably more praise than complaints. VBRRA staff consider this no small achievement in such emotionally fraught circumstances. Clean-up workers received psycho-social training so that they were prepared to work with families who had lost loved ones and experienced considerable trauma and loss. It was not the "tear down and build" job to which such contractors are more accustomed. Rather, the task was approached with the utmost sensitivity and respect.

If construction workers started to clean up a property and the owner asked them to stop for any reason—to save a rose bush, to give them more time to reflect—they stopped and waited. They avoided areas where family pets were buried. They preserved concrete slabs where children had pressed their hands. They retrieved precious items such as rings, watches and cufflinks.

Material Aid and Donations Management

Material Aid

People throughout Victoria, Australia and the world were shocked by the scale of destruction and wanted to help. They donated goods, which flooded into relief centres, community agencies and anywhere people thought they might be needed. Under existing emergency management arrangements, non-profit agencies were responsible for material aid distribution. However, these agencies were inundated by the unprecedented volume.

Head of Operations, Betsy Harrington, arrived at the VBRRA on the same day as six seconded staff from the Australian Defence Force. Their immediate task was to deal with 21,000 pallets of material aid. The Defence Force staff went on the road to study and analyze the situation. They wanted to know: What do we have? What is its value? Who needs it? Where is it" and Where should it be? The task was to match the needs of people with the donations—anything from clothing and household items to livestock and musical instruments.

Material aid presented logistical challenges. It needed to be managed, warehoused, sorted, stacked, transported and delivered. The VBRRA contracted a warehouse company to ensure that the bulk of the material aid was in one place and hired a logistics company to organize its transport. Teams of people—bank employees, Royal Australian Navy personnel and other volunteers—sorted through the goods. Regional distribution points were established. The VBRRA made arrangements with local non-profit agencies, setting up a simple process for them to know what was available and to ask people what they needed. Individuals and families were given the option to come to the main warehouse to collect material aid or to request its delivery.

When asked what could have been done differently, Betsy Harrington did not hesitate. "Early communications," she emphasized. Early communications would have encouraged potential donors to wait for information about what was needed and where it was needed.

Donations Management

The demand for some donated items outstripped supply. These included vouchers for department stores, furniture, homewares, airline travel and electronic goods. The VBRRA needed a system that was fair, equitable and manageable.

The VBRRA developed a needs-based donations management system. It was designed to meet client needs in a fair, equitable and timely manner in accordance with client and donor expectations. The system recorded what people needed, what was available and what had been given to whom. It included a "points system," which allocated 1,000 points to affected families. They could choose to "spend" their points as they wish on high-demand donated items. Points could be redeemed for store vouchers, airline travel and services, such as plumbing or architectural services. Popular items were released periodically through a ballot system. This recognized that some individuals needed more time than others to re-establish themselves and access donations. The ballot system avoided the exhaustion of high-demand items before everyone was ready.

Referral cards were issued to 6,000 affected individuals and families. This enabled easy accesses for cardholders to donated goods and services. People could also use the cards for other interaction with government agencies. The cards served as proof of their status as people affected by the fires and entitled to support services.

The VBRRA also delivered a "matching service" for high-value donations for community projects. This included asking communities what they wanted and turning the request into a scope document that could be taken to a corporate donor so a match could be made. Matching communities with donors was often complicated. Donors from the corporate and philanthropic sectors often have specific parameters for their contributions. In addition, community groups needed appropriate mechanisms to channel money and donated goods. They needed to have the right kind of tax and legal status. They also needed to have the capacity to manage money and projects. If the mechanisms or capacities were not in place, the VBRRA needed to find someone through whom donations could be channelled to the community. By March 2010, a total of 66 community projects had been supported in part or in full by a match.

Temporary Villages

The VBRRA constructed three temporary villages (Flowerdale, Kinglake and Marysville) and smaller temporary housing arrangements in Whittlesea. These areas were hardest hit by the bushfires and lacked sufficient housing for displaced individuals and families needing and wanting to remain in their communities. Victoria had no precedent for this kind of project. The VBRRA, a central agency of government, was confronted with the unique challenge of constructing the villages and equipping them for occupancy. The DHS manages the tenancies for the 253 temporary dwellings. This includes working with residents to transition them to secure permanent accommodation once the temporary villages close.

The VBRRA arranged access to land to construct the temporary villages. The villages include a mix of single, double and family moveable units. Constructing the villages went beyond providing sleeping quarters. It involved building communal cooking and family dining facilities, recreation space, laundries, showers, toilets, storage, pet facilities, storage and security.

Construction work used a mix of DHS knock-down buildings and donated and purchased goods and services. Buildings donated by BlueScope Steel, kitchens donated by Ikea and other assets will be handed over to local government councils for community use when the villages are decommissioned.

GOVERNANCE CHALLENGES

The VBRRA's operating environment is complex. It operates across jurisdictions, portfolios, sectors and geographically dispersed locations. One hundred and nine affected communities, each with its particular needs, are spread across 25 municipalities. The people in these communities experienced significant personal loss and trauma. They lost family members, neighbours and friends as well as homes, businesses and personal possessions.

The VBRRA continues to work in this complex environment without legislated powers to co-ordinate action for affected communities. The VBRRA is an administrative office of the Department of the Premier and Cabinet. This is an institutional form that can be established rapidly but does not necessarily come with legislative powers and functions. This means that the VBRRA must rely on partnerships, persuasion, negotiation and force of will to achieve consensus and co-ordination.

Four key factors enabled the VBRRA to operate effectively without statutory powers:
- Purpose and goodwill. Those involved in reconstruction and recovery efforts have a united purpose: to help affected communities recover and rebuild. There is widespread and genuine goodwill and dedication to achieving this purpose.
- Authorizing environment. The Premier and Prime Minister established an unequivocal authorizing environment. They consistently and publicly emphasized the importance of community-led recovery co-ordinated at a statewide level through the VBRRA.
- Leadership. The VBRRA's chairperson, Christine Nixon, has a well-established record of working with communities. She is also widely known and respected within the public sector. Her strong public profile strengthens the VBRRA's operating legitimacy.
- Budget. The VBRRA is the central co-ordinating body through which state budget decisions are channelled. Departments submit budget bids through the VBRRA as part of a co-ordinated package of initiatives. Local governments require access to state funding and resources to deliver recovery services and rebuild public infrastructure.

Strong working relationships are central to managing complex governance environments. For the VBRRA, this meant a lot of talking and listening. It meant creating the space to build relationships and have productive conversations with communities, state government departments, federal government departments, local government councils, business owners, non-profit agencies, corporate donors, insurance agencies, banks, lawyers, politicians, essential service providers, the building industry and the media.

VBRRA employees needed to become skilled at conversation, working with people and drawing on networks. This meant bringing everyone to the table, letting them know their help was needed and they were part of the solution. It meant asking the right questions of the right people and finding out what it would take to involve them. Building these relationships was not always easy. However, even when there was disagreement about decisions or processes, there was at least a shared recognition of an overarching objective to help affected communities recover and rebuild.

Relationship-building, although critical, was not always sufficient to meet governance challenges. In the absence of legislated powers and functions, the VBRRA needed an institutional mechanism to oversee recovery and reconstruction in the most severely affected municipality. The Shire of Murrindindi was the epicentre of Black Saturday's devastation. The fires killed 95 people in the shire and destroyed 1,242 properties. This amounted to significant individual and community trauma. It also meant a large volume of reconstruction projects at a time when local government services were stretched. In addition, the loss of so many properties substantially reduced the shire's capacity to raise revenue from ratepayers.

A special committee is managing bushfire reconstruction and recovery in the shire. Murrindindi Shire's Special Committee Responsible for Bushfire Recovery and Reconstruction has the delegated powers and duties of Murrindindi Shire Council under the *Local Government Act 1989*. A VBRRA representative chairs the committee, which also includes representatives from the DHS, the Department of Planning and Community Development and three members of the Murrindindi Shire Council. The committee provides a governance structure to co-ordinate and align policy, planning, community engagement, service delivery and reconstruction projects.

Committee meetings are open to the public. Each meeting agenda includes an open forum in which any recovery and reconstruction issues in the shire can be raised. Meeting agenda, papers and minutes are published on the council's website. Governance support through the committee is supplemented with a funded support package for recovery, which includes funding to build the necessary capabilities to deliver reconstruction projects within the shire.

What Is Resilience?

The New Synthesis of Public Administration contends that the ultimate role of government is to ensure a resilient society—that is, a society capable of adapting to unforeseen events. It envisages government working with individuals and communities to identify and mitigate vulnerabilities and build adaptive capacity.[8]

Resilience is the capacity to bounce back in the face of adversity. It refers to the ability to absorb disturbances and re-organize while undergoing change. The size of a shock that a system can absorb (without losing its fundamental purpose or identity) demonstrates its degree of resilience.[9]

Professor Bob Montgomery cites eight aspects of psychological resilience for individuals:

1. **Emotional awareness.** The ability to understand how an individual is feeling and why;
2. **Perseverance.** The ability to see things through and carry a greater than usual load in order to achieve goals;
3. **Internal locus of control.** A sense of being "in charge" rather than being a hopeless victim;
4. **Optimism.** A sense that there is a way out of the difficult situation;
5. **Social support.** The ability to tap into support;
6. **Sense of humour.** The ability to laugh even in difficult times;
7. **Perspective.** The ability not to be overwhelmed; and
8. **Spirituality.** A sense of spirituality (not necessarily religion).[10]

At a systems level, Professor Brian Walker notes that factors with a bearing on resilience include:

1. **Diversity.** Greater diversity mitigates vulnerability to single shocks;
2. **Modularity.** The impact of disturbances spreads less readily through modular systems than through intricately interconnected systems;
3. **Social capital.** Includes high levels of trust and leadership;
4. **Tight feedback.** Delays between a response and when the impact of the response is felt diminish resilience;
5. **Communication.** Includes inflow and outflow of information; and
6. **Overlapping institutions.** Sharing tasks across agencies rather than doing everything in one place.[11]

Resilience and the VBRRA

Individuals and communities in bushfire-affected areas are each recovering in their own time and in their own way. They continue to experience grief and trauma. Some have made decisions about their long-term future—whether to remain in affected areas or move on. Others are not yet ready to make those decisions.

One year on from the fires, it is possible to reflect on how the VBRRA's approaches to reconstruction and recovery co-ordination could have a lasting impact on community resilience. The VBRRA's emphasis on community-led recovery and local decision making has the potential to strengthen the communities' resilience and capacity to foresee and adapt to future challenges. This is consistent with the expectation that people recover better when they can participate and make decisions about their own recovery.[12]

Affected communities demonstrated their capacity to come together and plan for the future amidst unprecedented challenges. Communities worked together, in some cases for the first time, to collectively solve problems, debate issues and support each other to recover and rebuild. They demonstrated valuable skills in identifying issues, engaging stakeholders, setting priorities, developing plans, securing funding, working with public, private and non-profit agencies, and managing projects. These skills will likely equip communities to better meet future challenges.

In 2011, the VBRRA will withdraw from its central co-ordination role. It is currently developing transition plans so that communities, local government, state and federal departments and other agencies can continue to support long-term recovery and rebuild private and public infrastructure in its absence. Effective transition planning will be critical to ensure that case management, temporary housing, financial, health, planning and other forms of assistance leave individuals, households, community groups and local governments better equipped to manage their own long-term recovery. As services are gradually withdrawn or transition to more permanent arrangements, communities will need to be ready to adapt to these changes.

Rebuilding programs are well under way, but reconstruction will not be complete when the VBRRA ceases to exist. For this reason, the VBRRA has taken direct responsibility for only a limited number of reconstruction projects. The VBRRA's central role in reconstruction has been to ensure that households, communities and other organizations have the necessary capabilities to manage their own projects. Many of these projects have been highly challenging relative to their scale. Communities needed to establish consensus, engage with stakeholders, draw on multiple funding sources, co-ordinate pro bono services, use a mix of purchased and donated materials and adhere to new building standards. The scale of this challenge was magnified by the personally difficult circumstances of many members of the communities.

Communities affected by the bushfires require the resilience and capacity to lead their own long-term recovery. These communities continue to confront challenges arising from the bushfires. Central among the challenges for communities and government is addressing mental health and well-being needs, generating economic recovery and new jobs, and ensuring that communities are well prepared and protected for future fire seasons.

CONCLUSION

The VBRRA is government's central co-ordinating agency working with local communities to oversee the initial two-year phase of recovery and reconstruction from the most devastating bushfires in Australia's history. This large-scale effort crosses jurisdictional, portfolio, sectoral and geographic boundaries.

A clear sense of purpose and enormous goodwill has been central to the VBRRA's ability to operate in an environment of urgency and complexity. There is a genuine desire to support affected individuals, families and communities to recover and rebuild. This common purpose underpins new working relationships between the VBRRA and other agencies. It has been central to the VBRRA's capacity to respond with agility to emerging challenges, taking on both co-ordination and operational roles as required to anticipate and support communities' needs.

The VBRRA's focus on community-led recovery and local decision making is a building block for future resilience. There has been a strong emphasis on capacity building, engagement and decision making at the local level, even when this comes with time and resource costs. The VBRRA's level of success will become more apparent once the organization has reached its two-year sunset date. The degree to which communities are involved in decision making will likely determine how resilient and well-equipped they will be to continue to recover and plan for the future.

Chapter 13
Workfare In Singapore[1]

Koh Tsin Yen, Head (Social Strategy)
Social Programs, Singapore Ministry of Finance
Pamela Qiu, Researcher
Centre for Public Economics, Singapore Civil Service College

W orkfare is often thought to refer to the income supplement given to low-income workers to encourage them to stay in employment. It is more than that. In Singapore, Workfare embodies the philosophy that work is the best form of social assistance. People who are able to work should be helped to find a job and earn a salary that is enough to support them and their family. Manifested in concrete policies, Workfare reinforces the work ethic of Singaporeans and makes it worthwhile for anyone at the margin to offer up their labour to the economy.

The development of Workfare marks a milestone in the history of social assistance to low-income Singaporeans. When it was announced, it came as a surprise to some Singaporeans raised on a diet of strict anti-entitlement and anti-dependency rhetoric. However, Workfare is not a radical departure from the nation's policy approach: it reinforces the values of hard work and self-reliance that already exist in Singapore society. Workfare is first a pragmatic response to the effects of globalization and technology on wage stagnation and dispersion. Second, Workfare encourages the work ethic by providing incentives for working.

The case traces the evolution of Workfare in Singapore and illustrates Singapore's approach to policy making. Active scanning for policy ideas and experiences from around the world enabled Singapore's policy makers to adopt and adapt ideas to suit the local context. Testing the idea in incremental steps increased acceptance and enabled refinements along the way, eventually leading to policy innovation.

The case also explores the following elements of the New Synthesis Framework:
- The approach to building societal resilience by addressing the resilience of individuals and their families by encouraging work, enhancing employability and helping them grow assets for the future.
- The involvement of other stakeholders of society to achieve societal outcomes, such as encouraging citizens who are able to work to find employment, upgrading their skills to stay in employment and providing incentives to employers to

retain and re-train their employees.

- The use of early and multiple policy interventions at various levels: for example, a combination of income supplements, subsidies and a range of initiatives to increase opportunities for low-wage workers.

HOW IT ALL BEGAN...

The Context

The Asian financial crisis in 1998 and subsequent events (the global downturn in 2001, SARS in 2003) put an end to more than a decade of sustained non-inflationary growth and low unemployment in Singapore. Growth slowed and economic output shrank in real terms between 1998 and 2003. The resident unemployment rate jumped from an annual average of 2.0 percent in 1997 to 3.5 percent in 1998, and peaked at 5.2 percent in 2003. The number of retrenched workers (or those made redundant) tripled from 9,800 in 1997 to 29,100 in 1998. Net job creation was negative from 2001 to 2003 (see Table 1).

Table 1: *Economic Indicators (1998-2007)*

	1998	1999	2000	2001	2002	2003	2004	2005	2006	2007
Real change in GDP (%)	-1.4	7.2	10.1	-2.4	4.2	3.1	8.8	6.6	7.9	7.7
Unemployment rate (%)*	2.7	3.9	4.9	3.1	4.6	4.8	4.7	4.4	3.5	3.1
Net job creation ('000)	-23.4	39.9	108.5	-0.1	-22.9	-12.9	71.4	113.3	176.0	234.9

*Seasonally adjusted resident unemployment rate as at June.
Source: Department of Statistics, Singapore (www.singstat.gov.sg)

Singapore's income distribution, which was stable in the previous decade and improving before that, deteriorated sharply in the decade following the Asian financial crisis. A paper by the Department of Statistics (DOS) in 2005[2] revealed that real household incomes for the bottom two quintiles fell between 1998 and 2003 (the bottom 20 percent experienced the sharpest drop of 3.2 percent) even as they rose for those in the top 40 percent. This in stark contrast to the income growth for all households in the five years preceding the Asian crisis (see Table 2).

Table 2: *Change in Household Income (1993-2003)*

	Income (S$)			Average % change per annum	
	1993	1998	2003	1993-1998	1998-2003
All Households	857	1,298	1,457	8.7%	2.3%
Lowest 20%	240	304	281	4.8%	-1.6%
2nd Quintile	422	608	635	7.6%	0.9%
3rd Quintile	620	940	1,004	8.7%	1.3%
4th Quintile	929	1,424	1,572	8.9%	2.0%
Highest 20%	2,072	3,215	3,790	9.2%	3.3%

Source: Department of Statistics, Singapore, "Trends in Household Income and Expenditure," 2005

The widening wage gap was not peculiar to Singapore, but reflected global conditions. Growing labour mobility and the spread of technology, as well as the rise of China and India, contributed to polarizing the labour market, pushing up wages at the top and further depressing wages at the low end. There was the further concern that the most vulnerable low-wage workers were mostly older, had below secondary school-level qualifications and were ill equipped to succeed in the new economy.

Defining the Problem

Growing income inequality created tension in social policy. Since the 1960s, the government had warned against the dangers of a welfare state undermining economic growth and perpetuating high unemployment through its corrosive effects on the Singaporean work ethic. In 1998, as the impact of Asian economic crisis worked its way through the Singapore economy, then-Minister for Finance, Richard Hu, reiterated the government's position on welfare in the Budget Speech:

> The absence of large scale public assistance programs reflects the Government's stand on state welfarism. We believe that extensive welfare programs damage the fabric of our society as they diminish individual responsibility, self-reliance, community support and the work ethic. Even in the United Kingdom, the Government has realised that welfarism is not the right way to go, and is trying to roll back many of the welfare programs and policies introduced after the Second World War. Our approach is one of many helping hands, with co-funding from Government and public donations, and services rendered by volunteers and members of the community.[3]

Singapore's rejection of a welfare state was also based on the belief—backed by its own experience in the first 30 years of nationhood—that a rising tide would lift all boats, that people who were willing to work hard would be able to provide for their families, live in their own homes and give their children a better future. The widening income gap threatened this belief and challenged social cohesion. Then-Prime Minister, Goh Chok Tong, responding to concerns on income inequality, articulated the policy dilemma facing the government in his 2000 National Day Rally Speech:

> As a principle, we should not have measures that artificially raise the earnings of the lower-income Singaporeans. This will reduce the incentive for them to take the responsibility of improving their lot and that of their children. It will also turn away successful Singaporeans who are penalized for their achievements.
>
> That said, we cannot succeed as a nation if we operate strictly on the basis of every-man-for-himself. There would be no social cohesion if lower-income workers perceive that society is not willing to give them a helping hand to improve their lives. Or they fall so far down that they cannot afford even basic amenities.[4]

Contributing to the tension was a perception that foreign workers were taking jobs away from local workers and further depressing wages in low-skilled jobs. One option was to protect local workers and wages, either by restricting the influx of foreign workers or by enacting minimum wage legislation. Protectionism, however, would necessitate a radical overhaul of Singapore's social and economic policy. The latter is grounded on the need to keep Singapore competitive by keeping business costs low and increasing the skills and size of the labour force. A minimum wage policy would have introduced rigidities into the labour market at a time when the government was trying to enhance competitiveness by lowering wage costs through cuts in the employer Central Provident Fund (CPF) contribution rate and by diversifying the economy.[5] Foreign workers could boost growth in good times by providing the "full range and diversity of skills and experiences which the companies need[ed]"[6] and cushion the impact of job losses in bad times. As recently as June 2008, the National Trades Union Congress (NTUC) Secretary-General, Lim Swee Sway, felt compelled to remind Singaporeans that foreign workers, far from being a threat, were necessary to sustain economic growth.[7]

Nevertheless, something had to be done about low-wage workers. If the government would not adopt protectionist measures, then it had to consider redistributive measures. In introducing the first large-scale, one-off income redistribution program, the New Singapore Shares (NSS) scheme,[8] then-Prime Minister Goh laid the foundation for a "new social compact:"[9] the government would not shelter Singaporeans from global competition but would instead redistribute some of the benefits of economic growth to lower-income groups. The challenge was to find a way of doing so without "creating a dependency mentality among our people."[10]

The NSS scheme provided a piece of the puzzle, but was not in itself a permanent solution. It was deliberately conceived as an *ad hoc*, one-off scheme to avoid entrenching any expectation of handouts from the government. The problem of low-wage workers, on the other hand, appeared to be structural. Any long-term solution would have to include measures to enhance employability, raise incomes on a sustained basis and ensure that children were equipped with the skills needed to succeed in a more volatile and global economy.

Policy Options

The Ministerial Committee on Low Wage Workers was set up in June 2005 to recommend measures to improve employability and income security for low-wage workers and help their families break the cycle of poverty.

The Welfare Model: Hong Kong

One option was to enhance the financial assistance provided to unemployed workers and make such assistance conditional on job search and training efforts, such as expanding temporary programs like the Work Assistance Program set up in 2003 (later restructured into the Work Support Scheme). The idea was to minimize the disincentives associated with unemployment assistance work by reducing the welfare payment to a rate (known as the withdrawal rate) lower than 100 percent, so that every dollar the recipient earned from work would reduce the unemployment benefit by *less* than a dollar.

Hong Kong provided one example of such a system. High unemployment rates in the aftermath of the Asian financial crisis and again after SARS led to high welfare rolls at a time when government revenues were decreasing. In response, Hong Kong tightened eligibility conditions and imposed stricter work requirements for unemployed welfare recipients, first through the Support for Self-reliance (SFS) program in 1999, and then the Intensified SFS program in 2003. A system of disregarded earnings encouraged welfare recipients to work by phasing out the withdrawal of welfare benefits. These measures worked to some extent: from 2003 to 2005, the caseload for unemployed recipients in the Intensified SFS program dropped 5 percent annually, in contrast to other Comprehensive Social Security Assistance (CSSA) groups (such as single mothers, the disabled and the elderly) where caseloads *increased* 6 percent annually. Of the new applicants to the program, 40 percent returned to work within the month.[11]

The limited reforms in Hong Kong offer several lessons. First, the danger of entitlement creep was very real—even in a city characterized by Milton Friedman as the embodiment of free enterprise. "If you want to see capitalism at work, go to Hong Kong".[12] Second, reforms in Hong Kong did not do enough to strengthen incentives to work. Generous cash and healthcare benefits, even after the reforms, meant that a welfare recipient might quite rationally decide to remain on welfare rather than find a low-paying job.[13] Hong Kong's welfare program also required policing and enforcement to combat fraud. Applications were policed through intensive frontline screening, a whistle-blowing system for the public and a "risk management" approach for identifying potential fraud cases.

The Workfare Model: Wisconsin Works (W-2)

The 1996, American welfare reforms offered a radically different model to traditional welfare systems. One example of the new "welfare-to-work" system was the Wisconsin Works (W-2) program introduced in 1997, known for *both* its strict work requirements and its generous employment support package. The philosophy here was "pay more, demand more," as opposed to the "pay little, demand little" approach commonly found in traditional welfare systems and the "pay much, demand little" approach in European unemployment insurance systems.[14]

W-2 divided all participants into four tiers according to their readiness and ability to work. The idea was that all participants who *could* work *should* work. Participants who were able to take on market jobs were required to work, while participants who were able to work but lacked sufficient experience or regular work skills and habits were placed in trial jobs (wage-subsidized jobs) or community service jobs. Only participants who were not work-capable were not required to do so, though they were required to undergo training or perform basic jobs.[15]

In return for strict work requirements, participants who worked in market and trial jobs (the first two tiers) could receive earned income tax credits (EITC), which were payable once they had paid their income taxes. In addition to the federal tax credits, Wisconsin offered the highest state EITC for low-wage workers. It also mandated a minimum wage higher than the federal one. Cash grants were given only to participants who worked in community service jobs or who were unable to work because of severe barriers (the last two tiers), and this was subject to a maximum time period. All participants, including those in market jobs, qualified for a generous employment support package, which included healthcare benefits, job search and training assistance, co-payment for childcare services for low-income families, job access loans to help families meet immediate financial needs (such as car repairs or personal emergencies) and assistance with transportation to help parents get their children to daycare and themselves to work.[16]

W-2 proved remarkably successful in reducing the welfare rolls. The number of recipients receiving cash aid fell from 55,000 in 1996 to just over 10,000 in 2004, the largest decline experienced in the United States of America. Administrative data on case closures in the first two years of the program showed that more than 60 percent of the cases closed due to employment.[17]

However, the W-2 program was also criticized for its overwhelming concern with reducing welfare rolls and forcing participants into the job market at the expense of training and education programs that might increase the longer-term earning capacity of participants. A 2005 audit by the state Legislative Audit Bureau found that only about 20 percent of former participants earned more than the state poverty level in the year after they left W-2, although the proportion increased to 42 percent if the federal and state tax credits were included. The relatively high levels of recidivism in W-2 also suggest that the program was ineffective in increasing social mobility among needy families.[18]

Workfare in Singapore's Context

The W-2 experience offered several learning points for Singapore. Most importantly, it convinced policy makers that it was possible to provide institutionalized assistance to low-wage workers in a way that did not create disincentives to work or result in an overweening dependence on the state.

Welfare reforms elsewhere (as in Hong Kong) had focused on extending more help to welfare recipients and then providing incentives for them to return to work. But perversely, such efforts may have had the unintended effect of encouraging more people to be on welfare. The key insight of W-2 was that welfare recipients should not get a better deal than low-income individuals struggling on their own. More can be done for welfare recipients only if it is also done for other low-income individuals. In this way, government assistance does not create incentives for people to be on and stay on welfare.

Financial support and work requirements should not take the place of training and upgrading efforts, which are necessary to raise the longer-term earning capacity of workers and enable them to be self-reliant.

Support should not be limited to cash benefits or job search assistance, but should cover a range of services that support work, such as child care and healthcare. These benefits should be offered to all low-wage workers, not just welfare recipients.

The final report of the Ministerial Committee, published in January 2006, proposed Workfare as "a more effective alternative" to traditional welfare. The goal of Workfare is to ensure that all who can work find meaningful jobs and earn adequate wages to support themselves and their children. They should also be able to own their own homes, educate their children and put aside enough for their medical and retirement needs.[19]

Workfare is based on the principle that the government helps those who help themselves. To this end, the Committee outlined holistic approaches covering financial assistance for needy families, skills training and upgrading, expanding job opportunities, support for children from low-income families, surplus sharing schemes and financial support for low-wage workers.

MAKING INNOVATION POSSIBLE BY TAKING INCREMENTAL STEPS

One of the Committee's key recommendations was the Workfare Bonus Scheme (WBS). Although some studies had been done on the feasibility of introducing a wage supplementation scheme in Singapore, there was still some concern that a permanent income transfer program, however well intentioned, might create unintended distortions.

In announcing the details of the scheme in the 2006 Budget Statement, Prime Minister Lee warned that

> "...We should avoid creating permanent schemes unless we are very confident of how they will work. Instead, we should experiment with new schemes, see how they work out, and adjust and improve as we gain experience."[20]

The WBS was therefore conceived as a one-off scheme, though spread over two years and bundled with the rest of the Progress Package. It was targeted at older low-wage workers who were most vulnerable to structural changes in the economy. To encourage efforts at work, the bonus would be given only to workers who had worked for at least six months in the year of the payout. (See Annex A for details of the scheme.)

As the government had already given one-off cash transfers (for example, to offset increases in consumption tax rates or to provide short-term relief during economic slowdowns), the 2006 WBS was within the "possibility space" of current policy. On 1 May 2006, the first tranche of the Workfare Bonus was given to around 330,000 workers, at a cost of around S$150 million.

The smooth implementation of the WBS and the minimal evidence of abuse gave decision makers the confidence to make it permanent a year later. This was announced in the 2007 Budget Statement under the Workfare Income Supplement (WIS) scheme:

> The Workfare Income Supplement scheme is a major policy change. For the first time, the state will be supplementing the market wages that low-wage workers receive. But we have decided to make this change so as to help low-wage workers and encourage them to stay employed. This will strengthen social inclusion in Singapore.[21]

Between 2007 and 2009, the government paid out more than S$300 million to over 300,000 workers each year, which works out to about S$1,000 per worker, or 10 percent of income.

In 2010, the government further revised the WIS scheme. The income ceiling to qualify for WIS was raised from S$1,500 to S$1,700, widening the scheme's reach to 400,000 workers. The maximum payout was also increased from S$2,400 to S$2,800. (See Annex B for details of the WIS scheme and its 2010 revisions). The government also introduced a three-year Workfare Training Scheme (WTS) to complement the WIS scheme. The WTS provides 90-95 percent of absentee payroll and course fees to employers who send their older low-wage workers for training. In addition, WIS recipients receive a Training Commitment Award of up to S$400.

CONCLUSION

Workfare was a multifaceted approach to a global problem, customized to Singapore's unique social conditions and institutions. It was a creative attempt to combine elements of wage supplementation and subsidy models.

The approach involved multiple policy interventions coming together on multiple fronts to increase opportunities for low-wage workers so that they could support themselves and build up assets for the future. These changes were all based on coherent strategies (made possible by existing guiding principles of governance, such as the emphasis on self-reliance), the focus on achieving sustainable outcomes for the longer term (rather than adopting quick fixes that could create dependence on the state in the long run) and finally a whole-of-government framing rather than an agency-centric approach to achieving public results.

The policy-making process was enabled by the practice of active scanning for alternative models and learning from the experience of other countries, and adapting and contextualizing insight to Singapore's own challenges and needs. Innovation leaps did not happen overnight but through incremental steps, testing out the "adjacent possible" of existing policies and building on the go.

There are encouraging signs of Workfare's success. For example, WIS reaches over 300,000 workers. Each recipient receives an average of S$1,000 a year, which represents about 10 percent of their average annual income. This provides low-wage workers with assistance to help meet immediate needs and to build up savings for retirement.

Nevertheless, Workfare is still in its early days. The jury is still out on its success in meeting its other long-term objectives, such as facilitating social inclusion and providing income mobility across generations. These trends continue to be monitored.

Annex A
Workfare Bonus Scheme
(WBS)

ELIGIBILITY CRITERIA

Recipients are required to
- be Singapore citizens;
- be more than 40 years old;
- live in a property with an annual value (the estimated annual rent of the property, based on the market rents of comparable properties) of not more than S$10,000;
- have a monthly income of S$1,500 or less;
- have worked for at least six months in the calendar year; and
- sign up for the Progress Package in 2006.

STRUCTURE

- Two tranches: May 2006 and May 2007.
- Verification: For formal employees, employment and income are automatically verified using their Central Provident Fund (CPF) contribution records. Self-employed and informal workers who do not have tax or CPF records may declare their income to the CPF Board instead.
- Payout structure: 10 percent of the bonus is credited into the recipient's CPF Medisave account. The remaining 90 percent is given in cash.
- Amount: The amount of the payment depends on the recipient's average monthly income.

Annex B
Workfare Income Supplement (WIS) Scheme

(As announced in 2007)

ELIGIBILITY CRITERIA

Recipients are required to
- be Singapore citizens;
- be more than 35 years old;
- live in a property with an annual value of not more than S$10,000 (changed to S$11,000 from 2008 as a result of the revaluation of public residential properties in 2007);
- have a monthly income of S$1,500 or less; and
- have worked for at least three months in any six-month period in the calendar year, or at least six months in the calendar year. (Workers who have only worked three months out of the six-month period receive 50 percent of the payout.)

STRUCTURE

- Payouts are given to eligible recipients earning above S$50 and up to S$1,500 a month.
- Payments are made twice a year.
- Verification: For formal employees, employment and income are automatically verified using their CPF contribution records. Self-employed and informal workers contribute to their Medisave accounts to receive the WIS.
- Payout structure: For formal employees, a cash-to-CPF ratio of 1:2.5 is used. For self-employed and informal workers, the entire payout is credited to their Medisave accounts.

- Amount: The amount of the payout depends on the recipient's age, monthly income and employment status. Self-employed and informal workers who contributed to their Medisave accounts received two thirds of the total amount given to employees.

(Revisions in 2010)

In 2010, the government announced the following enhancements to the scheme:

ELIGIBILITY CRITERIA

- The monthly income threshold is extended from S$1,500 to S$1,700.
- The half-year payment for work done in the first six months of the work year is now assessed independently of the full-year annual assessment. This change allows recipients to keep the half-year WIS payment they receive.

STRUCTURE

- Maximum payouts for each age tier increased by between S$150 and S$400. Older workers received higher increases.
- As workers earn more, they do not lose their WIS benefits as rapidly.

These enhancements are expected to benefit about 400,000 workers at a cost of around S$440 million annually.

Chapter 14

Citizen-centred Public Services: Designing for Complex Outcomes

Tim Hughes and Sue Richards

The election in May 2010 gave Britain its first hung parliament since 1974. It was a watershed year for government. Subsequently, the Conservative and Liberal Democrat parties formed the first coalition government since the Second World War. Very soon thereafter, they began implementing a radical reform program intended to remove the fiscal deficit, shrink and decentralize the state machine and transform its relationship with citizens.[1]

In the years just before the election, the Labour government had already begun to change its approach to public service reform. The top-down, target-driven approach it had employed earlier was modified, and a new approach was developed that specified the role for central government as "strategic leadership rather than micro-management."[2]

The relationship between central and local government in the United Kingdom is not constitutionally codified and had become much more centralized since the 1980s. While many other jurisdictions experienced New Public Management as decentralization, the reverse occurred in the United Kingdom. From the early 1980s onwards, the central government imposed control over local governments' capacity to raise their own revenue, and it imposed other regulatory restrictions as well.

Moreover, the underlying design principles of the two levels of government tend to differ, creating frictions that reduce the effectiveness of the system as a whole. Central departments are designed primarily on "functional knowledge" criteria, (such as a department of health and a ministry of justice), powers are vested in the specific secretary of state, officials' careers are located primarily within the department, and organizational cultures that reflect that reality develop over time. Local authorities are typically more corporate and multi-functional, and seek to lead not only their own services but the "place" as a whole. Such differences mattered less when the system was more loosely connected, but a tighter link reduced the capacity of local government to respond to complex problems in a holistic way.

A centrally driven approach may be best when the goal is to deliver narrowly defined services. For example, a single and very efficient vehicle registration system that operates in a self-contained way offers the best value. But this approach is not the way to solve complex social problems. A more holistic and less mechanistic approach that integrates multiple contributions is needed. Grappling with the conundrum of inconsistent design principles has led to various initiatives over the years to get the best of both worlds so that specialization and integration mix in an optimal way, with central government providing strategic leadership rather than micro management.

This case study explores three such initiatives, one at the national or macro level and two at the local or micro level. Each illustrates the issues involved as government tackles complex issues through more holistic, integrated and participatory responses.[3]

The national-level *Total Place* program was initiated in 2008 and launched in 2009. It was designed to assess the gains to be made in efficiency and effectiveness by taking a less centralized, more holistic and place-based approach to public service. It was re-branded as Community Budgets by the incoming government in an announcement made in October 2010.

At the micro level, two collaborative endeavours to re-orient public services are described. The first example draws upon the work of the London borough of Croydon, through its Total Place pilot, to design holistic early years support for families. The second example considers the Family LIFE Program in Swindon where new approaches to family intervention and support are co-created with families.

Both local examples suggest that a new relationship is emerging between public services and citizens; one where services are designed with citizens and from their perspective. Citizens are not just seen as passive clients or users of public services, but as activists with knowledge and resources of their own. These examples also suggest a change of focus for public services, from coping with the symptoms of social problems to dealing with their underlying causes. That focus necessarily involves working with citizens, families and communities to build their social resilience by developing their capabilities and networks.

HISTORICAL AND PUBLIC POLICY CONTEXT

The early development of the modern state in the United Kingdom established the capacity of the central government to exercise power and ensure citizen compliance to laws passed by the legislature. This capacity in turn created norms and values that provide the foundation for legitimate government. It also created a powerful centrifugal force, especially in a unitary state where there is relatively little constitutional devolution.

In common with many other governments across the world since the 1980s, the emphasis in the United Kingdom has been on improving public service performance and increasing the cost-effectiveness of state action. However, in much of the rest of the developed world where constitutional and cultural settlements emphasized subsidiarity, performance was defined so that local service delivery specialists were free from central constraint and better able to use their local judgment to achieve outcomes for citizens. But in the United Kingdom, performance was defined in a way that reinforced centralizing tendencies.

These characteristics are long-standing and deeply embedded. While this model offers many advantages, such as clear accountabilities and economies of scale, it does not support coping with complex problems. There has therefore been a long history of special schemes meant to introduce the locality or citizen as an alternative design criterion around which services could be planned and delivered. Examples include the urban program in the 1960s, the City Challenge and the Single Regeneration Budget in the 1980s, and the idea in the late 1990s of "zones" (health action zones, education action zones) where funding from the central government was provided where organizers could prove that they were working in partnership with others from different specialities. Later, these onerous requirements for partnership were simplified through the creation of Local Strategic Partnerships, through which multiple streams of funding could be handled in a more coherent manner.[4]

But a re-emphasis on centralized control in the early 2000s sidelined these local partnerships, reinforcing the requirements of local bodies in priority fields— health service, education and crime—to respond to central directions.[5] This approach had some success at improving the delivery of service outputs (such as National Health System (NHS) waiting lists and clinic wait times), but it took attention away from partnerships in addressing more complex issues. There was a proliferation of centrally set targets. The whole system of mandating and funding local action suffered a loss of credibility.

Opinion leaders in local government criticized this approach, notably in the report produced by an inquiry into the purpose of local government, which defined it as "place-shaping" with the strategic leadership of "place" seen as the crucial factor in locality success.[6]

To address the situation, the central government began increasing its capability to respond to local needs through a significant number of senior appointments that drew people from local government. The top 200 cadres of public servants now contained a significant minority who had gained their experience in localities. Many of them gravitated towards the development of Total Place.

TOTAL PLACE

The Total Place initiative emerged in April 2009 in the context of a looming fiscal deficit, anticipated cuts in public expenditure and widespread disappointment with the results of an earlier surge of spending on public services. Its origins lie with the Calling and Counting Cumbria initiatives in 2008 that brought public agencies together to understand the needs of citizens, map public expenditure and explore how this information could better align in the county of Cumbria.

Treasury ministers asked the Executive Director of the Institute for Government, Michael Bichard, to lead a piece of work under the Operational Efficiency Program. A section of the program's final report on local incentives and empowerment recommended that government implement the Total Place program in at least 12 pilot sites. The goals were to identify efficiencies, incentives and barriers to collaboration and, with the support of ministerial sponsorship, ensure swift resolution of issues across government.[7]

The recommendation was adopted by the Department for Communities and Local Government (CLG) in partnership with the Treasury. Local Government Leadership, a non-profit organization, performed a co-ordination and intermediary role between central and local government. By May 2009, 13 localities across England had agreed to become pilot areas.

The Total Place approach was deliberately designed not to be a prescriptive central government program. A high-level group of officials was established in the central government that included director generals from across Whitehall (the British public service) and some chief executives from public agencies and local authorities. The group's role, however, was not to manage the pilots but rather to keep in touch with the emerging learning, share ideas and think about the barriers to local collaboration and innovation that the central government could remove. To aid this reflective process, each group member was assigned to one of the pilots to act as an advocate and intermediary, and to become involved in the work.

Each pilot involved a high-level count of how much public money was being spent and by whom. It involved a bottom-up tallying drawn primarily from discussion with local bodies. This stage was followed by a local decision to focus on particular themes, including early years, drugs and alcohol, mental health, high-deprivation neighbourhoods, unemployment, offender management, customer access and asset management. Pilot teams conducted a "deep-dive" for each theme, exploring how and where money was being spent, what effects were being felt and what opportunities and challenges existed for collaborative working arrangements.

The number and choice of themes were determined by the pilot teams according to local circumstances, as was the process of conducting the high-level counts and deep dives. There was some pressure from the central government to use the priority themes in the existing policy planning system but "it became clear it was important that the pilots went where the energy was in each locality and focused on issues most important to them."[8]

Each pilot submitted an interim report in September 2009 and a final report in February 2010 to CLG and the Treasury. In the interim period, the teams explored their themes and developed proposals, a process that varied across the locations but usually involved working across agencies and engaging with citizens as well as experimenting with some innovative methods of generating new conversations, insights and ideas. The final report summarized the journeys of the pilot teams, setting out their approach, the themes they had chosen, the evidence they had collected and the lessons they had learnt, as well as their visions and plans for the future, business cases for projects and recommendations to central government.

In March 2010, the Treasury, with input from CLG and Local Government Leadership, produced a summary report that recognized, "Total Place is demonstrating the greater value to be gained for citizens and taxpayers from public authorities putting the citizen at the heart of service design and working together to improve outcomes and eliminate waste and duplication."[9]

Postscript: From Total Place to Community Budgets

Total Place was the product primarily of the professional and political networks that connected local and central government, although it also had the stamp of approval of the then-government and it chimed well with the incoming coalition government's view that there should be greater decentralization of the United Kingdom state. It came as no surprise therefore that a re-branding process took place around a set of broadly similar design principles and the high-level group of officials was again put in place to guide its development.

The re-branded initiative focuses on families with complex needs and is being taken forward in 16 localities, including those that had already embarked on work in this area under Total Place.

As of February 2011, the coalition government's fiscal consolidation policies were being put into place. As a result, relationships between central and local government are suffering and there is a danger that Community Budgets will lose momentum, despite the fit with the government's overall strategy of decentralization. There is a mismatch between the strategic issues of decentralization and short-term media messaging regarding who gets the blame for cuts.

CROYDON TOTAL PLACE PILOT

Working from the recognition that "the public sector needs new models to improve public services,"[10] Croydon was one of the 13 localities to pilot the national Total Place initiative, beginning in May 2009 and ending in March 2010. While the borough had good previous experience with cross-agency integration of services, the pilot provided a catalyst for local agencies to come together and co-create with families a new vision and model for supporting families and children in the early years.

Co-led by the chief executives of Croydon Council and NHS Croydon, the local strategic health body, the partners decided on this focus because "the evidence is unarguable that a good start in life, in terms of physical, emotional and cognitive development, will result in better individual and social outcomes later in life."[11] Despite this evidence, overall expenditures were skewed towards addressing the consequences of poor early development later in young adulthood, rather than towards supporting families in the early years to prevent these problems arising.

The partners set the following success criteria for themselves:

- A new relationship between ourselves and our citizens, moving from "consultation" methods to collaborative co-design and co-production;
- A further deepening in the trust between organizations across Croydon;
- A new way of working taking root among professionals;
- A validation of our commitment to give specific time to shared problem framing, and doing this in new ways with new people;
- Significant financial savings in the short, medium and long terms.[12]

They did not immediately jump to developing solutions to an assumed problem, but rather adopted a system-design approach based on a four-stage process: discover (creating new information and insights), define (developing and testing a new formulation of the problem), develop (prototyping and refining new intervention methods) and deliver (supporting children and families during the early years across Croydon).

Discover

The partners worked across teams, organizations and sectors (using deep qualitative systems-thinking and traditional information gathering) to develop an understanding of their challenges and opportunities. This stage consisted of five work streams:

- Collecting and analyzing secondary data, including evidence from around the world on why early intervention is important and what works;
- Listening to families in new and creative ways to find out what life is really like for them;
- Engaging the 120+ frontline staff and managers from more than 20 organizations through a series of workshops and other collaborative techniques to develop a shared experience of what it means to design services around the needs of service users;

- Mapping activities and expenditures in the "early years system" to reveal the flow of resources to families from central government; and
- Mapping customer journeys through existing services by developing case studies (based on real families) of how services are actually experienced.[13]

This work uncovered a range of insights about the potential of early intervention, the experiences, needs and wishes of families, and the failures of the existing system.

Research reviewed from other localities and countries suggested there might also be significant financial savings from early intervention. These studies estimated "a 'not coping family' can cost an authority ten times the cost of a 'coping family', and 'a chaotic family' 75 times as much…early intervention makes good economic sense to strengthen their capability and resilience."[14]

Ethnographic research brought to life how families experience the existing system. The mapping of the journeys of 10 children through numerous interventions illuminated significant recurring themes, such as large time-gaps between problem identification and intervention, narrow service responses, a focus on service delivery rather than problem-solving, ad-hoc engagement, lack of continuity and decision making in silos.[15]

Mapping the money in the system showed that public agencies in Croydon spend £206 million each year on children from conception to age seven.[16] The mapping demonstrated there was very little opportunity for local discretion over how money was spent. It also showed that money was directed at services rather than solutions and that it was difficult to link investments to outputs and outcomes. The ethnographic work produced more worrying results. While a significant amount of money was spent on a limited number of children and families, each contact between those children and families with a public service only served a narrow purpose.

Together, the ethnographic research and money-mapping were powerful tools for breaking down organizational and cultural boundaries. Exposing frontline workers and managers throughout the system to the reality of people's lives helped develop a shared sense of purpose and energy that was vital to ensuring genuine collaboration. As one interviewee said, "Once people had confronted the current reality…you just built a momentum… It just got people thinking."

The need for joining up the cultural, geographical and technical aspects of the organizations involved was thus recognized. The shared learning experience at this early stage laid the groundwork for new relationships among partners, which in turn enabled more productive conversations about potential solutions.[17]

Critical to this process were "honest conversations" among people at all levels, but particularly among senior leaders. These shared, reflective conversations are an example of double-loop learning in action, highlighted by those leaders as having a major impact.

Define

The partners used the insight from new conversations to develop and refine a set of high-level propositions. These propositions shaped their new vision that "Children and their parents in Croydon…will experience a system from conception onwards which supports and invests in their parenting capabilities, resilience and ability to live independently…it will be a system that demonstrably supports the emergence of solutions for families, rather than merely delivering 'services'."[18]

More than 80 staff members from across the agencies took part in ethnographic insight and co-design training, and were challenged to go into the field to develop and test the propositions.

The importance of co-designing public services with their users was an important insight from the project. As a senior manager commented, "The really important issue is about the involvement of the citizens, the children, and the families in design and actually in delivery of the services…that's been the profound learning point from all this."[19]

The propositions were intended to fill the gaps in support to families. They included:

- geographically-based Family Partnership Teams, made up of professionals from across agencies, with shared budgets and outcomes;
- preparation for parenthood;
- early identification;
- family advocates;
- Peer2peer support networks;
- Family Space Croydon (web-based);
- the Life Passport for Disabled Children; and
- motivational support for return to work.

Develop and Deliver

At the time of writing, the partners, in collaboration with families and staff members from across public, voluntary and community organizations, were beginning to prototype and refine a number of propositions by "iterating and collaboratively designing a response in real time on the ground, making changes when they are identified, reflecting and refining to develop the best possible plan for implementation."[20]

In two of the most deprived areas in Croydon, the partners are implementing a selection of the prototyped propositions: the Family Partnership Team, the Peer-2peer Support Network and Family Space Croydon.

Family Partnership Teams are comprised of workers from various agencies seconded to a team with a devolved budget to address the needs of a particular locality. The final definition of each team is determined by local needs and "shaped through prototyping and co-design."[21] The team ensures a particular locality has sufficient capacity for focused preventative and early intervention services and that all contacts with families help develop parenting capacity, independence and resilience.

Peer2peer Support Networks build social supports for families in the greatest need so that parents are better able to access informal support and cope with problems before these escalate. Findings from the "discover" stage show that friends and family are the first port of call for parents for advice and information. The project works with communities to support the growth of parent networks, train parents in the community as peer mentors and develop networks of "virtual grandparents" who act as trusted friends and mentors.

Family Space Croydon is an online tool for parents and professionals that enables access to up-to-date information about local services and provides an opportunity for parent feedback.

By implementing these propositions across Croydon, the partners calculate that they can achieve significant savings: more than £8.3 million during spending period 2011/12–2013/14, £25 million by the end of the following spending period (ending 2016/17) and more than £62 million by the time the locality's current four year-olds turn 18 in 2023/24. These calculations are net of up-front costs and new revenue costs, and are based only on implementing the main propositions in four Croydon wards. The partners therefore believe their estimations are conservative.[22]

SWINDON FAMILY LIFE

The Family LIFE program is about "building new lives for individuals and families to enjoy."[23] It is an example of multiple public agencies in Swindon and the families themselves taking a new approach to interventions with families in crisis. At the core of the program is a new type of relationship between public services and families, including a focus on developing the capabilities, networks and resilience of families.

The LIFE program originated in 2008 when public agencies in Swindon recognized the need for a new approach regarding families with complex needs.[24] Local analysis shows Swindon has between 60 and 100 families living in the worst state of chronic crisis, suffering from numerous issues, such as susceptibility to illnesses, domestic violence, poor lifestyle habits, alcohol or drug abuse, poverty, child abuse or neglect, marginal living conditions and behavioural issues.[25]

Swindon Partners, the local cross-agency strategic partnership, was aware of rising numbers of children being taken into care and had evidence that interventions were not meeting the needs of families or enabling sustainable change. Swindon entered into a partnership with Participle, a private consultancy with expertise in public service design and a mission to create community-based change and develop a new approach for supporting families. "The intention has been to find what could bring about long-term sustainable positive change, not just for 'problem families' but also for other members of the community and government services."[26]

The approach to developing the Family LIFE program was based on a design methodology that included a participatory process in three phases: discovery, prototyping and delivery.

Discovery

The discovery stage brought together "cutting edge thinking in design with cutting edge thinking in social change."[27] An important aspect was reconsidering (rather than assuming) the nature of the problem before adopting solutions. Participants worked with 12 families during this discovery phase (which included six months when the Participle team lived in the community with families) shadowing frontline workers.

The picture that emerged was of disjunction between the approach of public services and the realities of the families: "We were just not speaking the same language."[28] It showed that government interventions were having little effect on the lives of families living in chronic crisis, and that the activity of the system was even creating a barrier to change. This system featured:

- impersonal delivery by professionals with a separate "professional" language;
- enforcement without relationships;
- lack of trust, honesty and transparency on both sides;
- negative systemic behaviours and cultural beliefs;
- service designs irrelevant to people's lives;
- high costs with few or no outcomes;
- a focus on reporting, risk management and monitoring; and
- an attempt to rescue rather than support people.

Families felt powerless: there was no safe place to ask for help, and they were exhausted from fighting the system. Families were building resilience against public agencies rather than social resilience. "For many, their career and expertise has become manipulating the system."[29]

However, richer conversations between families and public servants revealed that families in chronic crisis are "hungry for change and do have aspirations. There just wasn't the right kind of support there."[30]

Prototyping

Core to the prototyping stage was the recognition that change could not be achieved unless families themselves wanted it and were empowered to make it happen. The four families involved in prototyping were given control from the start: they worked with the multi-agency team (comprised of members interviewed and selected by the families) on a variety of projects and practical tasks (including cooking, shopping and managing home budgets). The intention was to enable families to develop the skills and knowledge they needed to begin to improve their lives, develop a new enriched relationship between the workers and the families, and build a sense of trust and a safe space for them to open up and talk about their aspirations and the issues they faced.

Delivery

During the delivery phase, the number of families involved in the LIFE program rose to nine, with participation ranging from six months to two years. Families were expected to move through the four stages of the program, albeit not necessarily in a linear fashion, acknowledging the likelihood of intensive periods, lulls, setbacks and breakthroughs. The amount and nature of contact between a team and family was to depend upon the needs and wishes of the family and the stage at which they found themselves.

In stage zero of LIFE, families are invited to participate in the program. During this period (which lasts for several weeks), the team builds a relationship with the family and helps them discuss the potential for change. Families that decline the initial invitation can participate at a later date.

In stage one, the team and family spend time together drawing out the aspirations and the potential of the family, as well as the values and capacities they wish to develop. Through a process of reflection, they begin to articulate a plan for the future and select a project that eventually they can work on independently from the team.

In stage two, the families explore opportunities for change in their activities, friendships, work and other relationships. They begin to experience the benefits of the changes and become engaged in outward-focused activities (for example, helping neighbours and volunteering).

In stage three, the families explore new social networks and relationships beyond their current friendship circles. They move towards independence (the team is needed less), build an exit strategy and eventually exit the program.

Multi-agency teams, comprised of up to ten workers, are used in the program. Members are seconded from the council, police or health and housing organizations. The model creates opportunities for different family members to bond with different people, lower the risk of burnout, increase the scope for questioning and challenge, and create more of a sense of "a team building something together."[31] Members recognize the danger of creating new dependency relationships or falling into the rescuing mode and so make an effort to avoid those traps. "We're all the time thinking, is this empowering the family?"[32]

The impetus of the program is not just on the families to change, but also for the team members to change. "The program is just as much a program for workers as it is for families. We found that building the capabilities of the team and working in a very different way was just as key as the work that needed to happen with the families."[33] Participle therefore trained the LIFE team workers to replace unhelpful working practices encouraged by the system with an ability to develop richer relationships with families.

The program saved £760,000 in the first year of the pilot. This includes £275,000 in reduced actual spending and £485,000 preventative value. Participle estimates that a further £720,000 will be saved in the second year, comprising £235,000 of actual and £485,000 value of preventative work.

As yet, none of the families has completed the program; however, a number of early positive outcomes have been achieved. There has been a reduction in domestic violence, the number of police call-outs, eviction orders and children taken into care. There has been an increase in children's school attendance, the number of adults seeking employment or training and the number of individuals seeking help for substance abuse. Mental health outcomes, emotional support skills among parents and relationships between family members and neighbours have improved.[34]

Encouragingly, participating families have not only invited other families to participate, but have also wanted to work with and support them. This development led the team to explore the creation of a position on the team for the mother from the first family engaged in the project. The LIFE Program is therefore showing signs of becoming a platform for peer-to-peer development. The LIFE team is working to increase the number of families and to institutionalize the approach across local public agencies.

LESSONS FROM THE CASES

The national Total Place initiative and the local Croydon Total Place and Swindon Family LIFE examples took place in the context of a unitary state with a strong record of achievement. That achievement was in areas where a centralized push can bring significant success, but not in areas where issues are complex. Five lessons, drawn from the examples above, may help inform how government can alter its thinking and behaviour to better handle complex issues, such as those revolving around families in chronic states of crisis.

Handling Complexity through Networks

Theories of complexity demonstrate that complex situations are full of emergent properties and unexpected consequences.[35] Complex problems will not be recognized unless an approach is developed that draws on many different perspectives and sources of intelligence and that adapts to new conditions. Recognizing the distributed nature of the knowledge required leads away from centralized prescription towards a networked mode of co-ordination.

Total Place is the flowering of the latter.[36] In particular, a set of people who already had the habit of connecting to professional peers through networks were recruited from local government to work at senior levels in central government. A critical mass of these appointments meant officials retained their previous orientation and contacts, rather than being socialized into a culture in Whitehall that normally puts hierarchy first. As important as the multi-level governance networks were, the existing horizontal networks in localities were also instrumental to the success of the initiatives.

The Importance of Tacit Knowledge

In both local examples, great efforts were made to engage local actors, including citizens, families and frontline professionals, in defining the problems and solutions. The design methodologies incorporated evidence gathered from elsewhere, but used to stimulate the thinking of those involved in the situation rather than to recommend a blueprint to be implemented. Addressing complex issues involves tapping the tacit knowledge of those involved, respecting knowledge that develops through experience and leaving space for collective sense-making and individual judgment.

Cultivating Resilience

Both local examples start from the proposition that human beings have built-in resilience and a desire to live a satisfying life and good relationships with others in their community. Where these outcomes are lacking, public service seems to treat the symptoms rather than the root causes. Both examples demonstrate the benefits of a citizen-centred approach, with an emphasis on building capability that should in due course reduce the need for public service. This capability needs to be grown. It is not possible to impose it from the top.

Leadership

If we think of an operating paradigm as "how we do things around here" along with the stories that have been developed over time to socialize people into doing things in that way, the development of a compelling, alternative narrative is an essential component of changing how things get done in the future. It can help people reframe their view of reality and to work together in new ways.

An academic literature had been developing since the 1990s about the need for "joined-up government" in the United Kingdom. The 1997 Labour government's first term of office involved much activity to overcome the silo nature of the British public policy system. These prepared the ground for new thinking. The breakthrough came when a number of former local government officials who became senior public servants at the national level played a significant part in re-framing the narrative. Michael Bichard was one of these people. Working with his network, he produced a critique that came to redefine the issues, successfully creating the climate for change.

In another lesson on leadership, Torbert suggests that we draw a distinction between conventional and post-conventional leadership.[37] The former plays a familiar part at various levels within organizations, but post-conventional forms are needed to work effectively within larger inter-organizational systems.

Both local and national examples in this case study demonstrate the presence of post-conventional leadership. The high-level officials group specifically rejected the conventional approach to program management and thus was able to create a framework that released innovative potential at the local level. The local-level senior managers and political leaders were then able to engage, rather than direct, local professional staff in a joint endeavour to find a better way, thus creating the opportunity to re-orientate professional practice in ways that accessed the knowledge of professionals *and* put citizen at the centre of the action.

Intermediaries as Resources for Change

Our two local cases would not have been as successful had it not been for the presence of intermediaries, such as Participle, that brought skills to facilitate change.[38] Intermediaries brought the capacity to listen to all perspectives, earn the trust of all participants, understand the highs and lows of change, synthesize workshop findings and pull together change narratives that made sense to all involved. Others like them were employed in Total Place and other local projects.

CONCLUSION

Public administration in the 20th century was dominated by large institutions and powerful professional groups. Grouping knowledge and expertise in this way has limitations, including the high cost of delivering unconnected silo services that make little headway in resolving underlying issues. In this approach, citizens have little involvement in decision making (beyond the ballot box) and are passive (rather than active) recipients of services.

In this case study, we explored these limitations and saw how this approach is insufficient to meet the challenges of the 21st century. Public service must harness new and diverse sources of knowledge and resources by unlocking and enhancing the insights, motivation, capabilities and networks of citizens and communities to boost social resilience, achieve greater public value and catalyze innovation. These new approaches present both challenges and opportunities for public services, and will require government leaders to re-frame consciously their views of governing in the 21st century.

Part Three

The New Synthesis
Journey

Chapter 15
The New Synthesis Journey

The overall approach and methodology used in the New Synthesis Project engaged the interests, energy and insights of an international group of senior public officials and scholars from the field of public administration and other disciplines.[1]

The approach used is not typical of how research is conducted in public administration. Instead, it:

- focused on the needs of practitioners;
- involved large-scale international collaboration;
- brought together in a common exploratory conversation the world of practice and the world of academia; and
- worked across borders and across disciplinary divides.

This methodology evolved over time.

This section reviews the evolution of the project, emphasizing the methodology that emerged and the success factors and lessons learned along the way. The process holds promise for addressing issues in public administration and public policy. It blends theorizing to advance ideas with experimenting to advance learning in practice as a way to modernize public administration.

SETTING THE STAGE

The ideas behind the New Synthesis Project started to take shape in 2006 when the International Institute of Administrative Sciences (IIAS) invited me to deliver the Braibant Lecture for that year.

Over my years in government, I had become increasingly worried about the growing gap between the Classic model of public administration that was held as the "gold standard" for practitioners and the reality faced by practitioners. Many of the concepts associated with New Public Management (NPM) were extensions of the Classic model. Even in renewed form, this model was inadequate to guide the actions of practitioners in a context characterized by increasing complexity, uncertainty and volatility.

Nothing is more useful than a good theory. But nothing more dangerous than a theory that has not kept up with the times, yet continues to be used as a normative reference, particularly when things go wrong. The damage done is most obvious in some developing countries that have been encouraged to implement the Classic model and NPM reforms too forcefully and in developed countries that struggle to maintain a degree of government-wide coherence.

I used the IIAS event to probe possible alternatives to the Classic model in a lecture called "Responsive, Responsible and Respected Government: Towards a New Public Administration Theory."[2]

Professor Christopher Pollitt, editor of the IIAS's International Review of Administrative Sciences,[3] listened to the lecture with surprise. Instead of putting forward a customary "five-step program…or some other apparently concrete and practical set of actions,"[4] the lecture argued that the practice of public administration is no longer consistent with the Classic model nor is it yet supported by a renewed, unifying philosophy. The presentation was an urgent call for dialogue between academics and practitioners to bring coherence to a quarter century of public sector reform initiatives.

The ensuing article, published in 2007, attracted some attention[5] but it did not mobilize people to action. Something else was needed if this work were to progress. The questions became: Who shared the view that this work was needed? and How could they be mobilized into a collective effort?

To overcome the divide between theory and practice, the process would need to include both theorists and practitioners. The project would engage people from multiple disciplines to address questions that could not be adequately broached within the traditional disciplines that constitute public administration. To create and sustain momentum, the work would need to progress quickly. To make it useful for practitioners, it should be action-oriented and grounded in practice. The project would not follow a traditional academic process with relatively long time-lines; but it would have a disciplined and structured approach, recognizing that flexibility would be needed to integrate new discoveries and findings along the way. The ideas generated would need to be relevant to practitioners working in a variety of contexts, circumstances and cultures. All of these specifications argued in favour of engaging a wide range of people from different countries.

Looking back, the project took shape over three distinct phases. The first was an exploration phase. This involved reviewing literature to find research that might be sufficient to address the challenges faced by practitioners. The hope was that most of the work had already been done, and that all that was needed was to integrate it and make it more usable by practitioners. We found many good ideas on specific problems and topics, but no integrated view of how they fit together. A coherent narrative had not yet emerged.

The exploration phase turned to a search for the main elements of a new narrative of public administration; one that would help map out a more modern and holistic way of thinking about the role of government in society.

To support this exploration, we looked for people and organizations interested in joining forces. This mobilization phase led to the creation of an international research network (NS6).

The last phase was a discovery phase. It took shape around a program of research and a series of international roundtables. This phase allowed the network to converge on a set of ideas and practices better aligned to the needs of practitioners who are called upon to face the challenges of the 21st century.

The overall approach was adaptive. It meant working systematically towards a common goal, while responding to situations and developments as they arose.

Much was learned along the way in terms of substance, process and human experience. Those who participated are better equipped to face the challenges of guiding public sector reforms in their country. The process helped us catch up on recent literature and discover inspiring experiences in many countries. The project provided practitioners with a safe space to discuss what works and what does not frankly and openly. It allowed them to express their views about emerging trends, their dreams for their country and their aspirations for preparing government for the challenges that lie ahead. Enduring friendships were formed. A network does not end when a project comes to an end.

The Exploration Phase

In embarking on collective endeavours that cross national boundaries, it is wise to start by gaining support at home.

The Canada School of Public Service (CSPS), where I have an honorary role as President Emeritus, came on board first. The project presented a number of benefits for the School. It would help modernize its thinking on public administration and, by extension, contribute to modernizing its leadership curriculum; contribute to its international profile; and help it connect with leading-edge thinkers and practitioners at home and abroad. The CSPS's support was invaluable.

The Privy Council Office (PCO) came on board next. In the fall of 2007, the then-

Secretary to the Cabinet and Clerk of the Privy Council, Mr. Kevin Lynch, agreed that I should dedicate a significant portion of my time to launch this project. This proved to be essential to garner support and ensure rapid progress.

Two more Canadian organizations, the Centre for International Governance Innovation (CIGI) and the University of Waterloo, both of which are recognized for encouraging innovation, joined the project in the fall of 2007. Their involvement provided academic support, some research funds and research assistants.

By the winter of 2008, a small team, resources and support were in place. This team started scanning literature for ideas and examples relevant to emerging lines of inquiry in the New Synthesis Project.

Early on, I had decided to expose the work in progress as frequently as possible to a variety of perspectives and in a variety of contexts. This approach played a key role in shaping the work and enlarging the circle of potential contributors. Each event enriched the team's thinking and expanded our understanding of the challenges faced by practitioners. Each encounter shed light on the weaknesses of the work in progress and strengthened the team's resolve to improve the ideas and arguments.

This process of rapidly assembling ideas and arguments, testing them on target audiences, accumulating and integrating insights and quickly moving forward became a key characteristic of the project's methodology. This is a practitioner's way of getting things done. It involves learning-by-doing and learning from and with others.

By the summer of 2008, we began to formalize the research. It took shape along a number of axes, including developing an initial research program and producing a number of background papers based on literature reviews.

The initial research program included validating the need for a new theoretical framework, developing a prototype framework, defining key elements of the framework and the relationships between them, conducting case studies and disseminating findings.

The first background paper aimed to identify authors who had argued there was a need for a new theory, model or conceptual framework for public administration.[6] It explored the evidence and arguments those authors put forward. It was interesting yet disquieting to discover the many authors who had written about the widening gap between public administration theory and practice. Some of the arguments referred to the changing context of public administration as a result of globalization, increasing complexity and uncertainty, the impact of information and communication technology (ICT), changing citizens' expectations, declining trust in public organizations, etc.

Three papers explored ideas from disciplines not traditionally associated with public administration. They focused on ideas to help build the capacity of government to anticipate and respond to global, complex issues and to build resilience to shocks, crises and unforeseen developments. These papers explored the implications of theories about complexity and emergence,[7] adaptive systems[8] and resilience.[9]

A sampling of literature was also reviewed to explore how government can engage citizens, tap collective intelligence[10] and promote social innovation.

Finally, a background paper was produced on the role of control, accountability and performance measurement systems in government to explore how they could support collaborative efforts.[11]

Throughout 2008, I used opportunities to participate in various international events to expose the work in progress to practitioners and scholars in various countries and to learn from a diversity of voices.

Asia-Pacific Economic Cooperation (APEC) Conference, Taipei, Taiwan

The first opportunity to expose the early work was at the Asia-Pacific Economic Cooperation (APEC) conference in March 2008 in Taipei, Taiwan. The conference theme was "Government Performance and Results Management." Delegates came from over 20 countries. Most were public sector auditors, comptrollers, or experts in performance measurement.

It was a tough audience to which to expose formative ideas and arguments because they challenged conventional thinking. My presentation was entitled "Performance Management: It's the Results that Count."[12] I observed that, while the focus on performance in government can be traced as far back as the early 1900s, under the influence of NPM, the focus became more extensive and intensive. Auditing expanded its focus from auditing for compliance to auditing for "value-for-money." Over time, the distinctions between audit and evaluation became blurred. Comprehensive audits started to cover some aspects of policy formulation as well as policy options and even policy decisions. I commented on the proliferation of performance measurement, the increasing cost of control systems and the perverse effects of the widespread use of performance targets.

I argued that it was necessary to disentangle control systems designed to reduce the risks of mismanagement from performance information systems designed to achieve better results. Both systems are valuable and necessary, but serve different needs and purposes. Control and compliance systems, while at their apogee, were at risk of becoming barriers to reasonable risk taking and innovation to achieve better public results.

A well functioning performance information system is one able to provide ministers and public administrators with the information they need to make better decisions in a timely way. An indicator of success is not the amount of information collected but whether the information is used, by whom and with what impact. Public policy decisions and policy implementation decisions are part of a common learning cycle that involves elected officials and professional public servants.[13] The role of performance information systems in this cycle is to help reveal the need for adjustments or course corrections to improve results.

I argued that many of the results most significant to citizens and ministers are beyond the reach of a single government program or agency; they require system-wide or societal action. Therefore, a meaningful performance information system must reach beyond agency results and situate the contribution of government agencies in the broader context of system-wide and societal results.[14] The presentation led to a lively discussion over the ensuing two days.

One of the most interesting conclusions of the conference was its recognition of the need to position government programs and agencies in the context of system-wide and societal results. No consensus emerged on how to disentangle compliance and performance functions, but a conversation had begun that would continue.

The Institute of Public Administration Australia (IPAA) National Conference, Sydney, Australia

The Institute of Public Administration of Australia (IPAA) conference in June 2008 in Sydney gathered a cross-section of experienced practitioners from the national and state levels and a large number of well-known scholars. The theme of the conference was "The Future of Public Service: Striking the Right Balance."

The title of my presentation, "The Future of Public Service: A Search for a New Balance," was meant to signal that no one way of serving is fit for all circumstances; instead, there is a continual search for balance.[15]

The presentation argued that, in future, public administration will continue to rely on the solid foundations of the past. Government will continue to contribute to stability and reduce uncertainties in society; it will continue to rely on and promote the rule of law; it will continue to value due process, respect for democracy, transparency and accountability. Not everything is changing or needs to change. A *compliance model* is here to stay.

Government should also retain the sharp focus that has been placed since the 1980s on efficiency, productivity, quality of service and user satisfaction. New ICTs enable governments to provide services in new ways, to integrate services when multiple actors are involved and to empower citizens to play a key role in public services. A *performance model* is also here to stay.

But more is needed to prepare government to serve in an unpredictable world characterized by complex problems, unpredictable crises, preventable failures, global cascading breakdowns and unprecedented breakthroughs. Government needs a more complete framework of public administration; one that complements the traditional and hierarchical structure of government with the use of expanded networks; one that recognizes the need for citizen engagement in policy design and service delivery by giving voice, choice and greater discretion to users of public services. There is a growing need to tap the collective intelligence of society to encourage innovation and to detect emerging issues and patterns. The role of government extends to building the resilience of society to "flourish in unpredictable circumstances, to shoulder the burden of inevitable crises, to avert preventable crises and to learn from adversity."[16]

At this event, I introduced for the first time a prototype of what would become the New Synthesis Framework. The presentation visually mapped out a broad frame of reference built on four distinct vectors delineating the subsystems of compliance, performance, emergence and resilience. It provided a mental map for exploring the role of government in predictable and unpredictable circumstances.

The presentation foreshadowed some notable global crises. It touched a nerve with practitioners because it captured some important aspects of their reality, however imperfectly.[17]

In the following months, a multi-year partnership agreement was reached with the Australia and New Zealand School of Government (ANZSOG) to pursue the work of the New Synthesis Project.

Public Administration Committee Annual Conference, York, United Kingdom

After the initial engagement with a large group of practitioners, I was looking for an opportunity to engage with academics and scholars in public administration. The opportunity presented itself in the form of an opening keynote address in September at the Public Administration Committee conference at the University of York. The participants were professors, scholars and graduate students from the United Kingdom and a few other European countries, most notably the Netherlands.

The theme of the conference was "New Directions in the Study and Practice of Public Administration." The keynote, entitled "New Directions in Public Administration: Serving Beyond the Predictable,"[18] was an important milestone for the New Synthesis Project. The work to scan the academic and practitioner literature was starting to pay dividends. The literature on complexity, complex adaptive systems, emergence and resilience was proving to be particularly relevant to the challenges faced by public administrators. This keynote provided the occasion to bring some of these ideas forward.

The presentation argued that an approach to public administration that focused predominantly on compliance and performance was no longer sufficient. Governments are increasingly working in uncertain, turbulent and complex contexts that involve a diffuse array of actors and distributed governance arrangements. The traditional approach needs to be complemented with a focus on *emergence* and *resilience*.

The role of government is to serve the collective interest in all circumstances, including predictable, less predictable and even improbable ones. This means building the capacity of government to anticipate, innovate and intervene before the cost of inaction becomes greater than the risk of exploring new avenues. It means reducing friction, avoiding preventable failures and ensuring an equitable sharing of the risks and benefits resulting from innovation. Furthermore, the increasing complexity of many public policy issues precludes government from acting alone. Governments are complex adaptive systems: complex because they are made up of multiple interconnected networks; adaptive because they have the capacity to learn, innovate and change. By working with others, governments have the added benefit of fostering resilience and building the social capital required to support collective actions.

Participants were particularly interested in discussing the concepts of emergence and resilience, and their implications for public administration. Conversations with delegates from the Netherlands revealed many common interests, foreshadowing the partnership that was to take shape in the coming months.

The 5ᵗʰ Quality Conference for Public Administration in the EU, Paris, France

The 5ᵗʰ Quality Conference, held in October 2008, brought together over 1,000 practitioners, leading thinkers and scholars from across Europe. The theme was "Le citoyen au coeur de la qualité publique" (The citizen at the heart of public quality).

By this time, a number of adjustments to the prototype had been introduced as a result of discussions in York. For instance, a definition was added for the four vectors that mapped out an expanding public space of modern governance. This addition helped reveal the tensions, trade-offs and choices open to government to achieve public results, including new ways of working with citizens and other actors. It made the framework more dynamic and potentially adaptive.

The presentation was entitled "The Citizen at the Heart of Public Sector Reforms."[19] It aimed to elaborate on the role of citizens in public administration. I argued that well performing public organizations must achieve public policy results and civic results. The role of government is to achieve results of increasing public value at system-wide and societal levels and in a manner that enhances civic capacity.

Public policy results build credibility, civic results build legitimacy; together, they build trust in government and public institutions.

Government needs to balance the drive for efficiency with the need to improve civic results. Civic results provide the basis from which to achieve more ambitious public policy results. Similarly, government must search for balance in using the authority of the state to leverage the collective power to achieve better public results. Using too much authority creates rigidities and dependencies; not enough dissipates the collective capacity to achieve results of public value and increases the risks borne by society.

Government can choose to act alone or as a partner, facilitator, leader or guardian of the collective interest. Whatever the choice, government will always be the "insurer of last resort" when the public interest demands it.

The presentation signalled the need for a different relationship between the state and citizens to achieve results of increasing public value. A different relationship can be achieved by giving citizens more voice, more choices and greater influence in the development and delivery of public services. This relationship requires government to recognize that citizen engagement has instrumental and intrinsic value. A growing number of issues require citizens to be active creators of public value.

The key elements of the presentation figured prominently in the concluding report of the conference. The presentation exposed the early work on the New Synthesis Project to prominent thought leaders in the field. It generated suggestions from other research groups as well as interested scholars and practitioners.

THE MOBILIZATION PHASE

By the end of 2008, a more complete prototype framework on the role of government in the future had been fleshed out. It evolved through interactive discussions and presentations to a diverse range of academics, experts and practitioners in different parts of the world. It was supported by some literature reviews and was documented in a number of articles that went to press in 2009. Working with limited resources, the team had taken the project as far as it could. It was time for a new phase.

From the start, I was of the view that a number of disincentives acting as contrary forces had prevented the modernization of public administration as a domain of practice.

One difficulty was the scope of such a modernization. No one individual could simultaneously grasp all the pieces of the puzzle.[20] A second difficulty was the disconnection (noted earlier) between scholars and practitioners. A third, and probably the most powerful disincentive, was the risk associated with such an undertaking. Whatever modernizing theory may be proposed, it will be immediately challenged. There are strong vested interests in preserving the status quo.[21]

To move the project forward, it was necessary to find a way to bridge the gap between theory and practice. At the same time, it was important to reduce the risks and costs to participating individuals and organizations.

The solution was to create a *collaborative international research network* of senior practitioners, academics and experts. However, building this network would require more capacity than my small team could muster.

In early 2009, the University of Waterloo, the Centre for International Governance Innovation (CIGI), the Canada School of Public Service (CSPS) and the Privy Council Office (PCO) reaffirmed their support.

The team could now count on three full-time staff and at least one graduate student. A website with the full suite of Web 2.0 tools was developed that would serve as a virtual platform for communication and collaboration among international partners.

The initial concept was to invite people and organizations from six countries representing the Americas, Europe and the South-East Asia and Pacific region to participate in the network. This would provide the necessary diversity of experiences and perspectives. It would allow ideas and findings to be tested from multiple points of view, ensuring that the emerging theoretical framework and narrative would be relevant in diverse circumstances and contexts.

Over the first half of 2009, the Netherlands, the United Kingdom, Singapore, Australia, Brazil and Canada were invited to join. The governments of these countries had led ambitious public sector reforms since the 1980s and had insights to share regarding these efforts and future trends. Together, they represented a diversity of governance approaches: parliamentary and presidential systems, unitary states and federations, more centralized and highly decentralized governments. They also represented different approaches to economic, social and democratic development, along with different political preferences.

While there was a rationale to selecting these six countries, the selection was also a pragmatic choice that took into account the network of relationships I had built over the years with senior practitioners in these countries. People who lead public sector reforms tend to know people who are leading reforms in other countries. They provide assistance to each other. They talk and exchange ideas. These conversations play a key role in shaping public sector reforms around the world. The ensuing relationships endure over many years.

The Netherlands

At the request of the Dutch Ministry of the Interior, I was invited to visit the Netherlands in January 2009 to explore areas of common interest and participate in an expert discussion on the co-creation of public goods and services. The program included a meeting with the State Secretary for the Ministry and a working session with Roel Bekker, then-Secretary General of the Central Government Reform Program.

The Dutch have a reputation for undertaking important public sector reforms. The Netherlands has a long tradition of citizen and community engagement supported and advanced by a vibrant academic community that contributes to advancing public debate. The work of Dutch scholars in public administration is at the leading edge in a number of areas, including less traditional topics such as the application of complexity and network theories to governance, administration and public policy.

The discussions revealed a powerful convergence of interests. The Netherlands was invited to join the network in January 2009 and was the first to sign a Memorandum of Understanding to this effect. The Ministry of the Interior, acting as lead partner, enrolled the contribution of scholars from the University of Rotterdam and Leiden University.

Australia

In February 2009, the Australia and New Zealand School of Government (ANZSOG) hosted a three-week program designed to expose a broad section of practitioners and experts to the ideas that underpinned the New Synthesis Project. In Melbourne, among other activities, the program featured a working session with managers of the State Government of Victoria to explore the relevance of the New Synthesis Project at the sub-national level. In Canberra, Terry Moran, then-Secretary to the Cabinet, brought together senior leaders to discuss ideas of mutual interest. The program ended with a public lecture hosted by the Department of the Prime Minister and Cabinet.[22]

The State Services Authority of Victoria (SSA) indicated its interest in joining the network since the New Synthesis Project complemented its own public administration research program. Through the Australian Public Service Commission and the SSA, ANZSOG and the Department of the Prime Minister and Cabinet formed a partnership and joined the network. This structure ensured powerful input from practitioners at the federal and state levels, as well as a strong academic input through ANZSOG's own network.

The United Kingdom

The United Kingdom is recognized for its thought leadership in public sector reforms and for the contribution of a robust academic sector and many NGOs to public debate.

I have the honour of serving as a member of the Board of Governors of the Institute for Government (IfG). The IfG is a non-partisan organization with a particular commitment to supporting the learning needs of elected public officials—a unique organization in Western democracies. The IfG pursues an ambitious research program and organizes learning events on major public policy and governance issues.

It seemed only natural to give the Institute the opportunity to join the network. Furthermore, there had been a strong relationship with the Canada School of Public Service and the United Kingdom National School of Government and between the Cabinet Secretaries in both countries over several decades.

In March 2009, the IfG, the United Kingdom National School of Government and the Cabinet Office formed a partnership and joined the network under the leadership of the IfG.

Canada

The Canada School of Public Service (CSPS) hosts an annual event that brings together representatives from the field of public administration from Canadian universities and senior public service leaders. The 2009 event, which took place in May, seemed like the ideal venue to brief Canadian public administration scholars on the New Synthesis Project.

The response to the presentation highlighted the need for greater clarity regarding my role as leader of an international initiative and the role of Canada as one of the six participating countries. The New Synthesis Project is an international initiative conducted through an international network. It is not a project of the Government of Canada, but one supported by the Government of Canada. These distinctions were necessary to ensure the independence of the network.

Canada joined the network, with the CSPS leading a partnership made up of the Privy Council Office, the Institute of Public Administration of Canada (IPAC) and the Canadian Association of Programs in Public Administration (CAPPA).

Singapore

Singapore was an early adopter of information and communication technologies (ICTs) in public service delivery. It is at the leading edge in thinking on how to improve the capacity of government to anticipate emerging trends and phenomena.

I have been associated in some way with Singapore Civil Service since the mid-1990s. I have served on the board of the Civil Service College (CSC) and had the honour of knowing and learning from successive heads of the Singapore Civil Service and some of the senior permanent secretaries.

In July 2009, I was invited as a Senior Visiting Fellow of the CSC to lecture on future trends in governance and public administration. The lecture was entitled "Serving Beyond the Predictable."[23]

This lecture added to the evolving New Synthesis narrative in a number of ways and expanded on the dynamic nature of the framework. It stressed the need for solid institutional capacity and strong organizational capacity for the compliance and performance systems of government to work effectively together. It proposed that governments need to improve their anticipative capacity to detect emerging issues. Governments need to rely more heavily on collective intelligence to detect emergent trends since important knowledge and insights can be developed by tapping multiple sources inside and outside government. Finally, it argued that governments need to improve their adaptive capacity and the adaptive capacity of society. Doing so will require a tolerance for redundancy and contingent capacity so that resources can be readily deployed to explore, experiment or ward off negative impacts in areas of greatest potential or vulnerability.

Singapore joined the network in July 2009, bringing an impressive track record in public service reform to the table. The CSC is the lead partner, working in close co-operation with the Public Service Division of the Prime Minister's Office.

The network received its name in Singapore during a meeting with Deputy Secretary, Lim Hup Seng, of the Ministry of Finance. He proposed the name NS6 to symbolize the search for a modern synthesis of public administration that the six participating countries were undertaking together. The name was adopted and reflected in the domain name of the virtual collaborative network that was subsequently developed.[24]

Brazil

Brazil's Escola Nacional de Administração Pública (National School of Public Administration, known in Portuguese as ENAP) has a long tradition of collaboration with Canadian institutions and particularly the Canada School of Public Service. Helena Kerr do Amaral, President of ENAP, and I had signed a bilateral co-operation agreement in 2003 involving ENAP and the CSPS. The two organizations have worked closely ever since.

I met with Helena in Helsinki in July 2009 to discuss the New Synthesis Project. We were both speaking at the IIAS conference. This was another important milestone for the New Synthesis Project. A few years after the Braibant Lecture, I was coming back to address the members of the IIAS. The 2007 lecture had been a call for action. The 2009 keynote, entitled "The History and Future of Nation-building: Building Capacity for Public Results," was a consolidation of the key ideas around the concept of a new synthesis of public administration.[25]

I agreed to present the New Synthesis Project at the XIV International Congress of the Centro Latinoamericano de Administracion para el Desarrollo (CLAD) in October 2009. The presentation, entitled "Public Purpose, Government Authority and Collective Power," built on the IIAS lecture. It explored what is different about serving in the 21st century.[26] It proposed that contemporary practitioners are the first generation to be called upon to address simultaneously difficult, complicated and a growing number of complex issues. This is a defining characteristic of the 21st century, resulting from a more global, networked and integrated world. Complex issues transform the role of government, the role of public organizations and the role of public servants. They require a shift from providing services to citizens to creating results of public value with others.

Following the CLAD, Brazil joined the network. ENAP led the country team, which included partner organizations as well as professors and researchers from Brazilian universities, such as the Universidade de São Paulo and the Fundação Getúlio Vargas, the Universidade Federal do Rio Grande do Norte and the Escola Nacional de Saúde Pública.

The Brazilian partners contributed a Latin American perspective and important insights from a unique history of governance. In just two decades since it emerged from a 20-year military dictatorship, Brazil has become a thriving democracy with a pronounced emphasis on public participation and social inclusion in which the pursuit of economic development is intrinsically associated with the reduction of poverty and inequality.

In the words of Helena Kerr, "Participation in the New Synthesis Network provides an invaluable opportunity to extend the discussion of public sector reforms in the 21st century in the context of an emerging nation such as Brazil facing simultaneously the challenges of overcoming poverty and exclusion, enabling social participation, promoting innovation and enhancing the framework for the rule of law."[27]

THE CONVERGENCE PHASE

By the end of 2009, the New Synthesis Project had come of age. It was supported by a dedicated team and a collaborative network of practitioners and academics from 24 organizations in six countries. The group had a common identity, the NS6, and a shared commitment to a common purpose.

A common process was also defined. The partners in each participating country agreed to take the lead on some research work and to contribute to the work of others. Each would develop two case studies to deepen the understanding in practice. Each would host an international roundtable or equivalent process that would address a key theme through a structured process of discussion enriched by the participation of leading thinkers and practitioners.

It was hoped this approach would increase the likelihood of producing results relevant to practitioners on a short timeline, while reducing the overall risks and cost to the contributors. At a minimum, the project would help participating individuals, organizations and countries better understand the emerging challenges. It would provide them with powerful examples and allow them to learn from their international peers. By the end of the process, the participants' thinking would be enriched by the work of others. Those leading reforms would be better prepared for the tasks.

Looking back, a number of factors helped the group coalesce. One of these was a shared sense of purpose and a powerful desire to help prepare our respective countries for the challenges of the 21st century. Of course, we could search for answers on our own, but the results might not be as rich or as rewarding without the diversity of ideas and experiences that a collective international network would provide. The project was designed to be a high value proposition at low cost and with minimum risks, the equivalent of which was not available without participating.

A final building block fell into place when, by chance, Cisco approached me to be a keynote speaker at its Public Services Summit in December 2009, in Stockholm. Participating in this event provided the opportunity to discuss the ideas emerging from the project with an international audience of leaders from the private sector, civil society and government. As important, it led to a productive longer-term partnership with Cisco that supported the project in a variety of ways. The network benefited from access to Cisco's Telepresence system for virtual meetings. The project also benefited from insights provided by experts in Cisco's public sector solutions team. Overall, the partnership with Cisco imbued the project with practical insights about the significance of modern information and communications technologies in the future of public administration.

With purpose, commitment, process, people and partnerships in place, the project was now entering a new phase.

Throughout 2010, the focus turned to deepening, enriching and continuing to debate the concepts relevant to the New Synthesis Project. The aim was to bring about some degree of convergence of ideas, supported by powerful examples that could help practitioners serve in the 21st century.

I know from experience that successful networks require a number of supporting conditions. They need a common purpose, trust among members, ongoing communication, a common platform for co-operation and distributed leadership, where different people provide the necessary leadership at different times to advance the work of the group. Networks are not owned by any one organization. Knowledge and expertise are not the monopoly of the "chosen few." Each contribution depends on the contribution of others and advances the work of the whole network.

Some of the groundwork for success had already been laid. A number of the people and organizations involved had existing good relationships and a productive history of working together. As well, a common purpose and a mutual understanding of the shared commitments were in place, along with some initial communication tools, including a virtual platform for collaboration.

By this time, the lead organization in each country had designated co-ordinators, and each country had laid out its specific research plans based on its key interests. While the initial impetus for the project in 2009 came from me and the people who work with me, the co-ordinators became the key drivers of the project in 2010. They ensured co-ordination among the participating organizations, guided the research and oversaw the preparation of case studies. They dedicated much effort to ensuring the success of the international roundtables. The co-ordinators supported each other and the members of my team. Their collaborative approach played a key role in the success of the network.

The network performed beyond expectations. We did not fully appreciate from the outset that we were collectively creating a unique and powerful methodology that holds promise for conducting research in public administration in the future.

The centrepiece of this innovation was the series of international roundtables. These events brought together world-renowned experts and leading practitioners in a process of deliberate discussions on key themes relevant to the research program. They offered a "safe space" that fostered free exchange and co-discovery. Participants were encouraged to expose their views, even if these were formative or speculative. The goal was to explore possibilities and convergence on ideas while avoiding the risk of agreeing on the lowest common denominator.

The roundtables were sequenced to accumulate and validate knowledge along the main lines of inquiry. A report was produced after each roundtable and made available in time for participants to prepare for the next one. Each event built on the findings and experiences of what came before. The roundtables became the locus of engagement, dialogue, knowledge production and organization as the work progressed.

The Hague, the Netherlands, 24-26 March 2010

Whenever the New Synthesis had been presented, the issue of how to deal with complex issues and how to build resilience in the face of shocks, crises and surprises generated much interest among practitioners. Based on the early research work, we all recognized that we needed to know more about this area. We also recognized that the approaches needed to address complex issues and cultivate resilience would have significant implications for the role of government and for public administration as a domain of practice.

The themes of emergence and resilience were the focus of the first roundtable in March 2010. This allowed us to deepen our understanding of these concepts and better prepare ourselves to understand their potential implications for the public administration systems and practices to be discussed at subsequent events.

The Dutch colleagues volunteered to host the first roundtable. There were many good reasons to start in the Netherlands. The Dutch have a reputation for trying out daring public policies and public sector reforms. They are pragmatic innovators and explorers—of new lands in the past and of new ideas in modern times. In addition, the Dutch academic community has a significant track record in exploring the implications of complexity science for public policy and administration. This was an opportunity to showcase some of these ideas and to test and discuss them with practitioners.

Our host, the Ministry of the Interior and Kingdom Relations, brought together experienced practitioners and leading thinkers to engage in an exploratory discussion on the themes of resilience and emergence. The event looked at the implications of these concepts on the practice of public administration and sought some guiding principles that could help practitioners.

Despite working to a very tight timeline with no pre-existing model, the event's design and its implementation set a very high bar for those that would follow. It provided a template that would be incrementally adjusted over the remaining events.

In the lead-up to the first roundtable, the Dutch organizers consulted regularly with my team. The event became a central item of discussion on the monthly network conference calls. A similar communication pattern held for all the subsequent events.

The first roundtable revealed the high level of commitment in the network. It took place over two and a half days, with the participation of over 40 senior practitioners and scholars. One full day was dedicated to resilience and one to emergence. The research questions were pursued through a mixed method of presentations, case studies, commentaries and open discussion. At the end of each day, the group was challenged to identify guiding principles for practitioners through a professionally facilitated process. The final half day emphasized the integration of findings and planning for the next roundtable.

The Dutch organizers took to heart the design concept of the New Synthesis Project to bridge theory and practice by having practitioners and scholars provide formal presentations and serve as commentators. General discussion brought the voices of practice and theory into a common conversation. The organizers invited resource people from multiple disciplines. Scholars from ecology, sustainable development, psychology and physics added their ideas to the mix with those from political science and public administration. Among this group of scholars was Professor Eve Mitleton-Kelly, an expert in complexity science and its application to organizations, who subsequently became a scientific advisor to the New Synthesis Project.

The Dutch introduced another design feature that was adopted in subsequent events. They used the event to showcase inputs from the network and inputs from their own country. This had a number of benefits. It turned the events into truly collaborative efforts and it enhanced the participants' understanding of the reforms under way in each country.

The partners in the Netherlands prepared a paper on emergence in public administration[28] and presented three case studies. One case was on Public Safety Centres,[29] one on Program Ministries[30] and one on Urban Renewal in Rotterdam.[31] A case from Australia on the State Government of Victoria's bushfire reconstruction and recovery efforts was also presented.[32]

At the end of the event, two rapporteurs—one from the host country and one from my team—summarized the findings. Their presentation provided an initial template for the report written immediately after the roundtable and made available in time to inform the next one. It was an important mechanism for ensuring knowledge was captured and avoiding repetition. The fast pace meant that these reports were not "perfect"—they only needed to be good enough to keep the collaborative process moving.

Ottawa, Canada, 4-5 May 2010

The Canadian partnership hosted its roundtable in May in Ottawa. The event focused on the core business of government, achieving public results. More than 30 senior practitioners, scholars and researchers explored the relationships between public policy results and civic results. They discussed ways in which government can shift from a focus on micro-level results to system-wide and societal results that include economic prosperity, wellness, life satisfaction and intergenerational fairness. They examined current research, experience and practice on when and how best to engage citizens and communities to improve public results. They also examined some of the obstacles to achieving better public results and how to overcome them.

The Canadian hosts adopted many of the features of the preceding event in the Netherlands. They struck a balanced mix of practitioners and academics, solicited material from the network and used the event to plan the Canadian contribution to the project. They provided a significant amount of material ahead of time to help the delegates prepare.

The Canadian hosts commissioned papers to constitute a base of findings in addition to those that would emerge through the presentations and discussions at the event.[33] They deliberately programmed fewer speakers and allowed longer periods for discussion than in the Netherlands.

The hosts designed the event to take full advantage of the power of the case studies that the network produced, placing case material foremost on the agenda and using it as a touchstone for the presentations and discussions that followed.

Canada provided a case study on the federal government's Homelessness Partnering Strategy[34] and another on Immigration and Settlement.[35] Both cases looked at system-wide and societal public policy results in light of multi-level, collaborative governance arrangements. Australia provided a case study on the Commonwealth Government's intergovernmental financial agreements with the state governments.[36] Singapore presented a case on the Singapore Prison Service's collaboration with the Community Action for the Rehabilitation of Ex-offenders (CARE) Network.[37] The case looked at how a high security, law enforcing agency engaged citizens, families and communities to reduce recidivism rates. Brazil presented a case on Bolsa Família, a direct transfer program designed to reduce poverty and hunger that illustrated how reducing unnecessary controls and conditions can improve results.[38]

The second roundtable needed to solve two key methodological challenges. The first was to ensure continuity from one roundtable to the next; the second was to bring new people into a conversation that had started several months before.

The first challenge was addressed by having two co-chairs. The role of the co-chair from the host country was to manage the meeting. The organizers arranged for Dr. Peter Aucoin, a highly regarded public administration scholar with a long history of working effectively with senior practitioners domestically and abroad, to serve as a co-chair. Dr. Aucoin subsequently became a scientific advisor to the New Synthesis Project. As the other co-chair, I was responsible for providing an overview at the beginning that summarized the findings to date and for nudging the discussion along. The latter role involved summarizing the discussion in real time and challenging participants from time to time to avoid repetition and to keep the ideas flowing.

The second challenge was addressed by ensuring that a core group of people from the previous roundtable attended the following one. On average over the course of the roundtables, one third of participants attended the previous roundtable and two thirds were newcomers. This ratio ensured continuity and served to expand and enrich the circle of contributors.

Both solutions became standard features of the subsequent roundtables.

The Canada roundtable coincided with another prestigious event of the Canada School of Public Service, the Manion Lecture. Each year, a renowned practitioner or expert gives a public lecture on an important, provocative topic related to public governance or public policy. Dr. Thomas Homer-Dixon, an expert in complexity science and innovation, was invited to give the lecture that year. His presentation helped integrate some of the concepts under discussion,[39] and he subsequently became a scientific advisor to the New Synthesis Project.

Rio de Janeiro, Brazil, 13-14 July 2010

The third roundtable, in Rio de Janeiro, Brazil, examined how new developments in society, such as the rise of shared governance, public participation, social networking and co-production, are transforming the role of government, public organizations and public servants. Twenty seven practitioners, scholars and researchers from eight countries explored the benefits and challenges of these developments and how to maximize their potential.

The Brazilian hosts integrated and refined many design features from the Dutch and Canadian roundtables. Some similarities included striking a balance between practitioners and academics from different backgrounds and experiences; using the research questions to guide the design and discussion; providing reading material ahead of time; briefing speakers and steering their contributions to address the research questions; and using case studies to ground the discussion.[40]

The Brazilian hosts introduced specific references to the Brazilian context—past, present and future. This proved to be an important improvement that was brought forward in subsequent events. It enabled the use of the host country's experience to be a "live case" or touchstone for the discussions, making the exploration process richer and more concrete for participants. It gave participants a tangible understanding of how practitioners in Brazil confronted challenges common to all the participating countries. It provided a comparative perspective that enhanced the value of the event for the other countries involved. The Brazilian reality and its history of reforms became part and parcel of the substance of the event.

Brazil's challenges are shared the world over. The lessons learned from the reforms in Brazil over the last ten years enriched the discussion and improved the research findings.

In the context of the New Synthesis Project, the National School of Public Administration (ENAP) introduced a number of innovations. After each roundtable, including Brazil's, it hosted a seminar at which participants discussed the key findings face-to-face and online with large groups of practitioners. This approach expanded the conversation at the national and state levels.

Singapore, 21-22 September 2010

The fourth roundtable, hosted by the Singapore Civil Service College (CSC), focused on the challenge of preparing governments to serve beyond the predictable. Building on the findings of the first three roundtables, 26 participants, scholars and researchers from seven countries explored how governments can improve their capacity to anticipate emerging trends and opportunities and to initiate proactive interventions that mitigate and improve the likelihood of more favourable outcomes. Participants explored how to build the capacity in government and society to experiment, innovate and adapt in the face of changing or unforeseen circumstances.

The theme was very well aligned with the reality of Singapore's economic and geopolitical context and with its governance experience. The event provided an opportunity for participants to learn from Singapore about its world-class capabilities in scenario planning, horizon scanning, risk assessment and innovation.

By the time we reached Singapore, we needed to shift the conversation from What is different about serving in the 21st century? to How can we prepare governments to serve? We also needed to probe the implications of the proposed changes on the current state of practice more deeply. In particular, we needed to deepen our understanding of how new ICTs are transforming the relationships between government and citizens.

Singapore's public service is well known for its ability to scan the world for the best ideas and practices and for its inventive capacity to improve and adapt them to the Singaporean context. The Singapore hosts displayed these qualities in designing their roundtable. The agenda focused on what could be done in practice while incorporating new avenues of inquiry. Drawing lessons from the strengths and challenges of previous events, they designed a powerful program and invited me to play a more active role in framing, summarizing and stewarding the discussions.

Singapore provided a case study on its response to Severe Acute Respiratory Syndrome (SARS).[41] Brazil presented a case on public service innovations.[42]

The hosts introduced some unique new elements to stimulate creative reflection and capture findings in real time. They organized a learning journey to NorthLight School, an internationally recognized success story in the education of young people at risk of being "left behind." A graphic artist produced a visual and textual record of findings as they emerged. During coffee breaks, participants recorded their suggestions on how to build capacity for serving beyond the predictable on a wall reserved for this purpose.

Australia and New Zealand, 28 September–14 October 2010

It was not realistic to hold six roundtables over a 12-month period. Instead, it was decided that I participate in a number of group discussions in Australia and New Zealand.

As part of the Australian contribution to the New Synthesis Project, meetings were held in Perth, Melbourne, Canberra, Wellington and Auckland between 28 September and 15 October 2010. The events engaged large groups of senior and executive practitioners to test the evolving New Synthesis Framework at the national, sub-national and local levels.

In Western Australia, ANZSOG and the Australian Public Service Commission organized the events, which included a policy dialogue on citizen engagement, an executive seminar on the New Synthesis Framework and a CEO forum on the challenges of serving in the 21st century.

The experience was revealing. From Rio to Perth, Ottawa to Singapore, practitioners defined the challenges they were facing in similar ways. Furthermore, they were experimenting with similar ideas. They used similar words to describe the growing gap between existing practices and their aspirations to adapt to a changing landscape. These participants from Western Australia would have felt at home at any of the international roundtables held so far.

In Melbourne, ANZSOG hosted a workshop that included representatives from the State Services Authority and academics from various fields. Participants discussed three papers, two of which were commissioned specifically for the New Synthesis Project. The papers explored the next phase of public management reforms,[43] the challenges of working across boundaries[44] and the concept of co-production.[45] These papers, which were used as advance reading materials for the final roundtable in London, made a significant contribution to the project.

There was a strong convergence of views on the macro elements of the New Synthesis Framework. But would it be useful to practitioners in line departments and agencies operating at a sectoral level? And to people dealing with issues relating to Indigenous Australians, aging or health? Meetings were arranged in Canberra with a number of sectoral departments to test the ideas.

This was the most important test of all. The network had made a commitment to produce something "useful and usable" for those willing to take on the responsibility of serving citizens. This was the *raison d'être* of this project. It was comforting to discover that the work was capturing "the essence of the multiple and varied challenges confronting busy executives…as they strive to deal with multiple expectations."[46] This was an important finding as we began to plan the last roundtable.

The group meetings in New Zealand continued to test the relevance of the New Synthesis Framework with practitioners in different contexts, roles and circumstances. A seminar with senior leaders was held in Auckland. In Wellington, the focus was on central agencies, including Cabinet and the New Zealand Public Service Commission, and on the professional-political interface.

Several New Zealand case studies enriched the material available to the network. The studies covered a range of topics, such as cross-government co-ordination, community engagement and shared accountability approaches.

The meetings in five cities across Australia and New Zealand enriched the network. It was a different way to test ideas and validate the relevance of the New

Synthesis Framework in practice. It provided a new way of exploring the expanding space of possibilities open to government.

London, United Kingdom, 16-18 November 2010

The United Kingdom roundtable was the last in a challenging process of exploration that had already taken us to The Hague, Ottawa, Rio de Janeiro and Singapore over eight months. The pace had been exacting but exhilarating, and the workload particularly demanding for those working closest to me and who had participated in all the roundtables.

The last roundtable, hosted by the Institute for Government (IfG) in London, was the most challenging. It was designed to look at how everything we had learned affected contemporary public institutions and organizations, and how to make these changes come about.

Immediately before the roundtable, a new coalition government in the United Kingdom was in the midst of defining its priorities. These circumstances were certainly challenging for the hosts, but they heightened interest among participants and senior officials in the British public service. An impressive mix of past and present British parliamentarians, senior public servants and thought leaders from civil society organizations, social enterprises, universities and consultancies attended the event. The trajectory of the roundtable shifted from consolidating the findings to getting a better appreciation of the reform agenda taking shape in the United Kingdom.

Forty-five practitioners, scholars and researchers came together to explore the issues, such as co-production, social enterprise and community involvement in public service and the accountability systems needed to enable distributed governance arrangements.

The event featured many of the successful design elements found in preceding roundtables. It drew some inputs from within the network, including a paper prepared by my team on disentangling performance, control and accountability regimes. The hosts presented a two-part case study on new approaches to public service design and management that placed a special emphasis on community-based budgeting processes and local experiments in co-designing public services with citizens. Singapore presented a case on workfare strategy, which revealed how it was designed to enlist recipients and other groups and organizations into a co-production process to alleviate income inequality and improve the skills and productivity of workers.

Overall, the energetic engagement of the British officials in a genuine search process and dialogue was particularly impactful. Their thirst for a fast-paced exploration was infectious. The discussion during the co-ordinators' meeting that immediately followed the roundtable focused entirely on the next steps. No one was ready to "down tools."

IN SUMMARY

Throughout 2010, a disciplined process of exploration, discovery and convergence took place. It was a collaborative effort enriched by the comparative discussions that naturally arise when representatives from several countries are involved. The rolling agenda of the roundtables allowed for knowledge to be tested and accumulated. It also provided for a continually expanding circle of players.

A number of lessons were learned through this process that may help others who wish to embark on similar initiatives.

First, the network would not have got off the ground without a common sense of purpose. An open-ended invitation to join a research project would not have enlisted partners. It was necessary to frame the issues and to risk advancing some initial hypotheses to spark people's interest. This work motivated substantive conversations out of which a common understanding emerged. In the end, the partners could see and pursue their own substantive interests while the collective interest of the group was simultaneously being realized.

Second, the invitation to join needed to be worthwhile. The proposition needed to be high value and low-cost for all involved. Participants and participating organizations had to be able to say, "I can only win by being involved."

Third, the process was agile and adaptive, yet retained a central structure and discipline. Commitment to this method never waivered, but the process was open to improvisation. There was a clear commitment to a result and a non-linear pathway for getting there—one that involved collaboration, experimentation and learning by doing.

Fourth, the rapid pace was necessary to sustain momentum and ensure a reasonable level of continuity. It was challenging but manageable.

Fifth, deliberately using an inclusive mix of practitioners, scholars and thought leaders from multiple disciplines and experiences and from multiple countries produced creative insights and innovative ideas. It also ensured that no single voice prevailed.

Sixth, the approach of rapidly producing, sharing, accumulating and analyzing ideas in a rolling agenda served its purpose. It derived a vast amount of creative, concrete ideas and examples that resonated as useful guidance for practitioners. The inclusive and open character of the process created a positive energy that drove it forward.

Seventh, at no time did partners in the network "free ride." They contributed their fair share according to their commitments, capacities and the context in which they worked. There was a tremendous amount of mutual support and respect.

Why did things turn out this way? One explanation is the quality and character of the people and organizations involved. But there was more. Another explanation is that it was also a function of the subject matter and of the process design. Everyone learned and everyone felt a deep sense of commitment to a collective endeavour that held meaning and relevance. At the Canadian roundtable, John Helliwell shared three factors associated with well-being: "positive trumps negative," "social trumps material" and "doing things for and with other people increases life satisfaction."[47] All three factors were at work in the New Synthesis Project.

The following chapters highlight some of the key findings, presentations and observations from the roundtables that influenced the work of the network and the development of the New Synthesis Framework. The chapters are not intended to provide a full account of each event, since reports are already available online for that purpose.

Chapter 16
The Netherlands Roundtable

The roundtable hosted by the Ministry of the Interior and Kingdom Relations in the Netherlands explored "emergence" and "resilience," two key themes of the New Synthesis Project.[1]

The event was convened to explore the implications for government of serving in increasingly complex and uncertain circumstances, where public issues regularly emerge as surprises and require equally emergent responses; to look at how these circumstances transform the role of government and the relationship between government and society; and to examine how to create more agile, innovative and adaptive approaches to governance and public administration.

The event also explored the role of government in promoting the resilience of individuals, communities and society to adapt and prosper even in the face of adversity—because unforeseen events will arise and unpredictable shocks will occur in spite of the efforts of governments and their citizens to explore, prevent, pre-empt or course-correct.

PERSPECTIVES ON RESILIENCE

A number of perspectives on resilience and its potential implications for public administration were provided. These included academic views from different disciplines and practitioner views, including case studies.

A Behavioural Science View on Resilience

The fundamental adaptive systems that humans have evolved to protect themselves naturally support resilience. The greatest risk to the resilience of individuals is when their adaptive capacity is undermined through dependency or neglect, or harmed through trauma or abuse. Another risk is that an individual's resilience can be hijacked; for example, by being drawn into a criminal gang.

Behavioural science has unearthed some key predictors of resilience. These predictors exist within individuals (for example, proper brain function and intrinsic motivation) and extend beyond the person into other systems, such as their relationships (for example, socially active peers and effective parenting), organizations (for example, effective schools and hospitals) and institutions (for example, effective policies and laws).

People can cultivate resilience by promoting positive development. This involves framing positive goals using an appreciative, strengths-based approach, and tracking successes and positive outcomes. It also entails using positive change strategies that focus on prevention (for example, reducing poverty), assets (for example, improving access to education), mobilizing elements of the adaptive system (for example, provide opportunities to develop talents) and using families, schools, peer systems and communities to provide cumulative protection.

A developmental focus helps cultivate resilience. There are periods of vulnerability during which prevention strategies are paramount. Stopping problems from snowballing, and monitoring and intervening during major transition periods are examples of this. During periods of change or recovery from adversity, positive promotion strategies are useful. Quick fixes may undermine long-term gains in resilience. The best interventions take advantage of existing strengths, mobilize the power of basic human adaptive systems and build competence as they reduce risk.

Too much intervention creates dependency and undermines resilience in citizens, communities and society; not enough dissipates the collective capacity to achieve better results. This gives rise to a number of challenges for public administrators and decision makers.

A Complex System View of Resilience

Governments play a special role in building societal resilience. Understanding the nature of complex adaptive systems, how they change and what makes them resilient can help governments deal with complex issues, shocks and unforeseen circumstances.

Dynamic relationships (such as interdependencies and feedback loops) are central to the functioning and evolution of complex adaptive systems. Resilience exists in how these relationships allow for continuity and change. This dynamic can be described as an adaptive cycle in which exploitation and conservation processes ensure continuity and routine changes, while release and reorganization processes promote continual change and adaptation. Governments can use their policy levers to support various phases in the adaptive cycle.[2]

An adaptive cycle needs a continual supply of innovation to sustain itself. Social innovation is an entry point to resilience. Governments can encourage social innovation by connecting social entrepreneurs, stimulating competition, providing support for successful ideas, spreading awareness of success and helping "scale up" proven innovations. Governments should use different approaches to evaluate social innovation at different phases of the adaptive cycle and take the learning curve into account.

A Practitioner View of Resilience: the Netherlands

Since the 1960s, the Dutch government has taken on an expanding range of responsibilities on behalf of citizens. As a result, citizens have become less accustomed to taking responsibility for themselves. Since the mid-1990s, the government has been rethinking its relationship with citizens, but the cycle of dependency and dissatisfaction continues. Changing from a cycle of dependency to an approach that encourages shared responsibility for achieving results means redesigning government programs, policies and services to encourage the active contribution of citizens.

Citizen participation does not make the job of public officials easier. It means creating conducive conditions that encourage the active role of citizens and communities. Above all, it represents a change of culture where government is no longer the sole decision maker and where results depend as much on government actions as they do on individual responsibility.

The roundtable participants heard that the Dutch are deeply aware of the need to reposition the role of government, even if they are uncertain about what role government can best play in the future. The choices are emotionally charged. Administrative reforms leading to greater efficiency gains have been undertaken, but the solution does not seem to lie there. It may lie instead in searching for a narrative about what government and citizens can achieve together.

Victorian Bushfire Reconstruction and Recovery Authority: Australia

The bushfires of February 2009 caused unprecedented devastation to the state of Victoria, Australia. Among the losses: 173 people died; 950 local parks, 467 cultural sites, 200 historic places, over 3,400 properties and almost 430,000 hectares of forest, crops and pasture were damaged or destroyed; and more than 55 businesses were lost, with hundreds more significantly affected.

Because of the scale and urgency of recovery tasks, the Government of Victoria needed to be agile and responsive. Within three days of the disaster, while fires were still burning, the government established the Victorian Bushfire Reconstruction and Recovery Authority (VBRRA) to co-ordinate the restoration and recovery of affected regions and communities. The VBRAA's organizational structure, decision-making and management processes facilitated speed and action. Six teams reported daily to the Chief Executive and Chair. The objective of each meeting was to give people the authority to act. Decisions were made quickly; if they were the wrong ones, they were corrected. The immediate establishment of the VBRRA injected a sense of optimism and hope into communities.

Recognizing that communities are better equipped to lead their own recovery, they were encouraged to establish a local recovery committee to prepare plans to support recovery under the VBRRA's guidance. Communities retained authorship over their plans and drew on their own resources, local organizations and networks to generate support and develop community-based approaches to recovery. Each committee set its own priorities and established its own pace. The idea of "recovery at your own pace" was central.

The VBRRA sought to avoid creating dependency while providing much-needed support. The VBRRA's focus on community-led recovery emphasized capacity building, engagement and decision making at the local level. This represented a significant departure from the traditional model of government-community consultation. Community-led recovery can strengthen communities in spite of the adversity involved. It can improve their resilience and their capacity to foresee and adapt to future challenges. It was noted that individuals and communities that had previously suffered disasters seemed to cope better with recovery.

This case study showed the need for government to work at different speeds and at multiple levels. The disaster required immediate responses at the local level and across government. The recovery process required fast action to create hope for the future and slower work to let people and communities recuperate and rebuild at their own pace.

Transforming Justice Program: United Kingdom

Despite falling crime rates, prison populations in the United Kingdom have more than doubled since the 1990s. Recidivism rates are high, as are public fear of crime and lack of confidence in the criminal justice system. Funding pressures to support a high incarceration rate have strained probation resources and pushed aside interventions known to prevent recidivism.

The Transforming Justice Program aims to divert young people away from the criminal justice system before they enter it. While criminal justice agencies play a major part in this effort, agencies in education, employment and other services relating to social and community well-being all play key roles. The program aims to bring all the relevant local agencies together to find ways of dealing with the seemingly intractable problems that plague the system.

One of the program initiatives was a workshop in Swansea to address policies and services for young people at risk of becoming offenders. Seventy people from 29 organizations came together in a disciplined and highly interactive process to develop ideas for improving outcomes for these people.

While this is a work in progress, the program hopes to demonstrate that putting citizens and multiple local agencies at the centre of a community-led approach can contribute to creating innovative ways of dealing with the problem, building long-term resilience and achieving better system-wide results.

The Rotterdam Urban Renewal Approach: Tarwewijk as a Resilient Community?

The Dutch Ministry of Housing, Communities and Integration reports that about 100 neighbourhoods face a combination of difficult issues, such as high unemployment, poverty, high dropout rates from school, crime and insufficient integration of new Netherlanders. These are instances of long-term erosion rather than a major disturbance or sudden crisis. Despite sustained attention and significant investments, national and local governments have not made major gains in addressing issues in these neighbourhoods.

Tarwewijk in Rotterdam is one of 40 neighbourhoods that the Dutch government targeted for intervention in 2007 to foster self-reliance by engaging citizens in the community. The targeted neighbourhoods received extra funding and support for housing, work, education, integration and public safety. The aim was to transform and improve these neighbourhoods using a collaborative approach in which the national government, municipal authorities, housing corporations, local organizations and the people living in the community work together to define their goals and how to reach them. According to the Minister, the approach is "based on the power of people...because the resilience of the city is in the people."[3]

Achieving success in Tarwewijk came with many challenges. The neighbourhood has a high percentage of transient residents, making it difficult to build constructive and close relationships. Many residents live close to the poverty line and deal with social disadvantages, such as insufficient language skills in Dutch. Many are primarily concerned with basic survival issues, including food and shelter. As a result, projects that aimed to involve residents in creating a "liveable neighbourhood" were not at the top of their priority list. Moreover, residents who did participate in such projects found a discrepancy between the government's slogan, "It's your neighbourhood, so it's your call," and their real impact on policy decisions. They were disappointed when their ideas were rejected at the planning stage due to a lack of funding, implementation capacity or conflicting priorities.

This case study provided important insights for roundtable participants. First, community-based approaches depend on the pre-existence of a community. This should never be taken for granted. The government's approach must be adapted to each neighbourhood's unique circumstances. Not all neighbourhoods are able to take their affairs into their own hands. In a neighbourhood such as Tarwewijk, community building may require a more hands-on approach by government to halt erosion and help address basic needs. Citizen participation is not synonymous with community resilience. To build credibility with communities facing a range of complex issues, it is advisable to under-promise and over-achieve.

IMPLICATIONS FOR GOVERNMENT IN FOSTERING RESILIENCE

Some areas of consensus emerged during the first roundtable. Shocks and surprises will continue to occur, and their frequency is likely to increase. Individuals, communities and societies are complex systems that, given the right conditions and capacities, will adapt even in the context of adverse conditions. Governments cannot create resilience, but they can nurture it and at least avoid undermining it in individuals, communities and society. Neither laisser-faire nor overly interventionist approaches help build the resilience of society. The former can be neglectful and deplete resources; the latter can create unhealthy dependencies. Supporting resilience is a delicate balancing act between government action and individual and community responsibilities. It is contextually and culturally specific. There are multiple pathways leading to enhanced resilience.

Participants in the roundtable identified nine principles to guide practitioners in cultivating resilience.

(1) Frame missions as positive, collective enterprises: A positive, appreciative outlook is an important building block of resilience. Emphasizing a positive mission involves story telling that taps emotions. Such an approach runs counter to modern political practices and media coverage that tend to focus on crises, problems and reducing deficits. The challenge is to emphasize strengths over deficits, learning and adaptation over risk avoidance, opportunities over problems, and accomplishments over failures.

(2) Make "smart" interventions: Resilience is contextually and culturally specific. Interventions should build on existing strengths in a given setting. Multilevel, multi-channel approaches provide cumulative protection.

(3) Take advantage of windows of opportunity: Resilience can be cultivated by using periods of adversity and crisis for renewal and growth (for example, the bushfires in the state of Victoria); by responding to early signs of resilience when they emerge (for example, citizens' groups eager to tackle a local issue); and by nurturing innovation and social innovators when they appear.

To take advantage of windows of opportunity, governments need to understand what to do and when. The concept of the adaptive cycle holds promise for helping practitioners make good decisions. Specific policy measures suit different phases in the cycle. Interrelated adaptive cycles take place at different scales (for example, individuals, groups, communities, organizations, institutions and culture), with smaller scales cycling more rapidly. Understanding this dynamic may help practitioners identify the best point at which to intervene and how an intervention at a smaller scale may affect resilience at larger ones.

(4) Foster adaptation: Adaptive capacity is already "out there." Governments need to cultivate and support it—or at minimum not weaken it (unless it is in the public interest to do so, as is the case of terrorist networks, for example). A basic adaptive system extends beyond individuals into their relationships with other people and systems, including public organizations and institutions.

Cultivating resilience requires three basic approaches: risk-focused (for example, mitigating vulnerabilities); asset-focused (for example, building on strengths); and process-focused (for example, mobilizing people and relationships). In general, governments have experience in managing risks and assets. Citizen engagement, public participation and shared governance arrangements are a means of tapping into that collective adaptive capacity.

(5) Experiment on small scales: A challenge for government is to balance the need to foster adaptive capacity to continual change while ensuring continuity and stability where needed. One approach is to experiment with change on a small scale, thus lowering the potential for undesirable effects to cascade across scales and create crises in the larger system. Small-scale successes can then be expanded over time.

(6) Support social innovation: Social innovation is a key strategy to support adaptation and build resilience. Governments can encourage social innovation by looking for social innovators, connecting them, setting conducive conditions for their work and helping them scale up successful innovations.

(7) Use participatory processes: Participation is at the core of resilience. It builds society's capacity to address public issues in ways that meet the needs of the people most affected. For this, governments must allow citizens and communities to participate in defining the nature of public issues and identifying solutions. This might not result in perfect solutions; but it can produce workable ones that enjoy community support.

Governments must learn to ask citizens for help and allow them to make real decisions. Naïve or disingenuous approaches will backfire and erode trust.

Participation processes can take many forms and involve different "publics." It is important to clarify the goals, participants, terms of reference, design and facilitation of such processes. Care must be taken to avoid favouring particular interests. Governments need to manage expectations and be clear on who has the authority to decide and act. Some participation processes will fail. Failed attempts may accelerate learning. The risk of failure is no justification for pursuing conventional approaches that are proven to be insufficient.

Participation is not the best approach in all circumstances. Some situations call for unilateral government action and a limited circle of influence.

(8) Slow down public policy: Allow citizens the time and space to find their own answers. Work with those affected, go at their speed and allow time for solutions to emerge. Governments sometimes rush to intervene before the solution has a chance to emerge naturally. While participation processes may appear slow, they may yield better and faster results than when governments act unilaterally. Governments need to treat policy decisions as a process of inquiry and experimentation and allow time for feedback and evidence to emerge. In many instances, it is advisable to start at a small scale and aim for "small wins" that yield better results over time. It is preferable to emphasize building capacity rather than finding perfect solutions so that capacity and ideas will be ready and available when needed.

(9) Build social capital: Both the bonding and bridging forms of social capital are important for resilience. Bonding social capital consists of establishing solidarity and trust among similar people. This solidarity helps weather adversity; however, tight bonds can also lead to rigidities and "brittleness" in the face of adversity if social groups are not open enough to allow for novelty. Bridging social capital consists of establishing networks of relationships among people, families and communities. It provides for diversity, variety and novelty, all of which are important for responding to surprises. It often takes intermediaries, such as social entrepreneurs or "connectors" to build these bridging connections. Social tolerance for diversity must exist for bridging to take place.

PERSPECTIVES ON EMERGENCE

The fact that the world is becoming more complex makes it necessary to anticipate emerging patterns so as to limit negative impacts and seize opportunities. By better understanding complexity and emergence (a feature of complexity), governments may be better able to address some of the more intricate challenges of our times.

A review of the literature on emergence in organizations suggests that the concept provides a useful analytical tool, but it should not be used as a normative concept.

The prevailing view in political science literature is that allowing for emergence (for example, improvisation and experimentation) in public organizations may lead to "breaking the rules" and therefore should be avoided. Taking the initiative may leave public services vulnerable to criticism and blame.

Since emergence encourages working across boundaries, organizational theory favours structure, procedures and rational planning over emergence. In the literature, emergence appears in discussion about organizational improvisation and bricolage, suggesting that it may help organizations adapt to changing circumstances. It is not always seen favourably since it can lead to challenging established practices.

The literature on systems theory offers another perspective: organizations should not be defined by their goals, structures and functions. Instead, they should be seen as a set of actors making decisions and acting on their knowledge and interests. Outcomes emerge as a result rather than being predetermined. Organizational action is not linear: trends are difficult to predict.

Approaching public administration in a way that encourages emergence can be complicated. Allowing too much emergence in organizations can make them vulnerable. If outcomes are emergent, performance cannot be easily measured. Emergence may affect efficiency. On the other hand, emergence helps organizations react quickly and has the advantage of making organizations more resilient.

Emergence and Complexity

Traditional strategic planning theory assumes that someone is in charge, that decisions can be determined centrally and that well designed procedures exist for implementing them.

The empirical study of the planning and implementation of large public projects provides a contrary perspective. Such projects are frequently plagued by cost overruns and delays. The response is generally to tighten controls, which makes matters worse because it does not take account of the complexity of the enterprise. Complexity theory offers insights that can help practitioners deal with large public projects. It suggests that the outcomes of complex projects do not flow directly from the decisions of officials. They result from a combination of actions and reactions in numerous subsystems. Outcomes emerge from the interaction among the actors involved and the context in which they interact.

Traditional planning approaches do not capture this dynamic, which is why they let practitioners down in steering action towards more desirable outcomes. Managers achieve better results when they have the discretion and flexibility to address the problem that confronts them as necessary rather than being held hostage to a predetermined pathway. This reveals the limits of conventional strategic planning.

Organizations are embedded in networks; each organization itself being a network. Actors and their relationships with others are more important than the structure of the organization. The quality of the actors and their interactions affects the quality of the processes. Interaction is the primary driver of performance. This has implications for the management of complex projects. Managers of complex projects need freedom to move. They need to be externally oriented. Creating trust among actors and paying attention to network activity and connectivity is more important for achieving results than central controls or organizational structure. Stakeholder involvement is positively correlated to project outcomes.

Co-creation, Complexity and Organizational Learning

Participants at the roundtable explored four approaches to learning: behaviour-based, cognitive, social constructivist and gestalt approaches. Complexity theory can be used to integrate these different theoretical approaches to organizational learning and bridge them. In doing so, it provides a framework to help understand organizational learning and how to enable it.

Organizations do not organically develop into learning organizations. An organization's ability to gain knowledge, understand its environment and produce creative solutions requires co-operation among individuals and groups, reliable communication systems and a culture of trust. Co-creation of an enabling environment is a pre-condition for learning.

Organizational learning is systemic and therefore more than the sum of its parts. It is the outcome of the interaction among learners. Organizational learning takes place in a social ecosystem. Organizations have a mutually adaptive or co-evolutionary relationship with their environment and all other organizations in that environment. The way each element influences and is in turn influenced by all other elements in the ecosystem is part of a process of co-evolution.

The exploration of different ways of working and relating is essential for innovation and the co-creation of an enabling environment. The search for a single optimal strategy is neither possible nor desirable in a changing or turbulent environment. Organizations will be more successful if they explore the space of possibilities through multiple, local micro-strategies.

When systems are pushed far from equilibrium, new structures and new order may emerge. Several alternatives are possible before settling into a new arrangement. It is a moment rich in innovative potential. When organizations are pushed far from established norms, they can make gains by attending to "the adjacent possible"—that is, deliberately scanning for ideas, practices and courses of action that hold untapped potential for meeting organizational needs and goals.

By seeing institutions, economies and societies as complex, co-evolving systems and by understanding the characteristics of these systems, it is possible to address apparently intractable problems.

A Practitioner View on Emergence: Singapore

Facing unpredictability and uncertainty requires a public service that is agile, innovative and adaptive. Overly lean policy units that focus on the problems of today are unlikely to take account of long-term possibilities or of the unintended consequences of today's actions. An over-emphasis on efficiency and cost-cutting can lock governments into rigid pathways that prove ineffective and costly in the long run.

To address this challenge, Singapore has made anticipative capacity a strategic priority. It embedded scenario planning in its annual budgetary and planning processes. This proved useful in bringing hidden assumptions and mental models to the surface. It helped forge a common language and frame of reference among senior leaders.

A Risk Assessment and Horizon Scanning (RAHS) program was developed to complement scenario planning. This computer-based tool helps analysts detect and investigate emerging strategic threats and opportunities.

Public Service for the 21st Century (PS21), which encourages the use of collaborative networking technologies, was introduced to develop a culture of openness to change and innovation. PS21 helps ensure that the public service is prepared to adapt to changing circumstances. This is complemented by strong leadership that fosters a favourable environment for new ideas.

Recently, the Singapore government established the Centre for Strategic Futures (CSF), a small dedicated group that serves as a focal point for futures-related work. The main tasks of the CFS are to challenge conformist thinking, calibrate strategic thinking processes, cultivate capacity to deal with uncertainty and shocks, and communicate emergent risks.

Program Ministries: the Netherlands

The Dutch government felt that it was not dealing with some social issues in an entirely satisfactory way. Two Program Ministries—virtual organizations that cut across ministries—were developed to help address youth care, housing and integration issues. These experiments were an extension of existing models, such as joined-up government and ministries-without-portfolio. It was hoped that, by unbundling vertical administration, a more fluid way of working would emerge that was better attuned to these challenging portfolios.

Creating virtual organizations was not without hurdles. First, Program Ministries are an odd structure within a context dominated by traditional ministries. The dominant model of traditional ministries hinders this new form to a great degree (for example, public servants within the Program Ministries are seen as outsiders).

Second, Program Ministries create matrix organizations that are an unfamiliar working model in the public service. Third, Program Ministries operate under the constraints of the traditional compliance and performance systems. The success of Program Ministries remains an open question.[4]

Participants noted that other countries are dealing with broad societal problems in other ways. Some countries are looking beyond the strict reliance on public sector organizations. Others are providing rewards for innovation in traditional ministries. While Program Ministries might have a short-term impact on performance, reorganization can be costly and time-consuming, with little evidence that it leads to better long-term results. Other options should be considered simultaneously.

Public Safety Centres: the Netherlands

Over the years, the Dutch government has created 47 Public Safety Centres (PSCs) whose mandate is to improve social safety at the local level. PSCs are networks of public services (for example, police, justice and social agencies) and non-public organizations that work together on some aspect of public safety and crime prevention. The main task of the PSCs is to deal with individual cases referred to them by any of the contributing partners. The networks share physical and digital space and use a co-operative approach. In essence, PSCs are a joined-up approach for addressing multifaceted problems.

The potential for success of the PSCs is linked to the motivation and talent of the participants who face a number of issues. For instance, tensions exist between the participants' formal accountabilities and reporting requirements to their home organizations and their responsibilities to each other in the context of the PSC. Managing multiple relationships and accountabilities is a challenge.

A promising development in the PSCs is that, over time, they have begun to organize around clusters of cases. This broadens their perspective and has potential policy implications because the appearance of clusters can signal emergent problems at local and national levels.

IMPLICATIONS OF EMERGENCE FOR GOVERNMENT

Emergence is a central concept in complexity theory. It is a descriptive term pointing to the patterns, structures or properties that develop through the multiplicity of interactions that continually constitute and reconstitute a complex system. Emergence can also be seen as a broader concept, pointing to the capability of society to develop new solutions to emerging problems. Complex systems cannot be controlled: they can only be constrained or enabled. This places a premium on the ability of actors—including government—to be agile and adaptive.

While organizational theory has long emphasized the need for organizations to adapt to their external environment, its main focus has been on organizational design—how best to align structures and functions to the context. Complexity theory is less optimistic than organizational theory about organizational design being the solution to emerging circumstances. For instance, research shows that there is no correlation between organizational form and outcomes. There are, however, strong correlations between policy outcomes and the use of multiple, local strategies, collaboration and trust. In this sense, complexity theory is a theoretical advancement: it provides an explanatory framework with concepts such as self organization, emergence and connectivity.

Understanding the concept of emergence and seeing institutions, economies and societies as complex, co-evolving systems can help governments address apparently intractable problems, such as conflict and major geopolitical issues. Difficult and complicated problems can be managed using a conventional approach that, based on evidence and rational planning, breaks the problem down into its constituent parts and tackles the parts in sequence. Complex issues require different approaches. The first challenge is to recognize when a problem is complex.

Participants at the roundtable identified nine principles to guide practitioners in addressing public issues that emerge from a complex operating context.

(1) Create space to recognize what might be emerging: Governments need to build anticipative capacity by employing foresight activities such as horizon scanning, scenario planning and pattern recognition to scan for long-term trends and canvass for weak signals and unexpected shocks.

(2) Listen to a variety of voices: Listening to different voices and views, inside and outside one's organization can improve one's understanding of what is emerging. This includes listening to the "silent voices" and paradoxical viewpoints.

(3) Embrace complexity: Complexity should be treated as a threat but also as an opportunity. New developments that emerge from complexity, including crises, represent opportunities for needed change and renewal. People can be enabled to deal with complexity by reducing organizational and operational barriers.

(4) Create spaces to explore: Discrete spaces can be created within organizations in which people can experiment and innovate. Multi-disciplinary groups can be tasked with identifying patterns and developing new narratives or understandings of complex reality.

(5) Create room for bricolage: Create room for bricolage by preserving some level of redundancy. Bricoleurs typically think and act beyond their current tasks and work units. They span boundaries and take initiative. For bricolage to

work, it needs some degree of social capital and trust. It can be inhibited by control and heavy compliance requirements.

(6) Use multiple strategies: It is neither possible nor desirable to search for an optimum strategy in a changing or turbulent environment. Instead, multiple, micro-strategies are essential for innovation and co-creating desirable outcomes. Mega-solutions are high risk. Pilot projects and experiments can reduce the risk of failure and improve the likelihood of success.

(7) Recognize the need for new approaches to deal with complex problems: There is a need for "neue Kombinationen" to tackle complex societal problems. Traditional strategic planning processes and traditional performance management systems have limitations. Sticking to rigid, pre-defined plans can lead to paralysis. Reorganization is generally not the answer. These responses could inadvertently constrain innovation and hinder public organizations in reacting effectively to complex problems.

(8) Promote organizational learning: Organizational learning helps people deal with complexity. Complexity provides an explanation of how environments can either inhibit or enable individual learning and the contribution of individuals to the learning process. In this learning process, it is necessary to take a holistic approach, which contributes to an understanding of how public organizations can co-evolve with emerging patterns in their environment.

(9) Focus on leadership competencies: Governments can benefit from bringing in leaders who are able to create trust, manage networks and who are non-hierarchical and connected with society. Leaders should be able to grasp opportunities to fulfill a mission and identify and use emerging trends, new policy paradigms and windows of opportunity to achieve outcomes. They should have a good understanding of their environment and be able to use this understanding to make proactive interventions.

SUMMARY OF FINDINGS

A number of important findings arose from the first roundtable.

Participants learned that resilience is supported by some fundamental adaptive systems and cycles that humans have evolved over time. Governments can cultivate resilience by supporting these systems and cycles. Resilience stems from self-reliance and supportive relationships, while neglect and dependency undermine it. The relationship between the state and society needs to continually strike a balance that promotes the former and avoids the latter. Optimism bolsters resilience. Governments should therefore emphasize strengths-based strategies and use positive narratives that provide direction and create hope.

To cultivate resilience, practitioners should involve those most affected by the issues. This approach may seem slower at first, but progress will be faster and more effective in the long run. Participation builds community capacity and resilience. Public administrators should be careful not to artificially separate politics and policy, as political leaders play a key role in promoting approaches that encourage resilience and collective capacity-building.

Multifaceted interventions (that is, numerous strategies at various points in adaptive cycles) at multiple levels (for example, individuals, families and communities) provide cumulative protection. The best solutions stem from collaboration across disciplines and levels. The role of government is to create conditions conducive to social innovators and help scale up promising innovations.

Four themes emerged from the roundtable to guide practitioners working in complex circumstances with unpredictable public issues.

First, governments have a wide range of options available for addressing complex issues. The conventional view of public policy as a series of authoritative decisions along a linear organizational pathway must give way to a view of public policy as results stemming from a dynamic combination of actions. The use of multiple micro-strategies and learning-by-doing are more effective than all-encompassing, single strategies. Oversimplifying complex problems makes them worse.

Second, many tools are available to help governments better explore and anticipate. Scenario planning, horizon scanning, risk assessment and other foresight methods help reveal assumptions, "blind spots" and emerging risks. They help calibrate medium- and long-term thinking. Organizational learning can help improve government capacity to deal with disruptions and shocks.

Third, working across scales is crucial when dealing with complex issues. Emerging issues that appear at one level may well appear in many other places and at other levels. A specific case may turn out to be the early manifestation of an emerging trend.

Finally, it is possible to improve the likelihood of "smart" interventions. Doing this starts with the ability to recognize complexity and work with the emergent properties that characterize it. It involves balancing the need for continuity and stability with the need for continual change. It entails recognizing the importance of anticipative, innovative and adaptive capacities.

Chapter 17
The Canada Roundtable

The Canada roundtable focused on achieving public results. Participants looked at how governments can shift from focusing on program results to system-wide and societal results, and what is needed to support this shift. They explored when and how to engage citizens and communities to achieve better public results. They discussed the barriers to achieving better public results and how to overcome them. Finally, they examined the relationships between public policy results and civic results, and strategies for pursuing ambitious policy priorities.[1]

ACHIEVING SOCIETAL AND CIVIC RESULTS

The participants explored the relationship between civic engagement and public policy results. Discussions highlighted that when public results are seen as a collective enterprise involving people, their families, their communities and society as a whole, government enjoys an expanding range of options to achieve them.

The three case studies that follow reveal some common elements that contributed to their success. These initiatives focused on societal results. They all reached beyond government circles. Government simultaneously played multiple roles, such as law enforcer, enabler and facilitator.

These cases provide positive reinforcement to the view that focusing on societal results is central to achieving better public results. They also show how pursuing policy results at the societal level and deepening civic results gives rise to new challenges. New forms of political leadership are needed to find solutions at the community level and to relate to the media in different ways. Public servants, for their part, must reach out beyond their agencies to fulfill their mission. New approaches are needed to monitor and encourage progress when collective efforts are involved.

Homelessness Partnering Strategy: Canada

In Canada, as elsewhere, homelessness is a complex, societal problem shaped by an array of issues related to housing, health, mental health, drug use, criminality, race, labour market, integration, etc. The majority of activities and services relevant to address homelessness are found at local levels.

The Canadian government's approach to homelessness is expressed in the Homelessness Partnering Strategy (HPS). As a result of this strategy, the government shifted its role from providing direct program funding to leveraging community efforts. The HPS helps communities organize, build capacity and fund their priority projects.

The HPS is notable, in part, because it brings players to the table who would not normally work together. It makes use of collective wisdom and resources in communities. It provides a model for how government can work with multiple stakeholders to tackle complex, pan-Canadian problems. The HPS recognizes that one size does not fit all. It enables diverse communities to organize and respond in unique ways that fit their local context. The approach encourages community endeavour. It focuses on capacity building at the community level and provides incentives for partners to connect related initiatives along the value chain of results. The continuation of the program despite two changes of government (at the time of writing) and a detailed program evaluation speak to the support of the general public for the initiative.

The HPS faced many challenges. The lack of alignment between traditional systems of accountability and the demands of a horizontal initiative involving multiple actors and stakeholders imposed a heavy burden on the participants in time and overall costs. With the array of parties working to address this complex issue, it proved difficult to monitor progress and attribute results. While the HPS was successful in bringing diverse groups together to address a shared societal problem, establishing a direct causal link to reducing homelessness remains tentative.

Labour Mobility/Foreign Qualifications Recognition: Canada

The Labour Mobility/Foreign Qualifications Recognition (FQR) initiative is a collaborative effort involving multiple levels of government and regulatory organizations to facilitate labour mobility across the Canadian federation. It also aims to ensure that immigrants who were trained abroad can practise their profession anywhere in Canada. The challenge is for federal, provincial and territorial governments and some 500 organizations that regulate a wide range of professions to construct and agree on a common system.

Efforts were first made to address labour mobility through the establishment of the Agreement on Internal Trade. Dialogue and collaboration among multiple levels of government and the organizations led to significant breakthroughs in labour mobility. Building on this success, a similar approach was used to establish the Pan-Canadian Framework for the Assessment and Recognition of Qualifications. The framework set out a shared vision, common guiding principles and desired outcomes for improving the assessment and recognition of foreign qualifications in Canada.

The federal department of Human Resources and Skills Development Canada (HRSDC) was responsible for engaging the 13 jurisdictions involved and their regulators. In playing this role, the government acted as facilitator and sought to build a relationship of trust among the stakeholders. The most important result was the creation of a platform for co-operation that allowed for new forms of collaboration to emerge.

A number of key findings emerged from the discussion of this initiative. First, collaboration and trust is essential to the success of multi-partner processes. Second, a bottom-up approach that enables all stakeholders to have a meaningful say in defining the solutions and a clear commitment to a common goal are critical. Third, shifting the focus from rules to outcomes—or from controlling training requirements for different professions to ensuring that people have the competencies to perform the work—allows real progress.

Singapore Prison Service: Singapore

During the first decade of the new millennium, the Singapore Prison Service (SPS) underwent a radical transformation from an organization plagued by overcrowded prisons, high staff turnover, low employee morale and poor public perception to a leading edge, award winning, public service agency. The genesis of this transformation was a focus on steering ex-offenders "towards becoming responsible citizens with the help of their families and the community." This vision was crafted with the help of over 800 staff, strategic partners in government and voluntary welfare organizations using a variety of means including retreats, facilitated dialogues and online intranet forums.

It soon became clear that internal structures and resources were not sufficient to support the vision. The desired outcomes called for community engagement to create a system of reintegration with a strong emphasis on family and community support. The initiative included a media campaign to improve the public's perception of ex-offenders, a networked governance structure to oversee the co-ordination of after-care services and an annual public education effort aimed at creating awareness of the benefits of giving second chances and at inspiring community action.

The SPS has seen dramatic improvements. Recidivism declined from 44.4 percent in 1998 to 26.5 percent in 2007. Nearly 2,000 employers have hired ex-offenders, and 1,400 volunteers have offered counselling and development activities for inmates. For the participants at the roundtable, this case study was a powerful example that illustrated the utility of the New Synthesis Framework in thinking about the pathways to better public results. The case showed that expanded possibilities exist when a policy problem is framed at the societal level. It revealed the diversity of roles that government must play to pursue better overall societal results, including law enforcer, but also leader, facilitator and enabler of change. Finally, it provided an example of the positive impact that can be achieved when government shares the responsibility for public results with other stakeholders and members of society instead of acting alone.

ACHIEVING RESULTS OF HIGH PUBLIC VALUE

Participants explored how recent research on well-being may help practitioners address public policy issues. Including this topic on the agenda was an important decision for the network. The key findings influenced the thinking of the group going forward.

Positive trumps negative. Positivity has a far greater impact on well-being than the absence of negativity. This supports the notion that, to promote societal well-being, public policy should not focus primarily on problem solving, deficit reduction and crisis management. Instead, it should focus on strengths and convey an elevated view of what people can accomplish together.

Social trumps material. Individuals are inherently relational. Social capital contributes as much, if not more, to societal well-being than material prosperity. This finding supports the use of collaborative networks and citizen engagement in public services.

Generosity pays. People are both individualistic and altruistic. They are social beings with deep attachments to their communities. This warrants a reassessment of public policy that is based on individual incentives. It may be possible to achieve better public results at a lower overall cost to society by designing public services so that helping others is built into the fabric of the service delivery system.

Measure the right things. Economic indicators are insufficient measures of societal progress. A more accurate assessment requires using a basket of indicators that measure economic results, quality of life, intergenerational fairness and life satisfaction. Measuring life satisfaction in national statistical agency surveys would help change the discourse around societal results and reveal areas that require collective action.

Support experimentation. Trust reduces the cost of experimentation and the risk of failure. In the government context, this signals the need to ensure that the measures to combat malfeasance do not create an environment where people are not willing to experiment for fear of failure. Failed experiments and learning-by-doing are part of the collective learning process.

Citizens are value creators. Citizens are much more than users and beneficiaries of public services. On many fronts, it is more effective to let people act on their own behalf and to incorporate engagement into public policy design. Furthermore, recent research indicates that people are happier when they have an opportunity to work together towards solutions. This in turn reinforces a positive feedback loop of increasing trust, positivity and well-being.

The science of well-being provided participants with important insights that could result in concrete and tangible improvements to government systems and practices.

Measures of well-being are deeply democratic. They involve asking citizens about their life satisfaction, social well-being and their satisfaction with public services. These measures provide a very different perspective than efficiency measures. Measures of life satisfaction can help policy makers compare and distinguish between priorities and enable a form of weighting among options based on what is really important to people.

Several determinants of well-being are not under individual control and can only be achieved by working with others. Citizen engagement is not about devolving responsibilities to citizens but about a shared arrangement in which parties take responsibility for what lies within their sphere of influence. An important aspect of well-being is rooted outside the paid economy and within social contexts at the family, neighbourhood, community and national levels.

Change takes place through experimentation. However, to take root, ideas must percolate from the bottom up, be shaped from the top down and be scalable. Learning by doing and learning from failure, in a process of experimentation and innovation, are significant drivers of progress.

Multiple layers of trust operate in the public sphere. Trust within government, between citizens and government, and among citizens is central to good governance. There is room for debate as to whether it is necessary to build trust inside and outside the public service simultaneously or whether internal trust creates the foundation for the public to trust the public service. There is, however, a relationship between trust and control mechanisms. Government control systems are often designed from the standpoint of distrust. Distrust breeds distrust, producing a self-fulfilling prophesy. Many practitioners have witnessed an increase in the layers of controls and reporting requirements that serve to increase the likelihood of errors and fuel a cycle of distrust.

A "narrative of hope" has substantial value for mobilizing collective efforts towards achieving ambitious public results. This narrative helps bridge the gap between public perception, public assumptions and reality on important public policy issues.

Further work is needed on how the media influence a sense of well-being and life satisfaction.

PUBLIC ENGAGEMENT AS A CONTRIBUTOR TO PUBLIC RESULTS

Public engagement provides an alternate way of thinking about how governments, citizens and society can work together to solve complex problems.

There are four basic steps in public involvement processes: gathering views; deliberating on the correct response; taking action; and evaluating the results. Evaluation is important for building trust and for improving the effectiveness of the process.

Various types of public involvement processes were discussed at the roundtable, including consultative, deliberative and engagement processes.

The traditional form of public involvement is through a consultative process, in which government seeks the views of the public, but deliberates and acts alone. This approach is not adapted to addressing complex problems; it presents a number of shortfalls. In a consultative process, government typically frames the issue. This may be appropriate when government controls the issue and may act to bring about the expected results. This approach sends a clear message that government is in charge and responsible for the solution. However, it is unlikely to work when the problem definition and its solution are beyond government reach and require the active contribution of multiple actors.

In a deliberative process, government seeks the views of citizens and encourages public participation in framing the issue and shaping solutions, but makes the final decision on how to proceed. This approach allows citizens to work together to overcome differences. The approach is not without risks, since the public may arrive at solutions that exceed government authority and willingness to implement or that do not take its other priorities and needs into account. The risks can be mitigated by setting clear parameters.

In a collaborative public engagement process, citizens are involved at all stages. They contribute to shaping the issue and are a part of implementing the solutions with government and other actors. In essence, public engagement is about enabling people to take back the responsibilities that belong to them and that they can best perform. Collaborative approaches are best suited to addressing complex issues.

Many government operations do not require direct citizen engagement. In the case of behaviour-based issues, such as smoking cessation, obesity, global warming or innovations, governments can only make progress with the support of citizens.

There are numerous examples of failed government-led public engagement process. In some cases, consultations were used to buy time or justify an existing decision. Many public engagement processes failed due to a lack of clarity on the objectives and design problems.

A number of factors contribute to the success of public engagement processes. They should be broad based and build on collective ownership of outcomes. This entails a collective effort at framing the issue, a shared responsibility for action and a deliberate effort at integrating diverse perspectives. The design is critical and should include experimentation, careful measurement and the ongoing evaluation of results.

Citizen engagement entails risks. Politicians may be concerned about processes over which they have less control. The public has little appetite for time-consuming processes without the assurance that their views will be taken seriously. Individual commitment to action may be difficult to sustain.

Citizen engagement requires new skills for public policy makers and public administrators. Facilitation skills are needed to navigate the process and help move an issue from the "I" of government acting alone to the "We" of collective and shared results.

Web 2.0 social networking tools are making collaboration easier and less costly. Through social networks, citizens are able to connect and help each other in ways not previously possible. Ideas can spread and collect support. Citizens can help one another in areas of common concern with or without government involvement.

Virtual communities are proliferating. They can be used to encourage experimentation and social innovation. These communities can be encouraged and supported but they cannot be created or commanded. They are reshaping and expanding the public space in our networked societies. They are redefining how public goods are created and how collective enterprises are taking shape. They represent a challenge and an opportunity to reposition and prepare government to face the challenges of the 21st century.

Bolsa Família Program: Brazil

Bolsa Família is a program of conditional transfer payments to low-income families that focuses on maternal and children's health, school attendance and social protection. It benefits approximately 50 million Brazilians and operates on an annual budget of US$7.4 billion.

The program originated as an assortment of small-scale, conditional cash transfer initiatives that evolved through learning and experimentation. After the success of the first initiatives, an increasing number of government agencies set up their own conditional cash transfer program to address goals related to a diverse range of issues, such as social work, health, education, food security, energy and child labour. Each agency used different registries, payment mechanisms, conditions and administrative processes.

The proliferation of programs created serious problems for recipients. Eventually, the programs were collapsed into a single national program. Bolsa Família was born with the understanding that "citizens are not divided into ministries." This consolidation was the first step towards empowering families to make their own decisions. Each of the earlier programs may have been efficient in its own right, but the sum total was neither efficient nor effective at reducing poverty or at eliminating the problems associated with it.

There were significant risks in removing conditions and allowing recipients to decide how best to use the money. The initiative was politically controversial. Much of the media attention focused on the risk of fraud or corruption. When mistakes were made inadvertently, media coverage provided no distinction between administrative errors and intentional fraud.

Perseverance paid off and the outcome has been positive. Bolsa Família has contributed measurably to reducing poverty, child undernutrition and inequality. It empowers citizens to make choices about their lives and to play a critical role in achieving the societal goal of alleviating poverty.

A number of important findings emerged from the discussion of the Bolsa Família case study. First, reducing layers of control can lead to better overall results. Indeed, in this case fewer conditions and controls were a necessary condition for better societal results. Second, better societal results are not synonymous with better departmental results. Third, mistakes will be made and, in these instances, political leadership is needed for the public to understand the difference between mistakes and wrongdoing. No organization, private or public, can guarantee error-free performance.

DISENTANGLING COMPLIANCE AND PERFORMANCE

Participants at the roundtable explored whether and how contemporary compliance and performance systems in government were serving their intended purposes or serving as barriers to better public results.

Participants observed that the role of controls is to ensure compliance with the laws and rules that govern the conduct of public officials and organizations and to reduce the risk of mismanagement. Controls in a public service context vary from "hard" rules that include constitutional conventions, legislation, regulations and policy requirements enforced with the threat of sanctions to "softer" forms, such as policy standards and guidelines, organizational culture and values.

In contrast, the role of performance information systems is to provide decision makers with the information they need to improve decisions to achieve better results. In practice, however, some sources of performance information (whether systematic and formal or unsystematic and informal) are used to both ensure compliance and measure performance. The use of performance targets is an example.

Increased layers of control affect the quality of services and the ability of public organizations to achieve results. Participants noted that, in some cases, public servants operate in a climate of fear that inhibits innovation. Controls may also hinder the functioning of third-party agencies. Participants noted there are examples of controls and reporting requirements consuming up to one-third of the resources of service agencies.

One easy improvement may be for government agencies to report publicly on the cost of controls and reporting requirements. This would allow for greater scrutiny by the public and by the legislative assembly on the cost to taxpayers to meet internal bureaucratic requirements.

Participants argued that disentangling compliance and performance systems would be a step forward but still insufficient to reduce substantially the barriers to achieving better public results. Ultimately, a reform agenda should focus on reducing the "culture of compliance" and reducing the cost of controls.

Several factors relative to changing the culture of compliance characteristic of public administration in many countries need more research. One such factor may be the reluctance of elected officials to allow management discretion. This reluctance, in effect, may limit the role of the public sector in carrying out predictable tasks. Government may find it increasingly difficult to adapt to serving in an environment characterized by complexity, uncertainty and volatility.

Another factor is the progressive blurring that has occurred in the private and the public sectors between audit for compliance, audit for value for money, comprehensive audit, program evaluation and policy research. Notwithstanding the need to disentangle compliance and performance systems, performance information systems need to be reoriented towards system-wide and societal results.

A number of factors impact the success of collaborative initiatives, including an explicit mandate and political support for interagency collaboration; whether the organizational culture encourages information-sharing and collaboration; and the use of incentive systems to reward government-wide actions.

A system of shared accountability for government-wide results is unlikely to be sustainable without some institutional adjustment to counter the dominance of vertical silos. A public administration fit for the future must find ways to reconcile the need of the legislative assembly to ensure that voted funds are used for the intended purpose, the need of public administrators and decision makers to initiate change to achieve better results and the need of citizens to be informed about the progress of their society.

Federal Financial Agreement: Australia

Under Australia's previous system of federal-state financial relations, tied grants from the federal government to states in areas such as healthcare and education were used to co-ordinate and promote societal outcomes. These grants were hampered by overlapping roles and responsibilities. Moreover, the conditions accompanying them were onerous and included detailed reporting requirements.

In January 2009, a national intergovernmental agreement on federal financial relations came into effect. The agreement reflects an understanding that it takes many levels of government and multiple agencies working together to tackle most social issues. It aims to help the federal government work more effectively as a partner with the eight state governments and create an enabling context for negotiating outcomes in key areas of social policy.

The agreement reshaped the relationship between levels of government. It removed the conditions accompanying transfer payments, eliminated non-essential reporting requirements and focused on accountability for outcomes rather than on inputs or processes. This gives the states the flexibility to direct resources in ways that will produce the best results in the unique context of each state.

The increased flexibility for allocating resources at the state level is balanced by an increased accountability for publicly reporting on results. States report against performance indicators and are assessed by an independent third party. Performance reports are produced in plain language to encourage public debate.

Participants learned important lessons in discussing this case study. First, it is difficult to let go of old habits and the silo mentality that characterize public administration in most countries. Politicians still demand reports on inputs. It takes time to develop meaningful performance indicators and timely information. Second, there is a need for new capabilities among public servants to support the change in roles, responsibilities and relationships.

SUMMARY OF FINDINGS

This roundtable concluded that focusing on societal and civic results enables public organizations to achieve public policy results of higher public value. An increasing number of public results cannot be achieved by government working alone or by imposing solutions from the top down. The challenges of the 21st century require greater collaboration across government agencies, between governments and with the public.

In this context, citizens are more than users or beneficiaries of government services: they are value creators. An increasing number of public policy results can only be accomplished by government and society working in synergy. This means modern governments are serving in an expanded public space. Serving in this space requires government to act beyond its traditional roles to generate a collective response to a multifaceted problem.

Research reveals that active participation increases trust among people and institutions and improves the quality of democratic governance. It also contributes to life satisfaction and well-being.

However, in many countries, the control mechanisms associated with government are rooted in distrust and breed distrust, imposing costs on society and increasing the likelihood of error. Institutional fear of failure and risk aversion is stifling experimentation, innovation and interagency collaboration. No organization, private or public, can guarantee error-free performance. Government must learn to fail small, fail fast and fail safely.

Chapter 18
The Brazil Roundtable

Participants at the Brazil roundtable explored how government and society can work in synergy in a co-evolving system of public governance. The event focused on how the state can effectively use its authority and resources to leverage the collective power of society to achieve better public results. It looked at the rise of public participation, social networking and co-production, and how these are transforming the role of government, public organizations and public servants.[1]

A SEARCH FOR BALANCE

Traditionally, public administration has focused on the role of the state as legislator, service provider and decision maker to serve the public and the collective interests. To a large extent, public administration has underestimated the contribution of other actors in society and undervalued the role played by citizens.

Public sector reforms since the 1980s have not addressed these issues. Some reforms embraced a market approach, and aimed at making government more efficient. Others were designed to bring services closer to users. Many countries now feature a blend of decentralization, delegation, disaggregation and devolution. While these two prevailing approaches helped governments address some issues that could not be handled in the traditional way, new problems emerged. Insolvency crises in the private sector and market failures point to the risk of relying too much on market solutions.

Concerns have been raised about the effect of market solutions and disaggregation on public sector values, such as accountability, equity and fairness and the primacy of politics for steering society. In response to these and other concerns, many countries are searching for a new balance between the role of the state, market and society. There is no going back to traditional approaches. New approaches are needed that take into account the increasing complexity of public policy issues, the need for collective action across sectors and the diversity of circumstances.

In the Brazilian Context

The roundtable provided the participants with an opportunity to gain a better appreciation of the reforms led by the Brazilian government to manage a successful transition from a military regime to democratic governance. The country has made constant economic and social progress. While many challenges and problems remain, it has made great strides in overcoming poverty and social exclusion.

Brazil's success in recovering from the global economic crisis that began in 2008 was due to the balanced approach the country took in regard to the role of the state, market and society. It is a source of inspiration for other developing and emerging economies.

The policy mix that helped Brazil weather the global economic storm included a sound regulatory framework (while considered outdated by some, this framework protected the country against the worst effects of the global financial crisis); strong public institutions, including three public banks that were able to extend credit when it was most needed; and a suitable mix of social policies that shielded people from the most negative impact of the crisis while encouraging adaptation.

Brazil will continue to improve its capacity for democratic governance and sound public administration. It will continue to pursue an agenda aimed at building capacity, encouraging innovation and promoting competitiveness.

In the Uruguayan Context

In 2005, the incoming government in Uruguay found a country confronted with significant challenges. Among its problems: rampant poverty among children, single mothers and temporary workers; and an undiversified economy vulnerable to external shocks.

The government created new public institutions and launched a number of structural reforms, including a comprehensive health system, a tripling of the budget for education, a substantial increase in child benefits, and tax reforms. It also included an *Investment Promotion Act* and a *Public-Private Partnership Act*.

The government achieved significant progress. The poverty rate fell from 31 percent in 2004 to 20 percent in 2008. As of 2009, Uruguay has the lowest income inequality in Latin America, based on the GINI Index. Public-private investments have led to new industries and products.

While Uruguay has modernized some of its public agencies, it did not invest as heavily in strengthening the capabilities of its central administration. Weaknesses remain in areas such as regulation, policy development, evaluation and the co-ordination of government-wide policies. Strengthening the centre of government will be necessary for future progress.

Developing core capacity in Uruguay's public sector has been limited by weaknesses in the budget, career management and information and national statistics systems and, until recently, by the absence of an e-government agenda for the public sector. The government has introduced a number of measures to address these problems.

PRACTICAL EXPLORATIONS

Participants observed that the New Synthesis Framework is trying to avoid the pitfalls of a mental map that conceives public governance and public administration as a series of binary choices. It does not suggest that practitioners choose between the private or public delivery of public services, centralized or decentralized governance, acting alone or working with multiple actors. Rather, the New Synthesis Framework points to the vast array of options available. The choice of approach must be context- and circumstance-specific. At the end of the day, however, it is important to remember that government will always remain the insurer of last resort when the collective interest demands it.

Good governance is more than what government can do on its own. It is about what government can achieve with the private sector, civil society and citizens. Modern communications technologies and social networking are transforming the landscape of modern governance. Dynamic relationships, participation and co-ordination are essential for good governance.

Ultimately, good governance requires taking care of the fundamentals, including a solid regulatory framework, respected public institutions and well performing public organizations. While accountability is a central feature of good government, contemporary demands in many countries for an increasing number of control mechanisms must be kept in check. The cost of control measures must be commensurate with the risk of mismanagement. Public sector organizations cannot perform well without being able to innovate—and this is not possible without reasonable risk-taking and learning-by-doing.

Homelessness Partnering Strategy: Canada

The homelessness case study, presented at the roundtable in Canada, was discussed again in Brazil. This time, the focus was on how best to balance the direct use of government authority with the need to build capacity at the community level to tackle complex public problems.

In 1999, the federal government created the National Homelessness Initiative to fund transitional housing and other services for homeless people across the country. By 2007, the complexity of the problem had become clearer and the government realized that focusing on housing would not be sufficient. Federal funding could only go so far in addressing the issue. The government needed to mobilize and align its actions with other levels of government, organizations and community groups to make progress. The national Homelessness Partnering Strategy (HPS) is based on an understanding that the federal government has limited capacity to act on its own. The government plays a convening role by creating a platform and incentives for collaboration.

The HPS assembles community groups, stakeholders and multiple levels of government who come to the table with their respective mandates, authorities and resources. The HPS distributes federal funds[2] and mobilizes existing sources of funding found within communities and other public organizations. The program is delivered through Community Advisory Boards (CABs) that review and recommend project proposals to the relevant authorities for approval. Local organizations work in horizontal networks or in joint arrangements alongside agencies from multiple levels of government to deliver the approved services.

This government-sponsored mechanism has been effective at building community capacity. The HPS does not undermine traditional accountability structures: rather, it aims to complement them. The government retains control over its funding allocations, and accountability structures apply fully on project proposals reviewed by the CABs and approved by the responsible authority.

However, it is difficult to achieve, monitor and attribute results for complex issues like homelessness, particularly when the actions are tailored at the community level and multiple parties are addressing the issue from different perspectives, ranging from mental health and poverty to housing and criminal justice. The HPS currently measures the results supported by government funding rather than following the chain of activities among actors that lead to broader societal outcomes. Establishing a link between the HPS and overall levels of homelessness has thus been tentative. Moreover, the lack of alignment between traditional reporting systems and the demands of a horizontal initiative has been costly for the participants in terms of time and resources.

National Health Conferences and Participatory Processes: Brazil

Social participation issues entered the mainstream Brazilian political agenda when military rule ended in the 1980s. The role played by new stakeholders, organized in various social movements, strengthened civil society and enabled its participation in various spheres of collective life. The 1988 Federal Constitution incorporated different forms of social participation at the local and federal levels into the political system. Participation takes place through a range of channels, such as public policy councils, conferences, hearings and public consultations.

Brazil's National Health Conferences are hailed as democratic spaces for the meeting of different sectors of society, interested in evaluating, discussing, criticizing and suggesting public policies. Representatives from across civil society and the state mobilize, discuss and evaluate policies, and produce proposals and guidelines to inform and influence the government's agenda and actions.

The 8th Health Conference, held in 1986, involved over 4,000 participants, including intellectuals, professionals, trade unionists and healthcare users. Half the delegates represented civil society; the other half came from public institutions and healthcare facilities. It was a watershed moment in the development of Brazilian health policy. The Conference's final report became the main input of the health chapter of the 1988 Constitution. The reforms it recommended were adopted and eventually led to the creation of Brazil's publicly funded universal healthcare system, the Unified Health System (SUS).

The 13th Health Conference, held in 2007, mobilized an unprecedented number and diversity of actors. Over 1.3 million people participated in the process. Over 4,400 Brazilian municipalities staged local conferences, followed by 27 state-level conferences and one final national conference. The process of debate, negotiation and consensus building resulted in a wide range of proposals for consideration at the national conference. Delegates at the national level included SUS users, health workers, public managers, union representatives and civil society organizations. The conference rules gave equal rights to all delegates, regardless of their sector. Discussions moved systematically through roundtables to thematic plenary sessions to a final plenary in which proposals that had received favourable votes in previous sessions were debated and voted upon. The result was a final report consisting of 857 proposals.

While the Brazilian government was not bound to implement these proposals, the national conference provided officials with information that represents the aggregate preferences of the majority of the people involved. It also gave officials important insight on emerging issues and potential solutions that public officials had not previously contemplated. This allowed them to develop policies that more closely reflected the reality and interests of society.

Working with others to achieve results entails sharing responsibilities, risks and power. Governments must build mechanisms that enable citizens to listen to each other and interact with public administrators to improve results. Social groups can generate public policy ideas, influence the agenda of government and even produce public goods.

Participatory spaces, such as the Brazilian conferencing systems, are an important instrument of modern governance. They add information, diagnoses and collective knowledge. They encourage respect for diversity and the open expression of ideas. They can contribute to building bridges and fostering consensus. They must involve some degree of tension as they give a voice to actors who have been previously marginalized. They enable the multiplicity of interests not previously considered to be recognized. They can be incubators for experimentation and innovation.

Social participation creates a number of challenges. The Brazilian health conferences case shows that, as the number and diversity of actors and interests increase, finding consensus and setting priorities becomes more difficult. The sheer number of proposals that emerge from large-scale participation efforts may be difficult to convert into effective public policy. The 13ᵗʰ Health Conference demonstrated that, in some instances, social participation may polarize delegates and crystallize opposition to government policies. As an example, delegates eventually rejected two significant proposals that the government supported.

Better Justice Outcomes through a Citizen-centred Approach: United Kingdom

Beginning in the 1980s, governments in the United Kingdom built momentum towards a high imprisonment approach to criminal justice. Since then, prison populations have grown dramatically, despite falling crime rates. Funding pressures to support a high incarceration rate have strained probation resources and pushed aside interventions known to prevent recidivism. In addition to these issues, the historical approach to delivering criminal justice services meant services were not integrated, control was centralized, and programs were over-specified, over-measured and focused on outputs rather than outcomes.

In the first decade of the new millennium, the British government concluded that it needed to improve the functioning of the criminal justice system, reduce recidivism and assist victims of crime. Through the Transforming Justice program, the government introduced a series of reform initiatives. It created the National Offender Management Service as an executive agency. The agency helped reduce short-term political pressures and focus attention on fostering innovation in the system and producing better results. The overall approach was to focus on geographic areas and contract with service providers in those areas to reduce the overall demand on the system and the resources needed to run it. The purpose was to make services more effective in achieving justice outcomes while reducing costs. Funding pressures were a key driver of reform.

A crisis can be important in destabilizing an old paradigm and legitimizing the need for change. The fiscal crisis moved the British government from providing a direct service to exploring different avenues, including the possibility of collective action among a wide set of people and organizations.

In Wales, for example, an innovative approach was taken to dealing with adult female offenders. There were many barriers to helping these offenders rehabilitate and re-enter society after their sentences. One such barrier was that prisons for Welsh female offenders were located hundreds of miles away in England. This distance meant the women were at risk of losing touch with their families, friends and support systems back home. Working with citizen groups and other stakeholders in Wales, new ways were found to ensure that some women could serve their sentences close to home and receive the support needed to avoid re-offending.

The path to this citizen-centred approach involved leadership on the part of public officials and the development of new skills in dealing with conflict in social participation processes in the community to establish conducive conditions for the program to work for all involved.

This approach illustrated how communities that have a sense of ownership of their problems can be central to solutions. This sense of ownership can be enabled or encouraged. Public officials can convene citizens and stakeholders to help bring issues to the surface and deal with conflicting interests on the way to a collective solution. However, this is not easy or straightforward. It requires significant skills and capabilities.

Examples abound of projects that prove their worth but are never scaled up to become mainstream because of rigidities across the system. In this case, it is not yet clear if the Welsh experiment will be extended into other parts of the system.

The Public Health System and Mechanisms of Institutional Governance: Brazil

Until the 1980s, the Brazilian healthcare system was institutionally fragmented. There was administrative discontinuity between the three levels of government, no integration between private and public health services, and most of the population had little or no access to healthcare.

By the end of the 1980s, one of the most important civil society organizations—the "Sanitary Movement" formed by intellectuals, professionals, trade unionists and users of healthcare—advocated a comprehensive health reform for the country. The movement designed and promoted a plan for an alternative health system. It eventually succeeded in having health enshrined in the 1988 Constitution as a citizens' right, requiring the state to provide universal and equal access to health services.

Under a subsequent health reform in 1996, Brazil established the Unified Health System (Sistema Unificado de Saúde—SUS) based on decentralized, universal access. Municipalities provide comprehensive and free healthcare to individuals, paying special attention to primary healthcare, which is a pillar of the system. The system serves more than 70 percent of the population and exists alongside a private system of for-profit and not-for-profit organizations.

The SUS demonstrates that it is possible to build a new model of primary health on the principles of fairness and solidarity—if there is political will and strong public support.

Decentralization to municipalities, community participation and complementing private and public services are some of the important features stemming from the SUS's innovative institutional design. All three levels of government (federal, state and municipal) work hard to encourage those living in poverty to use and benefit from the health system through initiatives such as the Family Health Program and the deployment of "agentes de saúde," members of local communities employed as the auxiliary assistants of the health professionals.

The SUS is implemented by health departments at municipal and state levels, financed by general taxes and co-ordinated by government entities through the Ministry of Health. The latter's normative power has positive aspects in terms of standardizing procedures, but can also have a negative dampening effect on local initiatives.

Developments in the SUS demonstrate that it matures through local experiments that are gradually institutionalized to produce health services of greater efficiency and quality. Examples include the use of health councils to allow communities and stakeholders to participate in planning and delivery; family health modules, which were originally organized in simple formats to target lower-income populations and poverty-hit regions but have now become more sophisticated and have expanded to major metropolitan areas; the Family Health Strategy, which has been diversified and structured into networks to promote the transformation of older primary care centres into "polyclinics;" and new emergency care structures that emerged in Brazil's southeast region and are being adopted in other metropolitan areas.

The Brazilian healthcare system demonstrates that experimentation is a mechanism for adaptability. The SUS had two major foci of innovation—service provision (for example, community participation as auxiliary workers) and governance (for example, intergovernmental co-operation). Social participation mechanisms (for example, health councils) allow citizens, all levels of government and health workers to participate actively.

Compensatory financial mechanisms related to large programs such as the SUS can help reduce regional disparities. Strong popular support for the SUS ensures its continuity and ongoing development through successive changes in government.

Group Discussion

The case studies allowed the roundtable participants to explore new ways of organizing government authority and new forms of accountability.

The case studies revealed how co-ordination can take place within governments, among governments and between government and society, as well as some of the issues and barriers that can arise. An important insight was that this co-ordination does not require a trade-off between centralization and decentralization. A strong central government can and must co-exist with strong local governments and communities. Each plays a different role and draws on different strengths and authorities. The centre must be able to monitor, course correct and be open to adapting its policies as local developments take shape.

The cases revealed that collective efforts require the development of shared responsibility arrangements, which, in the case of the Brazilian national health system, remain a work in progress. Social participation processes can be an important complement to representative democracy. They require that public servants be attentive to public debate. Processes also need to be well thought out.

Decentralization and devolution have been significant aspects of reinventing government. However, context is important. Reinventing government in an established democracy is different than in a country with a new democratic tradition. It also differs depending on whether a country has well established democratic institutions, the size of a country and whether it has a federal or unitary system.

Transferring public delivery to the private sector carries the risk of over-estimating the potential financial savings and under-estimating the public expenditures that may still be required.

Small-scale experiments are powerful first steps towards large-scale institutional changes. The challenge is scalability. Many good, small-scale projects fail to realize their potential because people do not know how to scale them up. Pilot projects should not be started unless there is a commitment to mainstream success if or when the case arises.

Experimentation is in the nature of the Brazilian healthcare system, which continually tests the limits of innovation. Successful innovations are readily shared and become incentives for change in national policies or in law.

Accountability can become more varied where responsibility is shared. When responsibility is shared with private entities, final accountability rests with the public body.

The test of a good policy is in its implementation. The public policy process is about delivering public policy outcomes at the lowest overall cost to society and with the fewest unintended consequences. Policy decisions and policy implementation are part of the same system leading to public results.

SUMMARY OF FINDINGS

One of the main findings of the Brazil roundtable was that the New Synthesis Project is not proposing yet another new model to guide public sector reforms. Instead, it is proposing a new framework of public administration. A model provides answers. It is a resting place. A framework is a way of thinking through the choices open to government and exploring a broadening space of possibilities. These choices involve a search for balance among multiple forces at play.

Public results are increasingly a collective enterprise. Governments must reach out to others to achieve the results of greatest interest to citizens. As a result, the role of government is expanding from decision maker, lawmaker, enforcer and service provider to include convenor, facilitator, negotiator, enabler, conflict manager and partner. The role of citizens is also expanding from that of voter, taxpayer and service user to decision maker, partner and co-creator of public goods. The expanding role of government requires greater capacity for co-operation in government and society. It requires a capacity for co-evolution as government transforms society and society transforms the role of government.

No one, not even government, can meet the challenges of the 21st century by working alone. Governments can create new public platforms for co-operation. They can collect and encourage the dissemination of public data as public assets. They can encourage the co-production of public goods with citizens and other actors. An active citizenry is the best protection against the abuse of dominant position. Citizens are the most important value creators in an increasing number of cases.

Collaborative processes are an important instrument in dealing with growing social complexity. These processes can identify issues and solutions that were hitherto unforeseen. They can build bridges among a range of interests.

Public participation processes have become an important complement to representative democracy. They can increase the legitimacy and credibility of government decisions. Governments need to use different technologies to pursue a dialogue with citizens. New information and communications technologies provide the tools to hear everyone. Public servants must learn to "listen" using modern tools, such as Web 2.0. These tools should supplement not displace old tools.

There will always be a place for government to act alone—when it can frame the issue and achieve the results by itself or when circumstances require it. However, government's legitimacy to use its authority to act alone is declining, and it must increasingly reach out to others. This is having a major impact on government, public sector institutions and public servants.

Modern information and communications technologies are transforming society. In a world of social networking and social media, government does not control participatory processes. Citizens engage in public policy debates and produce public results with and without government.

Participative processes, real or virtual, can open up space for debate, dialogue and collective action. They can bridge the gap between the information the public service has and information citizens have. They may lead to better public policy decisions, programs and services. Government must ensure equitable access to the information it and other parties hold and equitable access to the participatory processes.

Participatory processes influence and inform formal political institutions. They are a way of ensuring that civil society arguments reach government and the legislative assembly. While participatory and representative democratic processes can co-exist, public officials must determine when and how to use these processes to achieve public results. Public servants need to consider how to balance engagement activities with formal political accountability, and how to use engagement activities to complement and inform public and political debate. They need to ensure that the diversity of views is heard and that the dominant voices in society do not overwhelm those on the margins.

Finally, the discussions at the roundtable helped clarify a number of important principles and concepts. Good governance is concerned with the quality, fairness and justice of society. There is no good governance without good government, which consists of strong regulatory framework, solid public institutions and a multifaceted mix of policies to balance individual interests and collective aspirations. The stewardship role of government cannot be outsourced. Government will always be the insurer of last resort when the public interest demands it.

Chapter 19

The Singapore Roundtable

P articipants at the Singapore roundtable explored the ways in which governments can build their anticipative capacity to mitigate risks or improve the likelihood of more favourable outcomes. Participants discussed how to improve the capacity of society to innovate, prosper and adapt to emerging issues, unforeseen events and changing circumstances. They identified some of the practical implications for governments, public organizations and public servants in terms of undertaking this work.[1]

EXPLORATION AND ANTICIPATION

Foresight activities can contribute to good governance. They must be adapted to the particular situation of each country; there is no one-size-fits-all model. Countries can learn from each others' experiences and adapt what they learn to their own requirements.

Exploration and Policy Making: Finland

Finland has a high standard of living, a high adaptation of technology, ample natural resources and a rapidly aging population. It has a stable parliamentary democracy with multi-party governments and a strong focus on consensus building. It is a welfare state that invests heavily in innovation, education and research and development. It ranks highly in terms of international competitiveness and overall quality of life.

The Finnish government conducts futures research to provide background data for its foresight work. It produces one comprehensive futures report per government term before each general election. It also generates regular situation awareness reports that focus on physical threats and security. Ministries involved in business and employment systematically conduct situation awareness activities. Individual ministries undertake sectoral futures reviews before each election. These reviews look out a decade or more, but place special emphasis on the next four-year government term.

Finland's parliamentary Committee for the Future deliberates over documents referred to it and makes submissions to other parliamentary committees. It conducts futures research and facilitates dialogue between the government and Parliament about long-term priorities. In particular, it issues a formal parliamentary response to the government foresight report in time for each general election.

While Finland is ahead of many countries with the emphasis it places on looking ahead and on the focus it gives to mid- to long-term priorities, a number of possible improvements have been identified. They include:
(i)   widening the scope of futures research and linking the scanning processes used in various ministries;
(ii) involving civil society in the foresight work, including co-producing options for the future and exploring the use of public opinion surveys and social media;
(iii) improving links between anticipation activities and decision-making processes in Cabinet;
(iv) expanding the scope of foresight work across government; and
(v)   encouraging experimentation to test the validity of policy options.

A review is under way to improve the link between foresight work and decision making for the incoming government. It will explore how to strengthen horizontal coordination and link foresight work with decision making in Parliament and Cabinet.

Foresight Program: United Kingdom

Created in 1994 and reporting to the government's Chief Scientific Advisor and the Cabinet Office, the United Kingdom's Foresight Program helps government think systematically about futures issues by combining the latest scientific evidence with futures analyses, by understanding what alternative futures are possible and by challenging presumptions.

The program looks ahead 50 to 100 years. Each project takes 18 to 24 months to complete and must not duplicate other government work. Projects must focus on a significant issue that touches some aspect of science and technology. They must take a long-term view and have action-oriented outcomes, a cross-sectoral reach and buy-in from key stakeholders.

Projects involve stakeholder groups, science and engineering experts and international contributors. Participants use various techniques, such as scenario development, technology road mapping, influence diagrams and systems mapping. Typical outputs include an analysis of recent developments, visions of possible futures and recommendations for action.

Ten major projects have been undertaken since 1994, including projects on obesity, flooding and mental health. Current projects include global food and farming, the international dimensions of climate change, global environmental migration and computer trading in financial markets.

The program also launched a Foresight Horizon Scanning Centre in 2005 to serve as a centre of excellence for strategic futures thinking in government. The Centre encourages longer-term thinking and evidence-based analysis. It advises government departments on the use of horizon scanning, provides training and supports departments in creating their own futures capability. The Centre conducts futures projects that look five to 15 years out. It oversees Sigma Scan, an online and searchable set of research papers that look 50 years into the future.

Potential areas for improvement include strengthening the relationship between foresight work and decision making, and encouraging stronger buy-in from senior managers across the public sector.

Risk Assessment and Horizon Scanning Program: Singapore

Singapore has always been acutely aware of its vulnerability as a small country. Its development has been closely tied to long-term strategic planning and decision making. Over the years, Singapore has adapted its strategic planning approach to take account of the increasingly volatile and unpredictable regional and global contexts.

Scenario planning has played a key part in Singapore's strategic planning process since the 1980s. The government conducts national and global-level scenario planning exercises every few years and runs focused scenario studies on specific topics regularly. While valuable for exploring "what if" situations, the government has found scenario planning insufficient for anticipating short-range and potentially game-changing shocks, such as the Asian financial crisis or SARS.

In 2004, the government created the Risk Assessment and Horizon Scanning program (RAHS) to complement scenario planning. RAHS is a computer-based platform designed to help analysts detect and investigate emerging strategic trends by canvassing a wide range of sources for weak signals of potential future shocks.

In 2009, the government established the Centre for Strategic Futures on the combined strengths of scenario planning and RAHS to encourage experimentation and discovery. Individuals and teams are encouraged to learn by experimenting in a "safe to fail" environment. The Centre developed a toolkit to provide strategic planners with processes and methodologies to help them develop new insights into complex problems. The Centre cultivates networks capable of generating strategic conversations and harnessing divergent viewpoints across government, with non-government stakeholders and with the media.

Possible improvements include the need to identify and retain good strategic planners, enhanced capacity to deal with cognitive bias and measures to ensure that foresight work remains rigorously relevant to policy makers.

Group Discussion

Foresight activities must look at many scenarios, including the probable, the possible, the plausible and the preferable. It must scan for long-term trends and canvass for weak signals. Different forecasting activities require different capacities and skills. Futures work occurs in many places. There is no shortage of knowledge about future trends, but there is a shortage of capacity to integrate and make sense of it.

A small group of policy makers, a single agency or even a single government cannot possess all the information needed to anticipate and address complex problems. Foresight activities must bring together a broad range of talent, a diverse array of ideas and multifaceted perspectives, including dissenting voices, to avoid the risk of groupthink.

Foresight activities must be integrated into the political decision-making process and be relevant to policy makers. Building support with decision makers includes promoting a culture of looking ahead and framing issues from a futures perspective. Foresight activities will enjoy greater support from decision makers if they lead to better results and connect to issues of the day. When political demand for such activity is low, the public service should pursue its work of looking ahead and being prepared to provide the best possible advice as the need arises.

Foresight activities must also enjoy public support and contribute to public awareness. Support tends to peak at times of crisis and ebb before them. Involving citizens in the process of futures-thinking is a key part of sustaining public support. The process of engagement is itself an important result.

It is neither viable nor desirable to plan exhaustively for every contingency. Instead, government can probe, sense patterns and be ready to act with incomplete and imperfect information. Frequent transitions in political systems add a layer of difficulty in linking foresight work and decision making.

SOCIAL INNOVATION AND CO-PRODUCTION

Social innovation and co-production are important contributors to good governance. They enhance the capacity for improved public results.

Innovation Awards Program: Brazil

The Brazilian Innovation Awards is a non-monetary awards program designed to promote and disseminate social innovations and recognize teams that carry out their activities creatively. Since 1995, the program has given over 300 awards. The focus is on the delivery of services to citizens.

Three examples of award recipients include the Social Security Boat; the National Documentation Program for Rural Women Workers; and the Path to School program.

The Social Security Boat (Prevbarcos) program uses vessels to help riverside communities in the Amazon region access social benefits. This has allowed the government to provide services locally without establishing costly new agencies in municipalities with small or dispersed populations.

The National Documentation Program for Rural Women Workers provides proof-of-identity documents (a basic condition for accessing many government benefits). The program uses mobile units that issue documents on the spot, allowing individuals in rural areas who were previously excluded to access the benefits to which they are entitled.

Through the Path to School program (Caminho da Escola), the government provides supplementary financial support for school transportation, ensuring that children living in rural areas can attend school. The program has contributed to standardizing rural school transportation, renewing school buses to comply with rigid technical specifications and providing access to schooling for underprivileged children.

All these programs aim to improve service delivery to populations dispersed over large geographic areas. As such, they deal with the challenges of co-ordinating actions horizontally among agencies, vertically among levels of government and between government and social groups; delivering national policy at the local level in ways that meet unique local conditions and needs; and managing risk taking and innovation among public servants who break new ground to provide services to the public. They demonstrate the need to trust public service teams to discover innovative solutions to the problems they encounter in practice.

Total Place Initiative: United Kingdom

Through 13 pilot projects, the Total Place Initiative encourages local agencies to look beyond their location and consider how a "whole area" approach might improve public services at a lower cost.

The pilot projects revealed several barriers to innovation. There was often a lack of active collaboration across government systems, such that policies were developed in departmental silos with little support for working across boundaries. There was a lack of skill at developing genuine partnerships with civil society, due in part to a lack of knowledge about civil society organizations. There was a tendency of public organizations to manage to meet targets rather than to aim for better overall results. Risk aversion reinforced the focus on targets and on process. Other barriers included a bias in favour of reorganization as a way of solving problems rather than focusing on measures to make government-wide systems work as one.

Many Helping Hands: Singapore

The Singapore social services model is a collaborative partnership between government and community organizations. The government provides one-for-one funding to Voluntary Welfare Organizations (VWOs) to deliver social services. This has expanded the social safety net by involving a network of community groups to administer assistance. It has laid the foundation for shared responsibility between government, citizens and the private sector in working together to improve the lives of Singaporeans, especially those in need. The Many Helping Hands approach has empowered community agencies to be flexible and resourceful. By involving many stakeholders, the program contributes to building social capital.

A key factor for success is the shared ownership that provides the impetus for more open dialogue and collaboration among public servants. Shared ownership requires a delineation of roles and responsibilities. The government sets the direction and provides funding; the National Council of Social Service acts as facilitator and enabler; the VWOs serve as service providers and initiators at the ground level; citizens and service providers are "prosumers" (producers and consumers). The sustainability of the program depends on community support for co-funding as well as the capacity to adapt to citizens' needs in changing circumstances.

The changing social landscape has created a challenge to grow the VWO sector in scale and scope to meet a higher demand for services. In this context, the one-for-one funding formula may be difficult to maintain. The VWOs risk losing their inventiveness as they face an increasing number of controls and reporting requirements that come with increased reliance on government funding. In the context of this program, government must balance accountability with trust. It will need to take a risk management rather than a risk avoidance approach, which will require reining in the desire for increased regulatory control that could undermine social innovation.

A number of lessons can be drawn from the Singapore experience. The government and the VWOs need a mutual appreciation of each others' roles. VWOs are not an extension of government: government is more than a source of funds. Government needs to build a collaborative partnership to tap the knowledge of those closest to the service recipient. Power sharing, mutual risk taking, a tolerance for experiments and empowered citizens are keys to enabling change.

Group Discussion

Social innovations are social in their ends and in their means. Their benefits accrue to society as a whole. They respond to social needs and they enhance society's capacity to act. Some social innovations are transformative. Others are incremental improvements made by recombining existing elements. Social innovations are rarely either wholly top-down or bottom-up. They generally involve networks, collaboration and high quality relationships. Social innovations require trial and error and a willingness to accept "good enough" rather than searching for perfect yet elusive solutions.

Co-production can increase social capital, self-reliance and well-being. There are many barriers to social innovation and co-production, including a lack of co-operation across boundaries, a culture of compliance, risk aversion and a focus on structure. Civil society and the voluntary sector face their own internal challenges, including unpredictable funding, difficulty retaining good people and the danger of becoming a quasi-government organization.

The fiscal challenges that many governments face as a result of the global financial crisis that began in 2008 could encourage social innovation and co-production. For this to happen, governments should emphasize achieving public results and lower overall costs to society rather than cutting their expenditures in the short-term.

EXPERIMENTATION

Experimentation can be a powerful tool to improve policy making. It allows policy makers to identify the likely outcomes of a new program in a controlled environment. Governments have many reasons to encourage experimentation. It allows them to test ideas to spread innovation, promote collaboration among levels of government or stakeholders and quickly, with evidence, disavow bad ideas.

There are many kinds of experimentation, such as pilot projects, demonstration projects, random control trials and social experiments. Each needs rigorous analysis. Pilot and demonstration projects have been widely used. Random control trials are a powerful way to gain knowledge using a treatment group and a control group. Social experimentation, which consists of random control trials involving social policy ideas, has developed over the last 40 years as a major form of research activity.

Experimentation in the public sector requires a culture of evidence-based policy and dedicated funding. As experiments take time, experimentation as a key strategy needs anticipative capacity to identify issues well enough in advance to allow time to carry out experiments. Those with expertise in this area are working hard to find faster methods for experimentation in the public policy area.

To develop more expertise and nurture a culture of experimentation, public service management schools could help prepare public servants to conduct rigorous experimentation. This is not widely taught in the discipline.

NorthLight School: Singapore

The Ministry of Education launched the NorthLight School in 2007 to try a different approach to help students who repeatedly failed the national Primary School Leaving Examination and were at risk of dropping out. Within three years, the growth and motivation of NorthLight students and the results of the NorthLight experiment surpassed all expectations, and the school has attracted strong support from the community. Its innovative strategies and non-conformist approaches have been copied in primary schools throughout the country and internationally.

NorthLight School is an innovation that involves government, education professionals, students, families and communities working together to address a pressing social need. It demonstrates how public sector agencies can facilitate innovation and how governments can support experiments. The school has become an interesting laboratory for "spreading" a social innovation by teaching others who can then replicate successes in their own classrooms and schools.

Self-Sufficiency Project: Canada

The Self-Sufficiency Project is one of nine large demonstration projects carried out in Canada since 1995. This project was conducted to determine how earning supplements affect the participation of long-term, single-parent, welfare recipients in the labour market. The 9,000 participants were equally divided into an experimental group and a control group. Those in the experimental group received earning supplements for up to three years on condition that they left welfare for full-time work.

Results indicated that people in the experimental group returned to the labour market much sooner than those in the control group. However, over the long term, both groups participated at similar levels in the labour market. The results influenced the design of welfare and workfare schemes in Canada and elsewhere.

Local Enterprise Partnerships: United Kingdom

The coalition government in the United Kingdom has signalled the need to shift power from Westminster (the British Parliament) to the people. It supports decentralization, democratic engagement and balancing top-down government with enhanced powers to local councils, communities, neighbourhoods and individuals. To rebalance top-down prescription and voluntary collaboration, local private and public sector organizations have been challenged to form Local Enterprise Partnerships.

Nationally, these partnerships require a focus on innovation, a greater focus on collaboration and a whole-system approach. Locally, they require refocusing on the needs of citizens, moving away from providing funding with centrally-imposed conditions to pooled funding and community-based budgets.

The Local Enterprise partnership approach is built on the notion that open-source policy development is a promising way forward. This is based on the notion that "none of us is as clever as all of us." It recognizes the need to create a culture and environment that encourage innovation and the importance of a whole system approach to policy development.

Group Discussion

Experimentation builds the capacity for ongoing improvement. It provides a reality check against mental biases and preferences.

There are many forms of experimentation but they all value evidence—whether quantitative or qualitative. One provides statistically valid knowledge about probable outcomes: the other picks up situational factors that influence outcomes, such as the informed judgment of frontline workers and innovative leaders at the local level. Experimentation requires a blend of both.

Experimentation requires a cultural shift. How governments respond to reasonable mistakes and failed attempts is a powerful indicator of the prevailing culture. In some countries, the design of social experiments in which one group of people may be treated differently than another runs counter to a particular concept of "equal treatment," while it may be widely accepted elsewhere.

THE ENABLING ROLE OF INFORMATION AND COMMUNICATIONS TECHNOLOGY

Technology enables, accelerates and reframes many issues. Connectedness is a conversation about peoples' lives and how they live their lives using the technology of their times.

A centralized organizational model is well known to government. Decentralized models with multiple hubs and spokes have progressively become more prominent. Distributed networks are characteristic of how the connected world operates. The distributed model is the most resilient model of organizations. It is able to survive even if entire nodes are shut down.

Distributed operating models are less dependent on central command and control. They do not rely on centralized decision making when the knowledge, expertise and experience required to make informed decisions are at the edge. They depend on participative processes and use integrative thinking to create new choices and develop new solutions. This is the world to which the public sector must adapt.

Web 2.0 technologies and applications are creating new forms of social interaction among people. As more people participate on these platforms, governments will be called upon to move toward more open, collaborative, co-operative arrangements entailing a dispersion of power, authority and control.

The power of social networking can only be harnessed if organizations open up and share. Different organizations will follow different strategies. Gatekeepers will want to control access to knowledge. Connectors will encourage the recombination of knowledge. Distributed knowledge can be reassembled and recombined in unpredictable and powerful ways.

Several examples illustrate the potential of the transformation under way. These include Patient Opinion, NATO's Policy Jam, Opinion Space 2.0, Where Does My Money Go, Peer to Patent and Planetary Skin. A lesson learned from these initiatives is that "networks know more than we do—some of the smartest people don't work for us."

InfoComm Development Authority: Singapore

Singapore places a major focus on long-term planning to reduce the risk of costly mistakes. To prosper in the context of complex issues, "wicked" problems and "wildcards," government and society must future-sense, innovate when it cannot rely on the past, re-invent itself and become resilient.

Now that citizens no longer accept that government always knows best, a shift from a "government-to-you" to a "government-with-you" approach is taking shape. This means sharing public data to encourage the creation of innovative applications; making sense of data; involving citizens in the co-creation of public policies and services; accessing the collective wisdom of citizenry through social media platforms; adopting state-of-the-art technologies like cloud computing, social media and smart mobile technologies; and pursuing a "search and discover" approach.

Group Discussion

Participants noted that, for many years, the technology sector over-promised and under-delivered. But technology has caught up with the rhetoric and is becoming "game-changing."

Social networking and social media are causing a "disruptive shift" in the balance of knowledge between government and citizens. While the Internet and social networks provide a platform for disseminating information and obtaining feedback, government must also be aware of the pitfalls. Data and information can be problematically recombined, misconstrued and misused. In the Internet Age, good analysis, bad analysis, trustworthy information and misinformation all have the potential to "go viral." Monitoring and course correcting must be constant. Public servants must be able to distinguish between genuine feedback and "noise," avoid being co-opted by vocal minorities, and reconcile real-time responses with the longer timeline of deliberations.

E-government is not a substitute for representative democracy and electoral democracy. Societies need to explore how technology may enrich democratic processes.

Technology is creating the need for different skills in the public sector, including the ability to engage citizens and knowledge of the latest technologies.

ADAPTIVE CAPACITY

Shocks happen despite the best efforts to prevent them. The role of government, therefore, extends to mitigating their impact and building the adaptive capacity of communities and citizens to absorb them.

Planning for Pandemics: Singapore

Small, urbanized states are especially vulnerable to pandemics, for which it is preferable to over-prepare than to face the aftermath of under-reaction.

Singapore has a number of advantages in managing crises. It is a small island with a fixed number of entry points. It is a city state with no rural population. It has a strong, stable government and a professional public service. When confronted with the SARS outbreak, it had already learned from previous pandemics in southern China and Hong Kong.

Singapore used every communication tool at its disposal to explain the outbreak so as to build trust and manage the country's external image.

People trusted the government to take the necessary actions to contain the disease. However, while the government could act swiftly and decisively, trust had the side effect of slowing down responses in civil society as people looked to the government for direction and solutions instead of acting within the sphere of their own responsibilities and capabilities.

The lessons learned from the SARS crisis contributed to the government's response to subsequent situations, including H1N1 and avian flu. In crisis situations, there is a need for decisive leadership. This entails involving the highest levels of government and mobilizing all ministries and agencies. It requires transparent and honest communications to sustain the trust and confidence of the population. Most crises require a multi-disciplinary, multi-sectoral approach with no artificial boundaries between agencies, disciplines and levels of government.

Infrastructure (such as networked government), capability (such as use of scenario planning), legislative tools, learning best practices from others and from experience, and leadership at various levels allowed Singapore to come through the SARS crisis. While crises are seldom the same, the SARS experience in Singapore reinforced the importance of building a society's adaptive capacity with strong institutional, organizational and innovative capacity.

Victorian Bushfire Reconstruction and Recovery Authority (VBRRA): Australia

The scale and urgency of the recovery task from the devastating bushfires that raged through the state of Victoria in 2009 called for agile, responsive approaches to the recovery effort, and placed unpredictable demands on public agencies. The complexity derived from the need to operate across jurisdictions, portfolios, sectors and geographic areas and the scale of the devastation.

Within three days of the disaster, the Victorian Bushfire Reconstruction and Recovery Authority (VBRRA) had been established to oversee the largest rebuilding and recovery program in the state's history. It was a flat organization that could make decisions rapidly and fix them if they proved wrong.

The VBRRA established a recovery and reconstruction framework to address longer-term challenges related to issues, such as distributing goods to those in need, managing the clean-up effort, providing housing and promoting community-led recovery. From the start, the authority recognized that people who participate recover better. As a result, it used a participatory approach at the community level. This approach brought its own challenges, including reluctance from some communities, slower decision making, difficulties in achieving consensus and capability gaps. However, the solutions were better tailored to local needs, and the approach resulted in stronger, more resilient communities.

Group Discussion

Public agencies need agility to operate in unpredictable environments. The participants defined a number of measures to encourage agility and to support an "agility cycle." These include scanning for emerging trends and issues; working with communities to transform information into actionable solutions; responding to new problems with new approaches; transforming the future environment through prevention and mitigation; and building resistance to shocks.

Strong adaptive capacity requires strong institutional, organizational and innovative capacity. It requires long-term planning, the ability to scan and detect signals of emerging trends and to make sense of them, and the ability to intervene proactively and to ride through short-term crises.

Having multiple frames of analysis is critical. An empirical frame provides data and insight into events. A political frame provides insight on what to do and when to do it. A human resources frame provides information on the kinds of capabilities needed. A media frame provides a minute-by-minute narrative of what is happening and being done that shapes the public perception of the event. A symbolic frame tells the government what rituals and symbolic acts may make a difference in helping people respond to and weather the crisis.

In light of the rise of social networking and other modern communications technologies, the SARS crisis might be handled differently in today's world. The use of social media, such as Facebook and Twitter, would be of great importance in communicating with the public now. People would shape the news and perception of events by communicating among themselves using social media. But in a crisis situation, citizens would also want to hear from authority figures and experts. They want reliable information from people they trust. Social media must be used in conjunction with other communications tools.

Social media have a negative and positive potential. Sometimes, "the wisdom of the crowd can become the ignorance of the mob." While this dynamic is not new, the advent of social media has made it harder to counter, given the speed at which information can now travel and the vast audience it can now reach.

Governments often respond well to crises. They make quick decisions and work across boundaries. However, in the normal course of events, governments seem unable to use some of the practices that allow them to shine in exceptional circumstances.

Crises will happen. Their frequency and magnitude will most likely continue to increase. The key question is whether governments are able to learn and adapt, and whether they can use this learning to prepare to serve in "turbulent times."

SUMMARY OF FINDINGS

Participants concluded that building a culture of "looking ahead" requires a process of engagement between officials, experts doing foresight work, decision makers and citizens. Foresight activities will not only earn greater acceptance if they are connected to decision making in government, but if the process of engaging people in thinking about the future builds anticipative and adaptive capacity. Framing issues from a futures perspective and building a strong narrative to communicate what the future may hold are important to shaping an ambitious collective agenda.

In doing foresight work, continual scanning is preferable to one-time futures-related events. Foresight activities must guard against the dangers of groupthink. They need to maintain a multifaceted perspective, engage multiple networks, pursue a diversity of ideas and encourage dissenting voices.

Social innovation can help societies remain agile and adaptive. As a process, it can be messy, yet orderly. It entails building relationships, working across borders, taking risks and accepting variability. As enablers of social innovation, governments must focus on results and impact. Being an enabler is about allowing ideas to flourish and creating an environment in which it is possible to fail safely.

Experimentation improves the likelihood of desirable outcomes. Multiple approaches to experimentation are acceptable, ranging from quantitative, evidence-based analysis to qualitative analysis. Most experiments require a blended approach. Promoting a greater use of experimentation in government will require a cultural change, a structural change and a move away from a silo mentality.

Technology is both an enabler and a challenge. It is accelerating the speed at which issues emerge and can be addressed. Social networks and social media are shifting the balance of knowledge between government and citizens. Governments must move from providing "government-to-you" to creating "government-with-you;" from being the custodian and gatekeeper of public data to being the connector and sharer of data to encourage the creation of innovative solutions.

Chapter 20

The United Kingdom Roundtable

The United Kingdom roundtable explored key elements of the New Synthesis Project, including the co-design and co-production with users of public services and accountability systems for distributed governance arrangements. It looked at the institutional reforms needed to prepare government to do this. It built on the results of the previous roundtables and explored how to prepare future leaders.[1]

CITIZEN-FOCUSED PUBLIC SERVICE

In many countries, new possibilities are being explored to reconcile the predictability provided by the nation state, the solidarity offered by the welfare state and the agility provided by self-reliant people, resilient communities and efficient markets.

A search is under way to redefine the role of the state in the contemporary context. These concepts are being expressed with different names. For example, the idea of a relational state that emphasizes the nature and quality of government's relationships with citizens has emerged. Another concept is that of an affirmative state, which emphasizes the need for government to affirm and promote the collective interest in all circumstances by keeping a full range of options, capabilities, roles and relationships at the ready.

Participle: United Kingdom

A number of experiments are taking place in the United Kingdom that provide a laboratory for identifying promising avenues for new forms of governance.

Participle is an example. It is a social enterprise that is working with the end-users of public services to co-design new types of public services that will better meet their needs. The company is looking at issues through the lens of motivating participation and encouraging social contributions. Its vision knits the economic, social and emotional dimensions of life together.

Participle's process is based on rethinking public problems by working directly with those most affected by them. The process brings to bear a range of knowledge and skills from different professions, disciplines and walks of life, and scales up successes through social enterprise. This approach has been used successfully in a number of areas. One area was in designing services with seniors to help improve their quality of life; another was in working with families in crisis to have them design their own solutions to build new lives.

Commissioning: United Kingdom

The fiscal crisis in the United Kingdom is stimulating innovative ideas about the use of community-based organizations to deliver services. In practice, building a working relationship between government and these organizations may prove challenging.

One key challenge is for government to find ways of funding community-based organizations that allow the latter to retain their autonomy and local support, which are essential to success but which also provide the former with acceptable accountability arrangements. In the United Kingdom, commissioning has been identified as offering promise in these two areas.

Commissioning is defined as "understanding the needs of people to build better platforms to help them." In this sense, it may lead to a greater focus on user needs and a repositioning of the role of government. Commissioning works best when the desired outcomes matter as much to the public agency as they do to the community organizations involved and the end-users, when the market will not work on its own and when the results are measurable. Potential benefits include creating room for more innovative and flexible solutions, a greater focus on what works and cost savings to government.

Commissioning may take many forms: the concept is still evolving in practice. For example, in the United Kingdom's welfare-to-work program, commissioning began with payment for results, with the latter measured as sustained job outcomes. Then it progressed to "black box" contracts, which specified a minimum number of activities, giving providers the space to innovate to achieve better results. Then it went to "prime" contracts, which were large contracts to a main contractor that managed its own supply chain.

Based on experience, there are some important considerations in deciding on a commissioning approach. Size matters: most large-scale approaches ended up with a mixed model. Capacity matters: the capacity of local government and community groups needs to be taken into account.

There are risks associated with the commissioning model. Commissioning creates distance between the public service and citizens. There are also risks of "gaming" and "creaming" (community organizations picking the easiest clients to serve). This leads to questions about creating the right incentives for desirable behaviours and outcomes and disincentives for undesirable ones. There is also a risk that commissioning may amount to nothing more than contracting under a new name.

It is important to have a balanced, rigorous method for evaluating government-provided and government-commissioned services.

Citizen, Family- and Community-focused Public Services: United Kingdom

The Family LIFE program in Swindon, United Kingdom, is a framework to help families in chronic crisis build new lives by having them design their own solutions. Croydon is one of 13 pilot sites offering an early-life support initiative for children and parents.

The projects in Swindon and Croydon took a design methodology approach, beginning by understanding the lives of the people receiving assistance through a variety of government programs. Program officials discovered that many of these public services did not make sense to people whose lives cut across multiple public service silos.

Officials from both projects asked how they could design services that shift the focus from dealing with the consequences of a "chaotic family" to dealing with the underlying causes to promote a better outcome. For both, the answer lay in involving the families in designing the programs and the service delivery mechanisms.

The programs face a number of challenges, including maintaining momentum in the face of budget cuts, dealing with staff turnover and government restructuring, breaking down professional and institutional boundaries, and spreading the culture beyond the early adopters.

Workfare: Singapore

The government of Singapore had traditionally resisted the concept of public assistance payments because of their potential impact on economic growth and work ethic. The rationale for workfare was to address the stagnation of low and median wages that followed the Asian financial crisis in the late 1990s.

Workfare in Singapore consists of six strategies: increasing the individual's incentive to find and continue employment using workfare bonuses and housing grants; supporting low-wage workers with families through enhanced child care and training grants; providing access to training to raise the skill level of workers; expanding job opportunities by generating demand for low-wage workers; helping children succeed in school; and sharing budget surpluses through special transfers. The program provides higher payouts for older workers, and creates incentives for informal workers to join the national social security system. The program's objectives are to "make work pay" through stronger economic incentives and to strengthen the norms of inclusion and fairness.

The workfare program was developed through a rigorous process that included scanning for the best ideas and practices from around the world and recombining and adapting them to Singapore's context.

Group Discussion

The British context illustrates that expenditure reduction can provide an impetus for innovation, but it can also cause people to retreat into silos and compete for scarce funds. The possibility of innovation "leaking away" during times of fiscal restraint is a real risk. It is preferable to look at how services can be rethought and reinvented from the perspective of citizens while reducing costs and achieving results of higher overall value.

One of the main obstacles to innovation in the public sector is risk aversion. It is an ongoing challenge to find out how to create a more enabling environment for experimentation and innovation. The causes of risk aversion must be identified and addressed. A starting point is to distinguish between systemic failure, wrongdoing and failures that ensue from trying new ideas. While there can be no tolerance for wrongdoing, learning through trial and error must be encouraged. Innovation needs both bottom-up and top-down approaches. The top has to create the enabling environment and support infrastructure to allow experimentation and new ideas to emerge from the bottom up.

Innovation exists at all levels in the public sector. The challenge is to develop strategies to move from individual cases to routines that encourage dissemination. Most public organizations question how they can be simultaneously good at experimentation and at executing routines, and whether the same people can do both.

"Routines" are important. They can improve the efficient delivery of some services. They reduce the need for "reinventing the wheel." Routines can help people and organizations be more agile if the time and resources are reinvested in creative work. Routines must be distinguished from control mechanisms. The former codify the best known way of performing tasks, and can be changed and improved over time; the latter set an objective requirement against which those who do not comply can be disciplined or punished.

OPEN GOVERNMENT

Open government—making public data more available to the public—is taking hold as an important area of reform because it makes possible new relationships between government and citizens in creating public value. Many countries are making concerted efforts to ensure that public bodies maintain and publish inventories of their data and release machine-readable public data in a timely manner.

Some anticipated benefits of open government include increased citizen engagement and participation; increased transparency and accountability; increased economic and social value; improved public services; improved e-government effectiveness and interoperation; and reduced costs.

As governments make public data more broadly available, they also need to develop responses to the new challenges that emerge from doing so. Lower quality data can be improved through "crowd-sourcing" (for example, transit users fixing data about the location of bus stops). The risk of data being misinterpreted or contested can be mitigated by releasing information on how the data were collected along with any caveats or underlying assumptions associated with their use. Security and privacy concerns require judgment as to whether the benefits outweigh any downsides to the release of the information. These judgments may signal the need for new social conventions and greater agility with regard to regulations and legislation.

Under the aegis of the "Radical Transparency" initiated in the United Kingdom, a "five-star quality guide" has been developed to encourage openness in government: one star is awarded for putting public data on the Internet in any format; two for making public data available in a structured format; three for using open, standard formats; four for using URLs to identify data sets; and five stars for linking public data to other data.

Open data and the use of modern information and communication technologies (ICTs) for managing and releasing it do not, by themselves, constitute a strategy for open government. To be open, government must be networked, inclusive and participative. This can be encouraged through public services that include co-design and cross-organizational collaboration.

Group Discussion

Opening up public data may enable people to find ingenious ways of helping themselves. It may lead to co-creating, co-designing and co-producing public goods and services. In some cases, it may enhance public accountability and help reduce the risk of corruption.

Opening up data comes with a number of challenges for government. While privacy issues should not be an excuse, they cannot be overlooked. There are legitimate fears about releasing personal data. Opening data among public agencies would be a good start in many cases.

Collaborative platforms are blurring the lines between politics and administration. Politicians express discomfort in allowing public servants to engage with citizens using new communication technologies and tools. But changes are happening that cannot be ignored. They are transforming the role of government and of public servants.

The discussion revealed two perspectives on how to ensure open government. One view was that transparency and access to information issues are rights-based and therefore should be addressed separately from the issue of making public data publicly accessible. The former require a legal approach whereas the latter can be encouraged through incentives, policy directions, monitoring and reporting on progress. The other view was that, while the rights-based and publicly accessible data approaches can be separated conceptually, they are intertwined in practice. Technological developments are forcing governments to rethink access-to-information legislation and openness in government at the same time.

SHARED PUBLIC ACCOUNTABILITY

Accountability helps ensure that tax dollars are used for their intended purposes and that officials are using their authority in a manner that is respectful of the law and public sector values. There is no good government or good governance without accountability.

Many forms of public accountability exist, including government's accountability to the people for results and for accountability to the legislative body for the appropriation and use of public funds; accountability for due process to ensure fairness, transparency and equality of treatment; and accountability for conducting the affairs of government in a manner free of corruption and malfeasance. Given the need to move towards shared and distributed governance processes, one challenge has been to devise accountability systems suited to supporting interagency co-operation on collective results when multiple actors are involved.

Participants discussed three examples to explore how new forms of governance might transform the traditional accountability system in government: a program to support former military personnel, an initiative to integrate government services at the local level and the use of community budgeting.

Be the Boss (BtB): United Kingdom

Be the Boss (BtB) is a national project set up in April 2010 to provide former military personnel with funding and support to launch their own business. It is funded by the Department of Business Innovation and Skills, co-ordinated by the Royal British Legion and distributed by multiple partners and devolved administrations. The objective is to get multiple partners working together as one system to deliver results.

The challenge in establishing the BtB structure is that different locations have different infrastructure and cannot offer the same level or quality of assistance. The governance model and the accountability system are a work-in-progress and continue to evolve.

Local Service Boards: United Kingdom

Local Service Boards are shifting public services from a direct delivery role to one in which professionals work with citizens in a co-creation relationship. This work is still in the early stages.

Generally, the initial successes of Local Service Boards have stemmed from the use of a team concept, the co-location of a range of public services, the cross-fertilization of ideas and active, clear communications to build trust and understanding among organizations and with end-users.

Some challenges associated with Local Service Boards are maintaining the energy for innovation in a budget-cutting environment and introducing initiatives that strengthen cohesion and integration. How these challenges are addressed will affect the governance and accountability systems that evolve over time.

Community Budgets: United Kingdom

The British government spends £8 billion a year on 120,000 families that have multiple problems. Funding reaches local areas through hundreds of separate schemes and agencies. Despite significant public investment, many of these families are still experiencing problems.

As of April 2011, communities gained control over a portion of local spending. The first phase took place in 16 areas, where 28 local councils and their partners became responsible for community budgets. Various strands of government funding are pooled into one "local bank account" that communities can use to develop local solutions to local problems. The government intends to roll out community budgets nationally by 2013-14.

Ministers believe that community budgets help reduce overhead costs. Local authorities are expected to re-design and integrate frontline services across organizations and share management functions to reduce costs and produce the best local outcomes. Local authorities are being asked to operate with 30 percent less money.

The central government is looking at mechanisms for tracking funds and results. This initiative is also a work-in-progress. It remains to be seen what degree of authority will be exercised locally and what system of accountability will be put in place to monitor results and report publicly on the use of funds.

Group Discussion

Where government is relied upon to deliver services, directly or indirectly, accountability must be in place. The "Big Society" concept in the United Kingdom suggests that communities will exercise progressively more power. It raises certain questions. Who are these "communities?" Who will be accountable to taxpayers for program expenditures? Parliament needs to follow the changing configuration of government and ensure a consistent and coherent answer to accountability issues. It can play a key role in encouraging new forms of shared accountability for results when many agencies and multiple actors are involved.

New forms of accountability are needed to supplement traditional forms of accountability. Parliamentary committees tend to follow the traditional structures of government. If government is joining up, Parliamentary committees should reach beyond their structural boundaries and follow the chain of action leading to results.

Local budgeting takes different forms in countries with highly decentralized systems, in federations with multiple levels of government and taxation powers and in countries with a constitutional obligation for equal treatment.

FUTURE LEADERS

A leadership development approach to support the capacities embodied in the New Synthesis Framework needs to address such areas as leading across boundaries, relational leadership and leading beyond formal authority. The approach would encompass the key elements of the New Synthesis (compliance, performance, emergence and resilience) and their implications. It would pursue a collaborative enquiry and reflective learning methodology, including the exposure of assumptions. It would blend learning from individual, team, organizational, sector and system-wide contexts. It would focus on the ability to lead within a global context and to gain international experience.

Public Sector Leadership (the Netherlands)

The results of a study to find out if changes in society since the 1970s affect what makes top managers stand out showed that leadership abilities remained relatively stable. People recognize leaders when they see them in action. Then as now, people tended to identify leaders as those individuals with outstanding personal, social and cognitive skills. These attributes include flexibility, ability to network and managerial expertise. Leaders use bottom-up and top-down approaches as required, and have strong interpersonal, relationship- and community-building skills.

Political Leadership: United Kingdom

In the British context, a number of reforms are under way to promote inclusiveness. Measures consist of removing bureaucratic burdens, empowering communities to do things differently, increasing local control over spending, breaking open monopolies in the supply of public services, making public bodies transparent and strengthening accountability to the public.

Change is unlikely to percolate on its own. Government must act as an agent of change. The change agenda represents a shift in power to allow people to act on their own behalf. It requires community engagement and some tolerance for failure. There is no evidence that the failure rate in community organizations is any higher than in other kinds of organizations. Political leadership is needed at the national level to ensure that the fear of failure does not get in the way of the reform agenda. While latent capacity will be discovered in communities, capacity building will likely be required at the local level for people and organizations to take on more responsibility. Finally, it will be important to document success stories and spread best practices.

Developing Future Leaders

A rapidly changing environment is making the job of political and public sector leaders increasingly demanding. They need to build agile organizations, create a vision and communicate it with passion. They require emotional intelligence and must be capable of achieving results while relying less on the exercise of authority. They need self-confidence to implement change in a collaborative way.

Future leaders will need broad experience working in different organizations, situations and sectors, as well as experience in leading change agendas, team building and conflict resolution.

Group Discussion

Leadership is hard to define but easy to recognize. In addition to the personal, social and cognitive skills noted above, senior officials need to be capable of achieving results across organizational and sectoral boundaries. They need relational skills. They must know how to deal with elected officials, citizens, stakeholders, colleagues and staff. They need communication and active listening skills. They must be able to identify new patterns and to "see the new," respond and adapt as it emerges. They need the capacity to combine a short-term focus with mid-term action and long-term results.

Some current leadership development programs aim at building some of these skills. In Singapore, the model has moved from a focus on specialist skills to management skills and now to global leadership. Canada's leadership development framework focuses on the fundamentals of the job, preparing for the next level, networking, reflection, global issues, emotional intelligence and 360-degree feedback.

As they develop their careers, leaders will need a diverse set of experiences, including policy and operations, as well as experience working with civil society organizations and social enterprises. This will increase the cross-fertilization between the public and private sectors.

While all capacities cannot reside in a single leader, they should all exist in each organization. Evaluating the performance of leaders should include documenting the longer-term legacy of their contribution as they progress in their careers and their ability to achieve sustainable results.

Some of the learning needs of political leaders and public service leaders are the same. The need to build a better relationship between the public service and politicians could be addressed by developing joint learning activities.

SUMMARY OF FINDINGS

Beginning in the 1980s, the series of public sector reforms undertaken in many countries focused primarily on productivity and efficiency. Some advances were made, but reforms have not fully prepared public sector organizations to deal with today's challenges.

Faced with complexities, uncertainties and volatility, a significant shift in approach is needed to prepare governments to serve in the 21ˢᵗ century. The shift starts by thinking differently about the role of government in society. Among other things, this means understanding that knowledge and power are increasingly distributed rather than concentrated at the top; recognizing that solutions are as likely to come from outside the public sector as within it; focusing on prevention to develop sustainable solutions; being skilled at building relationships and understanding problems at the human level; valuing experimentation and learning by doing; working across boundaries between public organizations, sectors and disciplines, and with citizens; recognizing that a one-size-fits-all approach does not address the diversity of needs in a diversity of circumstances; and shifting the emphasis from government as the primary agent in serving the public good to the co-creation of collective results.

Taken together, these shifts represent a significant realignment of the role of government in society and of the relationships between the state, society and citizens.

In addition, a set of characteristics of future public organizations started to emerge through the earlier roundtable discussions. Agility, including the ability to work at multiple scales and at multiple speeds, is increasingly important. Openness is essential. It means being at the cutting edge in the use of modern ICTs to bring in knowledge and insights, share public knowledge, encourage innovation and achieve collective results. Inventiveness is another key characteristic. It involves scanning the world for emerging trends, learning from others, experimenting, learning by doing and adapting solutions to the context and circumstances. Inclusiveness means that public organizations must operate as platforms for public collaboration working across multiple boundaries. Public organizations need to be skilled at managing multiple relationships to co-produce public goods and services. They also need to be connected, to promote distributed leadership and to reconcile vertical accountability for delegated authority with the need to work in vast networks to achieve shared results.

In the end, the prevailing philosophy, values and political preferences will shape the public sector reform agenda in each country.

Chapter 21

Group Discusions
in Australia and New Zealand

As stated earlier, it was not realistic to hold six roundtables over a 12-month period. Instead, we decided to hold a series of group discussions with senior practitioners and scholars in Australia and New Zealand instead of a roundtable in Australia. These took place in between the Singapore and London roundtables.[1]

In advance of the discussions in Australia and New Zealand, the New Synthesis Framework garnered some attention as to how it could inform public sector reform agendas, especially with respect to collaboration between agencies and sectors, citizen engagement and innovation in service delivery.

Many participants at these discussions had not been exposed beforehand to the debates and ideas being pursued through the New Synthesis Project. What was particularly striking, therefore, was the degree of convergence between what was "top of mind" for these practitioners and their counterparts in the other countries involved in the project.

In Australia, considerable attention was paid to how to create a more collaborative public sector. In one discussion, the issue of "working across boundaries" was explored through the example of Indigenous Coordination Centres. In another discussion, the topic of co-producing public goods and services was addressed. Both discussions were supported with research papers.[2]

Managing complexity emerged as a general theme. Participants observed that governments have always dealt with complicated issues and developed appropriate capabilities for dealing with them. What characterizes the contemporary era is the number and extent of complex issues whose scope crosses temporal and geographic boundaries and for which solutions are contested and unclear.

Ministers, senior officials and decision makers have to come to terms with the fact that government does not have the power to solve every problem. Citizens and other actors need to be involved. Over-promising or pretending that government can "do it all for you" generates unachievable expectations, puts government in untenable positions and disempowers individuals and communities. When government fails to deliver, credibility and trust are undermined.

Despite the contemporary emphasis on citizen and community-oriented service delivery, not everything in government can or needs to join up with everything else. Many government activities require predictability and regularity. Government should act on its own where appropriate and work with others when the desired outcome requires collaboration.

Citizen engagement should be used when genuinely needed. Government should be transparent about the reasons for reaching out and be clear on how power, resources and risks will be shared.

The scope of many issues and the range of actors who need to be involved means that the appropriate sequel to public administration theory is no longer the "one best way" of the Classic model, nor is it "the next one best way." Rather, it is a much more nuanced suite of responses carefully tailored to normative and practical considerations. Public organizations need to undertake situational analyses and develop approaches in keeping with their context and the circumstances they face.

Participants observed that the New Synthesis Framework presents public officials with a menu of options, not a set of prescriptions. The framework is an intellectual map that focuses practitioners on the questions they need to ask. It is not a blueprint for a specific course of action. The most suitable approaches will take context, culture and mission into account.

The discussions also highlighted a number of key governance challenges, including the need to bridge the gaps between politics and administration, policy decisions and implementation in addressing complex policy issues; reconcile the short-term focus of media commentary with the long timeframes required to address complex issues; balance top-down leadership with the need for leadership at all levels; decide which challenges can be addressed with 19th century approaches, which 20th century skills are still needed and what is needed to address the complex challenges of the 21st century; find mechanisms to support exploration and experimentation, and to scale up successful innovations; determine how to work across governments and how to manage issues involving shared accountability for results; and find ways for developed countries to learn from the experience of developing countries, particularly with respect to cultivating more resilient indigenous and local communities.

Finally, leadership capabilities were raised in a number of discussions. It was observed that serving in the 21st century requires leaders who understand the distinction between authority and power, who have international literacy and the capacity to collaborate with others inside and outside government, and who can work effectively on short-, mid- and long-term issues simultaneously.

Appendix A

Names and Affiliations of Invited Speakers and Participants at NS6 International Roundtables

(listed alphabetically by event,
with titles as they were at the time)

The Hague, 24-26 March 2010

John Alford, Professor, Public Sector Management, Australia and New Zealand School of Government; Australia.

Roel Bekker, Secretary General, Central Government Reform; the Netherlands.

Kees Breed, Secretary, Advisory Council for Public Administration, Ministry of the Interior; the Netherlands.

Steven Broers, Director, Administrative Affairs, Municipality of The Hague; the Netherlands.

Gerard Van de Broek, Director, Knowledge Department, Ministry of the Interior; the Netherlands.

Jocelyne Bourgon, President Emeritus, Canada School of Public Service; President, Public Governance International (PGI); Canada.

Silvio Crestana, Researcher and Former President, Brazilian Agricultural Research Corporation (EMBRAPA); Brazil.

Roos van Erp-Bruinsma, Secretary General, Ministry of the Interior; the Netherlands.

Paul Frissen, Professor, Public Administration, University of Tilburg; Dean, Netherlands School for Public Administration; the Netherlands.

Martin Gagner, Researcher, Centre for Governance Studies, Leiden University; the Netherlands.

Merel de Groot, Knowledge Advisor, Ministry of the Interior; the Netherlands.

Lotte Helder, Policy Advisor, Ministry of the Interior; the Netherlands.

Peter Ho, Head, Singapore Civil Service, Public Service Division, Prime Minister's Office; Singapore.

Menno Hurenkamp, Professor, Sociology and Anthropology, University of Amsterdam; the Netherlands.

Jürgen de Jong, Partners + Pröpper Research and Consulting; the Netherlands.

Philip Karré, Senior Researcher and Lecturer, National School for Public Administration; the Netherlands.

Helena Kerr, President, National School of Public Administration (ENAP); Brazil.

Erik-Hans Klijn, Professor, Public Administration, Erasmus University; the Netherlands.

Natalia Koga, graduate student, University of Westminster; United Kingdom.

Harrie Kruiter, Researcher, Centre for Governance Studies, Leiden University; the Netherlands.

Anil Kumar, Ambassador of Singapore; the Netherlands.

Tobias Kwakkelstein, Strategy Advisor, Knowledge Department, Ministry of the Interior; the Netherlands.

Shaun Lednor, De Argumentenfabriek; the Netherlands.

Lena Leong, Senior Researcher, Centre for Governance and Leadership, Civil Service College; Singapore.

Derk Loorbach, Researcher and Lecturer, Social Sciences, Erasmus University; the Netherlands.

Igno Pröpper, Partners + Pröpper Research and Consulting; the Netherlands.

Ann Masten, Professor, Institute of Child Development, College of Education and Human Development, University of Minnesota; United States of America.

Eve Mitleton-Kelly, Professor, Institute of Social Psychology and Director, Complexity Research Program, London School of Economics; United Kingdom.

Janet Newman, Professor, Social Policy, Open University; United Kingdom.

Christine Nixon, Chair, Victorian Bushfire Reconstruction and Recovery Authority; former Police Commissioner, State of Victoria; Australia.

Gordon Owen, Director, General Partnerships and Best Practices, Canada School of Public Service; Canada.

Sue Richards, Professor and Senior Fellow, Institute for Government; United Kingdom.

Esther van Rijswijk, De Argumentenfabriek; the Netherlands.

Jill Rutter, Whitehall Secondee, Institute for Government; former Director of Strategy, Department for Environment, Food and Rural Affairs; United Kingdom.

Hironobu Sano, Professor, Federal University of Rio Grande do Norte; Brazil.

Marie Sassine, Visiting Assistant Deputy Minister, Canada School of Public Service; Canada.

Andy Scott, Andrews Senior Fellow in Social Policy, University of New Brunswick; former federal cabinet minister; Canada.

Mandy Smits, Project Manager, Ministry of the Interior; the Netherlands.

Martijn van der Steen, Associate Dean and Deputy Director, Netherlands School for Public Administration; the Netherlands.

Geert Teisman, Professor, Public Administration, Erasmus University; the Netherlands.

Mark van Twist, Director, Netherlands School for Public Administration; the Netherlands.

Steven van der Walle, Professor, Public Administration, Erasmus University, the Netherlands.

Frances Westley, JW McConnell Chair in Social Innovation, University of Waterloo; Canada.

Yee Ping Yi, Senior Director (Special Studies), Strategic Policy Office, Public Service Division, Prime Minister's Office; Deputy Dean, Civil Service College; Singapore.

André van der Zande, Secretary General, Ministry of Agriculture, Nature and

Food Quality; the Netherlands.

Ottawa, 4-5 May 2010

Peter Aucoin, Professor Emeritus, School of Public Administration/Department of Political Science, Dalhousie University; Canada.

Jocelyne Bourgon, President Emeritus, Canada School of Public Service; President, Public Governance International (PGI); Canada.

Elisabete Roseli Ferrarezi, Co-ordinator of Research, National School of Public Administration (ENAP); Brazil.

Francisco Gaetani, Deputy Executive-Secretary, Ministry of Planning, Management and Budget; Brazil.

Andrew Graham, Adjunct Professor, Policy Studies, Queen's University; Canada.

Jenifer Graves, Senior Advisor and Researcher, Canada School of Public Service; Canada.

Zoe Gruhn, Director of Learning and Development, Institute for Government; United Kingdom.

Frederico Guanais, Head, International Co-operation Office, National School of Public Administration (ENAP); Brazil.

June Gwee, Principal Researcher, Centre for Governance and Leadership, Civil Service College; Singapore.

John Halligan, Professor, Business and Government, University of Canberra; Australia.

David Halpern, Director, Research, Institute for Government; United Kingdom.

John Helliwell, Arthur J.E. Child Foundation Fellow, Canadian Institute for Advanced Research; Professor, Economics, University of British Columbia; Canada.

Thomas Homer-Dixon, Centre for International Governance Innovation Chair of Global Systems at the Balsillie School of International Affairs and Professor, Centre for Environment and Business, University of Waterloo; Canada.

Maria Rita Garcia Loureiro Durand, Professor, São Paulo Business Administration School of Fundação Getulio Vargas; Brazil.

Mike Joyce, Adjunct Professor and MPA/PMPA Program Director, Policy Studies, Queen's University; Canada.

Linda Kendell, Director, Evaluation and Research Group, Australian Public Service Commission; Australia.

Koh Tong Hai, Commander Cluster A, Singapore Prison Service; Singapore.

Tobias Kwakkelstein, Strategy Advisor, Knowledge Department, Ministry of the Interior; the Netherlands.

Don Lenihan, Vice President, Engagement, Public Policy Forum; Canada.

Bart Litjens, Director, Research, Partners + Pröpper Research and Consulting; the Netherlands.

Aaron Maniam, Head, Centre for Strategic Futures, Public Service Division, Prime Minister's Office; Singapore.

Paula Montagner, Director, Communication and Research, National School of Public Administration (ENAP); Brazil.

Gordon Owen, Director General, Partnerships and Best Practices, Canada School of Public Service; Canada.

Jessica McDonald, Executive Vice-President, Western and International Development, HB Global Advisors Corporation; Canada.

Sue Richards, Professor and Senior Fellow, Institute for Government; United Kingdom.

Jeremy Tan, Strategist, Centre for Strategic Futures, Public Service Division, Prime Minister's Office; Singapore.

Bernard Toh, Strategist, Centre for Strategic Futures, Public Service Division, Prime Minister's Office; Singapore.

Evelien Tonkens, Endowed Chair in Active Citizenship, Department of Sociology and Anthropology, University of Amsterdam; the Netherlands.

Thomas Townsend, Executive Head, Policy Research Initiative, Government of Canada; Canada.

Allan Tupper, President, Canadian Association of Programs in Public Administration; Head, Political Science, University of British Columbia; Canada.

Neil Yeates, Deputy Minister, Citizenship and Immigration Canada; Canada.

Rio de Janeiro, 13-14 July 2010

Pedro Vieira Abramovay, National Secretary, Justice, Ministry of Justice; Brazil.

Helena Kerr do Amaral, President, National School of Public Administration (ENAP); Brazil.

Leonardo Avritzer, Professor, Federal University of Minas Gerais; Brazil.

Rodrigo Ortiz Assumpção, President, Social Security Data Processing Company (Dataprev); Brazil.

Jocelyne Bourgon, President Emeritus, Canada School of Public Service; President, Public Governance International (PGI); Canada.

Gerard Van de Broek, Director, Knowledge Department, Ministry of the Interior; the Netherlands

Silvio Crestana, Researcher and former President, Brazilian Agricultural Research Corporation (EMBRAPA); Brazil.

Cibele Franzese, Professor, Getúlio Vargas Foundation; Brazil.

Katherine Graham, Professor, Public Policy and Administration, Carleton University; Canada.

Lena Leong, Senior Researcher, Centre for Governance and Leadership, Civil Service College; Singapore.

James Low, Senior Researcher, Civil Service College; Singapore.

Paula Montagner, Research Director, National School of Public Administration (ENAP); Brazil.

Alan Nymark, former Deputy Minister, Government of Canada; Fellow, Queen's University; Canada.

Lidewijde Ongering, Director General, Ministry of Transport, Public Works and Water Management; the Netherlands

Gordon Owen, Director General, Partnerships and Best Practices, Canada School of Public Service; Canada.

B. Guy Peters, Professor, University of Pittsburgh; United States of America.

Conrado Ramos, Deputy Director, Presidential Office of Planning and Budget; Uruguay.

José Mendes Ribeiro, Professor, National School of Public Health (ENSP); Brazil.

Sue Richards, Professor and Senior Fellow, Institute for Government; United Kingdom.

Hironobu Sano, Professor, Federal University of Rio Grande do Norte; Brazil.

Ronaldo Mota Sardenberg, President, Brazilian Telecommunication Agency(Anatel); Brazil.

Edna Tan, Senior Strategist, Centre for Strategic Futures; Singapore.

Yvonne Thomas, Operations Director and Director of Offender Management, Ministry of Justice; United Kingdom.

Singapore, 21-22 September 2010

Gareth Alston, Project Leader, International Dimensions of Climate Change, Government Office for Science; United Kingdom.

Michael Bichard, Founding Director, Institute for Government; Chair, United Kingdom Design Council; United Kingdom.

Jocelyne Bourgon, President Emeritus, Canada School of Public Service; President, Public Governance International (PGI); Canada.

Lim Yen Ching, Principal, NorthLight School; Singapore.

Tiago Falcão, Secretary, Management, Ministry of Planning Budget and Management; Brazil.

Merel de Groot, Knowledge Advisor, Ministry of Interior; the Netherlands.

James Kang, Assistant Chief Executive, InfoComm Development Authority; Singapore.

Sirpa Kekkonen, Counsellor, Head of Government Program Monitoring, Policy-Analyst Unit, Prime Minister's Office; Finland.

Karen Lau, Assistant Director, Public Policy and Organization Reviews, State Services Authority, Victoria; Australia.

Evert Lindquist, Director and Professor, Public Administration, University of Victoria; Chair, Applied Public Management Research, Crawford School of Economics and Government, Australian National University; Australia.

Lena Leong, Senior Researcher, Centre for Governance and Leadership, Civil Service College; Singapore.

Ang Bee Lian, Chief Executive, National Council of Social Service; Singapore.

Lim Chiew Ling, Senior Executive, Civil Service College; Singapore.

Lucas Lombaers, Director, Labour Affairs Public Sector, Ministry of Interior and Public Affairs; the Netherlands.

Donald Low, Head, Centre for Public Economics, Civil Service College; Singapore.

James Low, Senior Researcher, Civil Service College; Singapore.

Irene Lucas, Acting Permanent Secretary, Department of Communications and Local Government; United Kingdom.

Aaron Maniam, Head, Centre of Strategic Futures and Deputy Director, Strategic Policy Office, Public Service Division, Prime Minister's Office; Singapore.

K U Menon, Senior Consultant, Public Communications and Consultancy, Ministry of Information, Communications and the Arts; Singapore.

Paula Montagner, Director, Communications and Research, Brazilian National School of Public Administration (ENAP); Brazil.

Gordon Owen, Director General, Partnerships and Best Practices, Canada School of Public Service; Canada.

Sue Richards, Professor and Senior Fellow, Institute for Government; United Kingdom.

Tan Li San, Director, Centre for Governance and Leadership, Civil Service College; Director, Strategic Policy Office, Public Service Division, Prime Minister's Office; Singapore

Martijn van der Steen, Associate Dean and Deputy Director, Netherlands School for Public Administration; the Netherlands.

Martin Stewart-Weeks, Director, Public Sector Practice in Asia-Pacific, Cisco Systems Internet Business Solutions Group; Australia.

Jean-Pierre Voyer, Chief Executive Officer, Social Research Demonstration Corporation; Canada

John Wanna, Sir John Bunting Chair of Public Administration and Professor, Politics and International Relationship, Australian National University; Australia.

Lionel Yeo, Deputy Secretary (Development), Public Service Division, Prime Minister's Office; Dean, Civil Service College; Singapore.

Yee Ping Yi, Senior Director (Special Studies), Strategic Policy Office, Public Service Division, Prime Minister's Office; Deputy Dean, Civil Service College; Singapore.

London, 16-18 November 2010

Andrew Adonis, Director, Institute for Government; United Kingdom.

Roel Bekker, Professor, Employment Relations in Government, University of Leiden; the Netherlands.

Michael Bichard, Senior Fellow, Institute for Government; Chair, United Kingdom Design Council; United Kingdom.

Jocelyne Bourgon, President Emeritus, Canada School of Public Service; President, Public Governance International (PGI); Canada.

Rod Clark, Chief Executive Officer, National School of Government; United Kingdom.

Sarah Deeks, Business Operations Manager, Financial Services and Public Sector, Booz & Company; United Kingdom.

Jenifer Graves, Senior Advisor and Researcher, Canada School of Public Service; Canada.

Merel de Groot, Knowledge Advisor, Ministry of Interior; the Netherlands.

Zoe Gruhn, Director of Learning, Institute for Government; United Kingdom.

Tim Hughes, Researcher, Sunningdale Institute, National School of Government; United Kingdom.

Andrew Johnstone-Burt, Vice-President, Financial Services and Public Sector, Booz and Company; United Kingdom.

Philip Karré, Senior Researcher and Lecturer, National School for Public Administration; the Netherlands.

Eve Mitleton-Kelly, Professor, Institute of Social Psychology and Director, Complexity Research Program, London School of Economics; United Kingdom.

Helena Kerr, President, National School of Public Administration (ENAP); Brazil.

Natalia Koga, graduate student, University of Westminster; United Kingdom.

Tobias Kwakkelstein, Strategy Advisor, Knowledge Department, Ministry of the Interior; the Netherlands.

Lena Leong, Senior Researcher, Centre for Governance and Leadership, Civil Service College; Singapore.

Donald Low, Head, Centre for Public Economics, Civil Service College; Singapore.

Carmel McGregor, Deputy Commissioner, Australian Public Service Commission; Australia.

James Meddings, Vice President, Organizational Leadership and Innovation, Canada School of Public Service; Canada.

Gus O'Donnell, Cabinet Secretary and Head, Civil Service; United Kingdom.

Laura Ibiapina Parante, graduate student, University of Marne-la-Vallée/UMLV-Cité, President Itaca Consultoria e Pesquisa; Brazil.

Susan Phillips, Professor, Public Policy and Administration, Carleton University; Canada.

Sue Richards, Professor and Senior Fellow, Institute for Government; United Kingdom.

Tan Li San, Director, Strategic Policy Office, Public Service Division, Prime Minister's Office; Director, Centre for Governance and Leadership, Civil Service College; Singapore.

Rômulo Paes de Sousa, Vice Minister, Ministry of Social Development and Fight Against Hunger; Brazil.

Allan Tupper, President, Canadian Association of Programs in Public Administration; Head, Department of Political Science, University of British Columbia; Canada.

Martijn van der Steen, Associate Dean and Deputy Director, Netherlands School for Public Administration; the Netherlands.

Rapporteurs

Adrian Brown, Fellow, Institute for Government; United Kingdom.

Steven Dhondt, Netherlands Organization for Applied Scientific Research (TNO); the Netherlands.

Brian Johnson, President, Gladeview Consulting; Canada.

Andrew Kwok, Researcher, Civil Service College; Singapore.

Peter Milley, Senior Advisor, Canada School of Public Service; Canada.

Marie Sassine, Visiting Assistant Deputy Minister, Canada School of Public Service; Canada.

Laura Ibiapina Parente, graduate student, Université Marne-la-Vallée/UMLV-Cité, President Itaca Consultoria e Pesquisa; Brazil.

Endnotes

Introduction

1. See: Kettl, *The Transformation of Governance*; Osborne, "The New Public Governance"; Denhardt and Denhardt, *The New Public Service*; NS6 Project Leader's Team, "Literature Scan no.1: On the Need for a New Synthesis of Public Administration."

Chapter 1

1. Badger, Johnston, Stewart-Weeks and Willis, *The Connected Republic*.
2. Kettl and Fesler, *The Politics of the Administrative Process*, 4.
3. Organisation for Economic Co-operation and Development, Directorate for Employment, Labour and Social Affairs, "OECD Health Data 2010—Frequently Requested Data."
4. According to the United Nations Development Program "International Human Development Indicators," life expectancy in 2010 in Japan was 83.2 years versus 79.6 in the United States. According to United Nations Children's Fund (UNICEF) "Child Mortality Estimates" for 2009, child mortality in the United States is twice that of Japan.
5. According to the Organisation for Economic Co-operation and Development "Health Data—Frequently Requested Data," obesity rates in 2010 in Japan are 3.2 percent while in the United States they are 30.6 percent. According to Gapminder "GDP Per Capita Purchasing Power Parities," income per person in 2005 in Japan was approximately 12 percent less than in the United States.
6. On the institutionalization of dichotomies into public administration, see Svara, "The Myth of the Dichotomy"; and Lynn, "The Myth of the Bureaucratic Paradigm."
7. Denhardt and Denhardt, *The New Public Service*.
8. Kettl, *The Transformation of Governance*.
9. Bourgon, "Performance Management: It's the Results that Count"; NS6 Network, *A Public Service Renewal Agenda for the 21st Century*.
10. Bourgon, "The Future of Public Service: A Search for a New Balance."

11. See Kettl, *The Transformation of Governance*; Denhardt and Denhardt, *The New Public Service*; Osborne, "The New Public Governance"; NS6 Project Leader's Team, "Literature Scan No.1: On the Need for a New Synthesis of Public Administration."
12. Ostrom, "Crowding Out Citizenship."
13. Denhardt and Denhardt, *The New Public Service*.
14. Dagger, *Civic Virtues*.
15. Pranger, *The Eclipse of Citizenship*.
16. Organisation for Economic Co-operation and Development, *Participative Web and User-Created Content*.
17. Stone, *Policy Paradox*.
18. Kettl, *The Global Public Management Revolution*.
19. Salamon, *The Tools of Government*.
20. Rotmans, Kemp and van Asselt, "More Evolution than Revolution."
21. Bourgon, "New Directions in Public Administration."
22. Morgan, *Images of Organization*.
23. Klijn, "Complexity Theory and Public Administration."
24. Morgan, *Images of Organization*.
25. Mitleton-Kelly, "Ten Principles of Complexity and Enabling Infrastructures."
26. Morgan, *Images of Organization*.
27. Mitleton-Kelly, "Ten Principles of Complexity and Enabling Infrastructures."
28. Kahane, *Solving Tough Problems*.

Chapter 2

1. Paraphrase of Albert Einstein, according to Calaprice, *The New Quotable Einstein*, 292.
2. Bourgon, "Understanding the Public Leadership Environment."
3. Livi-Bacci, *A Concise History of World Population*.
4. Ibid.
5. United Nations Department of Economic and Social Affairs, Population Division, "World Population to 2300."
6. Westley, Zimmerman and Patton, *Getting to Maybe*.
7. Ibid.
8. Snowden and Kurtz, "The New Dynamics of Strategy."
9. Glouberman and Zimmerman, "Complicated and Complex Systems."
10. Snowden and Kurtz, "The New Dynamics of Strategy."
11. Leong, "Managing Complexity and Uncertainties."
12. Ho, "Governance at the Leading Edge."
13. Haynes, *Managing Complexity in the Public Services*.
14. Wagenaar, "Governance, Complexity, and Democratic Participation."
15. NS6 Network, *Resilience and Emergence in Public Administration*.
16. Bovaird, "Emergent Strategic Management and Planning Mechanisms in

Complex Adaptive Systems."
17. Kahane, *Solving Tough Problems.*
18. Ibid.
19. Ibid.
20. Wagenaar, "Governance, Complexity, and Democratic Participation"; Cottam, "Participatory Systems."
21. Snowden and Boone, "A Leader's Framework for Decision Making."
22. Kahane, *Solving Tough Problems.*
23. Duit and Galaz, "Governance and Complexity."
24. Gladwell, *The Tipping Point.*
25. Ho, "Governance at the Leading Edge"; Homer-Dixon, *The Upside of Down*; Homer-Dixon, *The Ingenuity Gap.*
26. Cottam and Leadbeater, *Health: Co-Creating Services.*
27. Snowden and Kurtz, "The New Dynamics of Strategy."
28. US-Canada Power System Outage Task Force, *Final Report on the August 14, 2003 Blackout in the United States and Canada.*
29. US Commodities Futures Trading Commission and US Security and Exchange Commission, *Findings Regarding the Market Events of May 6, 2010.*
30. Morgan, *Images of Organization*, 255.
31. Brooks, "Tools for Thinking."
32. Castells, *The Information Age.*
33. Koppenjan and Klijn, *Managing Uncertainties in Networks.*
34. Ho, "Thinking About the Future."
35. Duit and Galaz, "Governance and Complexity."
36. NS6 Network, *Resilience and Emergence in Public Administration.*
37. Ostrom, "A Communitarian Approach to Local Governance," 227.
38. Ostrom, "Crowding Out Citizenship."
39. Cahn, *No More Throw-Away People.*
40. Lindquist and Wanna, "Co-production in Perspective."
41. O'Flynn, "Adding Public Value."
42. Alford, *Engaging Public Sector Clients.*
43. Organisation for Economic Co-operation and Development, Program for International Student Assessment, *PISA 2009 Results.*
44. Ostrom, "Crowding Out Citizenship," 13.
45. Ostrom, "Crossing the Great Divide."
46. Helliwell and Putnam, "The Social Context of Well-Being."
47. Dale and Onyx, *A Dynamic Balance.*
48. Alford, *Engaging Public Sector Clients.*
49. Brooks, "Tools for Thinking."
50. Cahn, *No More Throw-Away People.*
51 Leadbeater, *We-Think.*
52. NS6 Network, *Preparing Government to Serve Beyond the Predictable*; Valdez, "Co-Creation Part of Singapore's 'Gov-With-You' Strategy."

53. Based on data from The World Bank, "Internet Users," and The World Bank, "Mobile Cellular Subscriptions."
54. Wikipedia, "List of Virtual Communities with more than 100 Million Users."
55. Leadbeater, *We-Think.*
56. Ibid.
57. NS6 Network, *Preparing Government to Serve Beyond the Predictable.*

Chapter 3

1. Bourgon with Milley, *New Frontiers of Public Administration*, 6.
2. Ibid.
3. See http://nsworld.org.
4. See Appendix A for a complete list of roundtable participants.
5. Salamon, *The Tools of Government.*
6. Moore, *Creating Public Value.*
7. See Organisation for Economic Co-operation and Development, "Society at a Glance 2011 – OECD Social Indicators"; and United Nations Development Program, "Human Development Reports."
8. See Stiglitz, Sen and Fitoussi, *Report by the Commission on the Measurement of Economic Performance and Social Progress*; the British Columbia Progress Board at http://www.bcprogressboard.com.
9. Helliwell, "Well-Being, Social Capital and Public Policy."
10. Halpern, *The Hidden Wealth of Nations.*
11. Organisation for Economic Co-operation and Development, *From Open to Inclusive.*
12. See NS6 Network, *Resilience and Emergence in Public Administration*; NS6 Network, *Achieving Public Results*; Helliwell and Putnam, "The Social Context of Well-Being."
13. New York City, "NYC DataMine."
14. New York City, "NYC BigApps2.0."
15. NS6 Network, *Governance in the 21st Century.*
16. Social Research and Demonstration Corporation, "What We Do."
17. Leadbeater and Cottam, "The User-Generated State: Public Services 2.0."
18. Ostrom, "Crowding Out Citizenship."
19. Mahbubani, "The Dangers of Democratic Delusions."
20. Fung and Wright, *Deepening Democracy.*
21. This idea is attributed to Chua Chin Kiat, Director of Prisons in Singapore, in the Singapore Prison Service case study in Part Two of this volume.
22. See the full case study on the Bolsa Família in Part Two of this volume.
23. NS6 Network, *Achieving Public Results*, 26.
24. See NS6 Network, *Resilience and Emergence in Public Administration.*
25. President Lula quoted from the full case study in Part 2 of this volume.
26. Mendoza and Vernis, "The Changing Role of Governments and the Emer-

gence of the Relational State," 390.

27. O'Flynn, Halligan and Blackman, "Working Across Boundaries."
28. Kelman, "The Transformation of Government in the Decade Ahead."
29. Ostrom, "Crossing the Great Divide."
30. Bourgon, "Responsive, Responsible and Respected Government."
31. Klijn, "Governance and Governance Networks in Europe."
32. Baran, *On Distributed Communications.*
33. NS6 Network, *Resilience and Emergence in Public Administration.*
34. See the full case study of the Public Safety Centres in Part Two of this volume.
35. See the full case study of the Public Safety Centres in Part Two of this volume.
36. KIPP, "Frequently Asked Questions."
37. KIPP, "About KIPP."
38. Balfanz and Legters, *Locating the Dropout Crisis,* 21.
39. KIPP schools are largely focused on serving students from grades 4-9, as these are seen to be the formative years in which successful attitudes and approaches to learning can be developed. For evaluation information, see KIPP, "Frequently Asked Questions" and "Independent Reports."
40. Australian Department of Finance and Deregulation, *Engage: Getting on with Government 2.0,* xxi and 53.
41. Scottish Centre for Telehealth, "About the Centre."
42. Grammond, "La Télémédicine à la Côte en Suisse."
43. Ibid.
44. Ushahidi-Haiti @ Tufts University, "About Us."
45. Smith, "Tufts Map Steered Action Amid Chaos."
46. Ushahidi, "About Us."
47. NS6 Network, *Achieving Public Results;* NS6 Network, *Governance in the 21st Century.*
48. See the full case study on the Homelessness Partnering Strategy in Part Two of this volume.
49. For example, in 2000 the World Health Organization identified the stewardship role of government as one of the four main functions needed to attain desired health outcomes in society. See Travis, Egger, Davies and Mechbal, "Towards Better Stewardship."

Chapter 4

1. Badger, Johnston, Stewart-Weeks and Willis, *The Connected Republic.*
2. Bourgon, "The History and Future of Nation-Building?"
3. A summary of the findings from the NS6 roundtables is presented in Part Three of this volume. Full reports from the events are available at http://nsworld.org.
4. Goldstein, "Emergence as a Construct."
5. Habegger, *Horizon Scanning in Government;* Schultz, "The Cultural Contra-

dictions of Managing Change."
6. For example, crime rates in England and Wales fell 50 percent between 1996 to 2009. See Ministry of Justice (United Kingdom), "Criminal Statistics: England and Wales 2009," 9. In Canada, crime rates have been on a steady decline since peaking in 1991. See Statistics Canada, "Crime Statistics."
7. Halpern, *The Hidden Wealth of Nations*, 65.
8. See Vandenbroeck, Goossens and Clemens, *Tackling Obesities*.
9. Ramalingam and Jones with Reba and Young, *Exploring the Science of Complexity*.
10. Habegger, *Horizon Scanning in Government*.
11. NS6 Network, *Preparing Government to Serve Beyond the Predictable*.
12. Habegger, *Horizon Scanning in Government*.
13. The website for Singapore's RAHS is http://rahs.org.sg.
14. Habegger, "Strategic Foresight in Public Policy."
15. Ho, "Thinking About the Future."
16. NS6 Network, *Preparing Government to Serve Beyond the Predictable*, 21-2.
17. The website for Singapore's PS21 initiative is http://www.ps21.gov.sg/.
18. NS6 Network, *Preparing Government to Serve Beyond the Predictable*, 19-21. The website for Finland's Parliamentary Committee for the Future is http://web.eduskunta.fi/Resource.phz/parliament/committees/future.htx.
19. Schuler, "Civic Intelligence and the Public Sphere."
20. Runge and Senauer, "How Ethanol Fuels the Food Crisis."
21. NS6 Network, *Governance in the 21ˢᵗ Century*; NS6 Network, *Preparing Government to Serve Beyond the Predictable*.
22. NS6 Network, *Resilience and Emergence in Public Administration*.
23. NS6 Network, *Governance in the 21ˢᵗ Century*.
24. NS6 Network, *Preparing Government to Serve Beyond the Predictable*.
25. NS6 Network, *Governance in the 21ˢᵗ Century*; NS6 Network, *Preparing Government to Serve Beyond the Predictable*.
26. Osborne and Brown, *Managing Change and Innovation in Public Service Organizations*.
27. Mulgan, *Ready or Not?* 4.
28 Borins, "Leadership and Innovation in the Public Sector."
29 Mulgan, *Ready or Not?*
30. Ostrom, "Crossing the Great Divide," 90.
31. Beddington, Agnew and Clark, "Current Problems in the Management of Marine Fisheries."
32. Muldavin, "The Paradoxes of Environmental Policy and Resource Management in Reform-Era China"; Rozelle, Huang and Zhang, "Poverty, Population and Environmental Degradation in China."
33. Yang, *Calamity and Reform in China*.
34. Waltner-Toews and Lang, "A New Conceptual Base for Food and Agricultural Policy."
35. King and Thomas, "Big Lessons for a Healthy Future."

36. Ho, "Governance at the Leading Edge."
37. Mulgan, "The Process of Social Innovation."
38. Bason, *Leading Public Sector Innovation*.
39. March, "Exploration and Exploitation in Organizational Learning," 71.
40. See the full case study of the transformation of the Singapore Prison Service in Part Two of this volume.
41. See the full case study of the implementation of the Bolsa Família in Part Two of this volume.
42. The RDSP was announced in the Government of Canada's 2008 budget. See Department of Finance Canada, "Backgrounder: Summary of Federal Tax Relief for 2008 and 2009." For details about the plan see Human Resources and Skills Development Canada, "Registered Disability Savings Plan (RDSP)."
43. Westley, Zimmerman and Patton, *Getting to Maybe*.
44. Van de Walle and Vogelaar, "Emergence and Public Administration."
45. Begun, Zimmerman and Dooley, "Health Care Organizations as Complex Adaptive Systems," 276.
46. Fonseca and Bastos, "Twenty-Five Years of the AIDS Epidemic in Brazil."
47. World Bank, *Controlling AIDS: Public Priorities in a Global Epidemic*.
48. Westley, Zimmerman and Patton, *Getting to Maybe*, 4.
49. Begun, Zimmerman and Dooley, "Health Care Organizations as Complex Adaptive Systems," 276.
50. Ibid.
51. Storey, "A Different Kind of Justice."
52. Ibid.
53. More than 21,000 people gave testimony in the TRC committees. See BBC News, "TRC: The Facts."
54. Kahane, *Solving Tough Problems*.
55. Hefetz and Warner, "Privatization and Its Reverse."
56. O'Flynn, Halligan and Blackman, "Working Across Boundaries."
57. See Freidman, *The World is Flat*.
58. In May 2008, United Nations Secretary General Ban Ki-moon stated that millions of people are cut off from the quality of life benefits enabled by the internet and concluded that narrowing the digital divide is crucial to global anti-poverty goals. See United Nations Department of Public Information, "Narrowing Digital Divide Crucial Part of Achieving Global Anti-poverty Goals."
59. See http://www.everyblock.com.
60. See Part Three of this volume for a summary of findings from the London roundtable.
61. NS6 Network, *A Public Service Reform and Renewal Agenda for the 21st Century*, 33.
62. Australian Government Department of Finance and Deregulation, *Engage: Getting on with Government 2.0*.

63. The European Commission's Social Innovation Europe website is http://ec.europe.eu/enterprise/policies/innovation/policy/social-innovation/index_en.htm.

64. Mulgan with Tucker, Ali and Sanders, "Social Innovation."

65. Westley and Antadze, "Making a Difference."

66. Voyer, "Experimentation for Better Policy-Making."

67. Mulgan, *The Art of Public Strategy*.

68. The Social Research and Demonstration Corporation website is http://srdc.org.

69. NS6 Network, *Preparing Government to Serve Beyond the Predictable*, 31.

70 See http://www.nls.edu.sg/home/.

71. MindLab, "Away with the Red Tape: A Better Encounter with Government." The MindLab website is http://www.mind-lab.dk/en.

72. Benjamin, "Small is Powerful."

73. See http://unreasonableinstitute.org.

74. Mulgan with Tucker, Ali and Sanders, "Social Innovation."

75. See Kelly, Mulgan and Muers, *Creating Public Value*.

76. Steffen et al., *Global Change and the Earth System*.

77. Walker and Salt, *Resilience Thinking*.

78. McManus, Seville, Brunsdon and Vargo, *Resilience Management*.

79. Menon, "National Resilience."

80. Bourgon, "New Directions in Public Administration."

81. Brondizio, Ostrom and Young, "Connectivity and the Governance of Multi-level Social-Ecological Systems."

82. Newman and Dale, "Network Structure, Diversity, and Proactive Resilience Building."

83. Berkes, "Understanding Uncertainty and Reducing Vulnerability."

84. A cornerstone of the New Zealand resilience strategy was the introduction of the *Civil Defense Emergency Management Act* in 2002 along with a dedicated fund for promoting resilient communities.

85. Resilience was also the subject of a substantial literature review in the project. See NS6 Project Leader's Team, "Literature Scan no. 3: Resilience and Public Administration."

86. The full case study on the Victorian Bushfire Reconstruction and Recovery Authority is included in Part Two of this volume.

87. NS6 Network, *Achieving Public Results*.

88. According to Masten and O'Dougherty Wright, "Resilience Over the Lifespan," research on resilience in human development is interested in understanding how people overcome risk and adversity to succeed in life. It explores the reasons behind the variability of outcomes among individuals who have experienced poverty, violence, disaster or trauma.

89. Masten, "Ordinary Magic: Resilience Processes in Development."

90. Masten, "Ordinary Magic: Lessons from Research on Resilience in Human

Development," 29-30.
91. Ibid, 31.
92. NS6 Network, *Achieving Public Results*, 19; Helliwell, "Institutions as Enablers of Well-Being: The Singapore Prison Case Study."
93. NS6 Network, *Achieving Public Results*, 20; Helliwell, "How Can Subjective Well-Being Be Improved?"
94. Coutu, "How Resilience Works."
95. McManus, Seville, Brunsdon, and Vargo, *Resilience Management.*
96. Dale and Onyx, *Dynamic Balance.*
97. Berkes and Folke, "Back to the Future."
98. Murphy, "Locating Social Capital in Resilient Community-Level Emergency Management"; Newman and Dale, "Network Structure, Diversity, and Proactive Resilience Building."
99. Litjens, Rouw, Hammenga and Prӧpper, "Rotterdam Tarwewijk, A Resilient Neighbourhood?"
100. Comfort, "Risk and Resilience"; Gunderson, Holling and Light, *Barriers and Bridges to the Renewal of Ecosystems and Institutions.*
101. Holling and Meffe, "Command and Control and the Pathology of Natural Resource Management."
102. Berkes and Folke, "Back to the Future."
103. Norris et al, "Community Resilience as a Metaphor, Theory, Set of Capacities, and Strategy for Disaster Readiness"; Scheffer et al, "Dynamic Interaction of Societies and Ecosystems."
104. Homer-Dixon, *The Upside of Down.*

Chapter 5

1. Ostrom, "Beyond Markets and States," 435.
2. NS6 Network, *A Public Service Reform and Renewal Agenda for the 21st Century*, 20.
3. Samuels, "Separation of Powers."
4. Livingston, "German Reunification from Three Angles"; Pfaff, *Exit-Voice Dynamics and the Collapse of East Germany.*
5. Kettl, *The Global Public Management Revolution.*
6. Ho, "Reinventing Local Governments and the E-Government Initiative."
7. NS6 Network, *A Public Service Reform and Renewal Agenda for the 21st Century*, 20.
8. Agranoff and McGuire, "Big Questions in Public Network Management Research."
9. NS6 Network, *A Public Service Reform and Renewal Agenda for the 21st Century*, 35.
10. Aucoin and Jarvis, *Modernizing Government Accountability.*
11. Bouckaert and Halligan, *Managing Performance.*

12. Gregory, "New Public Management and the Ghost of Max Weber," 232-33.
13. Lenihan, Godfrey, Valeri and Williams, "Accountability for Learning." Lenihan, Godfrey, Valeri and Williams, "What is Shared Accountability?"
14. Australian National Audit Office, *Whole of Government Indigenous Service Delivery Arrangements*, 105.
15. Office of the Auditor General of Canada, "Chapter 9: Modernizing Accountability in the Public Sector," 15.
16. Ibid.
17. Halligan, "Shared Accountability for Shared Results"; NS6 Network, *Achieving Public Results*, 30-31.
18. Bouckaert and Halligan, *Managing Performance*.
19. Aucoin and Heintzman, "The Dialectics of Accountability for Performance in Public Management."
20. Ibid.
21. NS6 Network, *Achieving Public Results*.
22. Ibid., 19.
23. Stiglitz, Sen and Fitoussi, *Report by the Commission on the Measurement of Economic Performance and Social Progress*.
24. Organisation for Economic Co-operation and Development, "Better Life Initiative."
25. British Columbia Progress Board, "Tracking Changes in the Economic Performance and Social Well-Being of British Columbia."
26. Finland Prime Minister's Office, "Findicator—Set of Indicators for Social Progress."
27. NS6 Network, *A Public Service Reform and Renewal Agenda for the 21st Century*, 39-40.
28. NS6 Network, *Resilience and Emergence in Public Administration*, 36-7; NS6 Network, *Achieving Public Results*, 20, 28-30; NS6 Network, *Governance in the 21st Century*, 15, 22, 31; NS6 Network, *Preparing Government to Serve Beyond the Predictable*, 25, 31; NS6 Network, *A Public Service Reform and Renewal Agenda for the 21st Century*, 38-39.
29. Radin, *Challenging the Performance Movement*.
30. Kroeger, "Accountability: Three Approaches."
31. Lépine, *The Web of Rules*.
32. Marsh and Spies-Butcher, "Pragmatism and Neo-Classical Policy Paradigms in Public Services," 243.
33. Power, *The Audit Society*, 127.
34. Rainey, *Understanding and Managing Public Organizations*.
35. Aucoin and Heintzman, "The Dialectics of Accountability for Performance in Public Management."
36. Gregory, "New Public Management and the Ghost of Max Weber," 232-3; Pollitt, "How Do We Know How Good Public Services Are?"
37. For example, Hood, James, Jones, Scott and Travers, "Regulation Inside Gov-

ernment."
38. Aucoin and Heintzman, "The Dialectics of Accountability for Performance in Public Management."
39. Barzelay and Armajani, "Innovations in the Concept of Government Operations."
40. Tonkens and Swierstra, "What Gets Measured Gets Moulded."
41. CCAF-FCVI, *Innovation, Risk and Control.*
42. International Federation of Accountants, *2010 Handbook of International Quality Control, Auditing, Review, Other Assurance, and Related Services Pronouncements.* International Organization of Supreme Audit Institutions "Guidelines for Internal Control Standards for the Public Sector."
43. Lonsdale, "Developments in Value-For-Money Audit Methods," 73.
44. Thomas, "The Rise and Fall of Enron."
45. Moore, Tetlock, Tanlu and Bazerman, "Conflicts of Interest and the Case of Auditor Independence."
46. Kelman, "The Kennedy School of Research on Innovations in Government."
47. Thomas, "Performance Measurement, Reporting and Accountability."
48. Sanderson, "Intelligent Policy Making for a Complex World," 713-14.
49. Aucoin and Heintzman, "The Dialectics of Accountability for Performance in Public Management"; Lenihan, Godfrey and Williams, "Results Reporting, Parliament and Public Debate."
50. Koppenjan and Klijn, *Managing Uncertainties in Networks.*
51. Kernaghan, Marson and Borins, *The New Public Organization,* 264.
52. For an example of the dynamics involved in working simultaneously in networks and hierarchies, see the case study on Public Safety Centres in the Netherlands in Part Two of this volume.
53. O'Flynn, Halligan and Blackman, "Working Across Boundaries."
54. Ibid.
55. Bourgon, "The Future of Public Service."
56. Digital 4Sight, *Governance in the Digital Economy.*
57. Borins, *Innovations in Government.*
58. Heritage Foundation and Wall Street Journal, "2011 Index of Economic Freedom."
59. National Economic Council, Office of the President of the United States of America, "A Strategy for American Innovation"; Government of Finland, *Government's Communication on Finland's National Innovation Strategy to the Parliament,* 3; Norwegian Ministry of Trade and Industry, *An Innovative and Sustainable Norway.*
60. State Government of Victoria, *Innovation Action Plan.*
61. Canadian Centre for Management Development, "Corporate Documents: Learning and Innovation Seed Fund."
62. Corporation for National and Community Service of the United States of America, "Social Innovation Fund."

63. Bason, *Leading Public Sector Innovation*.
64. Ibid.
65. Kao, *Innovation Nation*, 130.
66. Bason, *Leading Public Sector Innovation*, 101.
67. NS6 Network, *A Public Service Reform and Renewal Agenda for the 21st Century*, 33.
68. Australian Government, "Declaration of Open Government"; Australian Government, "Govspace: Enabling Online Engagement"; Kotwani, "Biometric Faces Will Be Your Passport at Singapore's Checkpoints."
69. NS6 Network, *Governance in the 21st Century*.
70. Junqueras and Lichtenberger, "Civil Rights on the Internet."
71. Sigmundsdottir, "Tech-savvy Iceland online for new constitution."
72. Australian Government, "Government 2.0 Taskforce."
73. Australian Government Department of Finance and Deregulation, "Government Response to the Report of the Government 2.0 Taskforce."
74. Bason, *Leading Public Sector Innovation*.
75. Dewar, and Dutton, "The Adoption of Radical and Incremental Innovations."
76. Voyer, "Experimentation For Better Policy-Making."
77. Behn, "Management by Groping Along."
78. Voyer, "Experimentation for Better Policy-Making."
79. Bason, "Use Co-Creation to Drive Public Sector Innovation"; Valdez, "Co-creation Part of Singapore's 'Gov-with-You' Strategy"; John F. Moore, "Washington, DC: Co-Creation in Action."
80. Bason, *Leading Public Sector Innovation*.
81. NS6 Network, *A Public Service Reform and Renewal Agenda for the 21st Century*, 23.
82. Brown, *Change by Design*.
83. NS6 Network, *Governance in the 21st Century*, 24-6.
84. de Carvalho Oliveira, Ferrarezi and Koga, "National Health Conferences and Participatory Processes in the Brazilian Federal Public Administration."
85. Ibid, 5.
86 See Canadian Health Services Research Foundation, "Paediatric Complex Care Coordination—A Pilot Project."
87. Warner, "Reversing Privatization, Rebalancing Government Reform."
88. Alford, *Engaging Public Sector Clients*.
89. Cahn, *No More Throw-Away People*, 87-8.
90. This example is based on presentation materials entitled "Innovation in Eldercare—Governing Strategies of Involvement: Lessons from Danish Municipalities" that were verified by a former Director of the Department of Elderly Care, Health and Labour Force in the Municipality of Fredericia, Denmark.
91. NS6 Network, *Resilience and Emergence in Public Administration*; NS6 Network, *Achieving Public Results*.
92. Ibid.

Chapter 6

1. Bourgon with Milley, *The New Frontiers of Public Administration*, 6.
2. See Part Three of this volume for a description of the NS6 Network and how it came together and worked.
3. See Appendix A of this volume for a list of participants in the international roundtables of the New Synthesis Project.
4. See Bourgon, "The Future of Public Service"; Bourgon, "The History and Future of Nation-Building?"
5. Moore and Braga, "Police Performance Measurement," 8-9.
6. Neo and Chen, *Dynamic Governance*.
7. Bovaird, "Developing New Forms of Partnership with the 'Market' in the Procurement of Public Services," 96.

Chapter 7

1. See http://www.nsworld.org.
2. NS6 Network, *Resilience and Emergence in Public Administration*, 14-26.

Chapter 8

1. The author would like to thank the management and staff of the Singapore Prison Service and the Singapore Cooperation of Rehabilitative Service (SCORE) for their assistance in the writing of this case study, in particular, Koh Tong Hai, who presented it at the NS6 International Roundtable in Ottawa, 4-5 May 2010.
2. Singapore Prison Service, *Annual Report*.
3. Singapore Prison Service, *Organisational Health Survey*.
4. Bourgon with Milley, *The New Frontiers of Public Administration*, 36-38.
5. The Singapore Prison Service (SPS) dates from the penal settlements established in 1825 to house convicts transported from British India; between 1841 and 1936, the British Colonial Government built four prisons in all. The prevalent philosophy of deterrence through punitive measures rather than rehabilitation led to an extremely high rate of recidivism which, in turn, led to prison crowding. In 1946, SPS was institutionalized as a department and today plays an important role in Singapore's Criminal Justice System, working closely with the Judiciary and other partner agencies under the Ministry of Home Affairs (MHA). Its mission is to "protect society through the safe custody and rehabilitation of offenders, co-operating in prevention and aftercare." SPS operates a total of 14 Penal Institutions and Drug Rehabilitation Centres; and three maximum, five medium and six low-medium security institutions. Total inmate population is about 13,400, of which 51 percent are drug addicts. About 3.4 percent serve the tail-end of their sentence in community-based

programs outside the prisons. SPS staff strength stands at 2,300, of which 23 percent are Senior Officers; 67 percent, junior ranks; and 10 percent, civilian. The inmate-to-staff ratio is about 7.6 inmates to 1 staff (Singapore Prison Service, www.prisons.gov.sg).

6. Singapore Prison Service, "Mission & Vision of Singapore Prison Service."

7. Lapses in the post-war years created concern that opening doors to volunteers would put security at risk and subject prisons staff to accusations of favouritism and corruption. This thinking was reinforced in the design of SPS' internal systems, rules and processes. The public hence lacked understanding of SPS activities and prisoners, resulting in fear and reluctance to associate with them in any way.

8. The Board of Visiting Justice comprised prominent members of society with the influence to rally public support and action towards the reintegration of ex-offenders.

9. SCORE was established in 1975 as a statutory board under the MHA to manage inmate-run enterprises within SPS. A key partner of SPS, its scope was expanded in 1987 to include rehabilitation and aftercare services to facilitate transition into the community. Today SCORE has four core functions: Work, Training, Employment Assistance, and Community Engagement. In 2009, SCORE provided work programs for 3,500 inmates, trained 2,980 inmates in market-relevant skills, assisted 2,517 ex-offenders and inmates to find jobs and maintained a total of 1,853 employers in its job databank. SCORE has about 130 staff members, of which about 24 percent are ex-offenders. It is a self-funding entity and does not receive any direct funding from the government (Singapore Corporation of Rehabilitative Enterprises, www.score.gov.sg).

10. Singapore Community Action for the Rehabilitation of Ex-Offenders (CARE) Network, "Yellow Ribbon Project."

11. Chung, *Making a Difference as Captains of Lives.*

12. Singapore Prison Service, *Singapore Prison Service's Singapore Quality Award.*

13. Senge, "The Leader's New Work: Building Learning Organizations," 10-13.

14. Senge, Kleiner, Roberts, Ross, and Smith, *The Fifth Discipline Fieldbook*, 235-237.

Chapter 9

1. Frederico Guanais is Health Senior Specialist at Social Protection and Health Division of the Inter-American Development Bank in Washington, DC. When the drafts of this paper were written, he was Head of the International Cooperation office at the Escola Nacional de Administração Pública (ENAP) in Brasília, Brazil. The findings, interpretations and conclusions do not necessarily reflect the view of the Brazilian government or the Inter-American Development Bank.

2. Brazil has a population of approximately 191 million, 84.3 percent of which

is urban. Its gross domestic product of US$1,573 trillion in 2008 (approximately 8,414 per capita) places the nation within the ranks of middle-income countries. However, despite remarkable progress in recent years, extremely high levels of inequality mean that the absolute number of poor citizens remains high. In 2009, the top one percent own 12.1 percent of income; while the poorest 50 percent take home only 15.5 percent, according to 2010 data (Instituto de Pesquisa Econômica Aplicada, 2010).

3. Rounded value for an exchange rate of US$1.00 = BRL 1.76 (April 2010). All figures in US dollars in this paper follow this rate.

4. Inflation in consumer prices for the year of 1993 was 2,489% (two thousand four hundred and eighty nine percent).

5. Instituto de Pesquisa Econômica Aplicada, "IPEADATA."

6. Ibid.

7. Salomon, "Graziano indica que Vale-Gás e Bolsa-Renda podem acabar."

8. Belchior, "Professionalism and consolidation". Note that the Interministerial Social Policy Commission is a working group coordinated by the President's Office to integrate different social policy areas.

9. The Programa de Erradicação do Trabalho Infantil remained separate until 2005 when it was also merged with Bolsa Família.

10. Betto, *Calendário do Poder*, 255-256.

11. Lula, Speech at the Meeting of CONSEA.

12. Lindert and Vincensini, "Bolsa Família in the Headlines."

13. Similar experiments have been implemented in most Latin American countries. Like Bolsa Família, Mexico's wide-scale and largely successful conditional cash transfer program is called Oportunidades.

14. Rocha, "Transferências de renda federais;" Soares, *O Ritmo de Queda na Desigualdade no Brasil É Adequado?*; and Kakwani, Neri, and Son, *Pro-Poor Growth and Social Programmes in Brazil.*

15. Santos, Paes-Sousa, Silva and Victora, "National Immunization Day."

16. Paes de Barros, *Sucessos e Desafios para a Proteção e Promoção no Brasil.*

17. Ibid.

18. Santos, Paes-Sousa, Silva and Victora, "National Immunization Day."

19. Ananias de Sousa, "El combate al hambre y el nuevo marco de las políticas públicas"; Soares, *Volatilidade de Renda e a Cobertura do Programa Bolsa Família.*

20. Kriger, Interview with Minister Patrus Ananias.

21. Pacheco, "Crise afeta menos a base da pirâmide."

22. According to January 2011 data provided by the Ministry of Social Development, 1.9 million beneficiaries (15 percent of the total number of families that receive Bolsa Família) already receive their cash payment through a personal bank account.

Chapter 10

1. "It will take common vision, collaboration, persistence and hard work over several years to resolve the longstanding problems that have led to the homelessness, untreated mental health, problematic substance use and crime that Victoria, and other communities across the country, are seeing in our downtowns" (Mayor's Task Force on Breaking the Cycle of Mental Illness, Addictions and Homelessness, "Executive Summary," 13).
2. Interviews were conducted in March 2010 with program staff from the Homelessness Partnering Secretariat, Human Resources and Skills Development Canada. The author would like to thank the program staff at the Homelessness Partnering Secretariat, Human Resources and Skills Development Canada and the Canada School of Public Service for their assistance with this case study.
3. Crooks, "Evidence."
4. Hulchanski, "Homelessness in Canada," 5.
5. Hopper and Baumohl, "Redefining the Cursed Word," 3, quoted in Hulchanski, op cit.
6. Echenberg and Jensen, *Defining and Enumerating Homelessness in Canada*, 2.
7. Ibid., 1-2.
8. United Nations Human Rights Council, *Report of the Special Rapporteur on Adequate Housing*.
9. Wente, "Urban Aboriginal Homelessness in Canada."
10. Edmonton Joint Planning Committee on Housing, *Out in the Cold*.
11. Gaetz, "The Struggle", 1-2.
12. Ibid, 2.
13. Smith, "Lessons from the Homelessness Initiative," 9.
14. Ibid., 6.
15. Eberle, "Evidence."
16. Hopper and Baumohl, "Redefining the Cursed Word," 3.
17. Gorman, *Government and Communities*, 14.
18. Weaver, "Evidence."
19. Senate of Canada, *In From the Margins*, 16.
20. City of Prince Albert, *Community Action Plan on Homelessness and Housing*, 8.

Chapter 11

1. In researching this case study, interviews were conducted with managers at four PSCs (November 2009 to January 2010) and with representatives of partner organizations at two PSCs (December 2009 to February 2010). Observations were made at meetings and discussions at two PSCs (January and February 2010). The following websites were consulted: Centre for Crime Prevention and Safety (www.hetccv.nl); Ministry of Justice (www.minjus.nl); Ministry of Interior Affairs and Kingdom Relations (www.minbzk.nl); offi-

cial website for all PSCs (www.veiligheidshuizen.nl); portal for PSCs (www.veiligheidshuis.nl); portal to PSCs in Breda, Tilburg, and Bergen of Zoom (www.veiligheidshuis.org); Scientific Research and Documentation Centre (www.wodc.nl); the Dutch Government (www.regering.nl).

2. The themes are (1) external relations, (2) the economy, (3) sustainability and the environment, (4) social cohesion, (5) public safety and security, and (6) the government's role in providing services.

3. The Balkenende IV Cabinet refers to the (fourth) coalition government headed by Prime Minister Balkenende. This government fell on February 20, 2010.

4. Ministerie van Algemene Zaken, *Samen werken – samen leven.*

5. Ibid, 70.

6. Ministerie van Justitie / Ministerie van Binnenlandse Zaken en Koninkrijk relaties, *Safety Begins with Prevention: Continuing Building a Safer Society.*

7. Ministerie van Justitie / Ministerie van Binnenlandse Zaken en Koninkrijksrelaties, *Naar een veiliger samenleving.*

8. Ministerie van Justitie / Ministerie van Binnenlandse Zaken en Koninkrijksrelaties, *Veiligheid begint bij Voorkomen. Voortbouwen aan een Veiliger Samenleving.*

9. Fijnaut and Zaat, *De sociale (on)veiligheid in Tilburg.*

10. It is difficult to determine the specific role played by the PSC in this development, as it cannot be isolated from other efforts. Nevertheless, these positive results are frequently attributed to the cooperative approach at the PSC.

11. Box 1 and Box 2 illustrate how problems are perceived and dealt with at two particular cluster tables.

12. The ISD measure has been available as a sentence since 2004, and is administered by the Ministry of Justice. Placement in an ISD is a fairly severe measure and requires a court order. Due to its severity and cost (which is paid by the Ministry of Justice), it is not widely or lightly applied.

13. The responsibility for providing post-incarceration care for ex-detainees was decentralized from the national level to the municipal government through agreements made in 2008. An "ex-detainee cluster" is now one of the most common clusters at PSCs.

14. Ministerie van Justitie, "Veiligheidshuizen effectief".

Chapter 12

1. In researching this case study, interviews were conducted with the following VBRRA officials in Melbourne from December 2009 to January 2010: Christine Nixon, Chairperson; Ben Hubbard, Chief Executive Officer; Betsy Harrington, Head, Operations; Penny Croser, Head, Policy, Secretariat and Business Services; Jeff Rosewarne, Interim Chief Executive Officer (February–June 2009); Deb Symons, Executive Adviser. The State Services Authority would like to thank and acknowledge these important actors for taking time to reflect on the VBRRA's first year. The State Services Authority would also like to thank John

Hanna for his support in coordinating the case study process.

2. State Services Authority (State of Victoria, Australia), *Welcome to Government*, 1.

3. Department of Planning and Community Development (State of Victoria, Australia), "Guide to Local Government".

4. Moncrief, "Worst Day in History."

5. The Victorian Bushfire Appeal Fund was established in the days after the fires by the Victorian Government, in partnership with the Australian Red Cross and the Australian Government, raising $379 million by the time the appeal officially closed in April 2009.

6. Ellis, Kanowski, and Whelan. *National Inquiry on Bushfire Mitigation and Management*; Emergency Management Australia, *Recovery*.

7. Tony Ferguson cited in the Victorian Bushfire Reconstruction and Recovery Authority, *12 Month Report*, 45.

8. Bourgon, "Serving Beyond the Predictable," Occasional Paper No. 8.

9. Australian Broadcasting Corporation, "Black Saturday Anniversary: Resilience."

10. Ibid.

11. Ibid.

12. Ellis, Kanowski, and Whelan. *National Inquiry on Bushfire Mitigation and Management*; Emergency Management Australia, *Community Development in Recovery From Disaster*.

13. Victorian Bushfire Reconstruction and Recovery Authority, *100 Day Report*, 4.

14. Ibid., i.

15. Victorian Bushfire Reconstruction and Recovery Authority, *Rebuilding Together*, 40-41.

Chapter 13

1. The case study on "Singapore Workfare" was first written in 2008 by then senior researcher from the Centre for Public Economics, Civil Service College, Koh Tsin Yen. It was further updated in 2011 for the purpose of the New Synthesis Project by Pamela Qiu, a researcher also from the Centre for Public Economics, Civil Service College. The authors would like to thank the management and staff of the Ministry of Manpower (Singapore) for their support in the development of this paper.

2. Department of Statistics (Singapore), "Trends in Household Income and Expenditure," 2005.

3. Hu, "Budget Speech, 1998."

4. Goh, "National Day Rally Speech, 2000."

5. Hu, "Budget Debate Roundup Speech, 2000."

6. Lee, "Budget Debate Roundup Speech."

7. Oon, "Keep stagflation at bay: Swee Say".

8. All adult Singaporeans who contributed at least S$50 to their CPF accounts

Chapter 13, continued

would get "shares" worth between S$200 and S$1,600, depending on their income and the annual value of their homes. The shares would earn an annual dividend pegged to the real GDP growth rate for the next six years.

9. Goh, "National Day Rally Speech, 2001."
10. Ibid.
11. Ministry of Finance (Singapore), "Study Team Report on Hong Kong's Welfare System," 2005.
12. Friedman and Friedman, *Free to Choose*.
13. For example, a household with five members (two parents, a child, two elderly grandparents) would be eligible to receive over HK$13,250 a year (about S$2,230) without working, plus free healthcare benefits while they remained on the CSSA scheme. If the parents took on jobs, their first HK$600 would be fully disregarded, the next HK$3,800 would reduce benefits by 50 percent, and any income earned thereafter would reduce CSSA benefits dollar for dollar. The 'disregarded' income of HK$2,500, in other words, represents only a 19 percent increase over his or her CSSA benefits.
14. Ministry of Finance (Singapore), "Study Team Report on Wisconsin-Works (W-2)."
15. Wisconsin Department of Children and Families, "Wisconsin Works (W-2) Overview."
16. Ibid.
17. Ibid.
18. State of Wisconsin Legislative Audit Bureau, *Financial Management of Selected W-2 Agencies*.
19. Ministerial Committee on Low Wage Workers (Singapore), *Report of the Ministerial Committee on Low Wage Workers*.
20. Lee, "Budget Speech, 2006."
21. Tharman, "Budget Speech, 2007."

Chapter 14

1. HM Government (United Kingdom), *The Coalition: our programme for government*.
2. Cabinet Office (United Kingdom), *Excellence and Fairness: Achieving world class public services*.
3. The case study was informed by interviews with more than 30 national and local government officials and experts in public service reform and design.
4. Department for Transport, Local Government and the Regions (United Kingdom), *Strong Local Leadership*.
5. Barber, *Instruction to Deliver*.
6. Lyons, *Lyons Inquiry into Local Government*.
7. HM Treasury (United Kingdom), *Operational Efficiency Programme: Final Report*.

8. Leadership Centre for Local Government, *Places, People and Politics*, 26.
9. HM Treasury (United Kingdom), *Total Place*, 5.
10. Croydon Council and National Health Service Croydon, *Child: Family: Place: Radical Efficiency to Improve Outcomes for Young Children*, 14.
11. Ibid., 9.
12. Ibid., 22.
13. Ibid., 50-53.
14. Ibid., 34.
15. Ibid., 54-55.
16. Of that amount, £103m (or 50 percent) goes directly to families as transfer payments, £71m is spent by Croydon Council and £32m by NHS Croydon.
17. Croydon Council and National Health Service Croydon, *Child: Family: Place: Radical Efficiency to Improve Outcomes for Young Children*, 87.
18. Ibid., 62.
19. Interviewee.
20. Croydon Council and National Health Service Croydon, *Child: Family: Place: Radical Efficiency to Improve Outcomes for Young Children*, 29.
21. Ibid. 71.
22. Ibid., 84-85.
23. National Health Service, Swindon (United Kingdom), "Family Life Programme."
24. Participants included the Borough Council, Strategic Health Authority, Primary Care Trust, and Wiltshire Police.
25. National Health Service, Swindon (United Kingdom), "Family Life Programme."
26. Ibid.
27. Interviewee.
28. Interviewee.
29. Interviewee.
30. Interviewee.
31. Interviewee.
32. Interviewee.
33. Interviewee.
34. National Health Service, Swindon (United Kingdom), "Family Life Programme."
35. Bourgon, with Milley. *The New Frontiers of Public Administration*.
36. Markets, hierarchies and networks are the usual categories of co-ordination explored in the academic literature. See Powell and diMaggio, *The New Institutionalism in Organizational Analysis;* Thompson, Frances, Levacic and Mitchell, *Markets, Hierarchies and Networks*.
37. Torbert, *Action Inquiry.*
38. On the role of intermediaries in improving public services, see Horne, *Honest Brokers.*

Chapter 15

1. In the initial phase of the project, over one thousand practitioners and academics were exposed to the formative ideas through keynotes addresses at conferences, lectures, seminars and other discussion venues. In the detailed research phase, more than two hundred practitioners, academics and thought leaders participated.
2. Bourgon, "Responsive, Responsible and Respected Government."
3. Bourgon, "Responsive, Responsible and Respected Government."
4. Pollitt, "Towards a New Public Administration Theory."
5. It was the most frequently cited article in the journal in 2007. As of February 2011, it was the eleventh most cited article in the history of the journal. See http://ras.sagepub.com/reports/mfc1.dtl.
6. NS6 Project Leader's Team, "Literature Scan No. 1: On the Need for a New Synthesis in Public Administration."
7. NS6 Project Leader's Team, "Literature Scan No. 2: Complexity Theories."
8. NS6 Project Leader's Team, "Literature Scan No. 6: Applications of Complex Adaptive Systems Theories."
9. NS6 Project Leader's Team, "Literature Scan No. 3: Resilience and Public Administration."
10. NS6 Project Leader's Team, "Literature Scan No. 4: Collective Intelligence."
11. NS6 Project Leader's Team, "Literature Scan No. 5: Disentangling Performance Management Systems from Control Systems."
12. Keynote speech published as Bourgon, "Performance Management: It's the Results that Count."
13. Majone and Wildavsky, "Implementation as Evolution."
14. Based on his work with Geert Bouckaert, John Halligan made a similar observation at the event, arguing the need for micro, meso and meta indicators of results. See Bouckaert and Halligan, *Managing Performance.*
15. Keynote speech published as Bourgon, "The Future of Public Service: A Search for a New Balance."
16. Bourgon, "The Future of Public Service: A Search for a New Balance," 402.
17. The paper received the 2008 Sam Richardson Award for the most influential article published in the Australian Journal of Public Administration.
18. Keynote speech published as Bourgon, "New Directions in Public Administration: Serving Beyond the Predictable."
19. Bourgon, "The Citizen at the Heart of Public Sector Reforms."
20. Pollitt, "Toward a New Public Administration Theory," 37.
21. Ibid.
22. Bourgon, "New Governance and Public Administration: Towards a Dynamic Synthesis."
23. Different versions of the keynote were published. See Bourgon, "Serving Beyond the Predictable."

24. The domain name of the website was ns6newsynthesis.com.
25. Keynote speech published as Bourgon, "The History and Future of Nation Building? Building Capacity for Public Results."
26. Bourgon, "Public Purpose, Government Authority and Collective Power."
27. Bourgon with Milley, *The New Frontiers of Public Administration*, 25.
28. Van de Walle and Vogelaar, "Emergence and Public Administration."
29. de Vries, Kruiter, and Gagner, "Public Safety Centres in the Netherlands." A revised version of this case study is included in Part 2 of the current volume.
30. Karré, Pen, van der Steen, and van Twist, "Organizing Government Around Problems."
31. Litjens, Rouw, Hammenga and Pröpper, "Rotterdam Tarwewijk: A Resilient Neighborhood?"
32. State Services Authority (State of Victoria, Australia), "Victorian Bushfire Reconstruction and Recovery Authority — A Case Study on Agility and Resilience."
33. The commissioned papers included Joyce, "Information, Control and Performance"; Halligan, "Shared Accountability for Shared Results."
34. Graham, "Tackling Homelessness in Canada." A revised version of this case appears in Part Two of this volume.
35. Lenihan, "Collaborative Federalism."
36. Australian Public Service Commission, "Case Study: Australia's New Cooperative Federal Financial Agreement."
37. Leong, "The Story of Singapore Prison Service."
38. Guanais, "Bolsa Familia Program."
39. Homer-Dixon, "Complexity Science and Public Policy."
40. Two Brazilian cases were presented, including Ribeiro, "Brazil Public Health System and Mechanisms of Institutional Governance" and Oliveira de Carvalho, Ferrarezi, and Koga, "National Health Conferences and Participatory Processes in the Brazilian Federal Public Administration." A revised version of the latter case appears in Part Two of the current volume. A case from the United Kingdom was also presented: Thomas and Richards, "Better Justice Outcomes Through a Citizen-centred Approach."
41. Menon, "SARS Revisited: Insights from Singapore."
42. Oliveira, "The Brazilian Innovation Award."
43. Alford and Hughes, "Public Value Pragmatism as the Next Phase of Public Management."
44. O'Flynn, Halligan, and Blackman, "Working Across Boundaries."
45. Lindquist and Wanna, "Co-production in Perspective."
46. Lindquist, "The New Synthesis and Antipodes Re-Visited," 5.
47. NS6 Network, *Achieving Public Results: Societal and Civic*, 19.

Chapter 16

1. For a complete report see NS6 Network, *Resilience and Emergence in Public*

Administration.

2. For example, regulation supports a conservation phase, decommissioning outdated programs supports a release phase, competition and reward programs support a reorganization phase, and targeted grants support an exploitation phase.
3. Litjens, Rouw, Hammenga, and Pröpper, "Rotterdam Tarwewijk, A Resilient Neighborhood?" 3.
4. Following the Dutch general election in June 2010, the new government cancelled the Program Ministry experiment.

Chapter 17

1. For a complete report, see NS6 Network, *Achieving Public Results.*

Chapter 18

1. NS6 Network, *Governance in the 21st Century.*
2. The federal government has provided C$390 million per year for five years (until 2014) for housing and homelessness programs as a financial incentive to convene groups, pool resources and collaborate.

Chapter 19

1. NS6 Network, *Preparing Government to Serve Beyond the Predictable.*

Chapter 20

1. NS6 Network, *A Public Service Renewal Agenda for the 21ˢᵗ Century.*

Chapter 21

1. For details on where these discussions were held and who was involved, see Chapter 15 in Part Three of this volume and Lindquist, "The New Synthesis and Antipodes Re-visited."
2. See O'Flynn, Halligan and Blackman, "Working Across Boundaries"; Lindquist and Wanna, "Co-production in Perspective."

BIBLIOGRAPHY

Agranoff, Robert, and Michael McGuire. "Big Questions in Public Network Management Research." *Journal of Public Administration Research and Theory* 11, no. 3 (2001): 295-326.

Alford, John. *Engaging Public Sector Clients: From Service-Delivery to Co-Production*. Baskingstoke, UK: Palgrave Macmillan, 2009.

Alford, John, and Owen Hughes. "Public Value Pragmatism as the Next Phase of Public Management." *The American Review of Public Administration* 38, no. 2 (2008): 130-148.

Ananias de Sousa, Patrus. "El combate al hambre y el nuevo marco de las políticas públicas: implementando un efectivo Estado de Bienestar en Brasil" [The fight against hunger and the new framework for public policy: implementing an effective Welfare State in Brazil]. *Revista española de desarrollo y cooperación* 22 (2009): 11-26.

Aucoin, Peter and Ralph Heintzman. "The Dialectics of Accountability for Performance in Public Management Reform." In *Governance in the 21st Century: Revitalizing the Public Service*, edited by B. Guy Peters and Donald Savoie, 244-80. Montreal-Kingston: McGill-Queen's University Press, 2000.

Aucoin, Peter, and Mark D. Jarvis. *Modernizing Government Accountability: A Framework for Reform*. Ottawa: Canada School of Public Service, 2005.

Australian Broadcasting Corporation. "Black Saturday Anniversary: Resilience." An episode of *Australia Talks*. ABC Radio National, 3 February 2010. http://www.abc.net.au/rn/australiatalks/stories/2010/2807733.htm.

Australian Department of Finance and Deregulation. *Engage: Getting on with Gov-*

ernment 2.0. Report of the Government 2.0 Taskforce. Canberra: Department of Finance and Deregulation, Government of Australia, 2009. http://www. finance.gov.au/publications/gov20taskforcereport/doc/government20task forcereport.pdf.

Australian Department of Finance and Deregulation. "Government Response to the Report of the Government 2.0 Taskforce." Canberra: Department of Finance and Deregulation, Government of Australia, 2010. http://www.finance. gov.au/publications/govresponse20report/index.html.

Australian Government. "Declaration of Open Government," http://www.egov. vic.gov.au/focus-on-countries/australia/government-initiatives-australia/ government-and-politics-australia/government-information-and-data-aus tralia/declaration-of-open-government.html.

———. "Government 2.0 Taskforce." http://gov2.net.au/about/index.html.

———. "Govspace: Enabling Online Engagement." http://govspace.gov.au/.

Australian National Audit Office. *Whole of Government Indigenous Service Delivery Arrangements.* Performance Audit Report No. 10, 2007–08. Canberra: National Audit Office, Government of Australia, 2007. http://www.anao.gov.au/ uploads/documents/2007-08_Audit_Report_101.pdf.

Australian Public Service Commission. "Case Study: Australia's New Cooperative Federal Financial Agreement: Focusing on Better Outcomes for Citizens." Paper presented at the NS6 International Roundtable, Ottawa, 4-5 May 2010.

Badger, Mark, Paul Johnston, Martin Stewart-Weeks, and Simon Willis. *The Connected Republic: Changing the Way We Govern.* San José, CA: Cisco, Internet Business Solutions Group, 2004. http://www.cisco.com/go/connectedrepublic.

Balfanz, Robert, and Nettie Legters. *Locating the Dropout Crisis: Which High Schools Produce the Nation's Dropouts? Where Are They Located? Who Attends Them?* Centre for Research on the Education of Students Placed at Risk, Report 70. Baltimore, MD: CRESPAR/Johns Hopkins University, 2004. http://www. csos.jhu.edu/crespar/techReports/Report70.pdf.

Baran, Paul. *On Distributed Communications: I. Introduction to Distributed Communications Networks.* Santa Monica, CA: RAND Corporation, 1964. http:// www.rand.org/pubs/research_memoranda/RM3420.

Barber, Michael. *Instruction to Deliver: Fighting to Transform Britain's Public Services.* London: Methuen Publishing, 2007.

Barzelay, Michael, and Babak J. Armajani. "Innovations in the Concept of Government Operations: A New Paradigm for Staff Agencies." In *Innovations in American Government: Challenges, Opportunities and Dilemmas*, edited by Alan A. Altshuler and Robert D. Behn, 119-25. Washington, DC: Brookings Institution Press, 1997.

Bason, Christian. *Leading Public Sector Innovation: Co-Creating for a Better Society*. Bristol, UK: The Policy Press, 2010.

———. "Use Co-creation to Drive Public Sector Innovation." *Innovation Management*, 4 October 2010. http://www.innovationmanagement.se/2010/10/04/use-co-creation-to-drive-public-sector-innovation/.

BBC News. "TRC: The Facts." London: British Broadcasting Corporation, 30 October 1998. http://news.bbc.co.uk/2/hi/special_report/1998/10/98/truth_and_reconciliation/142369.stm.

Beddington, J.R., D.J. Agnew, and C.W. Clark. "Current Problems in the Management of Marine Fisheries." *Science* 316, no. 5832 (2007): 1713-16. http://www.sciencemag.org/content/316/5832/1713.full

Begun, James, Brenda Zimmerman, and Kevin Dooley. "Health Care Organizations as Complex Adaptive Systems." In *Advances in Health Care Organization Theory*, edited by S.M. Mick and M. Wyttenbach, 253-88. San Francisco: Jossey-Bass, 2003.

Behn, Robert D. "Management by groping along." *Journal of Policy Analysis and Management* 7, no. 4 (1988): 643–63.

Belchior, Miriam. "Professionalization and consolidation of public service in the context of public policy reform." Speech at the Brazil-France Forum, National School of Public Administration (ENAP), Brasília, Brazil, 15 September 2009.

Benjamin, Alison. "Small is Powerful." *The Guardian*, 7 January 2009. http://www.guardian.co.uk/society/2009/jan/07/spain-basque-co-operative-business-collective-society-social-revolution.

Berkes, Fikret. "Understanding Uncertainty and Reducing Vulnerability: Lessons from Resilience Thinking." *Natural Hazards* 41 (2007): 283-295.

Berkes, Fikret, and Carl Folke. "Back to the Future: Ecosystem Dynamics and Local Knowledge." In *Panarchy: Understanding Transformations in Human and Natural Systems*, edited by Lance H. Gunderson and C. S. Holling, 121-146. Washington, DC: Island Press, 2002.

Betto, Frei. *Calendário do Poder*. Rio de Janeiro: Rocco, 2009.

Borins, Sandford. "Leadership and Innovation in the Public Sector." *Leadership and Organization Development Journal* 23, no. 8 (2002): 467-76.

———. *Innovations in Government: Research, Recognition, Replication*. Washington, DC: Brookings Institution Press, 2008.

Bouckaert, Geert, and John Halligan. *Managing Performance: International Comparisons*. New York: Routledge, Taylor and Francis, 2008.

Bourgon, Jocelyne. "Responsive, Responsible and Respected government: Towards a New Public Administration theory." Braibant Lecture, International Institute of Administrative Sciences, Brussels, 22 March 2006. http://www.iias-iisa.org/e/conferences/braibant/Pages/2006.aspx.

———. "Responsive, Responsible and Respected Government: Towards a New Public Administration Theory," *International Review of Administrative Sciences* 73, no. 1 (2007): 7-26.

———. "Performance Management: It's the Results that Count." *Asian Pacific Journal of Public Administration* 30, no. 1 (2008): 41-58.

———. "The Future of Public Service: A Search for a New Balance." *Australian Journal of Public Administration* 67, no. 4 (2008): 390-404.

———."The Citizen at the Heart of Public Sector Reforms." Keynote speech, 5th Quality Conference for Public Administration in the European Union, Paris, France, 20 October 2008.

———. "New Governance and Public Administration: Towards a Dynamic Synthesis." Public lecture hosted by the Australian Department of the Prime Minister and Cabinet, Canberra, 24 February 2009.

———. "New Directions in Public Administration: Serving Beyond the Predictable." *Journal of Public Policy and Administration* 3, no. 23 (2009): 309-30.

———. "Understanding the Public Leadership Environment: Preparing People to Serve People in the 21ˢᵗ Century." Keynote speech, Annual Conference of the Commonwealth Association of Public Administration and Management, Kuala Lumpur, Malaysia, 22 June 2009.

———. "Serving Beyond the Predictable." Lecture, Singapore Civil Service College, Singapore, 30 June 2009.

———. "Serving Beyond the Predictable." *Ethos* 7 (2009): 5-11.

———. "Serving Beyond the Predictable." Keynote speech, CISCO Systems Public Services Summit, Stockholm, Sweden, 9 December 2009.

———. "Serving Beyond the Predictable." Occasional paper No. 8, State Services Authority and the Australia and New Zealand School of Government, 2010. http://www.ssa.vic.gov.au/CA2571410025903D/WebObj/OccPaper_08_Bourgon/$File/OccPaper_08_Bourgon.pdf.

———. "Public Purpose, Government Authority and Collective Power." Keynote speech, XIV International Congress of Latin American Development, Salvador de Bahia, Brazil, 27 October 2009.

———. "The History and Future of Nation Building? Building Capacity for Public Results." *International Review of Administrative Sciences* 76, no. 2 (2010): 197-218.

Bourgon, Jocelyne, with Peter Milley. *The New Frontiers of Public Administration: The New Synthesis Project*. Ottawa: Public Governance International, 2010.

Bovaird, Tony. "Developing New Forms of Partnership with the 'Market' in the Procurement of Public Services." *Public Administration* 84, no. 1 (2006): 81-102.

———. "Emergent Strategic Management and Planning Mechanisms in Complex Adaptive Systems." *Public Management Review* 10, no. 3 (2008): 319-340.

British Columbia Progress Board. "Tracking Changes in the Economic Performance and Social Well-Being of British Columbia." http://www.bcprogressboard.com/.

Brondizio, Eduardo S., Elinor Ostrom, and Oran R. Young. "Connectivity and the Governance of Multilevel Social-Ecological Systems: The Role of Social Capital." *Annual Review of Environment and Resources* 34 (2009): 253-78.

Brooks, David. "Tools for Thinking." *The New York Times*, 28 March 2011. http://www.nytimes.com/2011/03/29/opinion/29brooks.html?_r=1&partner=rss&emc=rs.

Brown, Tim. *Change by Design: How Design Thinking Transforms Organizations and Inspires Innovation*. New York: HarperCollins, 2009.

Cabinet Office (United Kingdom). *Excellence and Fairness: Achieving world class public services*. London: Cabinet Office, 2008.

Cahn, Edgar S. *No More Throw-Away People: The Co-Production Imperative.* Washington: Essential Books, 2004.

Calaprice, Alice. *The New Quotable Einstein.* Princeton: Princeton University Press, 2005.

Canadian Centre for Management Development. "Corporate Documents: Learning and Innovation Seed Fund." Ottawa: Government of Canada, 2005. http://www.csps-efpc.gc.ca/aut/cdo/lisf05-eng.asp.

Canadian Health Services Research Foundation. "Paediatric Complex Care Coordination—A Pilot Project." http://www.chsrf.ca/Libraries/Taming_of_the_Queue_English/Day_1-9_Chantal_Krantz_Nathalie_Major_Cook.sflb.ashx

Carroll, Lewis. *Alice's Adventures in Wonderland and Through the Looking-Glass.* New York: Bantam Dell, 2006.

Castells, Manuel. *The Information Age: Economy, Society and Culture.* Oxford: Blackwell, 2004.

CCAF-FCVI. *Innovation, Risk and Control.* Ottawa: CCAF-FCVI, 2008. http://www.ccaf-fcvi.com/IRC/CCAF-IRC-English.pdf.

Chung, Sang Pok. *Making a Difference as Captains of Lives – Singapore Prison Service Transformation Journey.* Singapore: Civil Service College, 2007.

City of Prince Albert. *Community Action Plan on Homelessness and Housing.* Prince Albert, SK: City of Prince Albert, Community Services Department, 2007. http://intraspec.ca/CommunityActionPlanOnHomelessnessAndHousing.pdf.

Comfort, Louise K. "Risk and Resilience: Inter-Organizational Learning Following the Northridge Earthquake of 17 January 1994." *Journal of Contingencies and Crisis Management* 2, no. 3 (1994): 157-170.

Corporation for National and Community Service of the United States of America. "Social Innovation Fund." http://www.nationalservice.gov/about/programs/innovation.asp.

Cottam, Hilary. "Participatory Systems: Moving Beyond 20ᵗʰ Century Institutions." *Harvard International Review*, February 2010. http://hir.harvard.edu/big-ideas/participatory-systems.

Cottam, Hilary and Charles Leadbeater. *Health: Co-Creating Services.* London: Design Council, 2004. http://www.designcouncil.info/RED/health/REDPaper01.pdf.

Coutu, Diane. "How Resilience Works." *Harvard Business Review* 80, no. 5 (2002): 46-50.

Crooks, Tim. "Evidence." Senate Committee on Social Affairs, Science and Technology, 2nd Session, 39th Parliament, 6 December 2007. Cited in *In From the Margins: A Call To Action On Poverty, Housing And Homelessness*, Report of the Subcommittee on Cities, 107. Ottawa: Standing Senate Committee on Social Affairs, Science and Technology, 2009. http://www.parl.gc.ca/40/2/parlbus/commbus/senate/com-e/citi-e/rep-e/rep02dec09-e.pdf.

Croydon Council and National Health Service Croydon. *Child: Family: Place: Radical Efficiency to Improve Outcomes for Young Children.* http://www.croydon.gov.uk/contents/departments/democracy/pdf/617342/child-family-place.pdf.

Dagger, Richard. *Civic Virtues: Rights, Citizenship and Republican Liberalism.* New York: Oxford University Press, 1997.

Dale, Ann, and Jenny Onyx. *A Dynamic Balance: Social Capital and Sustainable Community Development.* Vancouver: UBC Press, 2005.

de Vries, Jouke, Harry Kruiter, and Martin Gagner. "Public Safety Centers in the Netherlands: A Case Study for the New Synthesis Project." Paper presented at the NS6 International Roundtable, The Hague, the Netherlands, 24-26 March 2010.

Denhardt, Janet Vinzant, and Robert B. Denhardt. *The New Public Service: Serving, Not Steering.* Armonk, NY: M.E. Sharpe, 2003.

Department for Transport, Local Government and the Regions (United Kingdom). *Strong Local Leadership: Quality Public Services* [CM5237]. London: Department for Transport, Local Government and the Regions, 2001.

Department of Finance (Canada). "Backgrounder: Summary of Federal Tax Relief for 2008 and 2009." Ottawa: Finance Canada, Government of Canada. http://www.fin.gc.ca/n08/08-115_2-eng.asp.

Department of Planning and Community Development (State of Victoria, Australia). "Guide to Local Government." http://www.dpcd.vic.gov.au/localgovernment/guide-to-local-government.

Department of Statistics (Singapore). "Trends in Household Income and Expenditure, 1993-2003." *Statistics Singapore Newsletter,* September 2005. http://www.singstat.gov.sg/pubn/ssn/archive/ssnsep2005.pdf.

Dewar, Robert D., and Jane E. Dutton. "The Adoption of Radical and Incremental Innovations: An Empirical Analysis." *Management Science* 32, no. 11 (1986): 1422-33.

Digital 4Sight, *Governance in the Digital Economy—The Governance Web: New Roles and Responsibilities for the Digital Era.* Toronto: Digital 4Sight, 2000.

Duit, Andreas and Victor Galaz. "Governance and Complexity—Emerging Issues for Governance Theory." *Governance: An International Journal of Policy, Administration, and Institutions* 21, no. 3(2008): 311–335.

Eberle, Margaret. "Evidence." *Proceedings of the Subcommittee on Cities,* Issue 4. Ottawa: Parliament of Canada, 2009. http://www.parl.gc.ca/40/2/parlbus/commbus/senate/Com-e/citi-e/04evb-e.htm?Language=E&Parl=40&Ses=2&comm_id=604.

Echenberg, Havi, and Hilary Jensen. *Defining and Enumerating Homelessness in Canada.* Ottawa: Parliamentary Library, Social Affairs Division, PRB 08-30E, 2008. http://www2.parl.gc.ca/content/lop/researchpublications/prb0830-e.pdf.

Edmonton Joint Planning Committee on Housing. *Out in the Cold: A Count of Homeless Persons in Edmonton.* City of Edmonton, Alberta, 2006. http://www.edmonton.ca/for_residents/CommPeople/HomelessCountOct2006.pdf.

Ellis, Stuart, Peter Kanowski, and Rob Whelan. *National Inquiry on Bushfire Mitigation and Management.* Canberra: Commonwealth Government of Australia, 2004.

Emergency Management Australia. *Recovery.* Australian Emergency Management Manual Series, Manual 10. Canberra: Commonwealth Government of Australia, Attorney-General's Department, 2002.

——. *Community Development in Recovery From Disaster.* Australian Emergency Management Manual Series, Manual 29. Canberra: Commonwealth Government of Australia, Attorney-General's Department, 2003.

Fijnaut, Cyrille, and I. Zaat. *De sociale (on)veiligheid in Tilburg* [The (Lack of) Social Safety in Tilburg]. Commission led by Cyrille Fijnaut, Tilburg, the Netherlands, November 2003. http://arno.uvt.nl/show.cgi?fid=57178.

Finland Prime Minister's Office. "Findicator—Set of Indicators for Social Progress." Helsinki: Government of Finland. http://www.findikaattori.fi/index_en/.

Fonseca, Maria Goretti P., and Francisco I. Bastos. "Twenty-five Years of the AIDS Epidemic in Brazil: Principal Epidemiological Findings, 1980-2005." *Cadernos de Saúde Pública* 27, sup. 3 (2007): S333-S344.

Friedman, Milton, and Rose Friedman. *Free to Choose: A Personal Statement.* San Diego: Harcourt Brace Jovanovich, 1990.

Freidman, Thomas. *The World is Flat: A Brief History of the Twenty-First Century.* New York: Farrar, Straus and Giroux, 2005.

Fung, Archon, and Erik O. Wright, eds. *Deepening Democracy: Institutional Innovations in Empowered Participatory Governance.* London: Verso Press, 2003.

Gaetz, Stephen. "The Struggle to End Homelessness in Canada: How we Created the Crisis, and How We Can End it." *The Open Health Services and Policy Journal,* no. 3 (2010): 21-26.

Gapminder. "GDP per Capita Purchasing Power Parities." http://www.gapminder.org/data/documentation/gd001/.

Gladwell, Malcolm. *The Tipping Point: How Little Things Can Make a Big Difference.* New York: Back Bay Books, 2002.

Glouberman, Sholom and Brenda Zimmerman. "Complicated and Complex Systems: What Would Successful Reform of Medicare Look Like?" Discussion Paper No. 8 of the Commission on the Future of Health Care in Canada, 2002. http://www.change-ability.ca/Health_Care_Commission_DP8.pdf

Goh, Chok Tong. "National Day Rally Speech, 2000." Singapore: Prime Minister's Office, 2000.

——. "National Day Rally Speech, 2001." Singapore: Prime Minister's Office, 2001.

Goldstein, Jeffrey. "Emergence as a Construct: History and Issues." *Emergence: Complexity and Organization* 1, no. 1 (1999): 49–72.

Gorman, Cheryl. *Government and Communities: Strengthening Neighbourhoods Together.* Ottawa: The Caledon Institute of Social Policy, 2006. http://www.caledoninst.org/Publications/PDF/593ENG.pdf.

Government of Finland. *Government's Communication on Finland's National Innovation Strategy to the Parliament.* Helsinki: Government of Finland, 2009. http://www.tem.fi/files/21010/National_Innovation_Strategy_March_2009.pdf.

Graham, Andrew. "Tackling Homelessness in Canada: The Federal Government's Homeless Partnership Strategy: A Case Study on Public Results." Paper presented at the NS6 International Roundtable, Ottawa, Canada, 4-5 May 2010.

Grammond, Stéphanie. "La Télémédecine à la Côte en Suisse." *La Presse* (Montreal), 9 April 2011: A19.

Gregory, R. "New Public Management and the Ghost of Max Weber: Exorcized or Still Haunting?" In *Transcending New Public Management: The Transformation of Public Sector Reforms*, edited by T. Christensen and P. Laegreid, 221-43. Aldershot, UK: Ashgate Publishing Limited, 2007.

Guanais, Frederico C. "Bolsa Família Program: Funding Families for Development: A Case Study for the 'New Synthesis' Project." Paper presented at the NS6 International Roundtable, Ottawa, Canada, 4-5 May 2010.

Gunderson, Lance, C.S. Holling, and S.S. Light. *Barriers and Bridges to the Renewal of Ecosystems and Institutions.* New York: Columbia University Press, 1995.

Habegger, Beat. *Horizon Scanning in Government.* Zurich: Centre for Security Studies, 2009. http://www.isn.ethz.ch/isn/Digital-Library/Publications/Detail/?ots591=0c54e3b3-1e9c-be1e-2c24-a6a8c7060233&lng=en&id=96274.

———. "Strategic Foresight in Public Policy: Reviewing the Experiences of the UK, Singapore and the Netherlands." *Futures* 42, no. 1 (2010): 49-58.

Halligan, John. "Shared Accountability for Shared Results." Paper presented at the NS6 International Roundtable, Ottawa, Canada, 4-5 May 2010.

Halpern, David. *The Hidden Wealth of Nations.* Cambridge, UK: Polity Press, 2010.

Haynes, Phillip. *Managing Complexity in the Public Services.* Maidenhead, UK: Open University Press, 2003.

Hefetz, Amir, and Mildred Warner. "Privatization and Its Reverse: Explaining the Dynamics of the Government Contracting Process." *Public Administration Research and Theory* 14, no. 2 (2004): 171-90.

Helliwell, John F. "Well-Being, Social Capital and Public Policy: What's New?" NBER Working Paper Series w11807. Cambridge, MA: The National Bureau of Economic Research, 2005. http://www.nber.org/papers/w11807.pdf.

Helliwell, John. "How Can Subjective Well-being Be Improved?" Unpublished paper presented at the Festschrift in Honour of Ian Stewart, Ottawa, Canada, 20-21 April 2011. http://www.csls.ca/events/2011/helliwell.pdf.

———. "Institutions as Enablers of Well-Being: The Singapore Prison Case Study." *International Journal of Wellbeing* (in press).

Helliwell, John, and Robert Putnam. "The Social Context of Well-being." *Philosophical Transactions of the Royal Society of London* B 359 (2004): 1435-46. http://www.ncbi.nlm.nih.gov/pmc/articles/PMC1693420/pdf/15347534.pdf.

Heritage Foundation and Wall Street Journal. "2011 Index of Economic Freedom." http://www.heritage.org/Index/explore.

HM Government (United Kingdom). *The Coalition: our programme for government.* London: Cabinet Office, 2010.

HM Treasury (United Kingdom). *Operational Efficiency Programme: Final Report.* London: HM Treasury, 2009.

——. *Total Place: A Whole Area Approach to Public Services.* London: HM Treasury, 2010. http://www.hm-treasury.gov.uk/d/total_place_report.pdf.

Ho, Alfred Tat-Kei. "Reinventing Local Governments and the E-Government Initiative." *Public Administration Review* 62, no. 4 (2002): 434-44.

Ho, Peter. "Governance at the Leading Edge: Black Swans, Wild Cards and Wicked Problems." *Ethos*, no. 4 (April 2008): 74–9. http://www.cscollege.gov.sg/cgl/pub_ethos_6m1.htm.

——. "Thinking About the Future: What the Public Service Can Do." *Ethos*, no. 7 (January 2010). http://www.cscollege.gov.sg/cgl/pub_ethos_10i4.htm

Holling, C.S., and G.K. Meffe. "Command and Control and the Pathology of Natural Resource Management." *Conservation Biology* 10 (1996): 328-337.

Homer-Dixon, Thomas. *The Ingenuity Gap: Can We Solve the Problems of the Future?* Toronto: Vintage Canada, 2001.

——. *The Upside of Down: Catastrophe, Creativity and the Renewal of Civilization.* Toronto: Alfred A. Knopf, 2006.

——. "Complexity Science and Public Policy." Public lecture, National Arts Centre, Ottawa, Canada, 5 May 2010. http://www.homerdixon.com/download/complexity_science_and_public_policy.pdf.

Hood, Christopher, Oliver James, George Jones, Colin Scott, and Tony Travers. "Regulation Inside Government: Where New Public Management Meets the Audit Explosion." *Public Money and Management* 18, no. 2 (1998): 61-68.

Hopper, Kim, and Jim Baumohl. "Redefining the Cursed Word." In: *Homelessness in America*, edited by J. Baumohl, 3-14. Phoenix: Oryx Press, 1996.

Horne, Matthew. *Honest Brokers: Brokering innovation in public services.* London: Innovation Unit, 2008. http://www.innovationunit.org/sites/default/files/Honest%20Brokers.pdf.

Hu, Richard. "Budget Speech, 1998: Expenditure Priorities, Operating Expenditure." Singapore: Ministry of Finance, 1998. http://www.mof.gov.sg/budget_1998/operating.html.

———. "Budget Debate Roundup Speech, 2000." Singapore: Ministry of Finance, 2000.

Hulchanski, J. David. "Homelessness in Canada: Past, Present, Future." Keynote address at Growing Home: Housing and Homelessness in Canada conference, University of Calgary, 18 February 2009. http://www.scribd.com/doc/14126679/Homelessness-Past-Present-Future-Hulchanski-2009.

Human Resources and Skills Development Canada. "Registered Disability Savings Plan(RDSP)," http://www.hrsdc.gc.ca/eng/disability_issues/disability_savings/index.shtml.

Human Resources and Social Development Canada. "The Homelessness Partnering Strategy: Partnerships that Work." Ottawa: Government of Canada, 2008. http://www.rhdcc-hrsdc.gc.ca/eng/corporate/success_stories/homelessness/2008/hps/page00.shtml.

Instituto de Pesquisa Econômica Aplicada. "IPEADATA." Brasília: Presidência da República Federativa do Brasil, 2010. http://www.ipeadata.gov.br.

International Federation of Accountants. *2010 Handbook of International Quality Control, Auditing, Review, Other Assurance, and Related Services Pronouncements.* New York: IFAC. http://web.ifac.org/publications/international-auditing-and-assurance-standards-board/handbooks.

International Organization of Supreme Audit Institutions. "Guidelines for Internal Control Standards for the Public Sector." http://intosai.connexcc-hosting.net/blueline/upload/1guicspubsece.pdf.

Joyce, Mike. "Information, Control and Performance: Disentangling and the Risk of Disconnection." Paper presented at the NS6 International Roundtable, Ottawa, Canada, 4-5 May 2010.

Junqueras, Oriol and Eva Lichtenberger. "Civil Rights on the Internet: The Experience of Brazil's Regulation Initiative," La-EX, http://la-ex.net/civil-rights-on-the-internet-the-experience-of-brazil-regulation-initiative.

Kahane, Adam. *Solving Tough Problems: An Open Way of Talking, Listening, and Creating New Realities*. San Francisco: Berrett-Koehler Publishers, 2004.

Kakwani, N., M. Neri, and H. Son. *Pro-Poor Growth and Social Programmes in Brazil*. Discussion paper no. 639, escola de pós-graduação em Economia, Fundação Getulio Vargas, December 2006. http://www.fgv.br/cps/pesquisas/ Politicas_sociais_alunos/BES/ee_639_pp_social_programs.pdf.

Karré, P.M., M. Pen, M.A. van der Steen, and M.J.W. van Twist. "Organizing Government Around Problems: A Case Study of the Two Dutch Programme Ministries for Youth and Family and for Housing, Communities and Integration." Paper presented at the NS6 International Roundtable, The Hague, the Netherlands, 24-26 March 2010.

Kao, John. *Innovation Nation: How America Is Losing Its Innovation Edge, Why It Matters, and What We Can Do to Get It Back*. New York: Simon and Schuster, 2007.

Kelly, Gavin, Geoff Mulgan, and Stephen Muers. *Creating Public Value: An Analytical Framework for Public Service Reform*. London: Strategy Unit, Cabinet Office, United Kingdom, 2002.

Kelman, Steven. "The Transformation of Government in the Decade Ahead. In *Reflections on 21st Century Government Management*, Donald F. Kettl and Steven Kelman, 33-55. Washington, DC: IBM Centre for Business and Government, 2007.

———. "The Kennedy School of Research on Innovations in Government." In *Innovations in Government: Research, Recognition and Replication*, edited by Sandford F. Borins, 29-35. Washington, DC: Brookings Institution Press, 2008.

Kernaghan, Kenneth, Brian Marson, and Sandford Borins. *The New Public Organization*. Toronto: The Institute of Public Administration of Canada, 2000.

Kettl, Donald F. *The Global Public Management Revolution: A Report on the Transformation of Governance*. Washington, DC: The Brookings Institution, 2000.

———. *The Transformation of Governance: Public Administration for Twenty-First Century America*. Baltimore: Johns Hopkins University Press, 2002.

———. *The Global Public Management Revolution*. Washington, DC: The Brookings Institution, 2005.

Kettl, Donald F., and James W. Fesler. *The Politics of the Administrative Process*. Washington, DC: CQ Press, 2011.

King, David A. and Sandy M. Thomas. "Big Lessons for a Healthy Future." *Nature* 449 (18 October 2007): 791-2.

KIPP. "About KIPP." http://www.kipp.org/about-kipp.

———. "Frequently Asked Questions." http://www.kipp.org/about-kipp/faq.

———. "Independent Reports." http://www.kipp.org/about-kipp/results/independent -reports.

Klijn, Erik-Hans. "Complexity Theory and Public Administration: What's New?" *Public Management Review* 10, no. 3 (2008): 299-317.

———. "Governance and Governance Networks in Europe: An Assessment of 10 years of Research on the Theme." *Public Management Review* 10, no. 4 (2008): 505-525.

Koppenjan, Joop, and Erik-Hans Klijn. *Managing Uncertainties in Networks: A Network Approach to Problem-Solving and Decision-Making.* London: Routledge, 2004.

Kotwani, Monica. "Biometric Faces Will Be Your Passport at Singapore's Checkpoints." *E-News,* 2011. http://www.e-news.com.bd/2011/05/20/biometric-faces-will-be-your-passport-at-singapores-checkpoints/.

Kriger, Gustavo. Interview with Minister Patrus Ananias, *Época* magazine, 29 August 2005.

Kroeger, Arthur. "Accountability: Three Approaches." *Literary Review of Canada* 14, no. 5 (2006): 9-11.

Leadbeater, Charles. *We-Think.* London: Profile Books, 2008.

Leadbeater, Charles, and Hilary Cottam. "The User-Generated State: Public Services 2.0." http://www.charlesleadbeater.net/archive/public-services-20.aspx.

Leadership Centre for Local Government. *Places, People and Politics: Learning To Do Things Differently.* London: Leadership Centre for Local Government, 2010.

Lee, Hsien Loong. "Budget Debate Roundup Speech, 2004." Singapore: Ministry of Finance, 2004. http://www.mof.gov.sg/budget_2004/roundup_speech/roundup_speech10.html.

———. "Budget Speech, 2006." Singapore: Ministry of Finance, 2006. http://www.mof.gov.sg/budget_2006/budget_speech/header3.html.

Lenihan, Don. "Collaborative Federalism: How Labour Mobility and FQR are Changing Canada's Intergovernmental Landscape." Paper presented at the NS6 International Roundtable, Ottawa, Canada, 4-5 May 2010.

Lenihan, Donald G., John Godfrey and John Williams. "Results Reporting, Parliament and Public Debate: What's New in Accountability?" *Policy, Politics and Governance* 3. Ottawa: Centre for Collaborative Government, April 2003.

Lenihan, Donald G., John Godfrey, Tony Valeri, and John Williams. "Accountability for Learning." *Policy, Politics and Governance* 4. Ottawa: Centre for Collaborative Government, June 2003.

Lenihan, Donald G., John Godfrey, Tony Valeri, and John Williams. "What is Shared Accountability?" *Policy, Politics and Governance* 5. Ottawa: Centre for Collaborative Government, November 2003.

Leong, Lam Chuan. "Managing Complexity and Uncertainties." *Ethos*, no. 4 (April 2008). http://www.cscollege.gov.sg/cgl/pub_ethos6n1.htm.

Leong, Lena. "The Story of Singapore Prison Service: From Custodians of Prisoners to Captains of Life." Paper presented at the NS6 International Roundtable, Ottawa, Canada, 4-5 May 2010.

Lépine, Genevieve. *The Web of Rules: A Study of the Relationship Between Regulation of Public Servants and Past Public Service Reform Initiatives*. Ottawa: Public Policy Forum, 2007.

Lindquist, Evert. "The New Synthesis and Antipodes Re-Visited: Summary Report on Madame Bourgon's Reconnaissance to Australia and New Zealand." Working paper. Australia: The Australia and New Zealand School of Government, 2010. http://nsworld.org/sites/nsworld.org/files/New_Synthesis_Revisited.pdf.

Lindquist, Evert, and John Wanna. "Co-production in Perspective: Parallel Traditions and Implications for Public Management and Governance." Unpublished working paper prepared for the Australia and New Zealand School of Government, Australian Public Service Commission, and Victoria State Services Authority, November 2010.

Lindert, Kathy, and Vanina Vincensini. "Bolsa Família in the Headlines: An Analysis of the Media's Treatment of Conditional Cash Transfers in Brazil." Washington, DC: World Bank, April 2008. http://siteresources.worldbank.org/SAFETYNETSANDTRANS FERS/Resources/281945-1131468287118/1876750-1215011470670/Lindert-BF_ Media_Paper_QandA_7-1-08.pdf.

Litjens, Bart, Mark Rouw, Rob Hammenga, and Igno Pröpper. "Rotterdam Tarwewijk, A Resilient Neighborhood? A Case Study for the New Synthesis Project." Paper presented at the NS6 International Roundtable, The Hague, the Netherlands, 24-26 March 2010.

Livi-Bacci, Massimo. *A Concise History of World Population*. Malden, MA: Blackwell Publishers, 1997.

Livingstone, Robert Gerald. "German Reunification from Three Angles." *German Politics and Society* 50, no.1 (1999): 127-36

Lonsdale, Jeremy. "Developments in Value-For-Money Audit Methods: Impacts and Implications." *International Review of Administrative Sciences* 66, no. 1 (2000): 73-89.

Lula, da Silva, and Luiz Inácio. Speech at the Meeting of CONSEA, 25 October 2004.

Lynn, Laurence E. "The Myth of the Bureaucratic Paradigm: What Traditional Public Administration Really Stood For." *Public Administration Review* 61, no. 2 (2001): 144-60.

Lyons, Michael. *Lyons Inquiry into Local Government: Place-shaping: a shared ambition for the future of local government*. London: The Stationery Office, 2007.

Mahbubani, Kishore. "The Dangers of Democratic Delusions." *Ethics and International Affairs* 1, no. 23, (2009): 19-25.

Majone, Giandomenico, and Aaron B. Wildavsky. "Implementation as Evolution." In *Implementation*, edited by Jeffrey L. Pressman and Aaron Wildavsky. Berkley: University of California Press, 2004.

March, James G. "Exploration and Exploitation in Organizational Learning." *Organization Science* 2, no. 1 (1991): 71-87.

Marsh, Ian, and Ben Spies-Butcher. "Pragmatism and Neo-Classical Policy Paradigms in Public Services: Which is the Better Template for Program Design?" *The Australian Journal of Public Administration* 68, no. 3 (2009): 239-55.

Masten, Ann S. "Ordinary Magic: Resilience Processes in Development." *American Psychologist* 56, no. 3 (2001): 227-38.
——. "Ordinary Magic: Lessons from Research on Resilience in Human Development." *Education Canada* 49, no. 3 (2010): 28-32.

Masten, Ann S., and Margaret O'Dougherty Wright. "Resilience Over the Lifespan: Developmental Perspectives on Resistance, Recovery, and Transformation." In *Handbook of Adult Resilience*, edited by John W. Reich, Alex J. Zautra and John Stuart Hall, 213-37. New York: Guildford Press, 2009.

Mayor's Task Force on Breaking the Cycle of Mental Illness, Addictions and Homelessness. "Executive Summary." City of Victoria, Canada, 19 October 2007. http://www.victoria.ca/cityhall/pdfs/tskfrc_brcycl_exctvs.pdf.

McManus, Sonia, Erica Seville, David Brunsdon, and John Vargo. *Resilience Management: A Framework for Assessing and Improving Resilience in Organizations.* Canterbury, NZ: Resilient Organisations Program, University of Canterbury, 2007. http://www.resorgs.org.nz/pubs.shtml.

Mendoza, Xavier, and Alfred Vernis. "The Changing Role of Governments and the Emergence of the Relational State." *Corporate Governance* 8, no. 4 (2008): 389-96.

Menon, K.U. "National Resilience: From Bouncing Back to Prevention." *Ethos* (January-March 2005): 14-17. http://www.cscollege.gov.sg/cgl/EthosPast/05Jan/06National.pdf.

———. "SARS Revisited: Insights from Singapore: A Case Study on Adaptive Capacity, Managing Risk, and Innovation." Paper presented at the NS6 International Roundtable, Singapore, 21-22 September 2010.

MindLab. "Away with the Red Tape: A Better Encounter with Government." http://mind-lab.dk/en/cases/away-with-the-red-tape-a-better-encounter-with-government. The MindLab website is http://www.mind-lab.dk/en.

Ministerial Committee on Low Wage Workers (Singapore). *Report of the Ministerial Committee on Low Wage Workers.* Singapore: Government of Singapore, 2006.

Ministerie van Algemene Zaken. *Samen werken – Samen leven. Beleidsprogramma Kabinet Balkenende IV, 2007-2011.* [Working together – Living together. Policy programme of the Balkanende IV Government, 2007-2011]. The Hague: Ministry of General Affairs, 2007.

Ministerie van Justitie. "Veiligheidshuizen effectief" [PSCs are effective]. Press release from the Ministry of Justice, The Hague, the Netherlands, 30 October 2009.

Ministerie van Justitie / Ministerie van Binnenlandse Zaken en Koninkrijksrelaties. *Naar een veiliger samenleving* [Towards a safer society]. The Hague: Ministry of Justice and Ministry of Interior Affairs and Kingdom Relations, 2002.

———. *Safety Begins with Prevention: Continuing Building a Safer Society.* The

Hague, the Netherlands: Ministry of Justice and Ministry of Internal Affairs and Kingdom Relations, 2007.

——. *Veiligheid begint bij Voorkomen. Voortbouwen aan een Veiliger Samenleving* [Safety begins with Prevention: Continuing Building a Safer Society]. The Hague: Ministry of Justice and Ministry of Internal Affairs and Kingdom Relations, 2009.

Ministry of Finance (Singapore). "Study Team Report on Hong Kong's Welfare System." Internal Report, Ministry of Finance, Singapore, 2005.

——. "Study Team Report on Wisconsin-Works (W-2)." Internal Report, Ministry of Finance, Singapore, 2005.

Ministry of Justice (United Kingdom). "Criminal Statistics: England and Wales 2009." *Statistics Bulletin*, October 2010. London: UK Ministry of Justice. http://www.justice.gov.uk/publications/docs/criminal-statistics-annual.pdf.

Mitleton-Kelly, Eve. "Ten Principles of Complexity and Enabling Infrastructures." In *Complex Systems and Evolutionary Perspectives of Organizations: The Application of Complexity Theory to Organizations*, edited by Eve Mitleton-Kelly, 23-50. Kidlington, UK: Elsevier Science, 2003.

Moncrief, Marc. "'Worst Day in History': Brumby Warns of Fire Danger." *The Age*, 6 February 2009. http://www.theage.com.au/national/worst-day-in-history-brumby-warns-of-fire-danger-20090206-7zf1.html.

Moore, Don A., Philip E. Tetlock, Lloyd Tanlu, and Max H. Bazerman. "Conflicts of Interest and the Case of Auditor Independence: Moral Seduction and Strategic Issue Cycling." *The Academy of Management* 31, no. 1, 2006: 10-29.

Moore, John F. "Washington, DC: Co-Creation in Action," Government in the Lab. http://govinthelab.com/washington-dc-co-creation-in-action/.

Moore, Mark H. *Creating Public Value: Strategic Management in Government*. Cambridge, MA: Harvard University Press, 1995.

Moore, Mark H., and Anthony A. Braga. "Police Performance Measurment: A Normative Framework." *Criminal Justice Ethics* 4 (2004): 3-19.

Morgan, Gareth. *Images of Organization*. Thousand Oaks, CA: Sage Publications, 2006.

Muldavin, Joshua. "The Paradoxes of Environmental Policy and Resource Management in Reform-Era China." *Economic Geography* 76, no. 3 (2000): 244-71.

Mulgan, Geoff. "The Process of Social Innovation." *Innovations* 1, no. 2 (2006): 145-62.

———. *Ready or Not? Taking Innovation in the Public Sector Seriously.* London: National Endowment for Science, Technology and the Arts (NESTA), 2007. http://www.nesta.org.uk/library/documents/readyornot.pdf.

———. *The Art of Public Strategy: Mobilizing Power and Knowledge for the Common Good.* Oxford: Oxford University Press, 2009.

Mulgan, Geoff with Simon Tucker, Rushanara Ali and Ben Sanders. "Social Innovation: What It Is, Why It Matters and How It Can Be Accelerated." Working paper, Skoll Centre for Social Entrepreneurship, Said Business School, Oxford University, 2007.

Murphy, B. L. "Locating Social Capital in Resilient Community-Level Emergency Management." *Natural Hazards* 41, no. 2 (2007): 297-315.

National Economic Council, Office of the President of the United States of America. "A Strategy for American Innovation: Driving Towards Sustainable Growth and Quality Jobs." Washington, DC: National Economic Council, Office of the President of the USA, September 2009. http://www.whitehouse.gov/administration/eop/nec/StrategyforAmericanInnovation/.

National Health Service Swindon (United Kingdom). "Family Life Programme." Report to NHS Swindon Board, 27 May 2010. http://www.swindonpct.nhs.uk/Library/Publications/Board_papers/2010/04_May/PCT_10_68_Family_Life_Programme.pdf.

Neo, Boon Siong, and Geraldine Chen. *Dynamic Governance: Embedding Culture, Capabilities and Change in Singapore.* Singapore: World Scientific Publishing, 2007.

Newman, Lenore, and Ann Dale. "Network Structure, Diversity, and Proactive Resilience Building: A Response to Tompkins and Adger." *Ecology and Society* 10, no. 1 (2005). http://www.ecologyandsociety.org/vol10/iss1/resp2/.

New York City. "NYC BigApps2.0." http://nycbigapps.com/.

———. "NYC DataMine." http://www.nyc.gov/html/datamine/html/home/home.shtml.

Norris, Fran .H., Susan P. Stevens, Betty Pfefferbaum, Karen Wyche, and Rose L. Pfefferbaum. "Community Resilience as a Metaphor, Theory, Set of Capacities, and Strategy for Disaster Readiness." *American Journal of Community Psychol-*

ogy 41, no. 1-2 (2008): 127-50.

Norwegian Ministry of Trade and Industry. *An Innovative and Sustainable Norway.* Short Version of the White Paper, Report No. 7 to the Storting. Oslo: Norwegian Ministry of Trade and Industry, 2008. http://www.regjeringen.no/upload/NHD/Vedlegg/brosjyrer_2008/innomeld_kortv_eng.pdf.

NS6 Network. *Resilience and Emergence in Public Administration: The Netherlands Roundtable Report.* Edited by Jocelyne Bourgon. Ottawa: Public Governance International, 2010.

——. *Achieving Public Results: Societal and Civic: The Canada Roundtable Report.* Edited by Jocelyne Bourgon. Ottawa: Public Governance International, 2010.

——. *Governance in the 21st Century: Using Government Authority and Collective Power: Brazil Roundtable Report.* Edited by Jocelyne Bourgon. Ottawa: Public Governance International, 2010.

——. *Preparing Government to Serve Beyond the Predictable: Singapore Roundtable Report.* Edited by Jocelyne Bourgon. Ottawa: Public Governance International, 2010.

——. *A Public Service Renewal Agenda for the 21st Century: United Kingdom Roundtable Report.* Edited by Jocelyne Bourgon. Ottawa: Public Governance International, 2010.

NS6 Project Leader's Team. "Literature Scan No. 1: On the Need for a New Synthesis in Public Administration." Unpublished working paper. Ottawa: NS6 Project Leader's Team, 2009.

——. "Literature Scan No. 2: Complexity Theories: What are They and What Do They Tell Us About Public Administration in the 21st Century?" Unpublished working paper. Ottawa: NS6 Project Leader's Team, 2009.

——. "Literature Scan No. 3: Resilience and Public Administration." Unpublished working paper. Ottawa: NS6 Project Leader's Team, 2009.

——. "Literature Scan No. 4: Collective Intelligence: What Is It and How Can It Be Tapped?" Unpublished working paper. Ottawa: NS6 Project Leader's Team, 2009.

——. "Literature Scan No. 5: Disentangling Performance Management Systems from Control Systems." Unpublished working paper. Ottawa: NS6 Project Leader's Team, 2009.

———. "Literature Scan No. 6: Applications of Complex Adaptive Systems Theories in Governance, Public Administration and Public Policy." Unpublished working paper. Ottawa: NS6 Project Leader's Team, 2009.

O'Flynn, Janine. "Adding Public Value: A New Era of Contractual Governance?" Paper presented at the Public Administration and Management Conference, University of Nottingham, UK, September 2005.

O'Flynn, Janine, John Halligan, and Deborah Blackman. "Working Across Boundaries: Barriers, Enablers, Tensions and Puzzles." Paper presented at the 14th Annual IRSPM Conference, Berne, Switzerland, April 2010. http://www.irspm2010.com/workshops/papers/32_synopticpaper.pdf.

Office of the Auditor General of Canada. "Chapter 9: Modernizing Accountability in the Public Sector." In *Report of the Auditor General of Canada to the House of Commons*. Ottawa: Office of the Auditor General of Canada, 2002. http://www.oag-bvg.gc.ca/internet/docs/20021209ce.pdf.

Oliveira, Clarice. "The Brazilian Innovation Award: Identifying Government Practices that Contribute to the Improvement of Service Delivery." Paper presented at the NS6 International Roundtable in Rio de Janeiro, Brazil, 13-14 July 2010.

Oliveira de Carvalho, Mariana S., Elisabete Ferrarezi, and Natália Koga. "National Health Conferences and Participatory Processes in Brazilian Federal Public Administration." Paper presented at the NS6 International Roundtable in Rio de Janeiro, Brazil, 13-14 July 2010.

Oon, Clarisa. "Keep stagflation at bay: Swee Say." *The Straits Times*, 22 June 2008. http://www.asiaone.com/News/AsiaOne%2BNews/Singapore/Story/A1Story20080622-72238.html.

Organisation for Economic Co-operation and Development (OECD). "Better Life Initiative," http://www.oecdbetterlifeindex.org/.

———. Directorate for Employment, Labour and Social Affairs. "OECD Health Data 2010—Frequently Requested Data." http://www.oecd.org/document/16/0,3343, en_2649_34631_2085200_1_1_1_1,00.html.

———. *From Open to Inclusive: Building Citizen-centered Policy and Services.* Paris: OECD, 2008. http://www.olis.oecd.org/olis/2008doc.nsf/ENGDATCORPLOOK/NT00000E9A/$FILE/JT03243619.PDF.

———. "Health Data—Frequently Requested Data." http://www.oecd.org/document /16/0,3343,en_2649_34631_2085200_1_1_1_1,00.html.

———. Program for International Student Assessment. *PISA 2009 Results: What Students Know and Can Do: Student Performance in Reading, Mathematics and Science*. Paris: OECD, 2009. http://www.oecd.org/dataoecd/54/12/46643496.pdf.

———. *Participative Web and User-Created Content: Web 2-0, Wikis and Social Networking*. Paris: OECD, 2007.

———. "Society at a Glance 2011—OECD Social Indicators." http://www.oecd.org/document/24/0,3746,en_2649_37419_2671576_1_1_1_37419,00.html#data.

Osborne, Stephen P. "The New Public Governance." *Public Management Review* 8, no. 3 (2006): 377-87.

Osborne, Stephen P., and Kerry Brown. *Managing Change and Innovation in Public Service Organizations*. New York: Routledge, 2005.

Ostrom, Elinor. "A Communitarian Approach to Local Governance." *National Civic Review* 82, no. 3 (1993): 226-33.

———. "Crossing the Great Divide: Coproduction, Synergy, and Development." In *State-Society Synergy: Government and Social Capital in Development*, edited by Peter Evans, 85-118. Berkeley: University of California, 1997.

———. "Crowding Out Citizenship." *Scandinavian Political Studies* 23, no. 1 (2000): 3-16.

———. "Beyond Markets and States: Polycentric Governance of Complex Economic Systems." Nobel Prize Lecture, Stockholm, Sweden, 8 December 2009. http://nobelprize.org/nobel_prizes/economics/laureates/2009/ostrom_lecture.pdf.

Pacheco, P. "Crise afeta menos a base da pirâmide" [Crisis affects less the bottom of the pyramid]. *O Estado de Sao Paulo* newspaper, 11 May 2009.

Paes de Barros, R. *Sucessos e Desafios para a Proteção e Promoção no Brasil* [Successes and Challenges for Protection and Promotion in Brazil]. Presentation at the International Symposium on Social Development, Social Policies for Development: Overcoming Poverty and Promoting Inclusion, Brasília, Brazil, 2009.

Pfaff, Steven. *Exit-Voice Dynamics and the Collapse of East Germany*. Durham, NC: Duke University Press, 2006.

Pollitt, Christopher. "How Do We Know How Good Public Services Are?" In *Governance in the Twenty-First Century: Revitalizing the Public Service*, edited by B. Guy Peters and Donald J. Savoie, 119-52. Montreal and Kingston: Canadian

Centre for Management Development and McGill-Queen's University Press, 2000.

——. "'Towards a New Public Administration Theory': Some Comments on Jocelyne Bourgon's 5th Braibant Lecture." *International Review of Administrative Sciences* 73, no.1 (2007): 37-41.

Powell, Walter W., and Paul J. DiMaggio, eds. *The New Institutionalism in Organizational Analysis.* Chicago: The Chicago Press, 1991.

Power, Michael. *The Audit Society: Rituals of Verification.* Oxford: Oxford University Press, 1997.

Pranger, Robert J. *The Eclipse of Citizenship: Power and Participation in Contemporary Politics.* New York: Holt, Rinehart and Winston, 1968.

Radin, Beryl A. *Challenging the Performance Movement: Accountability, Complexity and Democratic Values.* Washington, DC: Georgetown University Press, 2006.

Rainey, Hal G. *Understanding and Managing Public Organizations.* San Francisco: Jossey-Bass, 2003.

Ramalingam, Ben, and Harry Jones, with Toussaint Reba and John Young. *Exploring the Science of Complexity: Ideas and Implications for Development and Humanitarian Efforts.* London: Overseas Development Institute, 2008. http://www.odi.org.uk/resources/download/583.pdf.

Ribeiro, José Mendes. "Brazil Public Health System and Mechanisms of Institutional Governance." Paper presented at the NS6 International Roundtable in Rio de Janeiro, Brazil, 13-14 July 2010.

Rocha, S. "Transferências de renda federais: focalização e impactos sobre pobreza e desigualdade" [Federal income transfers: focalization and impacts on poverty and inequality]. *Revista de Economia Contemporânea* 12, no. 1 (2008): 67-96.

Rotmans, Jan, René Kemp, and Marjolein van Asselt. "More Evolution than Revolution: Transition Management in Public Policy." *The Journal of Futures Studies, Strategic Thinking and Policy* 3, no. 1 (2001): 15-31.

Rozelle, Scott, Jikun Huang, and Linxiu Zhang. "Poverty, Population and Environmental Degradation in China." *Food Policy* 22, no. 3 (1997): 229-251.

Runge, C. Ford, and Benjamin Senauer. "How Ethanol Fuels the Food Crisis." *Foreign Affairs*, 28 May 2008. Washington, DC: Council on Foreign Relations.

http://www.foreignaffairs.com/articles/64909/c-ford-runge-and-benjamin-senauer/how-ethanol-fuels-the-food-crisis.

Salamon, Lester M., ed. *The Tools of Government: A Guide to the New Governance.* New York: Oxford University Press, 2002.

Salomon, M. "Graziano indica que Vale-Gás e Bolsa-Renda podem acabar" [Graziano indicates that Cooking Gas Subsidy and Income Fund may end]. Interview with Mr. José Graziano in *Folha de São Paulo*, 2 February 2003.

Samuels, David. "Separation of Powers." In *The Oxford Handbook of Comparative Politics*, edited by Charles Boix and Susan C. Stokes, 703-26. Oxford: Oxford University Press, 2009.

Sanderson, Ian. "Intelligent Policy Making for a Complex World: Pragmatism, Evidence and Learning." *Political Studies* 57 (2009): 699-719.

Santos, L., R. Paes-Sousa, J.B. Silva, and C.G. Victora. "National Immunization Day: A Strategy to Monitor Health and Nutrition Indicators." *Bulletin of the World Health Organization* 86 (2008): 474-479.

Scheffer, Marten, Frances Westley, William A. Brock, and Milena Holmgren. "Dynamic Interaction of Societies and Ecosystems—Linking Theories from Ecology, Economy, and Sociology." In *Panarchy: Understanding Transformations in Human and Natural Systems*, edited by Lance H. Gunderson and C. S. Holling, 195-240. Washington, DC: Island Press, 2002.

Schuler, Douglas. "Civic Intelligence and the Public Sphere." In *Collective Intelligence: Creating a Prosperous World at Peace*, edited by Mark Tovey. Oakton, VA: Earth Intelligence Network, 2008.

Schultz, Wendy L. "The Cultural Contradictions of Managing Change: Using Horizon Scanning in an Evidence-Based Policy Context." *Foresight* 8, no. 4 (2006): 3–12.

Scottish Centre for Telehealth. "About the Centre." http://www.sct.scot.nhs.uk/about.html.

Senate of Canada. *In From the Margins: A Call To Action On Poverty, Housing And Homelessness.* The Standing Senate Committee on Social Affairs, Science and Technology, Report of the Subcommittee on Cities. Ottawa: Government of Canada, 2009. http://www.parl.gc.ca/40/2/parlbus/commbus/senate/com-e/citi-e/rep-e/rep02dec09-e.pdf.

Senge, Peter. "The Leader's New Work: Building Learning Organizations." *Sloan Management Review* 32, no. 1 (1990): 7-23.

Senge, Peter, Art Kleiner, Charlotte Roberts, Richard Ross, and Bryan Smith. *The Fifth Discipline Fieldbook*. London: Nicholas Brealey Publishing, 1994.

Sigmundsdottir, Alda. "Tech-savvy Iceland online for new constitution." *Yahoo! News*, 10 June 2011. http://news.yahoo.com/s/ap/20110610/ap_on_hi_te/eu_iceland_constitution

Singapore Community Action for the Rehabilitation of Ex-Offenders (CARE) Network. "Yellow Ribbon Project." http://www.yellowribbon.org.sg.

———. *Yellow Ribbon Project Manual*. Singapore: CARE Network, 2007.

Singapore Corporation of Rehabilitative Enterprises (SCORE). "The Community Action for the Rehabilitation of Ex-Offenders (CARE) Network." http://www.score.gov.sg/CARE_network.html.

Singapore Prison Service. *Singapore Prison Service's Singapore Quality Award, Executive Summary*. Singapore: Government of Singapore, 2006. http://www.spring.gov.sg/QualityStandards/be/beaw/Documents/SQA_Singapore_Prison_Service_2006_Summary_Report.pdf.

———. "Mission & Vision of Singapore Prison Service." http://www.prison-volunteers.gov.sg/sop/vw/mission.jsp#mission.

———. *Annual Report, 2009*. Singapore: Government of Singapore, 2009.

———. *Organisational Health Survey*. Singapore: Government of Singapore, 2009.

Smith, James F. "Tufts Map Steered Action Amid Chaos." *The Boston Globe*, 5 April 2010. http://www.boston.com/news/world/latinamerica/articles/2010/04/05/tufts_project_delivered_aid_to_quake_victims/.

Smith, Ralph. "Lessons from the Homelessness Initiative." In *Policy Development and Implementation of Complex Files*, 1-32. Ottawa: Canada School of Public Service, Special Studies, 2004.

Snowden, David J. and Mary E. Boone. "A Leader's Framework for Decision Making." *Harvard Business Review* (November 2007): 69-76.

Snowden, David J. and C.F. Kurtz. "The New Dynamics of Strategy: Sense-Making in a Complex and Complicated World." *IBM Systems Journal* 42, (2003): 462-83.

Soares, Sergei. *O Ritmo de Queda na Desigualdade no Brasil É Adequado? Evidências do Contexto Histórico e Internacional* [Is the rate of decline in Brazil adequate? Evidence from the Historical and International Context]. Instituto de Pesquisa Econômica Aplicada, Texto para Discussão no 1339, 2008.

——. *Volatilidade de Renda e a Cobertura do Programa Bolsa Família* [Income volatility and coverage of the Bolsa Família Program]. Instituto de Pesquisa Econômica Aplicada, Texto para Discussão no. 1459, 2009.

Social Research and Demonstration Corporation, "What We Do." http://www.srdc.org.

State Government of Victoria (Australia). *Innovation Action Plan: Create. Collaborate. Change.* Melbourne: Department of Premier and Cabinet, 2009.

State of Wisconsin Legislative Audit Bureau. *Financial Management of Selected W-2 Agencies.* Madison: Government of the State of Wisconsin, 2005. http://legis.wisconsin.gov/lab/reports/05-W2Agencies_Ltr.pdf.

State Services Authority (State of Victoria, Australia). *Welcome to Government, Your introduction to Working in the Victorian Public Sector.* Melbourne: State Services Authority, State Government of Victoria, 2009

——. "Victorian Bushfire Reconstruction and Recovery Authority—A Case Study on Agility and Resilience." Paper presented at the NS6 International Roundtable, The Hague, the Netherlands, 24-26 March 2010.

Statistics Canada. "Crime Statistics." *The Daily,* 17 July 2008. http://www.statcan.gc.ca/daily-quotidien/080717/dq080717b-eng.htm.

Steffen, W., A. Sanderson, P.D. Tyson, J. Jäger, P.A. Matson, B. Moore III, F. Oldfied, K. Richardson, H.J. Schellnhuber, B.L. Turner II, and R.J. Wasson. *Global Change and the Earth System: A Planet Under Pressure.* New York: Springer-Verlag, 2004.

Stiglitz, Joseph, Amartya Sen, and Jean-Paul Fitoussi. *Report by the Commission on the Measurement of Economic Performance and Social Progress.* Paris: Commission on the Measurement of Economic Performance and Social Progress, 2009. http://www.stiglitz-sen-fitoussi.fr/en/index.htm.

Stone, Deborah. *Policy Paradox: The Art of Political Decision Making.* New York: W.W. Norton, 1997.

Storey, Peter. "A Different Kind of Justice: Truth and Reconciliation in South Africa." *New World Outlook* (July-August 1999). http://gbgm-umc.org/nwo/99ja/different.html.

Svara, James H. "The Myth of the Dichotomy: Complementarity of Politics and

Administration in the Past and Future of Public Administration." *Public Administration Review* 61, no. 2 (2001): 176-83.

Tharman, Shanmugaratnam. "Budget Speech, 2007." Singapore: Ministry of Finance, 2007. www.mof.gov.sg/budget_2007/budget_speech/subsection14.6.html.

Thomas, Paul. "Performance Measurement, Reporting and Accountability: Recent Trends and Future Directions." Policy Paper 23, Public Policy Paper Series, Saskatchewan Institute of Public Policy (2004): 3-10.

Thomas, Yvonne, and Sue Richards. "Better Justice Outcomes Through a Citizen-Centred Approach." Paper presented at the the NS6 International Roundtable in Rio de Janeiro, Brazil, 13-14 July 2010.

Thomas, William C. "The Rise and Fall of Enron." *Journal of Accountancy* (April 2002): 41-48.

Thompson, Grahame, Jennifer Frances, Rosalind Levacic, and Jeremy Mitchell. *Markets, Hierarchies and Networks: The Coordination of Social Life.* London: Sage Publications, 1991.

Tonkens, Evelien, and Tsjalling Swierstra. "What Gets Measured Gets Moulded: From the Audit Explosion to Restrained Accountability." Unpublished working paper, University of Amsterdam, 2010.

Torbert, William R. *Action Inquiry: The Secret of Timely and Transforming Leadership.* San Francisco: Berrett-Koehler Publishers, 2004.

Travis, Phyllida, Dominique Egger, Philip Davies and Abdelhay Mechbal. "Towards Better Stewardship: Concepts and Critical Issues." In *Health Systems Performance Assessment: Debates, Methods and Empiricism,* edited by Christopher J.L. Murray and David B. Evans, 289-300. Geneva: World Health Organization, 2003.

United Nations Children's Fund (UNICEF). "Child Mortality Estimates." http://www.childmortality.org/cmeMain.html.

United Nations Department of Economic and Social Affairs, Population Division. "World Population to 2300." New York: United Nations, 2004. http://www.un.org/esa/population/publications/longrange2/WorldPop2300final.pdf.

United Nations Department of Public Information. "Narrowing Digital Divide Crucial Part of Achieving Global Anti-poverty Goals." Text of speech of UN Secretary-General Ban Ki-moon to the Ministerial Meeting on the Future of the Internet Economy, Seoul, Korea, June 2008. http://www.un.org/News/

Press/docs/2008/sgsm11577.doc.htm.

United Nations Development Program. "International Human Development Indicators." http://hdrstats.undp.org/en/indicators/69206.html.

——. "Human Development Reports." http://hdr.undp.org/en/statistics/.

United Nations Human Rights Council. *Report of the Special Rapporteur on Adequate Housing as a Component of the Right to an Adequate Standard of Living, and on the Right to Non-Discrimination in This Context, Miloon Kothari: addendum: mission to Canada (9 to 22 October 2007).* Geneva: UN Human Rights Commission, 17 February 2009. http://www.unhcr.org/refworld/docid/49b7af2c2.html.

US-Canada Power System Outage Task Force. *Final Report on the August 14, 2003 Blackout in the United States and Canada.* Governments of USA and Canada, 2004. http://www.ferc.gov/industries/electric/indus-act/reliability/blackout/ch1-3.pdf.

US Commodities Futures Trading Commission and US Security and Exchange Commission. *Findings Regarding the Market Events of May 6, 2010.* Washington, DC: US Commodities Futures Trading Commission and US Securities Exchange Commission, 2010. http://www.sec.gov/news/studies/2010/marketevents-report.pdf.

Ushahidi. "About Us." http://www.ushahidi.com/about-us.

Ushahidi-Haiti @ Tufts University. "About Us." http://www.ushahidi.com/about-us.

Valdez, Adrienne. "Co-creation Part of Singapore's 'Gov-with-You' Strategy," Asia Pacific FutureGov. http://www.futuregov.asia/articles/2011/feb/14/co-creation-part-singapores-gov-you-strategy/.

Van de Walle, Steven, and Merel Vogelaar. "Emergence and Public Administration: A Literature Review for the Project 'A New Synthesis in Public Administration.'" Paper presented at the NS6 International Roundtable, The Hague, the Netherlands, 24-26 March 2010.

Vandenbroeck, Philippe, Jo Goossens, and Marshall Clemens. *Tackling Obesities: Future Choices—Building the Obesity System Map.* London: UK Foresight Program, Government Office for Science, 2007. http://www.bis.gov.uk/assets/bispartners/foresight/docs/obesity/12.pdf.

Victorian Bushfire Reconstruction and Recovery Authority. *Rebuilding Together:*

A Statewide Plan for Bushfire Reconstruction and Recovery. Melbourne: State Government of Victoria, 2009. http://www.wewillrebuild.vic.gov.au.

———. *100 Day Report*. Melbourne: State Government of Victoria, 2009. http://www.wewillrebuild.vic.gov.au.

———. *12 Month Report*. Melbourne: State Government of Victoria, 2010. http://www.wewillrebuild.vic.gov.au

Voyer, Jean-Pierre. "Experimentation for Better Policy-Making." Paper presented at the NS6 International Roundtable, Singapore, 21-21 September 2010.

Wagenaar, Hendrik. "Governance, Complexity, and Democratic Participation: How Citizens and Public Officials Harness the Complexities of Neighborhood Decline." *American Review of Public Administration* 37, no. 1 (2007): 17–50.

Walker, B.H., and D. Salt. *Resilience Thinking: Sustaining Ecosystems and People in a Changing World*. Washington, DC: Island Press, 2006.

Waltner-Toews, David, and Tim Lang. "A New Conceptual Base for Food and Agricultural Policy: The Emerging Model of Links Between Agriculture, Food, Health, Environment and Society." *Global Change and Human Health* 1, no. 2 (2000): 116-30.

Warner, Mildred E. "Reversing Privatization, Rebalancing Government Reform: Markets, Deliberation and Planning." *Policy and Society* 13 (2008): 1-12.

Weaver, Liz. "Evidence." Subcommittee on Cities, 2nd Session, 40th Parliament, 3 June 2009. Cited in *In From the Margins: A Call To Action On Poverty, Housing And Homelessness*, Senate of Canada, 114-5. Ottawa: Government of Canada, 2009. http://www.parl.gc.ca/40/2/parlbus/commbus/senate/com-e/citi-e/rep-e/rep02dec09-e.pdf.

Wente, Maggie. "Urban Aboriginal Homelessness in Canada." Toronto: Faculty of Social Work, University of Toronto, 2000. http://action.web.ca/home/housing/resources.shtml?x=67148&AA_EX_Session=e010a84c0d8c4b55b5b9a1b9a5a44b7f.

Westley, Frances, Brenda Zimmerman and Michael Patton. *Getting to Maybe: How the World is Changed*. Toronto: Random House, 2006.

Westley, Frances and Nino Antadze. "Making a Difference: Strategies for Scaling Social Innovation for Greater Impact." *The Innovation Journal: The Public Sector Innovation Journal* 15, no. 2 (2010). http://sig.uwaterloo.ca/sites/default/files/documents/MAKING_A_DIFFERENCE_SiG_Format.pdf.

Wikipedia. "List of Virtual Communities with more than 100 Million Users." http://en.wikipedia.org/wiki/List_of_virtual_communities_with_more_than_100_million_users.

Wisconsin Department of Children and Families. "Wisconsin Works (W-2) Overview." Madison: Department of Children and Families, Government of the State of Wisconsin. http://dcf.wisconsin.gov/w2/wisworks.htm.

World Bank. *Controlling AIDS: Public Priorities in a Global Epidemic.* New York: Oxford University Press, 1997.

——. "Internet Users." http://data.worldbank.org/indicator/IT.NET.USER.

——. "Mobile Cellular Subscriptions." http://data.worldbank.org/indicator/IT.CEL.SETS.P2

Yang, Dali L. *Calamity and Reform in China.* Stanford: Stanford University Press, 1996.

Index